THE ILLUSTRATED
ENCYCLOPEDIA *of*
OPERA

PUBLISHER AND CREATIVE DIRECTOR: Nick Wells

COMMISSIONING EDITOR: Polly Willis

GENERAL EDITOR: Stanley Sadie

EDITOR AND PICTURE RESEARCHER: Julia Rolf

LAYOUT: Axis Design and Jake

Special thanks to:

Katharine Bushell, Freeman Gunter, Sarah Goulding, Chris Herbert, Dorothy-Jean Lloyd,
Olivia Robinson, Sara Robson, Stewart Spencer, Helen Tovey, Claire Walker

First Published 2004

FLAME TREE PUBLISHING

Crabtree Hall, Crabtree Lane

Fulham, London, SW6 6TY

United Kingdom

www.flametreepublishing.com

© 2004 Flame Tree Publishing

Flame Tree Publishing is part of
The Foundry Creative Media Company Limited

05 07 09 08 06 04

1 3 5 7 9 10 8 6 4 2

The CIP record for this book is available from the British Library.

ISBN 1 84451 026 3

Printed in Italy

THE ILLUSTRATED ENCYCLOPEDIA of OPERA

GENERAL EDITOR: STANLEY SADIE

FOREWORD BY PHILIP LANGRIDGE

Jane Bellingham, Richard Langham Smith, Dorothy-Jean Lloyd,
Robin Newton, Brenda Ralph Lewis, Julia Rolf, David Rose, Stewart
Spencer, David Vickers, Richard Wigmore

FLAME TREE
PUBLISHING

Contents

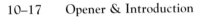

The Roots of Opera

The Early and Middle Baroque

Late Baroque

Classical

Early Romantic

# High Romantic

# The Twentieth Century

# Turn of the Century

# Resources

How To Use This Book

ABOUT THE ENCYCLOPEDIA

The Encyclopedia comprises an introductory section on the development of opera, from its roots in the musical theatre of ancient Greece, followed by seven chronologically organized chapters from the Early & Middle Baroque to the Twentieth Century.

Each chapter is divided into a number of sections. Common to each chapter are the following:

INTRODUCTION

Gives vital information about the relevant period, clarifying the backdrop against which the music developed and setting it and its protagonists into their social, historical and cultural context.

GENRES & STYLES

Details the creation of new musical styles, performance styles and compositional techniques, as well as the development of those that already existed. (NB there is no Genres & Styles section in Chapter 5.)

KEY COMPOSERS

Major biographical sections on the main composers of each era, including timelines and comprehensive lists of the operas they composed. There then follows a section in which a number of their most popular operas are discussed in more detail, together with synopses of the works.

OTHER COMPOSERS

Comprises shorter entries, organized alphabetically and outlining the lives and works of the era's less prolific composers, with synopses and further details of the more popular operas.

LIBRETTISTS

Biographies of the main librettists of each era, including poets, playwrights and novelists whose works were used as the bases for opera libretti.

SINGERS

A guide to the celebrated opera singers of the time, including some of music history's greatest divas, prima donnas and colourful characters.

THEMES

Six themes run throughout the book, the entries for which can be found in colour-coded boxes in broadly similar positions on each spread:

TECHNIQUES

 Introduces developments in the composition and structure of opera, with discussion of the innovations and various genres particular to each era.

HOUSES AND COMPANIES

 Provides information about the world's most celebrated opera houses and performance companies, as well as famous patrons and related societies and factions.

THE VOICE

 Explores developments in vocal techniques, the different types of voice that dominated each era and style, and how the composers tailored their operas to showcase the singers' vocal abilities.

PERFORMANCE

 Highlights different types of opera-related performance and developments in how the operas themselves were performed and staged, including contemporary eyewitness accounts of opera stagings.

STAGE AND SCENE

 Examines the more practical side of opera's history, including set designs and stage machinery, as well as issues such as censorship.

SYNOPSES

 Provides the plot outlines for over 200 operas, detailing the events and characters portrayed.

A thematic entry is indicated by an active icon at the top of the spread. The page references guide you to the previous and following examples of the relevant theme.

ADDITIONAL BOXES

POPULAR MELODY

Popular Melody boxes can be found throughout the book; these introduce pieces of music that may be familiar to the reader through their use in the popular media.

'LARGO AL FACTOTUM' (ROOM FOR THE FACTOTUM)
In Act I, Figaro, the barber of Seville, introduces himself to the audience by singing, rather ruefully, a catalogue of the many different tasks he must perform. He confides how hard it is to have to try and please everyone.

POPULAR MELODY

RECOMMENDED RECORDING

Recommended Recording boxes appear throughout the book; these suggest well-known or outstanding recordings of the works discussed in the text. You will find recommendations for audio CDs and also for DVD recordings – a wonderful way to familiarize yourself with opera in your own home.

Il barbiere di Siviglia, **Failoni Chamber Orchestra**
Will Humburg, **conductor**
Naxos 8 660027/9
Soloists: Sonia Ganassi (Rosina), Ingrid Kertesi (Berta), Ramón Vargas (Almaviva), Roberto Servile (Figaro), Angelo Romero (Dr Bartolo), Franco de Grandis (DonBasilio)

RECOMMENDED RECORDING

CROSS-REFERENCING

A system of cross-referencing has been used whereby a name, term or opera mentioned in the text that has a more detailed entry elsewhere in the book is followed by the page number, in bold, where the further information can be found.

NAMES, DATES AND TRANSLATIONS

Full names and dates are given for musicological figures the first time they are mentioned. Opera titles are translated the first time they are mentioned if not in English, and the year in which they were first performed is given. Titles of arias and excerpts are also translated where necessary.

USING THE ENCYCLOPEDIA

The information in the Encyclopedia can be accessed in a number of different ways:

The themes listed on page 6 can be traced throughout the book, using the buttons at the top of each spread, which give page references to the previous and following boxes of the same theme.

Cross-references indicate where to find further information about a person, opera or style mentioned in the text.

The introductory paragraph in each section provides a summary of information, acting as a quick reference guide and allowing the reader to explore the subject without reading the entire section.

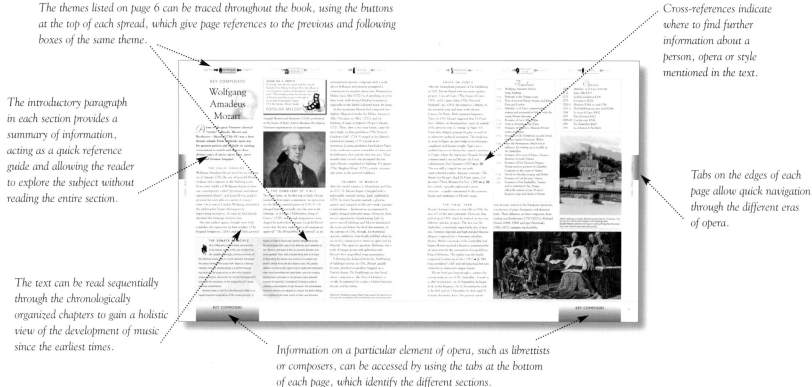

Tabs on the edges of each page allow quick navigation through the different eras of opera.

The text can be read sequentially through the chronologically organized chapters to gain a holistic view of the development of music since the earliest times.

Information on a particular element of opera, such as librettists or composers, can be accessed by using the tabs at the bottom of each page, which identify the different sections.

Foreword

"One who strives to create beauty, to liberate from the marble mass of language the slender forms of an art…." sings Gustav von Aschenbach in Benjamin Britten's *Death in Venice*. This could be written on my tombstone. It is the very essence of an artist's work. It is what we strive to do and what we hope to see and hear in performance. When I am performing as a singer, I often ask myself if I am communicating successfully with the listener. This in part also depends upon whether the listener is able to enter fully into the discussion, because that is how we should describe a performance: a discussion between performer and audience. The audience needs to take part in order for it to be a real discussion. This is one reason for using a book like this, to have a better understanding of the language, history, style, story etc. of any opera in order to take part in the discussion.

I know that *The Encyclopedia of Opera* looks a pretty forbidding title, but flicking through the pages it seems much more like a novel by the same name. For instance, you can easily imagine what it must have been like around the year 1600 when the good old Camerata were creating this magic formula, when real horses were used in performances of Monteverdi's *Il Combattimento di Tancredi e Clorinda*, and when the words, the music and the drama were of equal importance. Just imagine creating such a wonderful art form which has survived for 400 years, almost unchanged.

We have, of course, strayed quite a lot from those early ideals, having seen some terribly grand singers, before whom everyone bowed, the great and mighty conductor under whose baton everyone cowered, and finally the rise of the director, who has reigned supreme with all those seemingly crazy ideas on stage. In addition, there have been the opera companies begging for money to support themselves, with the politicians not far behind, and all of us musicians, singers, designers, and directors trying to stage the operas as works of art.

I myself have been fortunate in singing in so many of the styles which you will find discussed in this book. Monteverdi has always been a particular favourite of mine, and his *L'incoronazione di Poppea* comes top of my list. I love the way in which Monteverdi contrasted between a tragic scene (Senaca's Death for example) and a comic one (the scene with Lucano and Nero), placed right next to one another. Mozart did the same in his operas (*Die Zauberflöte* for instance), and one can trace this expressive device down through the years.

Singing Rameau's *Les Boreades* was a huge thrill, and at that time we were probably performing it for the first time ever. I found it to be an opera which points forward to Wagner and back to Monteverdi at the same time. His use of the recitative as aria and vice versa is extraordinary. How on earth did these composers get their inspiration? Inspiration? That is what Pfitzner's *Palestrina* deals with. It tells of the awful dilemma a composer finds himself in when his inspiration dries up. Interesting thought: a composer composing an opera about a composer with writer's block! I can only marvel at the brilliance of these composers, who just seem to come up with such amazing ideas.

So what is happening now in the world of opera? Are we still doing interesting and innovative things? Well, Sir Harrison Birtwistle's new opera *The Passion of Io* has just received its first run of performances and was conceived with composer, librettist and director all working together over a number of years, and that is pretty well what those chaps did in 1600. So perhaps we have not strayed so far from their ideals after all.

Janáček said that speech melodies are windows into people's souls. Debussy said that music is a dream from which the veil has been lifted, and that it is not even the expression of a feeling, it is the feeling itself. With words like that ringing in your ears you would be foolish not to join the discussion. You can visit any opera house to hear a live performance, listen to CDs of any of these operas and even see them on DVD. It really could not be easier. Opera is more popular now than ever, and much more accessible. Even schoolchildren get to see live performances. Personally I cannot imagine life without music, and when this is allied to words and theatre, the sky is the limit.

Come on in: it is lovely!

Philip Langridge July 2004

Introduction

Opera is perhaps the most elaborate of all art forms. It may call on the skills of poet, composer, scenographer, director and choreographer to create a 'complete art-work' (or, to call on Wagner's term, *Gesamtkunstwerk*). It can offer its creators a breadth of resource unknown to most other art forms, partly because of the simultaneous appeal it makes to several different susceptibilities, but also because music can open up possibilities of strengthening, subtilizing or inflecting, or even contradicting, any words that are uttered on the stage, and may even carry information about words or feelings or the characters that are left unspoken or are indeed unknown to the characters themselves.

In Gluck's *Iphigénie en Tauride*, for example, when Orestes tells himself and us that '*Le calme rentre dans mon coeur*' ('Calm returns to my heart'), we in the audience know – from the uneasy throb of the violas in the orchestra – that his newfound calm is illusory. When, in Wagner's *Die Walküre*, Sieglinde tells the tale of the mysterious stranger who intruded upon her wedding feast, the orchestra tells us precisely who this was. The music may elucidate the emotional relationship between characters in an ensemble, as in the famous quartet in Verdi's *Rigoletto*. It can symbolize and powerfully reinforce what is expressed: for example, when two lovers begin a duet singing singly and end it singing in mellifluous thirds or sixths – as they usually do – it will stress their growing mutuality of feeling and identity of purpose.

In everyday life, people do not very often sing to convey their thoughts; in opera they do. Opera is not a naturalistic art; it depends on the acceptance by its audience of a series of conventions, of which the coupling of music and words is the central one. But in the course of its history there have been numerous attempts to make it less dependent on what, in a changing society, has come to be regarded as artificiality and, often, as representative of an outmoded world. The "reforms" of the early eighteenth-century Italian librettists, of Gluck and his colleagues, of Wagner, and of various groups in the twentieth century have all been of this kind. The disputes to which they gave rise have sometimes focused on the claims of primacy between words and music (a topic which several composers have even treated as the subject matter of an opera, for example Salieri and Richard Strauss).

Often such disputes devolve on the issue of "set piece" arias or duets and whether they should be separated, by clear breaks in musical texture, or should be welded into a more nearly continuous whole. Traditions differ, geographically and temporally, and are closely related to social and linguistic factors. Verdi once remarked: 'If only there could be no cavatinas, no duets, no trios, no choruses, no finales etc., and if only the whole opera could be, as it were, all one number, I should find that sensible and right'. But he knew better than to compose operas like that for an Italian audience.

What music can tell us about human behaviour, and the different ways in which composers have chosen to use music to enrich our understanding: that is the central stuff of the history of opera, and it is what this book tries to clarify and illuminate.

Stanley Sadie, GENERAL EDITOR

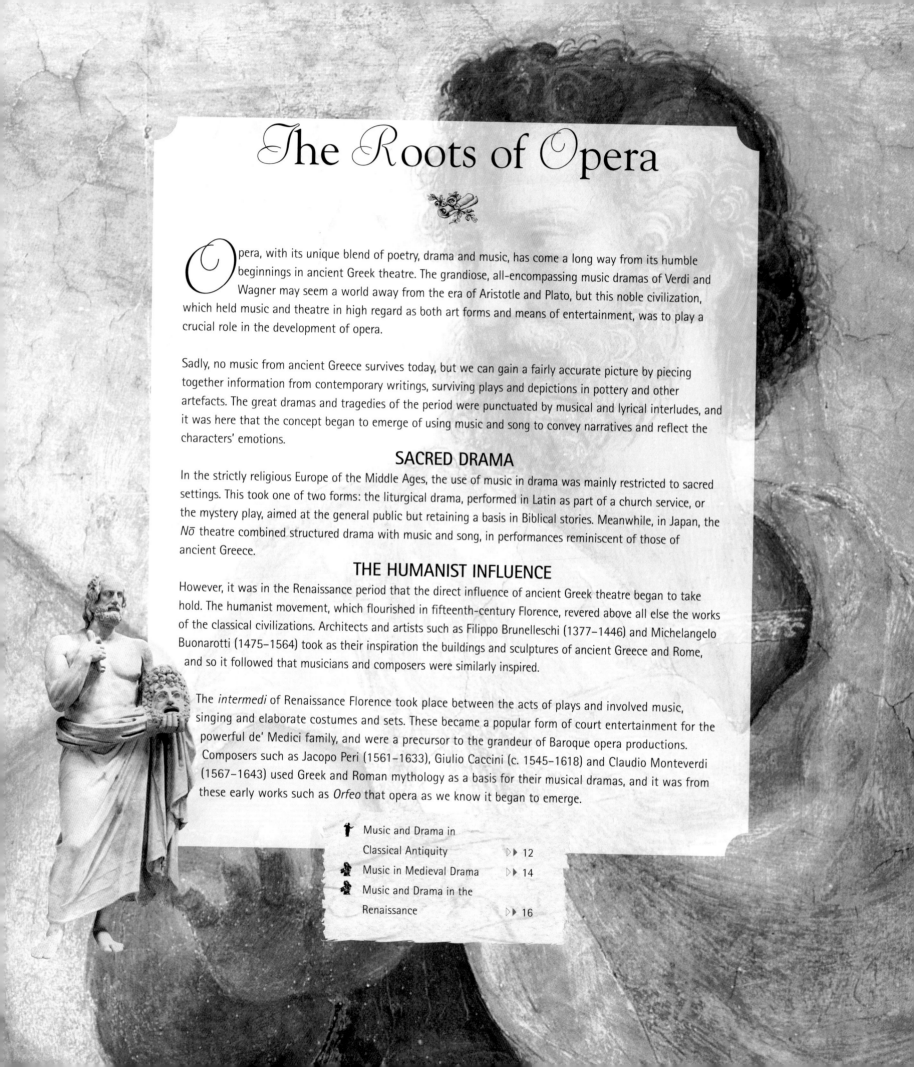

The Roots of Opera

Opera, with its unique blend of poetry, drama and music, has come a long way from its humble beginnings in ancient Greek theatre. The grandiose, all-encompassing music dramas of Verdi and Wagner may seem a world away from the era of Aristotle and Plato, but this noble civilization, which held music and theatre in high regard as both art forms and means of entertainment, was to play a crucial role in the development of opera.

Sadly, no music from ancient Greece survives today, but we can gain a fairly accurate picture by piecing together information from contemporary writings, surviving plays and depictions in pottery and other artefacts. The great dramas and tragedies of the period were punctuated by musical and lyrical interludes, and it was here that the concept began to emerge of using music and song to convey narratives and reflect the characters' emotions.

SACRED DRAMA

In the strictly religious Europe of the Middle Ages, the use of music in drama was mainly restricted to sacred settings. This took one of two forms: the liturgical drama, performed in Latin as part of a church service, or the mystery play, aimed at the general public but retaining a basis in Biblical stories. Meanwhile, in Japan, the *Nō* theatre combined structured drama with music and song, in performances reminiscent of those of ancient Greece.

THE HUMANIST INFLUENCE

However, it was in the Renaissance period that the direct influence of ancient Greek theatre began to take hold. The humanist movement, which flourished in fifteenth-century Florence, revered above all else the works of the classical civilizations. Architects and artists such as Filippo Brunelleschi (1377–1446) and Michelangelo Buonarotti (1475–1564) took as their inspiration the buildings and sculptures of ancient Greece and Rome, and so it followed that musicians and composers were similarly inspired.

The *intermedi* of Renaissance Florence took place between the acts of plays and involved music, singing and elaborate costumes and sets. These became a popular form of court entertainment for the powerful de' Medici family, and were a precursor to the grandeur of Baroque opera productions. Composers such as Jacopo Peri (1561–1633), Giulio Caccini (c. 1545–1618) and Claudio Monteverdi (1567–1643) used Greek and Roman mythology as a basis for their musical dramas, and it was from these early works such as *Orfeo* that opera as we know it began to emerge.

THE ROOTS OF OPERA

Music and Drama in Classical Antiquity

The musical culture of ancient Greece has had a profound influence on the history of Western music, even up to the present day. However, its legacy is particularly evident in the emergence of opera in the early seventeenth century. Even though we have little idea about what ancient Greek music actually sounded like – composers and musicians did not write their music down, but committed it to memory or improvised around traditional patterns – there are plenty of sources of information about it. Philosophers, such as Plato and Aristotle, discussed it in their treatises, music theorists analyzed its melodies and rhythms, craftsmen painted musical scenes on their pottery bowls, and, of course, we have the works of the great tragedians themselves – the plays of Aeschylus, Sophocles and Euripides – that formed the highpoint of Greek music drama.

GREEK DRAMA

In the fifth century BC, the city-state of Athens witnessed a great flourishing of artistic and intellectual achievement, among the greatest of which must be counted the development of tragedy. The dramas of ancient Greece had their origins in choral dances performed by ordinary citizens as part of ritual ceremonies, and these two aspects of the tragedy – the ritual and the choral – remained among the most important of its defining features, even when the element of story-telling (drama as we understand it today) assumed a more prominent role.

Greek tragedies were performed as part of the formal celebrations at the Great Dionysia, a festival of Dionysos, the god of wine, music and poetry. During this festival, three poets entered into a competition by each writing three new dramas for performance in front of the citizens of Athens. The poet not only wrote the words of the drama, but also acted as composer, choreographer, director, designer and producer, and his stories were retellings of the Greek myths with a serious, "tragic" character.

The winner of the competition was decided by public acclamation and prizes were also awarded to the best actor.

The three most famous tragedians were Aeschylus (525–456 BC), Sophocles (c. 496–406 BC) and Euripides (c. 485–c. 406 BC), and their works were revered in antiquity just as much as they are today. Aeschylus was the oldest of the trio. He wrote over 90 plays, of which only seven survive. Of these, the *Oresteia*, a trilogy of three tragedies, is perhaps the most famous: it was performed in 458 BC and won the festival competition.

Sophocles wrote over 120 dramas, but again, only seven survive, among them the famous *Oedipus Tyrannos* ('Oedipus the King'). He introduced the

GREEK TRAGEDY

The performers in the Greek tragedy were of two distinct types: the *choros* and the solo actors. The *choros* was a group of 12 or 15 adult men drawn from the general citizenry of Athens. Its role was largely passive in the drama, usually commenting upon the action, or sympathizing with the solo characters.

Although the *choros*, particularly its leader, the *choregos*, did engage in dialogue with the solo actors, its most important role was the performance of lyric songs. These were formal episodes in the tragedy, reflecting upon the action, and involved dancing, poetry and singing, often to the accompaniment of the *aulos*, a type of wind instrument rather like an oboe.

Sometimes the *choros* was divided into two groups, with one answering or debating with the other. The solo actors in the tragedy – of whom there were no more than three – were also all adult males, even when representing female characters. They were professional performers, skilled in acting and singing. They wore masks over their faces that showed the essential character of their role. Although they did perform formal songs, such as laments, their singing was probably more a kind of chant – more musical than everyday speech, but not quite the same as song.

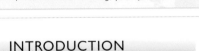

ROOTS OF OPERA

third actor into tragedy and increased the number of *choros* members from 12 to 15. Euripides, the youngest of the great tragedians, wrote about 90 plays, of which 19 are still known today.

THE GREEK THEATRE

The Theatre of Dionysos in Athens where the tragedies were performed stood at the foot of the south-eastern end of the Acropolis in the sanctuary of Dionysos. It was originally constructed at the beginning of the fifth century BC, but was rebuilt in the middle of the fourth – and this is basically the theatre whose remains can be seen today.

Like other Greek theatres, it was a vast space, wholly open to the sky, and, by the fourth century, could seat around 20,000 spectators. The audience sat in tiers of seats that were arranged in a horseshoe shape carved out of the rock of the Acropolis, and looked down upon the action below them. This was known as the *theatron*, "the place for seeing". At the centre of the horseshoe was a flat, circular piece of ground, called the *orchêstra*, "the place for dancing", that housed the altar of Dionysos and was where the *choros* of citizens performed their songs and dances. Behind this, facing the audience, was the *skêne*, or stage. In the fifth century BC this was a temporary, single-storey, wooden building, sometimes painted with rudimentary scenery to represent the setting of the drama. It had a platform slightly raised above the level of the *orchêstra*, on which the solo actors performed. Characters representing gods often appeared on the roof of the *skêne* to address the mortals below. Later, in the fourth century, when the Theatre of Dionysos was enlarged, the *skêne* was rebuilt of stone in two storeys and decorated with statues of the great dramatists. Inside the *skêne* and invisible to the audience, was the "backstage" area, which also housed the *mêchane*, "mechanical device", "machine" – a kind of crane or hoist that, from the time of Euripides onwards, was used to lift characters into the air, usually to represent flying.

MUSIC IN ANCIENT GREEK CULTURE

In performances of tragedy, as in other forms of Greek poetry, the words and the musical sounds were closely bound together. In particular, the melodic line exactly followed the intonations of the poetic language, reflecting the rise and fall of the singer's recitation of the text, and the rhythms were precisely those of the poetic metre used in the verse. Greek music was monodic – that is, it was a single melodic line, without harmony of any kind. In fact, so intimately connected were poetry, music and dance, that the Greek idea of music – or *mousikē* – encompassed all these aspects of performance – not just what we today understand as "music".

Music held a particularly important place in the culture of ancient Greece. It was not regarded as simply a pastime or mere entertainment, but exerted serious moral and emotional effects on the character of both performer and listener. Music was therefore of great concern in the education of children and in the everyday lives of adults. As music theory progressed and different styles of music were analyzed and given names, so philosophers began to assign moral characters to each style. This theory, known as the doctrine of *ēthos* ("character"), found its most influential proponent in the works of Plato (c. 485–c. 406 BC). According to Plato, the Dorian style of music was associated with virility and courage and was especially appropriate for choral music, the Phrygian was sober and thoughtful, and the Ionian and Lydian styles induced excitability, moral weakness and effeminacy. These views were shared by Plato's pupil, Aristotle (384–322 BC), but whereas Plato argued that the power of musicians and poets over people's emotions and characters was so great that they were a danger to citizens and should be banished from the city, Aristotle took a more moderate view. For him, music could be used educationally – by using the Dorian mode – to instil the ideal, manly virtues, but was also valuable as a means of entertainment and relaxation. In his view, the strong and varied emotions, which the music and poetry of tragedy produced in the audience, had a beneficial effect: by providing an outlet for extreme feelings, tragedy had a purifying effect (*catharsis*) on the soul.

ABOVE: The Theatre of Dionysos in Athens, Greece.
LEFT: Euripides, whose plays were widely performed in ancient Greece.
ABOVE LEFT: Images on Greek pottery have taught us about their music.

INTRODUCTION

THE ROOTS OF OPERA

Music in Medieval Drama

*I*n the Middle Ages, two distinct forms of music drama existed: the liturgical dramas that took place in churches as a part of the service – and were therefore in Latin; and the "mystery" or "miracle" plays that were performed outside churches in the everyday language of the people.

LITURGICAL DRAMAS

Liturgical dramas were performed only by members of the clergy, and formed part of the church service on particular occasions. The earliest known drama dates from the ninth century and recreates the scene from the Gospels when the Marys visited the tomb of Christ and spoke with an angel. It was often performed as part of the Mass on Easter Day. Later plays also took place on other major Christian festivals, particularly Christmas. There is some evidence that basic scenery and costumes were occasionally used, especially for the more elaborate plays.

In the Middle Ages, all the words of the Mass and other church services were chanted or sung, with each set of words having its own melody. The music for the liturgical dramas was no different, with the texts and verses of the plays set in the same traditional plainchant style. Sometimes chants were drawn directly from the liturgical services, but melodies were also often written specially for the plays.

"MYSTERY" PLAYS

"Mystery" plays were performed throughout Europe from the fourteenth century to the Reformation in the sixteenth. Their subject matter was religious and they were generally enacted out in the open air as part of the celebrations of a holy day (or "holiday"). Many of the plays tell of the whole history of the world,

Calcearius. Der Schuwmacher.

Qvi ventosa regunt hominum vestigia passim,
Calceolos docta consuo sutor acu.
Glorior humano quicquid de semine cretum
Esse vides, artis semper egere meæ?

ROOTS OF OPERA

JAPANESE NŌ THEATRE

Several other non-Western cultures have developed genres of musical performance similar to that of opera – i.e. they combine music, song, story-telling and theatrical presentation. The most famous of these is the *Nō* theatre of Japan.

Nō theatre was essentially established in the fourteenth and fifteenth centuries by the two great playwrights Kan'ami (1333–84) and his son Zeami (1363–1443). These two men drew upon earlier traditions of music and drama to form the highly stylized art that is still performed today. There are five types of *Nō* play: plays about gods; plays about men; plays about women – usually young and beautiful; plays featuring mad women; and plays concerning supernatural beings. Originally, a performance consisted of a play from each category, with a comic play known as a *kyōgen*, inserted between each *Nō*.

Such performances could last an entire day.

Nō actors – all of whom are men – are of three types: the principal, who wears a mask and represents the main character of the story; the secondary, who enters into dialogue with the principal; and the comic actor who performs the *kyōgen*. There is also a chorus of eight people that sets the scene and comments on the action, often voicing the other characters' thoughts and feelings. Accompanying the actors and chorus, as well as performing purely instrumental music and dances, are a flute-player (who plays the bamboo *nō kan*) and three drummers.

Nō theatre is performed on a square stage, with a pillar in each corner supporting a roof. The instrumentalists sit at the back, and the chorus kneels on either side of the stage. Traditionally, *Nō* plays took place outside, but for the last 100 years or so they have often been performed inside buildings specially constructed for the purpose. Today, Tokyo has several such theatres, including the National *Nō* Theatre, and other major cities in Japan also have dedicated theatres. *Nō* theatre is still a popular form of entertainment in Japan.

from the Creation to the Last Judgement, taking in all the major stories from the Bible. These plays were performed by craftsmen, with each guild being responsible for a particular scene. The choice of guild was often closely connected to the subject matter of the scene – for example, the carpenters might be in charge of the story of Noah's Ark, and the butchers of the telling of the Crucifixion. While some plays were designed for performance on a fixed wooden stage, others took place on a succession of wagons as part of a procession through the town's streets.

Although these plays were largely spoken, they also included many musical items – songs, instrumental music and dances. Unfortunately, very few of these pieces were written down in notation, because they were usually already well known to the performers and audience. The melodies were generally taken from popular songs, liturgical plainchant and dance tunes. Almost no music was specially written for the mystery plays.

RIGHT: A young Judi Dench in a 1950s revival of a mystery play.
TOP: Zeami Motokio in a scene from Japanese Nō theatre.
LEFT: Medieval guilds, such as the cobblers, performed liturgical plays.

INTRODUCTION

THE ROOTS OF OPERA

Music and Drama in the Renaissance

The Renaissance, with its renewed interest in the music of the ancient world, is where the true roots of opera lie. The word "Renaissance" means "rebirth" and refers to the revival of the artistic and intellectual ideals of classical civilization following the intervening Middle Ages. The Renaissance began in Italy in the late fourteenth century and later spread to other countries throughout Europe, but it was in Italy that the immediate predecessors of modern opera began to take shape in the fifteenth century.

INTERMEDI

One of the most important precursors of opera was the *intermedio*. *Intermedi* were a series of interludes that were inserted between the acts of a play, initially as a means of dividing up the action or marking the passage of time between events in the main drama. They were an aristocratic entertainment, often performed to celebrate occasions such as court weddings, and usually involved singing, dancing, instrumental music and elaborate stage effects. Their subject matter often reflected the fashionable Renaissance themes of stories from classical myths, allegories and pastoral scenes.

The earliest *intermedi* took place in Ferrara in the late fifteenth century, but the genre reached its height at the court of the Medici family of Florence in the sixteenth. By this time, the *intermedi* were often more important parts of the entertainment than the original drama. The scenery and costumes could be spectacular and the finest musicians, singers and dancers were employed to perform the musical numbers. The importance of the

ABOVE: Florentiae civitas *(city of Florence), birthplace of the Renaissance movement and of opera's early incarnations.*

intermedi for the development of opera at the very end of the sixteenth century lies in the close association between drama and music, and in the intellectual environment in which the most influential *intermedi* were performed. The 1589 *intermedi* of Florence, for example, involved many of the musicians and thinkers who were later responsible for the first genuine operas. They used these courtly entertainments as a means of presenting their ideas and putting their theories about the music of the ancient world in to practice.

THE FLORENTINE CAMERATA

The Camerata ("club" or "society") was a group of intellectuals, with aristocratic connections, that met in Florence during the 1570s and 1580s. Led by Count Giovanni de' Bardi, it came together principally to discuss the music of the ancient Greeks with the aim of influencing the composition of contemporary music. Among its chief members were Vincenzo Galilei, an expert in the music of the ancient world (and the father of Galileo), and the composers Guilio Caccini and Jacopo Peri, both of whom went on to write the earliest genuine operas.

THE FLORENTINE INTERMEDI OF 1589

The six *intermedi* composed to celebrate the marriage of Ferdinando de' Medici of Florence and Christine of Lorraine in 1589 were the most spectacular and expensive ever seen. So lavish was the presentation that it completely dominated the play it accompanied – *La pellegrina* ('The Pilgrim') by Girolamo Bargagli. All the texts and music survive, together with the designs for the costumes and sets. The *intermedi* were devised by Giovanni de' Bardi (1534–1612) on the theme of the

power of music in the ancient world, with texts written by Bardi, Ottavio Rinuccini (1562-1621) and Laura Guidiccioni (fl. 1550). The music was composed largely by Cristofano Malvezzi (1547–99) and Luca Marenzio (1550–99), with contributions by others, including Jacopo Peri (1561–1633), Giulio Caccini (1545–1618) and Bardi.

The individual scenes included: the Harmony of the Spheres (*Intermedio* 1); the contest in song between the Muses and the Pierides (*Intermedio* 2); the story of the singer Arion and his rescue by a dolphin (*Intermedio* 5); and the descent of Rhythm and Harmony from heaven to earth (*Intermedio* 6). The music for each of these scenes began with an instrumental *sinfonia*, and continued with a mixture of solo songs performed by virtuoso singers and elaborate choral madrigals requiring 60 singers and over 20 instruments.

RIGHT: Engraving after Bernardo Buonatalenti of the third intermedio from the Florentine festivities of 1589, celebrating the wedding of Ferdinando de'Medici. The subject of this scene, Apollo's victory over the python, formed the basis of Caccini and Peri's early opera Dafne.
BELOW: Plato and Aristotle, two key figures studied by the Camerata, from Raphael's fresco in the Stanza della Segnatura, Vatican City.

THE RECREATION OF THE GREEK IDEAL

The principal concern of the Camerata was to recreate as far as possible the character of ancient music. Although they had no actual examples of Greek melodies to go on, they closely studied the writings of the classical music theorists and philosophers (particularly Plato and Aristotle). Several ideas particularly interested the Camerata: the complete union of melody and poetry that its members saw in the performance

of song and dramas (especially tragedies) in the ancient world, and the legendary powers of music over the human soul and emotions. As a result of their discussions, the Camerata proposed an ideal style of music in which poetry and melody became equals. The music should not obscure the words – for example by having more than one melody performed at the same time, or by distorting the natural rhythms of speech. It should also reflect the subject matter of the poetry and reinforce the meaning of the words in order to achieve the maximum emotional impact on the listener. Music was reunited with drama and poetry once more.

The Early and Middle Baroque

As part of the Renaissance (literally "rebirth"), which began in Italy in around 1450 and featured a renewed interest in ancient Greek and Roman culture, the Baroque era was a revolution within a revolution. It saw a break from the Medieval view of humanity as innately sinful and in need of salvation. Instead, Renaissance thinking cast individuals as a dynamic force in their own right and gave freer rein than ever before to human imagination, ingenuity and self-expression. The breakaway Protestant movement, which rejected the ethos of the established Catholic Church after 1517, was typical of the often aggressive individuality that marked the Renaissance age.

A CHANGE IN MINDSET

The meaning of the word "baroque", coined by opponents of the new and shocking departure from ascetic Christian tradition, reflected the fundamental change in mindset the Renaissance involved. It derived from the Italian *barroco*, meaning "an obstacle to logic", or from the Portuguese *barroco* and Spanish *barrueco*, meaning an "irregularly shaped pearl". "Baroque" later came to mean anything imperfect, bizarre, contorted or generally contrary to established rules.

The impact was intense and all-pervasive. The flamboyant Baroque style affected all artistic forms, giving a new grandeur to architecture, rich, brilliant colour to painting and a more sensuous and fluid realism to sculpture. In particular, painting and sculpture depicted real, flesh-and-blood humans rather than stiff, insipid figures who looked as though they had never inhabited the real world.

A NEW VISUAL ATTRACTION

In the theatre, plays plumbed new depths of emotion and explored the dark complexities of love, hate, revenge and despair. The recasting of music was just as startling. Until the Baroque style evolved, music had been dominated by the simpler, restrained sound of sacred works designed to invoke religious devotion and typify the other-worldliness of faith. Baroque composers broadened these horizons by turning musical performances into entertainments that explored emotional depths and rich harmonic textures. Baroque opera introduced interplay between orchestra and performers and an entirely novel feature, the visual attractions of costumed performers and stage scenery.

Introduction

Opera began as an elite art. The first operas were created and performed for small, select audiences at wealthy courts in such cultural centres as Florence, Mantua, Parma and Rome. However, in 1637 the first public theatre in Venice, the Teatro San Cassiano (see below) opened, and the "invitation only" nature of opera changed. The Venetian opera houses were funded by Venice's patrician families, and paid for mostly by the sale of subscription boxes to the wealthy. Opera was expensive to produce, and although the opera houses were "public", access to the productions was usually limited to those with money to spare.

ITALIAN ORIGINS AND MONTEVERDI

Opera, a tradition that brings together art, architecture, music and literature, was the most enduring result of the Baroque's dramatic impulse. The operas of the seventeenth century are an index of the latest developments in all these arts. The plots of the operas were drawn mostly from mythology or history, but the telling of these tales reflected the current literary ideals.

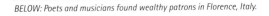

BELOW: Poets and musicians found wealthy patrons in Florence, Italy.

THE TEATRO SAN CASSIANO, VENICE

When the Teatro San Cassiano, the first public opera house, opened in 1637, the Venetian nobility rapidly decamped from the private homes in which performances had previously been given and rented the best box seats for each opera season. The public had to make do with the lower *parterre*, or "pit". The San Cassiano was built and owned by an aristocratic family, the Trons. The first opera staged there was *L'Andromeda* (1637), with music by Francesco Manelli and libretti by Benedetto Ferrari. Ferrari and Manelli were in charge of production for two years before handing over control to a company led by the composer Francesco Cavalli (1602–76). For the next six years, Cavalli wrote all the operas performed at San Cassiano except for Claudio Monteverdi's (1567–1643) *Il ritourno d'Ulisse in patria* ('Ulysses' Return Home', 1640). As more and more opera houses opened in Venice – 11 by the end of the seventeenth century – fewer and fewer operas were produced at San Cassiano.

Ultimately, the Teatro was upstaged by larger opera houses that were able to stage more elaborate performances. Although in decline, San Cassiano remained open for another century until it finally closed in 1807, after 170 years.

INTRODUCTION

ABOVE: Venice, Italy soon became the centre of Italian opera. This English miniature of the city was painted around 1400.
RIGHT: A poster for Jean-Baptiste Lully's Armide et Rénaud. Lully developed his opera style as court composer to Louis XIV.

L'Orfeo, favola in musica ('Orpheus, a Legend in Music', 1607), written by Claudio Monteverdi and first staged in Mantua, recounted the tragic tale of the legendary musician Orpheus, who never recovered from the death of his wife, Euridice: he spent the rest of his life mourning for her and singing of his loss. The popularity of this poignant theme was evident from the start. Within a year, another opera had been written on the same subject, and before the seventeenth century was out, a further 21 had been performed.

Monteverdi was an undisputed trendsetter, and in more than his choice of subject. *L'Orfeo* displayed a novel approach – more dramatic, more lyrical and much more expressive than its predecessors. The popular appeal of this first undisputed masterpiece of Baroque opera and the works that followed it was soon evident. Within a short time, Venice, where Monteverdi settled in 1613 as *maestro di cappella* at the Cathedral of St Mark's, became the first centre of Italian opera. There, opera began to evolve, as audiences demanded more drama and more action on stage. An overture, at first consisting of a short fanfare of instruments, was introduced to start the performance. Opera plots became more violent and exciting and stage effects more spectacular. The aria introduced by Monteverdi became more prominent. The seamless musical style known as *bel canto* – "beautiful singing" ⟶ **p. 24** – also developed in Venice. By that time, Rome had replaced Venice as the centre of Italian opera. Rome was succeeded later in the seventeenth century by Naples.

THE ARRIVAL OF OPERA IN GERMANY AND FRANCE

The popularity of opera quickly spread outside Italy. Italian opera was adopted wholesale in Germany and Austria and dominated the scene for several years. German-language operas did not appear until after 1678, when the Oper am Gänsemarkt was established in Hamburg. Italian opera arrived in France in 1645 but had only limited success. In the event, the individualistic French preferred to develop their own genre. In 1664, Jean-Baptiste Lully (1632–87), court composer to King Louis XIV, started to compose *comédie-ballets*, which bore some resemblance to opera in their use of recitative and melodious airs, with dances added to the performances.

VERNACULAR OPERA IN FRANCE AND SPAIN

The first French opera was *Pomone* (1671), composed by Robert Cambert (*c.* 1628–77), with a libretto written by the poet Pierre Perrin. Spain developed its own native form of opera, the *zarzuela*, also in the seventeenth century. This musical drama with spoken dialogue took its name from the hunting lodge owned by King Philip IV near Madrid, where *zarzuela* and other dramatic performances took place. Although characteristically Spanish, *zarzuela* was Italianate in form and included arias, recitatives, duets, choruses and dances, as well as popular songs performed between the acts.

FINALLY AN ENGLISH OPERA

The typically English opera was slow to develop, and did not appear in full form until the twentieth century. Instead, English audiences were offered French-style "semi-operas" that featured spoken dialogue. One brilliant exception was *Dido and Aeneas* (1689) ⟶ **p. 33** by Henry Purcell (1659–95), an outstanding all-English, all-sung opera that was written for a girls' school in Chelsea, London.

1475 — 1700 EARLY & MIDDLE BAROQUE

I.V. Duplessis inv.   L. Desplaces sculp.

ARMIDE TRAGEDIE

PROLOGUE.

Le Théâtre Repréſente vn Palais

Genres and Styles

Opera developed from a mixture of genres, styles and techniques that combined to create a distinctly new form of music. Among opera's many novel aspects, one of the most significant was its secular nature. Opera essentially upended the basic principle of church music. For religious purposes, words had to predominate over the music. With opera, it was the other way around; plots, characters and lyrics were important, but they served the musical agenda.

A BREAK WITH SACRED TRADITION – DRAMMA PER MUSICA

In Renaissance times, secularism was tantamount to heresy, and heresy incurred very severe punishment, including torture and burning. It was no small matter, therefore, when the effect of secularism on opera made it an obvious culprit. The evidence was there in opera's reliance on the pagan myths of ancient Greece, its strong emotional content, its emphasis on human, rather than religious motivations and the flamboyant materialism of its spectacular staging. Opera broke another basic tradition of religious music – that the "libretto" should consist of sacred texts. Instead, opera had its own libretto, the

dramma per musica ("drama for music"), which dealt with heroic or serious but not necessarily religious themes. In these circumstances, it was inevitable that opera should become subject to papal prohibition orders.

NEW MUSICAL FORMS EVOLVED – MONODY

The pope, however, could not exercise a blanket ban in Italy, which in Renaissance times was a mass of city-states with their own rulers, their own laws – and their own opera houses. Religious authorities were able to exert less pressure of the sort that had controlled the arts in Medieval times, so that new musical forms were able to evolve. One of them was monody, the solo song that

MONTEVERDI'S INNOVATIONS

Claudio Monteverdi was a great innovator who achieved the quantum leap of musical style that largely freed opera from its Medieval and religious origins. To achieve this, he broke some rules, put his own interpretations on others and made changes that, in seventeenth-century terms, were revolutionary. The recitative, for example, was already an established pattern in singing, but Monteverdi used it in a new way, as a lead-in to an aria.

Orchestras in the seventeenth century were relatively small, which limited their dramatic impact. Monteverdi expanded the size of his orchestra to some 40 instruments, thus broadening and deepening the sound. It was common practice, too, for music to be played by any available combination of instruments. Monteverdi sought more precise effects by allocating certain passages of music in his operas to instruments of his choice. A further innovation, again uncommon in seventeenth-century orchestration, was Monteverdi's frequent changes of harmony and key. This variability increased an opera's dramatic feel, alerted the audience to new musical developments in the score and generally kept their attention at a peak of interest.

RIGHT: Although small in size, seventeenth-century orchestras could feature up to 40 different instruments.

became popular in Florence and Venice in the first half of the seventeenth century. Monody, which was accompanied by a *continuo* (bass line), often played on a harpsichord or lute, came in two forms. The first was the madrigal type, which had an elaborately decorated vocal line. The second, established by Caccini around 1601–2, was the aria type, in which the principal melody was repeated with variations. Monody was emotional and highly ornamented, with varied rhythms and vocal leaps between notes that greatly heightened its dramatic effect.

RECITATIVE

Recitative, a part-spoken, part-sung musical line based on natural speech rhythms and pitch, was regarded as largely synonymous with monody. During the seventeenth century, recitatives acted as a link between one aria and the next, but this was not their only function. Their words could also further the plot or give insights into the characters, but without letting go of the musical line. Another French innovation, the *ballet de cour*, or "royal court ballet", featured a recitative at the start of each act, where it served as a narrative to explain the action or "plot" demonstrated by the dance.

RIGHT: The emergence of the aria allowed soloists, such as French soprano Marie-Louise Desmatins, to become stars in their own right. BELOW: A hugely popular instrument in Baroque times, the lute was used to accompany monody and is still played today.

ENSEMBLE

Like the ballet, opera was a genre requiring the precise, skillful teamwork known as ensemble playing. The expression came from the French word *ensemble*, meaning "together". As opera scores began to include duets – usually "love" duets – trios, quartets and quintets, great precision, timing and tone control were required of the singers. This is not to suggest that the solo performer, singing an aria and therefore responsible for delivering the major share of the music, was under less demanding discipline. In early Baroque opera, the aria – which in Italian meant "air" and was a lyrical piece for solo voice – was usually accompanied by a *continuo* with *ritornellos*, or short orchestral interludes between the verses. In early Baroque arias, there were four or more verses. The number of verses was reduced to two after 1650, and subsequently, the two-verse aria became standard. In Venice, until 1660 arias were written in double or triple time or a mixture of both.

GENRES AND STYLES

SACRA RAPPRESENTAZIONE IN ITALY

Opera, however, did not have a monopoly of the aria. Arias were also centrepieces in cantatas, the vocal chamber music of the Baroque era, and in oratorios. Although the oratorio shared with opera the basic ingredients of soloists, chorus and orchestra, oratorios placed much more emphasis on choral than on solo singing, and the two genres had different purposes. Opera rapidly developed as a secular art form, whereas oratorio was firmly planted in sacred music. In the mid-sixteenth century, some time before it helped to "father" opera, the groundwork of oratorio was laid in "spiritual exercises" at the Congregation of the Oratorio of St Filippo Neri in Rome. In its turn, oratorio had its own "sire", which also contributed to the development of opera – the *sacra rappresentazione*, or "sacred opera", a religious play with musical accompaniment.

DIVERTISSEMENT IN FRANCE

While Italy was the chief and most prolific influence in developing "true" opera, other European countries took to the new genre with enthusiasm and developed their own operatic traditions. The French, for example, introduced the *divertissement* ("entertainment"), a section of vocal solos, ensembles and dances that are usually

---

MELODIES FROM THE OPERA – THE OVERTURE

The Florentine composer Pietro Cesti (1623–69) introduced the idea of putting melodies in an opera into its overture, as a kind of "trailer" to the music that was to come and to set the mood of the opera itself. He first did this in his famous *Il pomo d'oro* ('The Golden Apple', 1668).

POPULAR MELODY

---

ancillary to the work's main action. The *grands divertissements* devised for King Louis XIV in 1664 and 1674, complete entertainments in their own right, featured two or more singers who represented allegorical or mythological figures.

Like these "big diversions", the *tragédie en musique* or *tragédie lyrique* – the musical or lyrical tragedy – had links with the French royal court. The *tragédie en musique*, which normally opened with a prologue extolling royalty, was first established by Robert Cambert and afterwards developed by Jean-Baptiste Lully and Jean-Philippe Rameau (1683–1764). The libretto concentrated on the themes of courtly love and knightly behaviour, and the performance included ballet scenes, recitatives, choruses and airs, which used minuet and other dance rhythms.

AIR

The French shared another innovation, the air, with the English. The air – a term for a light tune or song – appeared in France after 1571 as the *air de cour*, or court song. The first *airs de cour* were solo or ensemble songs with lute accompaniment. The genre reached England in 1597 with the publication of the first of four books of *Ayres for Voice and Lute* by John Dowland (1563–1626). The other three appeared in 1600, 1603 and 1612.

BEL CANTO

Bel canto – beautiful singing – is a vocal technique that is deliberately designed to sound effortless but is, in reality, extremely difficult to achieve. Although the technique reached full flower in the nineteenth century, especially in the operas of Vincenzo Bellini (1801–35), elements of *bel canto* style first appeared in the Baroque era, in Venetian opera of the mid-seventeenth century. The technique goes back even further, though, to Medieval teachers who encouraged singers to achieve an even continuity of tone and pass from one musical phrase to the next without a pause. The smooth, sustained *legato* characteristic of *bel canto*, in which the singer scarcely seems to take a breath, requires superlative tone, elegant phrasing and expressive delivery, all combined in seamless fashion to provide an uninterrupted musical line. Although *bel canto* can appear to lack vocal fire when compared to the extra-musical dramatics of *verisimo*, it is by no means without drama or emotion and was used to great effect by its most illustrious twentieth-century practitioners, Maria Callas (1923–77) and Tito Schipa (1888–1965). Long identified as the traditional Italian art of singing, the term *bel canto* was first used some time before 1840 by Italian composer and singer Nicola Vaccai.

GENRES AND STYLES

Overall, however, the English failed to make a characteristic mark on opera. The only noteworthy example to come out of England in the Baroque era was Henry Purcell's *Dido and Aeneas*. Purcell was nevertheless a considerable composer for the theatre. He wrote songs and instrumental music for plays and co-wrote five semi-operas. These were more spoken dialogue than opera but included *divertissements* and various musical scenes and shared some characteristics with the English court entertainment known as the masque.

MASQUES

The masque developed out of fifteenth-century English and Italian entertainments in which masks were used as a disguise. Introduced at court by King Henry VIII (1491–1547), the masque was a mixture of songs with recitatives, dialogue, dances, energetic "revels" and provocative interplay between performers and audience. The staging of masques could be extremely elaborate. After 1660, they moved from the royal court to the theatre, to become a public entertainment.

RIGHT: This costume design was drawn by Inigo Jones for a masque ball. It shows the Oberon costume worn by Prince Henry, son of James I. BELOW: A score for Cantata No. 188, by Johann Sebastian Bach (1685–1750). Cantatas were vocal works that included arias. OPPOSITE: Tito Schipa (1888–1965) was an Italian tenor and early protagonist of bel canto, a difficult vocal technique.

GENRES AND STYLES

KEY COMPOSERS

Claudio Monteverdi

EARLY & MIDDLE
BAROQUE

1475 — 1700

Claudio Giovanni Antonio Monteverdi (1567–1643), born in Cremona on 15 May, began his illustrious career as a choirboy in the town's cathedral. By the time he was 20, he had already published the first of his eventual nine books of secular madrigals. He was also a skilled composer of motets. Monteverdi's horizons expanded in 1591 when he joined the court orchestra of Vincenzo Gonzaga, Duke of Mantua, as a string instrumentalist.

LAMENTO D'ARIANNA ('ARIANNA'S LAMENT')

Lamento d'Arianna ('Arianna's Lament') is the only music from Monteverdi's opera *Arianna* to survive. It was arranged in various guises, as a monody in 1623, a madrigal in 1624 and a sacred song in 1638. In consequence, the *Lamento* is the best-known piece in Monteverdi's operatic output.

POPULAR MELODY

AN AMBITIOUS YOUNG MAN

The young Monteverdi was full of ambition and aspired to succeed the Flemish composer Giaches de Wert as *maestro di cappella* in Mantua. In the event, he was upstaged by an older musician, Benedetto Pallavicino, and was forced to wait for five years, until Pallavicino's death, before he achieved his goal. Once he had reached his goal, however, his new position did not bring Monteverdi a comfortable berth. The influence of the Camerata group in Florence and the push for heightened emotion and expression in opera were already spreading. Monteverdi was attracted by these radical changes and was soon regarded as the leading exponent of the new forms of harmony and orchestration. This led him into conflict with the conservative theorist Giovanni Maria Artusi. The argument brought Monteverdi to the fore as a leader of the progressives, who embraced the new, if revolutionary, style in opera.

AN INNOVATIVE OPERA: ORFEO

Monteverdi's *Orfeo* ➤ **p. 28**, produced in Mantua in 1607, made the case for the progressive approach, and the message was reinforced by his next work, *Arianna* (1608). This was a particularly fraught time for Monteverdi, for both these operas were accompanied by tragedy in his personal life. In 1607, the year of *Orfeo*, Monteverdi's wife, Claudia de Cattaneis, died and left him with three young children. In 1608, Caterina Martinelli, a young singer who lived with Monteverdi and who was due to take the title role in *Arianna*, died of smallpox. A replacement took over, and the first performance of *Arianna* went ahead as scheduled. Like *Orfeo*, the opera was a great

success, but the achievement had its down side: the acclaim appeared to intensify the dispute with Artusi and other conservatives, and a disenchanted Monteverdi left Mantua for his home town of Cremona. He pleaded poor health and insufficient pay but could not entirely free himself from Mantua. However, the Gonzaga family still had a lien on his services and did not release him until Duke Vincenzo died in 1612.

MAESTRO DI CAPPELLA AT ST MARK'S

The following year, Monteverdi was appointed *maestro di cappella* at the Cathedral of St Mark's in Venice, a prestigious post he held until his death 30 years later. His duties were not onerous, however, and left Monteverdi with plenty of time for other work. He was now a prestigious figure in the music and opera world, and commissions regularly came his way. Two, ironically from Mantua, included a ballet, *Tirsi e Clori* (1616), and another opera, *La finta pazza Licori* ('Licori's Fake Madness', 1627). Meanwhile, Monteverdi's books of madrigals continued to appear. The eighth was published in 1638, the ninth, printed posthumously, in 1651.

MONTEVERDI'S MASTERPIECE

In 1637, when the world's first public opera house, San Cassiano ➤ **p. 20**, opened in

Venice, Monteverdi was already on hand to compose operas for performance there. *Arianna* was revived for San Cassiano in 1640, and three new Monteverdi operas were premiered in the next three years. The third was Monteverdi's masterpiece, *L'incoronazione di Poppea* ('The Coronation of Poppea', 1642) •• p. 29, which was first performed in the autumn. Soon afterwards, Monteverdi went home to Cremona for the last time. He died on 29 November 1643, soon after his return to Venice.

BELOW: The cathedral in Cremona, Italy, where Monteverdi was a choirboy. The cathedral dates from the twelfth to the thirteenth century.
OPPOSITE: Claudio Monteverdi (1567–1643) wrote 13 operas in his lifetime. Sadly, many of these have been lost.

WORDS FOR THE MUSIC – THE LIBRETTO

A libretto – Italian for "small book" – enabled audiences to read the words of an opera or, in the case of a foreign language, a translation. Some of the earliest libretti were quite substantial in size, around 21.6 cm. However, they were not too unwieldy and were read by members of the audience, in confined seating space, while the performance was going on. The auditoriums of opera houses and theatres were lit by candles, which were dimmed while the performance was taking place. Instead, individual candles were available as an aid to reading. Some early libretti that have survived show grease spots where candle wax dripped onto the pages.

A libretto normally began with a preface dedicated to the librettist's patron and then went on to a prologue explaining the context of the opera's action. A list of characters came next, then details of the scene-changes, the dances to be featured and sometimes notes about the scenic effects on stage. In Italy, where the Church was always on the lookout for pagan references in the texts of Baroque operas, the librettist also had to affirm his own devout Roman Catholic faith.

Timeline

1567	Claudio Monteverdi born in Cremona, Italy
1587	Publishes first of nine books of secular madrigals
1591	Joins court of Duke Vincenzo I Gonzaga, Mantua, as string player
1601	Monteverdi becomes *maestro di cappella* at Vincenzo I's Mantuan court
1605	Fifth book of madrigals published
1607	Premiere of *Orfeo* in Mantua; Monteverdi's wife dies
1608	*Arianna* (music of which is now mostly lost) premieres in Mantua
1610	*Vespers* first performed, Mantua
1612	Released from court of Gonzaga after death of Vincenzo I
1613	Moves to Venice; becomes *maestro di cappella* at St Mark's Cathedral
1624	Composes *Il combattimento di Tancredi*
1630	Austrian troops sack St Mark's and destroy 12 of Monteverdi's operas; plague ravages Venice
1632	Monteverdi admitted to holy orders
1637	World's first public opera house, San Cassiano, opens in Venice
1638	Eighth book of madrigals published
1640	Monteverdi writes *Il ritorno d'Ulisse in patria* for Venetian public opera
1642	Composes *L'incoronazione di Poppea*
1643	*Poppea* premieres in Venice
1643	Monteverdi dies in Venice
1651	Ninth and final book of madrigals published posthumously

KEY COMPOSERS

EARLY & MIDDLE BAROQUE
1475 — 1700

L'Orfeo, favola in musica
('Orpheus, a Legend in Music')

L'Orfeo, favola in musica by Monteverdi

Composed   1606
Premiered   1607, Mantua
Libretto   by Alessandro Striggio, after
Ottavio Rinuccini and Ovid

L'Orfeo, favola in musica, consists of a prologue and five acts, a prolonged performance for its time. Monteverdi used several devices to extend the action of the opera. He wrote recitatives to be performed between the duets, as well as polyphonic madrigals, of which he was a master. Further additions included dances.

The opera, commissioned by the Gonzaga family for the carnival of 1606–7, was first produced privately in Mantua at the Accademia degli Invaghiti in February 1607. The performance was something of a relief to Monteverdi, who had been forced to overcome a crisis – a shortage of castrati (male sopranos) in Mantua. Monteverdi had to recruit a castrato from Pisa, but he intensified the crisis by arriving late. Monteverdi had to give him a crash course to enable him to memorize words and music in record time. Copies of Striggio's libretto were specially printed and distributed among the audience so that they could follow the performance while it was in progress. It was so successful that Duke Vincenzo Gonzaga ordered a second performance. A third was planned but never took place. Orfeo was published in 1609, with a dedication to the Duke.

LEFT: Demons wait to take Euridice back to the underworld.

Orfeo, **Le Concert d'Astrée**
Emmanuelle Haïm, **conductor**
Virgin Classics 7243 5 45642 2
Soloists: Natalie Dessay (Musica), Patrizia Ciofi (Euridice), Alice Coote (Silvia), Ian Bostridge (Orfeo), Christopher Maltman (Apollo)

RECOMMENDED RECORDING

Synopsis
L'Orfeo, favola in musica by Monteverdi

PROLOGUE
The figure of Music welcomes the audience and flatters the patrons (the Gonzaga family), telling of the magic and power of music and asking for silence during the performance.

ACT I
In the fields of Thrace, nymphs and shepherds gather to celebrate the long-awaited marriage of demi-god Orfeo to beautiful Euridice. Amid joyous dancing and singing and teasing lovers' games, Orfeo delivers a romantic aria to Euridice. The pair then leave for the wedding.

ACT II
Returning from the wedding, Orfeo sings with the shepherds about how wonderful life is now that he has married Euridice and how miserable his life was before the wedding. A messenger, Silvia, arrives with bad news; she tells Orfeo that Euridice has suffered a snake bite and has died, whispering Orfeo's name in her final breath. The grieving Orfeo resolves to fetch his bride back from the underworld, while Silvia, mortified by the terrible news she has had to bear, shuts herself away.

ACT III
Hope escorts Orfeo to the entrance of the underworld, where she then leaves him. There he encounters Charon, the boatman of the dead, who ferries souls across the River Styx. Charon is unwilling to let him pass, but Orfeo sings to him and plays his lyre until the boatman is lulled to sleep. Orfeo then crosses the river and enters the underworld.

ACT IV
Proserpina, the wife of Plutone, ruler of the underworld, is profoundly affected by Orfeo's music and pleads with her husband to release Euridice. Plutone agrees that Euridice may follow Orfeo out of the underworld, on the condition that Orfeo does not turn around. As they make their way along, Orfeo is seized with doubt and looks behind him to check that Euridice is there. Euridice must now leave Orfeo and remain in the underworld for eternity.

ACT V
Back in the fields of Thrace, the inconsolable Orfeo is comforted by Eco. His divine father, Apollo the sun god, descends from the heavens on a cloud. He then returns into the sky, taking Orfeo with him. From this heavenly viewpoint, Orfeo can gaze forever upon Euridice's starry image, as she has been transformed into a constellation.

THE CASTRATI

A castrato was a male singer whose boyish singing voice was preserved by castrating him before his voice changed during puberty. The castrato had an important part to play in the performance of opera, since women were barred from performing on stage and the male soprano or contralto was employed instead. If anything, a castrato's voice was the more effective, since castration did not entirely eliminate maleness. This was especially significant in terms of the strength of the lungs, which made the castrato voice more flexible, more penetrating and more sensuous than female voices could normally manage.

Castrati were first mentioned as early as 1562, when they were employed in religious services; the church went on using castrati for another three centuries. The advent of opera in the seventeenth century gave these singers an additional outlet – and a chance for riches and fame that the church could not offer. The opera house also provided an opportunity for lavish praise that flattered the proverbial vanity of the castrati. For example, the tone of one castrato was said to put a nightingale to shame with a sound that seemed barely human. The creation of castrati became illegal in 1870.

LEFT: Carlo Scalzi was a well-known Italian castrato. He was painted by French artist Charles Joseph Flipart in 1738.

KEY COMPOSERS

L'incoronazione di Poppea
('The Coronation of Poppea')

L'incoronazione di Poppea by Monteverdi

Composed	1642
Premiered	1643, Venice
Libretto	by Gian Francesco Busenello, after Tacitus and Suetonius

L'incoronazione de Poppea, has been called Monteverdi's greatest opera. It was one of the first operas to be based on history rather than mythology. The action takes place in Rome in AD 65. The eponymous heroine is the mistress and, later, wife of the Emperor Nero. The libretto was by Gian Francesco Busenello (1598–1659), who took his text from the annals of the ancient Roman historian Tacitus (AD 55–120). The opera received its first performance in Venice in 1643. *Poppea* was written when Monteverdi was 76 and, by the standards of the seventeenth century, a very old man. Comparisons have been made with Giuseppe Verdi (1813–1901), who wrote his last opera, *Falstaff* (1893), in old age. Modern research has revealed that *Poppea* may not have been all Monteverdi's own work. It was ascribed to him by Cristoforo Ivanovich (1628–89), an Italian librettist and theatre historian, but neither of

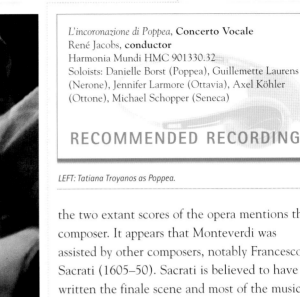

LEFT: Tatiana Troyanos as Poppea.

the two extant scores of the opera mentions the composer. It appears that Monteverdi was assisted by other composers, notably Francesco Sacrati (1605–50). Sacrati is believed to have written the finale scene and most of the music sung by Ottone, who attempts to kill Poppea after she has jilted him.

Synopsis
L'incoronazione di Poppea by Monteverdi

PROLOGUE

The figures of Fortuna (Fortune) and Virtù (Virtue) argue over who has the most power over mortals. Amore (Love, or Cupid) joins them, insisting that his superior power will shortly be proven.

ACT I

Poppea's husband, Ottone, returns to her palace to find Nero's guard outside, confirming that she has taken Nero as her lover. Poppea and Nero take leave of each other, and Poppea confides in her nurse, Arnalta, her desire to be crowned empress. Meanwhile, Nero's wife, Empress Octavia, laments her husband's infidelity and is comforted by Seneca, a statesman and philospher. Returning home to his palace, Nero declares his intention to divorce Octavia and marry Poppea, making her empress. Seneca argues against this on both moral and political grounds, causing Nero's temper to rise against him.

Later, Poppea, overheard by Ottone, convinces Nero that Seneca is an obstacle to their love and must die. Ottone is then rebuked by Drusilla, a noblewoman who is in love with him, over his continuing love for Poppea. Ottone pledges himself to Drusilla.

ACT II

The captain of Nero's guards, Liberto, delivers Seneca's death sentence from the emperor. Seneca gathers the members of his household around him and kills himself. While Poppea, overjoyed at the news of Seneca's death, prays to Amore, Octavia orders Ottone to kill Poppea. He hesitates, torn between his love for her and her cruel betrayal, but eventually he agrees and asks Drusilla to help him by lending him some of her clothes. Dressed as Drusilla, Ottone creeps into Poppea's chamber as she sleeps and tries to kill her. Cupid, however, protects her, and Ottone is unsuccessful. Poppea sees Ottone fleeing, pursued by Arnalta, and assumes that the figure is Drusilla.

ACT III

Drusilla is arrested for the attempted murder of Poppea and, to shield Ottone, pleads guilty and is sentenced to death. Ottone then comes forward, explaining that he was acting under Octavia's orders. This makes the situation fairly straightforward for Nero, who can now banish Octavia, as well as Ottone and Drusilla, and crown Poppea empress as planned. Poppea is invited to ascend the imperial throne and is crowned by consuls in the name of the Roman Senate. Amore then descends from heaven with Venus and crowns Poppea goddess of beauty on Earth.

ABOVE: A performance of Monteverdi's L'incoronazione di Poppea *by the San Fransisco Opera. The opera was first performed in Venice in 1643.*

EARLY & MIDDLE BAROQUE

1475 — 1700

KEY COMPOSERS

Jean-Baptiste Lully

Jean-Baptiste Lully (1632–87) was a French composer with an Italian background. He was born in Florence on 28 November 1632. His original name, later gallicized, was Giovanni Battista Lulli. In 1646, aged 14, he was placed with a noble household in Paris as a singer, dancer and violinist, and he became familiar with both French and Italian music. In 1653, he caught the attention of King Louis XIV.

COMPOSITIONS FOR THE COURT OF LOUIS XIV

Although discomfited by the composer's homosexual tendencies, King Louis thought a great deal of Lully and appointed him royal composer of instrumental music. By 1662, Lully was a naturalized Frenchman and he became music master to the French royal family. He produced numerous scores for the *comédies-ballets* performed at Louis' lavish court. After 1671, when Robert Cambert's *Pomone* received its first performance, Lully progressed to opera. Devious and opportunistic, Lully bought the "franchise" to present oprea that had been reserved to Cambert's librettist, Pierre Perrin (1620–75), after Perrin was imprisoned in 1672. Subsequently, Lully became a prolific composer of opera in the peculiarly French genre known as *tragédie lyrique*, which he promoted together with his librettist, Philippe Quinault (1635–88). Lully wrote 13 operas of this type, beginning with *Cadmus et Hermione* (1673) and ending with *Armide et Rénaud* (1686). Quinault was librettist for all but two.

MORE SOBER COMPOSITIONS

After 1683, when King Louis married the highly respectable Mme de Maintenon, the tone of the court became much more sober.

ABOVE: Jean-Baptiste Lully, composer and court musician.

Lully turned to writing sacred music and produced 13 "great" and 14 "small" motets, as well as his *Te Deum* (1677) and *De Profundis* (1683). Sadly, during a performance of the *Te Deum* early in 1687, Lully injured his foot with the point of the cane he was using to beat time. The injury became gangrenous and Lully died on 22 March 1687.

Operas

1672	*Les fêtes de l'amour et de Bacchus*
1673	*Cadmus et Hermione*
1674	*Alceste, ou le triomphe d'Alcide*
1675	*Thésée*
1676	*Atys*
1677	*Isis*
1678	*Psyché*
1679	*Bellérophon*
1680	*Proserpine*
1682	*Persée*
1683	*Phaéton*
1684	*Amadis de Gaule*
1685	*Roland*
1686	*Armide et Rénaud*
1686	*Acis et Galathée*
1687	*Achille et Polixène*

Timeline

1632	Born as Giovanni Battista Lulli in Florence, Italy
1646	Moves to France and changes name to Jean-Baptiste Lully
1653	Enters service of Louis XIV as ballet dancer and instrumental composer
c. 1656	Becomes leader of band of *les petits violins du Roi*
1662	Appointed music master to the royal family
1664	Collaborates with Molière on *Le marriage force*, first in series of *comédies-ballets*
1664	Writes *Miserere*
1670	Lully performs in his *comédie-ballet*, *Le bourgeois gentilhomme*
1672	Obtains exclusive rights from King Louis to arrange operatic performances in Paris
1673	Produces his first *tragedie lyrique*, *Cadmus et Hermione*
1674	*Alceste* premieres spectacularly in Paris
1677	Lully composes *Te Deum*
1683	Louis XIV marries, and Lully composes *De Profundis*
1686	Premiere of *Acis et Galathée*
1687	Lully dies of gangrene of the foot in Paris
1687	Posthumous production of *Achille et Polixène*

BELOW: Louis XIV was King of France from 1643 until his death in 1715. Lully produced numerous scores for Louis as court musician.

Alceste, ou le triomphe d'Alcide

Alceste by Lully

Composed	1674
Premiered	1674, Paris
Libretto	by Philippe Quinault, after Euripides

Jean-Baptiste Lully's *Alceste, ou le triomphe d'Alcide* ('Alceste, or the Triumph of Alcide'), a *tragédie lyrique* with a prologue and five acts, had a double link with ancient Greek culture. The libretto, by Philippe Quinault, was based on *Alcestis*, a tragedy by the ancient Greek dramatist Euripides that in turn derived from the legend of Alcestis, wife of Admetus, King of Thessaly: Admetus had been promised immortality as long as he could find someone to die in his place. Alcestis volunteers to die

ABOVE: This seventeenth century French engraving shows a performance of Alceste *given in the marble court of Château de Versailles, France, on the first day of the fête at Versailles in 1674.*

ALCESTE: PROLOGUE

In the prologue to *Alceste*, the purpose of the opera is made clear by the mythological Nymph of the River Seine, as she laments the absence of King Louis XIV who is away fighting against the forces of the Burgundian state of Franche-Comté.

POPULAR MELODY

for him but is prevented by the hero Hercules, who fights off Death in order to save her.

Lully wrote *Alceste*, which debuted at the Paris Opéra in 1674, to celebrate King Louis XIV's triumph in battle in Franche-Comté. Much of Lully's output while in Louis' employ was produced to satisfy the King's own taste in music, and *Alceste* was no exception. The

Alceste, **La Grande Ecurie et la Chambre du Roy**
Jean-Claude Malgoire, **conductor**
Astrée E 8527
Soloists: Colette Alliot-Lugaz (Alceste), Sophie Marin-Degor (Céphise), Howard Crook (Admète), Gilles Ragon (Lychas), Jean-Philippe Lafont (Alcide), François Loup (Lycomède)

RECOMMENDED RECORDING

staging of the opera was suitably spectacular, and knowing the French fondness for dancing, Lully provided ballet interludes. He also catered for audience preferences by providing a comic sub-plot and catchy tunes. This made *Alceste* a popular success, although the sensibilities of some critics were affronted, perhaps because they resented Lully's power.

Synopsis

Alceste by Lully

PROLOGUE

Nymphs on the banks of the River Seine sing and dance with La Gloire (Glory), eagerly awaiting the victorious return of the King from battle.

ACT I

The beautiful and widely courted Alceste selects as her husband Admète, King of Thessaly. Present at her wedding, and also in love with Alceste, are Alcide (Hercules) and Licomède, King of the island of Scyros. A sub-plot is introduced that reflects the main story, involving the confidants of Alcide and Licomède courting Alceste's confidante. Licomède organizes a feast, that various nymphs and spirits of the sea attend. In the confusion, he abducts Alceste, assisted safely to his homeland by his sister, the sea-nymph Thetis, and other supernatural beings.

ACT II

On Scyros, Licomède is unsuccessful in wooing Alceste. Alcide and Admète arrive to rescue her, and a fierce battle ensues. Due largely to Alcide's strength and valour, Licomède is vanquished, but Admète is mortally wounded in the battle and exchanges poignant dying words with Alceste. However, the divine Apollon intervenes, declaring that he will return Admète's life to him if someone will agree to die in his place.

ACT III

Alceste grieves for Admète and ponders over the problem of who is to die in order to restore her husband's life. Her confidante and Admète's father each outline their unsuitability for the task. Shortly Admète enters, desiring to know to whom he owes his return to health. It transpires it is Alceste who has sacrificed her life for his; Admète is heartbroken. Alcide declares his love for Alceste and offers to go down to the underworld to retrieve her, on the condition that Admète give Alceste up to him on their return. Admète agrees.

ACT IV

Alcide descends to the underworld and crosses the River Styx. There is a feast in progress, given by Pluton and Proserpine in honour of Alceste, which is interrupted by the news that Alcide has arrived to claim her and return her to the world of the living. Pluton, ruler of the underworld, is impressed by Alcide and agrees that the pair can leave.

ACT V

An *arc de triomphe* is erected and a huge feast given by Admète, to celebrate Alceste's and Alcide's return. Alceste reveals to Alcide that all of her love for Admète has returned, and Alcide heroically restores Alceste to her husband; the couple are reunited amid much rejoicing. Apollon and the Muses join in the celebrations, praising the happy couple and Alcide's noble sense of honour.

KEY COMPOSERS

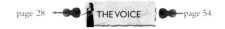
EARLY & MIDDLE BAROQUE

1475 — 1700

KEY COMPOSERS
Henry Purcell

*H*enry Purcell (1659–95) was one of the greatest Baroque composers and, as the diarist John Evelyn put it after his death, was "esteemed the best composer of any Englishman hitherto". Often compared to Mozart, Purcell exercised a similar mastery over many different types of composition – dramatic, sacred, vocal and instrumental. Tragically, like Mozart, Purcell died young, in his mid-thirties, leaving behind a prolific body of work.

FROM A MUSICAL FAMILY

Purcell came from a musical family. Apart from Henry himself, the most notable member of the family was his younger brother Daniel

BELOW: Henry Purcell (1659–95) wrote seven operas and the songs and incidental music for more than 40 stage plays in his brief but hugely successful career.

Operas

1689	*Dido and Aeneas*
1690	*Dioclesian*
1691	*King Arthur*
1692	*The Fairy Queen*
1695	*The Indian Queen*
1695	*The Tempest, or The Enchanted Isle*

(c. 1660–1717), who served as organist at Magdalen College, Oxford and at St Andrew's Church in London. In 1695, the year Purcell died, Daniel sought to follow in his illustrious brother's footsteps and became a composer of music for the London theatre.

A BRIEF BUT METEORIC CAREER

Henry Purcell began his short but brilliant career as a chorister in the Chapel Royal where his father was a gentleman. He went on to become organ maker and afterwards keeper of instruments to King Charles II in 1683, at a salary of £60 a year. Already Purcell had begun to compose, producing his first instrumental music in 1680 and his first songs three years later. Purcell's first foray into music for the theatre, *Dido and Aeneas*, was also his first and only true opera, in that it featured music throughout. Although he never wrote another opera as such, Purcell did not abandon the genre entirely. He wrote songs and incidental music for more than 40 stage plays. In 1690 he contributed a considerable portion of the music to *Dioclesian*, the first of five "semi-

Timeline

1659	Henry Purcell born in London
c. 1668	Becomes chorister in the Chapel Royal
1670	First musical composition in honour of Charles II's birthday
1674	Appointed as tuner of organ, Westminster Abbey, London
1677	Purcell becomes court composer
1679	Succeeds John Blow as organist of Westminster Abbey
1680	Writes first welcome ode, 'Welcome, Viceregent', for Charles II
1680	Completes his fantasies for viols; marries and eventually has six children
1682	Appointed one of three organists at the Chapel Royal
1685	Writes 'My Heart is Inditing' for coronation of James II
1689	Writes ode for Queen Mary, 'Now does the glorious day appear'
1689	*Dido and Aeneas* premieres in Chelsea
1691	*King Arthur* is produced
1692	Premiere of *The Fairy Queen*
1694	'Te Deum' and 'Jubilate' are performed for St Cecilia's Day
1695	Purcell's music accompanies Queen Mary's funeral
1695	*The Indian Queen* appears
1695	Purcell dies from tuberculosis in London, and is buried at Westminster Abbey

operas", providing *divertissements*, songs, choruses and dances. *Dioclesian* was followed by *King Arthur* (1691), *The Fairy Queen* (1692), *The Tempest* (c. 1695) and *The Indian Queen* (1695). Purcell died of consumption at Westminster on 21 November 1695.

SINGING VIBRATO IN BAROQUE OPERA

The revolution in opera that came about in the Baroque period required singers to acquire new techniques and disciplines. The idea was to elicit a greater emotional response from opera audiences, hold their attention and engage them more fully in the plot and its characters. One way these aims could be achieved was through judicious use of vocal ornamentation, such as *vibrato*. Singing *vibrato* required a singer to make the voice fluctuate in pitch, intensity and in its own distinctive sound, the timbre. Getting it right required great skill and control, since *vibrato* could easily degenerate into an unattractive "wobble". However, when it was performed by well-trained singers, either as a group or solo, *vibrato* gave added depth and expressiveness to the music. Lavish use of *vibrato* was not a general rule in Baroque opera. Controlled *vibrato*, known as "intensity *vibrato*", was preferred, and this was normally confined to the cadence point, the "full stop" at the end of a musical phrase. This ornamentation was always sung on the beat. Sometimes the ornament was notated on the opera score; at other times it was left to the singer to interpolate into the performance.

Dido and Aeneas

Dido and Aeneas by Purcell

Composed	1683–4
Premiered	c. 1689, London
Libretto	by Nahum Tate, after Virgil

Although ostensibly "English", *Dido and Aeneas* owes its ancestry to Italian and French operatic influences. Although the recitatives follow the rhythms and inflexions of the English language, they were clearly modelled on Italian monody. Purcell followed the already established tradition of taking the plots of operas from ancient myth and legend. This one came from ancient Rome, as the hero, the Trojan prince Aeneas, was by tradition an ancestor of the Romans. The story for *Dido and Aeneas* was taken from Book Four of the *Aeneid*, a drama in verse by the Roman poet Virgil who took 11 years to complete it.

Purcell's opera comprises a prologue and three acts, with a libretto by Irish dramatist Nahum

ABOVE: Virgil was a Roman poet who lived from 79–19 BC. Purcell based his opera Dido and Aeneas *on his writings.*

'WHEN I AM LAID IN EARTH'

At the end of Purcell's Baroque opera *Dido and Aeneas*, Dido, Queen of Carthage, is faced with the grievous fact that her lover, Aeneas, is going to leave her. Unable to bear the parting, she says farewell to life in the lament 'When I am laid in earth' and dies.

POPULAR MELODY

Tate. The first performance took place at Josias Priest's School for Young Gentlewomen in Chelsea, in the spring of 1689. This work is not *grand opéra*, despite its elemental theme, but makes fairly modest vocal demands on its small cast. It is therefore likely that the first performers of *Dido and Aeneas* were the Chelsea schoolgirls. The initial public performance was given in London in 1700. The opera was not revived again until the bicentenary of Purcell's death in 1895.

ABOVE: An illustration of the burial of Dido, taken from a fifteenth-century manuscript of Virgil's works.

𝒮*ynopsis*
Dido and Aeneas by Purcell

PROLOGUE

The Trojan Prince Aeneas has arrived at Carthage, having been shipwrecked on his way to Italy, where he was bound by Fate to found a new Troy. Belinda, lady-in-waiting and confidante of Dido, Queen of Carthage, sees Aeneas approaching the castle and requests that the court present him with an entertainment. There follows an allegorical dance featuring Phoebus and Venus.

ACT I

Dido is tormented by her love for Aeneas, but Belinda reassures her that the Prince returns her feelings. The courtiers, eager for a union between Carthage and Troy, offer further encouragement. Aeneas arrives with his attendants and declares his love for Dido, causing her to accept her own love for him. The act concludes with a triumphal dance.

ACT II

A sorceress summons witches to her cave, and together they gleefully plot Aeneas' departure, Dido's ruin and the destruction of Carthage. Their idea is to send one of their kind, disguised as Mercury, to persuade Aeneas that the gods want

him to leave Carthage immediately. They then conjure up a storm so that a royal hunting party will be obliged to return to the palace. Meanwhile, Dido and Aeneas are in the forest with a group of courtiers when the witches' storm breaks, and they flee for cover. Aeneas is approached by "Mercury", sent by the sorceress; he tells Aeneas that on Jove's command he must leave Carthage. Aeneas accepts his destiny, but not without sorrow for having to leave Dido. The act ends with a witches' chorus.

ACT III

On the quayside, Aeneas' men prepare for their departure with a sailors' song. The sorceress and witches look on with much joy and laughter; they comment on the proceedings and further plan Aeneas' death at sea, Dido's suicide and Carthage's ruin by fire. A witches' dance ends the scene. Back at the palace, Dido laments her cruel fate. Aeneas goes to her and declares that he will defy Fate and stay in Carthage, but Dido in her anger and self-pity rejects him. After Aeneas has left, Belinda attempts unsuccessfully to console Dido. The queen sings her final lament, considered to be one of opera's most beautiful and moving arias, and then kills herself. The opera concludes with the dance of the Cupids, who gather around Dido's tomb and scatter roses.

Other Composers

BLOW, JOHN
(1649–1708, ENGLISH)

John Blow, an influential figure in English music, was a gentleman of the Chapel Royal, organist there and later, in 1700, its official composer. Among his students was the brilliant Henry Purcell. Blow's own compositions were considerable. Besides his church music, which included over 100 anthems, he provided music for entertainments at the royal court. These were typically Baroque in their emphasis on emotion and included some 90 songs, together with duets, 70 pieces for harpsichord and his only work for the stage, *Venus and Adonis* (c. 1682). This short opera, which Blow described as a "masque for the entertainment of the king", was written for King Charles II, who had appointed him court composer. *Venus and Adonis*, in which Charles' mistress and her

ABOVE: John Blow (1649–1708) taught Henry Purcell and was court composer for Charles II.

daughter took part, showed distinct French influences in the dances. Blow's opera foreshadowed Purcell's *Dido and Aeneas*, composed two years later. Blow's 'Ode on the

Death of Mr Henry Purcell (1696)', a duet with instrumental accompaniment, eloquently expressed his sadness at the untimely demise of his young friend and sometime student.

CACCINI, GIULIO
(1551–1618, ITALIAN)

At age 13, Giulio Caccini arrived at the court of the Medici family in Florence and very quickly proved himself immensely gifted in several musical skills – as singer, composer, teacher, lutenist and harpist. In 1598, Caccini helped Jacopo Peri compose *Dafne*. In 1600 he became superintendent of musicians and actors at the ducal court of Tuscany. Also in 1600, Caccini wrote his first opera, *Il rapimento di Cefalo* ('The Kidnapping of Cefalo') and his second, *Euridice*, with libretto by Rinuccini. This *Euridice* was first performed in 1602. There was some dispute with Peri, who also used Rinuccini's text and acknowledged that his score included some of Caccini's music: this was not good enough for Caccini, who claimed that he, and not Peri, had "invented" the operatic style. However, Caccini's greatest contribution to music and

ABOVE: An illustration from Ovid's Metamorphoses. Musicians often used classical writers as inspiration for operatic works.

Synopsis
Euridice by Caccini
Premiered 1602, Florence
Libretto by Ottavio Rinuccini, after Ovid

PROLOGUE

The figure of Tragedy introduces the opera, explaining that to make the story suitable for marriage celebrations, the original ending has been altered.

ACT I

The act opens in an Arcadian village, with Euridice preparing for her marriage to Orfeo, along with nymphs and shepherds who sing of the couple's beauty. Orfeo is similarly celebrating with his friend Arcetro and other shepherds, when a messenger, Dafne, enters bearing bad news: Euridice has been bitten by a snake and has died, whispering Orfeo's name with her dying breath. The nymphs and shepherds join Orfeo in a melancholy lament.

ACT II

Orfeo, escorted by Venere, arrives in the underworld. He pleads with Plutone, the ruler there, to return Euridice to him, but Plutone explains that this is not how things happen in the underworld. However, the beauty of Orfeo's song touches the hearts of Proserpina (Plutone's wife), Venere and Charon, the boatman of the dead. These divinities add their pleas to Orfeo's, and Plutone eventually agrees to free Euridice.

ACT III

Meanwhile, the nymphs and shepherds are concerned about what has happened to Orfeo and Euridice. A shepherd, Arminta, arrives with the happy news that the couple are well and are on their way home. When Orfeo and Euridice return to the village, Orfeo sings a song of joy, which is followed by much rejoicing and dancing throughout the village. The opera closes with a celebration of the victory of love over death.

opera did not lie with his compositions but with his book *Le nuove musiche* ('The New Music'). In this book, published in 1602, Caccini made a powerful case for the radical changes of style and mood that revolutionized music in the Baroque period and prompted the birth of opera.

CAMPRA, ANDRÉ
(1660–1744, ITALIAN)

Despite his French name, André Campra was of Italian descent. Born in Aix-en-Provence, he became a church musician in Arles and Toulouse and composed sacred music that was much admired. In 1694 Campra moved to Paris to become master of music at the cathedral of Nôtre Dame. Three years later, he produced his *opéra-ballet*, *L'Europe galante* (1697). With this work, Campra was straying into secular territory and became worried that his church position might be jeopardized. This was why *L'Europe galante* was published anonymously and why Campra borrowed his brother's name for his other early compositions of the same type. Fortunately he did not have to maintain this subterfuge for too long. He left Nôtre Dame in 1700 and embarked on a prolific career as a composer of opera. Campra's sizable output included some 40 dramatic works, from short *divertissements* to full-length operas. Jean-Baptiste Lully, the "father" of French opera, exerted a strong influence over Campra's output, which won him great popularity and acclaim. Among his many honours and awards was an appointment, in 1722, as *Sons Maître de Musique de la Chappelle Royale* (Deputy Music Master of the Chapel Royal).

BELOW: Nôtre Dame Cathedral in Paris, France. In 1694, Campra was master of music here.

OTHER COMPOSERS

CAVALIERE, EMILIO DEL
(c. 1550–1602, ITALIAN)

Emilio del Cavaliere, composer, teacher, dancer and organist, was born in Rome. At the Medici court in Florence, he organized the family's spectacular celebrations and was also involved with the innovative Camerata group and their experiments into the *stile rappresentativo* (representative style). In 1589 Cavaliere contributed madrigals and concluding music for the *intermedi* (interludes) staged in Florence; the chorus that began the finale became one of the most popular melodies of its time. However, like Peri, Cavaliere fell foul of Caccini. Cavaliere wrote *La contesa fra Guinon e Minerva* ('The Dispute between Guinon and Minerva', 1600) for the wedding of King Henry VI of Spain. Caccini's *Il rapimento di Cefalo* was also to be performed on this occasion, but Caccini sabotaged Cavaliere's attempts to take control of the production. In disgust, Cavaliere returned to Rome. There he introduced the new style of music to a new

'DALLE GELOSE MIE' (BY MY JEALOUSY)
This soprano aria from Cavalli's *La Calisto* is set on the plains of of Erymanthus in the Peloponnese, Greece, where Giunone – the Roman goddess Juno – sings of her jealousy and fury at the love affair that is taking place between her unfaithful husband, the god Jupiter and the beautiful nymph Calisto.

POPULAR MELODY

BELOW: An illustration of the marriage of Louis XIV and Marie Thérèse of Austria. Francesco Cavalli wrote Ercole amante *for the occasion.*

audience with a sacred opera, sometimes called the first oratorio, *La rappresentazione di anima e di corpo* ('The Story of the Soul and the Body'). This presaged the role of Rome as a major centre of Baroque opera some 30 years later.

CAVALLI, FRANCESCO
(1602–76, ITALIAN)

Francesco Cavalli was in the right place at the right time when the first opera house, the

ABOVE: Personifications of the virtues, such as Prudence, were often used to introduce operas of this period.

Synopsis
La rappresentatione di animo e di corpo
by Cavaliere
Premiered 1600, Rome
Libretto by Agostino Manni and
Dorisio Isorelli

PROLOGUE
The figures of Avveduto and Prudenzio (both mean "Prudence") discuss at length the various facets of human nature and appeal to the audience to learn from what they will see in this allegorical opera.

ACT I
The character Tempo (Time) presents a monologue on the transience of human life and Intelletto (Intellect) discusses spiritual hopes and desires. There follows a dialogue between Corpo (Body) and Anima (Soul) about their contrasting needs The act concludes with a chorus that discusses the role of the heavens in helping men overcome everyday obstacles and dangers.

ACT II
Consiglio (Counsel) arranges a test for Anima and Corpo, in which they must resist the sins of the flesh offered by Mondo (the World) and Vita Mondana (Worldy Life). Piacere (Pleasure) appears with some cohorts and attempts to seduce Anima and Corpo. Corpo is about to give in, but Anima, disgusted, sends Piacere away. Anima appeals to the heavens for help and is answered by an echo. A guardian angel descends and assists them in resisting the temptations. The seduction ends when the silhouette of Morte (Death) is seen. Corpo laments the difficult choices he must make, and the chorus praises heavenly rewards.

ACT III
Intelletto and Consiglio present the two afterlife existences. They are aided alternately in their descriptions by damned spirits (who sing in a low register) and blessed spirits (who sing at a brighter pitch). Anima, Corpo, Consiglio and Intelletto discuss each issue as it is raised. Anima and Corpo resolve to reach heaven and invite everyone to rejoice in praise of the Lord.

OTHER COMPOSERS

Teatro San Cassiano, opened in Venice in 1637. The following year, Cavalli, with Orazio Persiani (fl. 1640) as librettist, produced *La nozze di Teti e di Peleo* ('The Wedding of Teti and Peleo', 1638) for the San Cassiano. In the next 10 years, Cavalli composed 10 more operas, including *Egisto* (1643). He also became manager of the San Cassiano, together with the librettist Giovanni Faustini (1619–51). Together, they firmly established the *stile rappresentazione*. In 1650 the San Cassiano closed due to financial difficulties, but it re-opened in 1658. Cavalli returned as musical director, contracted to write one opera a year. He was banned from working for any other Venetian opera house but was permitted to accept work from outside Venice. In 1660, he wrote *Ercole amante* ('Hercules in Love') for the marriage of King Louis XIV of France, but it was so badly received that Cavalli refused to write any more operas. In the end Cavalli relented, but two works he wrote in 1668 and 1673 were never performed, possibly because his style had become outdated.

Synopsis
Egisto by Cavalli
Premiered 1643, Venice
Libretto by Giovanni Faustini

BACKGROUND

Egisto and Clori, two lovers from Delos, have been captured by pirates and sold to different masters. On the day of her marriage to Lidio, Climene has also been captured and sold to the same master as Egisto.

ACT I

One year later Egisto and Climene have escaped and returned to her home island of Zakynthos, both anxious to be reunited with their former lovers. Unfortunately, however, they discover that Clori and Lidio have fallen in love. Climene's brother, Ipparco, also happens to have fallen for Clori and is encouraged by his servant Dema to take his vengeance against Lidio. After overhearing the declarations of love between Clori and Lidio, Egisto and Climene appeal to Amor to help them exact their revenge; instead of helping them however, he is encouraged by Venus to drive Egisto mad.

ACT II

Clori pretends not to recognize Egisto, claiming that he must be mad to think they were ever lovers. When confronted by Climene, Lidio tells her that she has been replaced in his affections by Clori. Egisto advises Lidio that his love for Clori will bring nothing but sorrow. Amor is captured by Semele, Fedra, Didone and Hero, all of whom had been wronged by love, and Amor appeals to Apollo (an ancestor of Egisto) to release him.

ACT III

To uphold his sister's honour and rid himself of a rival, Ipparco resolves to kill Lidio. He captures him and then urges Climene to stab her former lover, but she hesitates, asking the gods to forgive him and requesting her own death instead. This reawakens Lidio's love for Climene and they are reunited. Egisto has now been driven mad, but Clori's heart is softened by his suffering. All four lovers return to their original pairs through the power of Amor.

STAGING BAROQUE OPERA

Baroque opera featured lavish staging, spectacle and excitement. Stages were given added depth to allow for greater perspective and more vivid scenic effects. Steps were built leading from the stage into the auditorium, bringing the audience closer to the action. The "chariot and pole" device enabled scene changes to be made in seconds. 15 or 20 scene changes could be involved. Candles, torches and smoke depicted blazing hellfire or provided effects for the "magical" descent of golden chariots from heaven that brought the gods to Earth. Flashes of lightning were produced by the covering and uncovering of flaming torches. "Thunder" sounded as cannon balls were rolled down a stepped incline. Careful siting of the lights in the wings and the practice of dropping or raising cylinders or boxes of tin or black metal over the lamps made it possible to dim the stage for some scenes yet switch quickly to scenes requiring more illumination. To avoid the greatest danger of the candlelit era – setting fire to the theatre – lights were placed where they could not be dislodged, however vigorous the action on stage and however much the scenery might shake.

ABOVE: A Baroque stage design by Ferdinando Bibiena. The vast scale of the set was thought appropriate to the larger-than-life action.

OTHER COMPOSERS

EARLY & MIDDLE BAROQUE

1475 — 1700

CESTI, PIETRO
(1623–69, ITALIAN)

Musically speaking, Florentine composer Pietro Cesti led a double life. He wrote operas for the Venetian opera houses but also provided music for the courts at Innsbruck and Vienna. Either way, he was involved in basically secular entertainment, despite the fact that he was in holy orders. At age 14, Cesti had joined the Minorite friars, but his roving eye, which ill-suited him for the religious life, was encouraged by his contacts with Venice and the glamorous ducal courts of Austria. A series of scandals and indiscretions led him to resign from the Church in 1659, but earlier he had written *Orontea* (1649) and *Cesare amante* ('Caesar in Love', 1651) for Venetian audiences. In 1652, Cesti was appointed *Kappellmeister* to the Austrian Archduke Ferdinand Karl and produced several operas, including the most successful,

La Dori (or 'The Faithful Slave', 1657). From there, Cesti moved to imperial Vienna, where his most famous opera, *Il pomo d'oro* ('The Golden Apple') was staged in 1668. Another opera, *Genserico* (1669), was also produced in Vienna the year Cesti died in Florence.

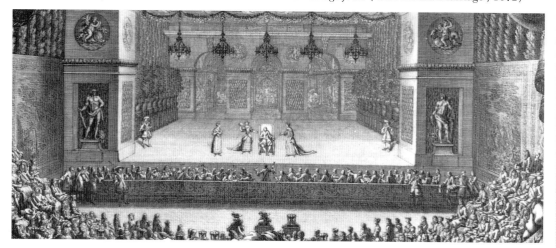

BELOW: A 1674 performance of Molière's La Malade imaginaire *at Versailles, for which Charpentier wrote the music.*

CHARPENTIER, MARC-ANTOINE
(c. 1645–1704, FRENCH)

Marc-Antoine Charpentier, a Parisian, was on hand to step into the breach after Lully quarrelled with the French playwright Molière (1622–73), whose works Lully had been setting to music. As a result, Charpentier wrote the music for Molière's *Le mariage forcé* ('The Forced Marriage', 1672)

Synopsis
Il pomo d'oro by Cesti
Premiered 1668, Vienna
Libretto by Francesco Sbarra

ABOVE: Il pomo d'oro *is another version of* The Judgement of Paris, *painted here in 1788 for the Count of Artois.*

PROLOGUE
Personifications of the Habsburg territories gather in praise of Austria and its emperor, Leopold I.

ACT I
During a banquet in Giove's palace, Discordia, goddess of strife, throws a golden apple inscribed "to the most beautiful" among the assembled goddesses. Venere, Pallade and Giunone all claim it, and Giove decrees that the prince Paride will decide. Paride and the nymph Ennone are together on Mount Ida when Mercurio brings news of Giove's decree. The shepherd Aurindo reveals his love for Ennone. At Paride's palace Giunone, Pallade and Venere try to win the apple, which goes to Venere when she offers Elena in exchange.

ACT II
Paride prepares to leave to claim Elena, but still affirms his love for Ennone. At the mouth of hell Caronte is cheered at the prospect of many new arrivals resulting from the coming war. Pallade calls on Cecrope, King of Athens, to defend her honour.

ACT III
Giunone orders Eolo, god of the winds, to destroy Paride's ship. Ennone laments her loss, while Aurindo's hopes are raised. Venere persuades Marte to support Paride and the Trojans. When Eolo unleashes the winds, Venere also persuades Nettuno to calm the seas so that Paride can continue to look for Elena. Marte defeats the Athenians and captures Cecrope.

ACT IV
The temple of Pallade is destroyed by an earthquake, and the remaining Athenian forces depart for battle. Venere and Marte taunt Cecrope, but news comes of the approaching Athenians, whom Pallade helps in the battle.

ACT V
Ennone accepts that she has lost Paride and submits to Aurindo. Giove destroys the tower on which the golden apple is standing, and it is finally awarded to Empress Margherita.

OTHER COMPOSERS

and *Le malade imaginaire* ('The Hypochondriac', 1673). Lully, however, was an expert at court intrigue, and he managed to sideline Charpentier. Molière had great regard for Charpentier and his abilities, but the renowned playwright died in 1673. All the same, Charpentier maintained his connection with Molière's theatre, the Comédie-Française, and many of his *divertissements* were staged there, including *Les amours de Vénus et d'Adonis* ('The Loves of Venus and Adonis', 1678). *Vénus et d'Adonis* proved so popular that it was still being performed there more than 70 years later. Charpentier's pastorales, such as *La noce du village* ('The Village Wedding', 1692), were

equally well received. His masterpiece, however, was a *tragédie lyrique*, *Médée* (1693), based on a play of the same name by Pierre Corneille (1606–84).

HIDALGO, JUAN
(c. 1612–85, SPANISH)

Most works by Juan Hidalgo, who was born in Madrid, were intended for church performance. However, Hidalgo was greatly attracted to Italian opera. While it would not have been acceptable for him to use the opera style in church music, he did introduce it into several of his secular songs and other vocal settings. This

led to collaboration with the famous Spanish dramatist Pedro Calderón de la Barca (1600–81), who was master of the revels of the Spanish king, Philip IV. The partnership was to be epoch-making in the context of Spanish music. Together, Hidalgo and Calderón produced the first Spanish opera, *La púrpura de la rosa* ('The Colour of the Rose', c. 1660). Unfortunately, neither the text nor the music of *La púrpura* have survived, but it was followed in the same year by another opera that is still extant, *Celos aun del aire matan* ('Even Jealousy of the Air Can Kill', c. 1660). Another important composition by Hidalgo was the first *zarzuela*, his *Los cielos hacen estrellas* ('The Skies have Stars', 1672) which established the traditional form of Spanish opera.

KEISER, REINHARD
(1674–1739, GERMAN)

Reinhard Keiser was born in Teuchern, Germany. When his mentor, Johann Sigismud Kusser (1660–1727) reloted to Hamburg in around 1693, Keiser succeeded him as *Kappellmeister* in Brunswick. In Brunswick, Keiser produced Kusser's first opera, *Basilius* (1694), and wrote several operas of his own, but after only three years, he followed his mentor to Hamburg. There, Keiser formed a partnership with the librettist Christian Heinrich Postel (1658–1705). A series of successful operas staged at the Theater am Gänsemarkt followed, beginning with *Adonis* (1697) and continuing at the rate of five every season. As co-proprietor of the theatre after 1702, Keiser oversaw performances of the early works of George Frideric Handel (1685–1759), among others. Afterwards, as sole director, Keiser made Hamburg the premier operatic centre in Germany. His own music contributed much to this reputation. Keiser's *Claudius* (1703), *Octavia* (1705) and *Croesus* (1710) demonstrated a lyricism and emotional power that was said to match the best of the Italian and French operas. The number of operas written by Keiser has been variously reckoned as being between 75 and 125, but only some 30 of these survive.

ABOVE: A bust of the Emperor Nero, who ruled the Roman Empire from the age of 16. He eventually committed suicide in AD 68.

Synopsis
Octavia by Keiser
Premiered 1705, Hamburg
Libretto by Barthold Feind

ACT I

King Tiridates of Armenia and his queen, Ormoena, have been captured and brought to Rome, where Nero falls in love with the beautiful Ormoena. Before he can marry her, however, Nero must first rid himself of his own virtuous wife, Octavia.

ACT II

Nero orders Octavia to commit suicide, either by poison or with a dagger. Ever obedient, Octavia prepares to stab herself but is stopped at the last minute by the patrician Piso, who is devoted to her. He swears to avenge Nero's treatment of Octavia and raises a rebellion that forces Nero to flee the city.

ACT III

Octavia, however, has other plans. Acting on a suggestion by the philosopher Seneca, she dresses as her own ghost and appears before Nero. He is horrified at the thought of what he has done and is stricken with remorse at Octavia's "death". Meanwhile, the rebels have been defeated. His loyal supporters tell Nero that Octavia is still alive. He is overjoyed at the news and even pardons Piso, since it was his action that saved Octavia's life. Tiridates is restored to his kingdom, and Ormoena happily returns to her husband.

OTHER COMPOSERS

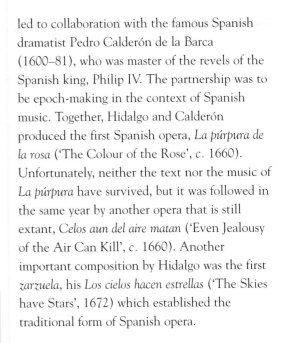

LANDI, STEFANO
(c. 1586–1639, ITALIAN)

Stefano Landi, who was born and gained his musical training in Rome, became *maestro di cappella* to the bishop of Padua in around 1618. The next year, Landi's *La morte d'Orfeo* ('The Death of Orpheus', 1619) was performed in Rome, where the composer returned in 1620. Four years later, Landi was appointed *maestro di cappella* at Santa Maria dei Monti, and he joined the papal choir in 1629. Landi's opera *Il Sant'Alessio* (1632) was performed at the opening of the opera house in the Barberini palace (see box). Both *La morte d'Orfeo* and *Il Sant'Alessio* were innovative and seminal works. The forme, the first secular opera to be performed in Rome, began a tradition for impressive choral scenes and spectacular endings that became characteristic of Roman opera.

THE BARBERINI FAMILY
(PATRONS OF OPERA)

The writing and performance of Baroque music and opera relied heavily on wealthy patrons, who often employed musicians in their private orchestras and opera houses. Among these patrons were the aristocratic Barberini family, who made their fortune in the Florentine cloth business. Moving to Rome, the Barberini became one of the city's most powerful family dynasties. Maffeo Barberini (1568–1644), elected Pope Urban VIII in 1623, was an influential opera enthusiast, and Roman opera basked in the favours that flowed from his direction. Composers such as Landi and Rossi received financial support and a magnificent new opera house for their works: the family had the auditorium – audience capacity 3,000 – built in the Barberini palace. Landi's *Il Sant'Alessio*, performed in 1632, was among many operas staged there. However, the golden age of Barberini opera was brief. After Pope Urban died, his family was sued by his successor, Innocent X, for lavishing papal funds on expensive opera productions. The Barberini fled to Paris, where their cause was championed by chief minister Cardinal Jules Mazarin. The family was reconciled with Innocent and reinstated in Rome after Mazarin threatened to invade the Papal States. Their opera house reopened in 1653 and, with occasional closures, was used until the end of the seventeenth century.

RIGHT: Maffeo Barberini (1568–1644), who was elected Pope Urban VIII in 1623, was a wealthy patron of the arts.

Il Sant'Alessio was on an even grander scale than its predecessor, with greater realism and drama and a hero who broke with established practice by typifying, not the mythological figures of earlier Baroque opera, but a real-life human being. In *Il Sant'Alessio*, Landi anticipated the opera overture with orchestral *sinfonias* that were performed before the start of each act.

Synopsis
Il Sant'Alessio by Landi
Premiered 1632, Rome
Libretto by Giulio Rospigliosi

PROLOGUE
The figure of Roma (Rome), surrounded by a chorus of slaves, dedicates the performance to the Prince of Polonia (Poland).

ACT I
Eufemiano, a Roman senator and Alessio's father, encounters Adrasto, a knight returning from war. While pleased to see Adrasto, Eufemiano mourns the disappearance of his son Alessio. Meanwhile, Alessio, an ascetic, is offered lodgings at his father's house by the pages Marzio and Curzio. Taking him for a beggar, they mock him. In hell, the devil resolves to tempt Alessio away from his holy life. Alessio's grieving wife and mother are comforted by their nurse. Curzio arranges a rustic dance to entertain everyone.

ACT II
Eufemiano laments the loss of his son. The devil reveals his plan to trick Alessio into returning to the joys of worldly pleasures: Alessio's wife will go off in search of him, and Alessio will feel guilty and reveal himself. Dressed as a pilgrim, Alessio's wife prepares to leave, accompanied by Alessio's mother. Alessio, as the beggar, tries to dissuade them. Seeing the grief he is causing his family, he considers revealing his identity and is encouraged to do so by the devil, disguised as a hermit. An angel appears, warning Alessio against the devil and comforting him with news of his approaching death and the joys that he can expect in heaven. Alessio sings of the pleasure he will find when his earthly existence is over. A light-hearted scene follows in which the devil and Marzio taunt each other. The figure of Religione (Religion) then praises Alessio's constancy, urging others to follow his example. Eufemiano, still grieving, is comforted by news of a celestial voice that has been heard in the cathedral.

ACT III
His mission unaccomplished, the devil returns to hell. A papal ambassador brings news of Alessio's death, and his family mourns as they hear a letter he has written to them. Angels encourage everyone to celebrate along with Religione, who praises Alessio's admirable conduct and dedicates a church to him.

LEGRENZI, GIOVANNI
(1626–90, ITALIAN)

Giovanni Legrenzi composed his first operas at Ferrara, where he became *maestro di cappella* at the Accademia dello Spirito Santo in 1656. He began with *Nino il giusto* ('Nino the Just', 1662) and in the next three years produced *Achille in Sciro* (1663) and *Zenobia e Radamisto* (1665). Subsequently, Legrenzi led a nomadic life, travelling around Europe until 1677, when he was appointed director of the Ospedali dei Mendicanti (the Beggars' Hospital) in Venice. Legrenzi wrote some 14 operas for the opera houses in Venice; many of these works have been lost. After becoming the first *maestro di cappella* at St Mark's in 1685, he abandoned the theatre and instead confined himself to instrumental and church music. The Venetian operatic tradition culminated with Legrenzi's works, which were partly modelled on those of Monteverdi and Cavalli and included an ingenious genre, the heroic-comic opera, including *Totila* (1677), *Giustino* (1683) and *I due Cesari* ('The Two Caesars', 1683). In all these operas, Legrenzi provided elaborate musical treatment for historical themes, as well

OTHER COMPOSERS

BELOW: Apollo, the ancient Greek god of music, poetry, archery, prophecy and healing, was the role played by Peri himself in his work Dafne.
BELOW LEFT: This engraving of a viol player dates from c. 1715. French composer Marais was renowned for his mastery of this instrument.

his virtuoso instrumental performances, and in 1676 he was summoned to the Palace of Versailles to play for the King. In 1679, he was appointed to an official post as a viola da gamba performer. Marais remained at Versailles until he retired in 1725. His instrumental music was much admired, and so were his four operas, which he modelled on those of his teacher, Jean-Baptiste Lully. All Marais' operas were produced in Paris. The first, *Alcide*, premiered in 1693, followed by *Ariane et Bacchus* (1695) and *Alcyone* (1706). *Alcyone* was noteworthy for its musical representation of a storm, one of the earliest to be produced in opera. Marais' fourth opera, *Sémélé*, was produced in 1709.

as dramatic and also comic scenes. One important innovation by Legrenzi was his emphasis on orchestral accompaniment and instrumental melodies, which anticipated practices later developed by the so-called Neapolitan school.

MARAIS, MARIN
(1656–1728, FRENCH)

Marin Marais, who was born in Paris, was both a composer and a player of the viola da gamba. He spent his life in Paris or Versailles, where he was among many musicians employed by King Louis XIV. Marais became a member of the Académie Royale de Musique and co-directed its orchestra with Pascal Colasse. For 15 years, between 1695 and 1710, Marais became renowned for

PERI, JACOPO
(1561–1633, ITALIAN)

Like his rival and fellow Roman Giulio Caccini, Jacopo Peri possessed several musical talents. He was a composer, singer and harpist. In 1588, also like Caccini, Peri joined the Medici court in Florence. At age 27, he was, it seems, an attractive addition to one of the most glittering courts in Europe, where his singing was greatly admired and his long blond tresses earned him the nickname *Il Zazzerino* ("little shock of hair"). Peri sang in the spectacular entertainments at the Medici court, composing some music for the performances, and he also became drawn to the Camerata and their promotion of the *stile rappresentativo*, the radical "representative style" in music. In 1598, Peri became the first to write a complete work, *Dafne*, in the new style. Peri also took a major part in his own composition, as the ancient Greek god Apollo. *Euridice* followed in 1600, with Peri this time taking the important role of Orpheus, Euridice's bereaved husband. The opera was written to celebrate the marriage of King Henri IV of France to Maria de' Medici. Published in 1601, *Euridice* is the earliest opera for which the complete score survives.

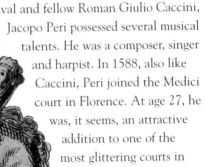

OTHER COMPOSERS

ROSSI, LUIGI
(c. 1597–1653, ITALIAN)

Luigi Rossi served for a time at the Neapolitan court before joining the Borghese family in his native city of Rome in 1621. Twenty years later, he entered the service of the Barberini family, who were influential patrons of opera. Rossi's first opera, *Il palazzo incantato* ('The Enchanted Palace', 1642), received its first performance in the Barberini palace. The production was lavish, and Rossi's opera became one of the most admired in the Italian Baroque repertoire. The Barberini family were exiled from Italy in 1644, and in 1646 Luigi Rossi followed them to Paris, where King Louis XIV's influential chief minister, Jules Mazarin, invited the composer to attend the court. Rossi's arrival was fortuitous, since Mazarin had been attempting for some time to introduce Italian opera in France. Rossi's *Orfeo* (1647) was all Mazarin could have hoped for. The opera represented the height of the luxurious and spectacular Roman opera of the seventeenth century, and it created enormous interest in France. This *Orfeo* was strong on visual effects, and Rossi's music was both lyrical and expressive.

ABOVE: Cardinal Mazarin (1602–61), an influential minister, invited Luigi Rossi to join King Louis XIV's court.

Synopsis
Orfeo by Rossi
Premiered 1647, Paris
Libretto by Francesco Buti

PROLOGUE

The figure of Vittoria (Victory) and French soldiers sing of their victories and the power of their kingdom.

ACT I

Euridice and her father, Endimione, consult a soothsayer regarding her forthcoming wedding to Orfeo. The omens are bad. Orfeo and Euridice celebrate their love for each other, while Aristeo, son of Bacco (Bacchus), laments his fate: he too is in love with Euridice. Having confided in his satyr, he calls for Venere (Venus) to prevent the marriage. Venere descends with Amore (Love) and the three Grazie (Graces), promising to help. Venere plans to trick Euridice into returning Aristeo's love. During the wedding ceremony, the torches are extinguished – a bad omen. Orfeo and Euridice proclaim their love.

ACT II

Disguised as an old woman, Venere approaches Euridice. She speaks of the bad omens surrounding Euridice's marriage to Orfeo and offers Aristeo as an alternative husband, but Euridice refuses. The gods scold Amore for his part in the deception; he promises to help Orfeo and Euridice, and reveals the truth to Orfeo. The Grazie tell Venere of Amore's betrayal; she swears vengeance. Endimione and the soothsayer pray to Venere, but Guinone (Juno) tells them to pray to her instead; she will protect the lovers. At the temple, Euridice sings of love, but she is bitten by a snake and dies.

ACT III

As all mourn Euridice's death, Orfeo is escorted to the underworld. Aristeo is driven mad by Euridice's spirit and, mocked by Momo and the satyr, kills himself. Giunone sends Gelosia (Jealousy) to Proserpina and argues with the jubilant Venere. Gelosia tells Proserpina that her husband, Plutone (Pluto), may betray her for Euridice; Proserpina and Caronte (Charon) persuade Plutone to listen to Orfeo. Orfeo asks to be reunited with Euridice. Plutone agrees, on the condition that Orfeo not look back as they leave. Caronte reveals that Orfeo has not obeyed, and Euridice disappears. Venere entices Bacco to avenge Aristeo's death; he orders the deaths of Orfeo and Euridice. Giove (Jupiter) transforms the two lovers and Orfeo's lyre into constellations.

SARTORIO, ANTONIO
(1630–80, ITALIAN)

Nothing is known of the first 30 years of Antonio Sartorio's life, except that he was Venetian. He made his first appearance in the historical records in 1661, when the first of his 15 operas, *Gl'amori infruttuosi di Pirro* ('Pirro's Hopeless Love', 1661) was performed in Venice. In 1664, Sartorio was appointed *Kappellmeister* at the ducal court of Brunswick-Lüneberg, and he remained in the post until 1675. However, he journeyed every year to Venice, where he hired musicians and oversaw the production of his operas at carnival time. In 1676, Sartori returned to Venice as *maestro di cappella* at St Mark's. His operas mark the height of the Venetian opera tradition and introduced several ingredients that later became standard fare: most notable among them was the lament. Sartorio was yet another composer to produce an opera on the tragic theme of Orpheus, in his case in 1672. His *Orfeo* created such a sensation that it eclipsed Cavalli's opera *Massenzio* (1673), which seemed so dull by comparison that the management of the Teatro San Luca feared an anticlimax and its performance was cancelled.

SCARLATTI, ALESSANDRO
(1660–1725, ITALIAN)

Sicilian-born Alessandro Scarlatti came to the attention of the Italian opera world with his first opera, *Gli equivoci nel sembiante* ('Mistaken Identities', 1679), which he wrote when he was only 19. The work was soon being staged by opera houses outside Rome, but this was not the limit of Scarlatti's new renown. At around the same time, he was appointed *maestro di cappella* to the generous patron of the arts Queen

OTHER COMPOSERS

ABOVE: Alessandro Scarlatti (1660–1725) wrote his first opera at the tender age of 19. He went on to write over 40 operas.
BELOW RIGHT: Alessandro Stradella (1642–82) was an Italian composer, singer and violinist. This portrait was painted by Gaetano D'Agostino.

'MI RIVEDI' (YOU SHALL SEE ME AGAIN)

In Scarlatti's opera La Griselda, the shepherdess Griselda is persecuted by her husband, King Gualtiero of Sicily, because she is low-born. Dejected at being sent away by the King, she sings this aria, telling him that he will see her again. Griselda returns and, in the second section, sings of her joy at coming home.

POPULAR MELODY

Christina of Sweden. By the time he was 24 and the composer of six operas, Scarlatti was *maestro di cappella* to the Viceroy of Naples and also director of the city's Teatro San Bartolomeo.

By 1702, Scarlatti had written at least 40 operas, but life and work in Naples seemed to pall and Scarlatti resigned his position. He hoped to join the Medici court in Florence and sent four operas to Prince Ferdinand de Medici as proof of his abilities, but nothing came of this. In 1708, Scarlatti returned to Naples where he scored two of his most brilliant successes, with *Tigrane* (1715) and *Cambise* (1719). Ultimately Scarlatti's connection with Naples helped to establish the city as a centre of opera during the eighteenth century.

STRADELLA, ALESSANDRO (1639–82, ITALIAN)

Alessandro Stradella was in his native Rome, writing *intermezzi* and other music for revivals of operas by Cavalli and Cesti, when he became embroiled in a quarrel with the Catholic authorities. He then had to leave Rome and decamped to Genoa, where he arrived in 1678. By that time, Stradella had composed several operas, and three were performed at Genoa's Teatro Falcone: *Trespolo tutore* ('The Guardian Trestle', 1677), *La forza dell'amor patterno* ('The Power of Paternal Love', 1678) and *Le gare dell'amor eroico* ('The Contests of Heroic Love', 1679). The first was a comic opera and one of the first in which a bass was cast in the leading male role. Stradella's operas have been considered by some to prefigure the Neapolitan opera later developed by Alessandro Scarlatti. In addition to composition, Stradella was a music teacher and one of his students was a nobleman's mistress. Stradella abducted her. The nobleman gave chase and almost killed the composer. Far from being cured by this experience, Stradella became involved with another woman associated with vengeful men: her brothers, who disapproved of the liaison, ambushed Alessandro Stradella and murdered him.

Synopsis

Mitridate Eupatore by Scarlatti
Premiered 1707, Venice
Libretto by Girolamo Frigimelica Roberti

ACT I

King Farnace and Stratonica, Mitridate's mother, have usurped the Pontus throne by killing Mitridate's father. Mitridate, the true heir, has sought refuge in Egypt; his sister, Laodice, awaits his return and dreams of avenging her father's death. Egypt and Pontus are set to form an alliance and Laodice is called to court, where she is mocked by Farnace and argues with her mother.

ACT II

Mitridate and his wife, Issicratea (calling herself Antigono), arrive at court, disguised as Egyptian ambassadors. They tell Stratonica that Mitridate is nearby and Farnace calls for his death; the "ambassadors" agree to bring him Mitridate's head in exchange for peace between their kingdoms. Laodice promises to help the "ambassadors", if they will spare her brother's life.

ACT III

In front of the temple, Farnace addresses his people. Stratonica tells the crowd that she is willing to sacrifice her son for their benefit. Mitridate also appears, as the ambassador, promising to honour their agreement. Laodice's husband, Nicodemo, tells her what the "ambassador" has announced. Laodice resolves to intervene and save Mitridate.

ACT IV

On the shore with Pelopida, Farnace's confidant, Laodice sees armed men arrive with the urn. Believing it to contain Mitridate's head, she mourns the loss of her brother. Mitridate recognizes her and, when they are alone, reveals his identity. The siblings are joyfully reunited. With renewed hope, Laodice shows her contempt for Stratonica and Farnace.

ACT V

Farnace arrives to claim the urn containing Mitridate's head and attempts to kill the "ambassador"; Mitridate's sword is quicker, and Farnace is killed. Stratonica launches herself at her son but is killed by Issicratea. Nicodemo announces to the people that Farnace's tyranny is over and Mitridate has returned. Laodice crowns Mitridate, who then crowns Issicratea. Everyone rejoices at the siblings' revenge and the restoration of peace to the land.

OTHER COMPOSERS

Librettists

BUSENELLO, GIAN FRANCESCO (1598–1659, ITALIAN)

Venetian-born Gian Francesco Busenello had a particular talent for the commercial operas that became fashionable in Italy in the first half of the seventeenth century. Busenello possessed a certain cynical realism about life that served him and his composers well when it came to insights into human behaviour. Busenello was never judgemental in his treatment of his operatic characters, even the most villainous. Instead, he viewed them with sardonic tolerance and an acute sense of humour, which made them more believable. Busenello began writing libretti somewhat late in life, and his output was not extensive. He wrote only five or six libretti, starting with Francisco Cavalli's *Gli amore di Apollo e di Dafne* ('The Love of Apollo and Daphne', 1640). Busenello provided libretti for three other Cavalli operas, but his greatest achievement was his work for Claudio Monteverdi in *L'incoronazione di Poppea* (1642).

CALDERÓN DE LA BARCA, PEDRO (1600–81, SPANISH)

Pedro Calderón de la Barca, one of Spain's greatest playwrights, made an important venture into the world of opera with his libretto for Hidalgo's *La púrpura de la rosa* ('The Colour of the Rose', c. 1660), the first Spanish opera performed in Madrid. The same year, Calderón provided Hidalgo with another libretto, this time for the composer's *Celos aun del aire matan* ('Even Jealousy of the Air Can Kill', c. 1660). Although Calderón's output for opera was not great, the plots of his plays – notably his so-called "revenge" dramas – explored similar territory. Calderón's work also retains a modern appeal. His most famous play, *La vida es sueño* ('Life Is a Dream', 1635), which dealt with free will and predestination, was turned into an opera by the American composer Lewis Spratlan (b. 1940) and won the Pulitzer Prize in Music in 2000.

'REVENEZ, AMOUR REVENEZ' (COME BACK, LOVERS, COME BACK)
The "lovers" in Lully's aria from his opera *Thesée*, sung by the Roman goddess Venus, represent dissatisfied Sport and Pleasure. They retreat into the forest because they have no purpose at the Palace of Versailles due to the absence of King Louis XIV. In this aria, Venus begs them to return.
POPULAR MELODY

ABOVE: Spanish dramatist Calderón de la Barca (1600–81).

CICOGNINI, GIACINTO (1606–51, ITALIAN)

Florentine librettist Giacinto Cicognini followed in a famous father's footsteps. His father, Jacopo (1577–1633), had been among the pioneers who first introduced Spanish theatre to Italian audiences. Jacopo Cicognini was also a librettist; he wrote *Andromeda*

(1618) for another Florentine, the composer Domenico Belli. Giacinto Cicognini initially intended to become a lawyer, but the stage proved much more seductive, and he renounced the courts for the theatre. Naturally enough, considering his father's work and interest in Spain, Giacinto's libretti show strong Spanish influences. This is especially strong in the elegance of Giacinto's verse. His best-known libretto was written for Francesco Cavalli's *Giasone* (1649) and, in the same year, he wrote *Orontea* for Pietro Cesti. Another libretto for *Gli amore di Alessandro Magno e di Rossana* ('The Love of Alexander the Great and Roxane') by Francesco Luzzo (1628–58) appeared in 1651, the year Giacinto died.

ABOVE: French writer Pierre Corneille (1606–84) wrote many heroic verse dramas that were later turned into operas.

CORNEILLE, PIERRE
(1606–84, FRENCH)

Pierre Corneille, the renowned playwright, wrote verse dramas on heroic and classical themes that were tailor-made for operatic treatment. Corneille's list of plays that were turned into libretti is not nearly as long as William Shakespeare's or Sir Walter Scott's, but it is impressive enough. Corneille's verse dramas were still attracting composers in the early twentieth century. In all, 13 of his plays were turned into 41 operas between 1664 and 1916. By far the most popular was Corneille's *El Cid* ('The Lord', 1637): El Cid, more properly called Rodrigo Diaz de Vivar, was the Spanish folk hero of numerous legends that told of his fight on behalf of Christian kings against the Moorish rulers of Spain. Between 1706 and 1916, no fewer than 20 operas were based on this play with music by such composers as George Frideric Handel (1685–1759) and Jules Massenet (1842–1912).

DRYDEN, JOHN
(1631–1700, ENGLISH)

John Dryden, the poet, playwright and critic, made his name writing "heroic" verse and other dramas in the Restoration period, which followed the return of King Charles II (1630–85) from exile in 1660. The restoration of the king to his throne was fortuitous for Dryden and other playwrights. During the dreary years of Puritan rule that followed the English Civil War and the execution in 1649 of the new King's father, Charles I, all theatres had been closed, and performances elsewhere – even in taverns or private houses – were forbidden by law. Dryden took full advantage of the re-opening of

ABOVE: John Dryden (1631–1700) enjoyed much success following the austere rule of Charles I under the patronage of his son, Charles II.

the theatres in 1660. He wrote two plays for operatic performance – *Albion and Albianus* (1685) and *King Arthur* (1691). Dryden, together with another dramatist, Sir Robert Howard, also provided the text for Henry Purcell's semi-opera *The Indian Queen* (1695).

FAUSTINI, GIOVANNI
(1615–51, ITALIAN)

Librettist and theatre manager Giovanni Faustini, who was born in Venice, wrote 11 libretti for Venetian opera houses in nine years – between 1642 and 1651 – and 10 of them were set to music by Francesco Cavalli. Cavalli owed a great deal to Faustini's skill and to his unerring "feel" for the pseudo-historical subjects of most of his libretti. Faustini also possessed an instinct for devising plots that had maximum popular appeal and would ensure financial success. His libretti were beautifully constructed and designed to wring the utmost drama out of the situations depicted on stage. He had a good understanding of the music and how it could heighten drama and made sure that his libretti offered composers plenty of scope for musical characterization. Faustini's best-known libretti, both written for Cavalli, were *Ormindo* (1644) and *Calisto*, which was first performed in 1651, the same year as Faustini's premature death.

FEIND, BARTHOLD
(1678–1721, GERMAN)

In 1705, Barthold Feind – whose real name was Aristobulos Eutropius or Aristobulos Wahrmund – was practicing law in his home city, Hamburg, when he wrote his first libretto for Reinhard Keiser, *Octavia*. Keiser needed a replacement at this time, after the death of Christian Heinrich Postel, who had been his librettist for nine years. Feind, however, was more than a substitute. He had his own strengths as a librettist. Feind's forte was his handling of the comic elements in his libretti and his deft way with satire and parody. In 1706, Feind produced two more libretti for Keiser and another text in 1708 for Christophe Graupner. The mixture of German and Italian elements found in Feind's libretti had been typical of Postel's work and, together with French influences, also marked the music of Reinhard Keiser.

LIBRETTISTS

EARLY & MIDDLE BAROQUE

1475 — 1700

MINATO, COUNT NICOLO
(c. 1627–98, ITALIAN)

Poet and librettist Count Nicolo Minato wrote 11 texts for the Venetian opera houses, including Cavalli's *Pompeo Magna* ('Pompey the Great', 1666). In 1669, the Emperor of Austria, Leopold I, appointed Minato his court poet, and some very exciting opportunities opened up for the Count. At that time, the court composer was Antonio Draghi. Minato joined forces with Draghi to produce no fewer than 170 libretti. Another member of the team was the designer Ludovico Burnacini, who staged the Draghi-Minato operas. As he had already demonstrated in Venice, Minato had a particular fondness for historical subjects, and he produced *Gundeberga* (1672), one of the earliest libretti, based on a story from German history. Other libretti were set in the ancient world – *Temistocle in Persia* ('Themistocles in Persia', 1681) in ancient Greece, and *Sciopione preservatore di Roma* ('Scipio, Saviour of Rome', 1690) in ancient Rome.

MOLIÈRE, JEAN-BAPTISTE POQUELIN
(1622–73, FRENCH)

The playwright, actor and impresario Molière was the brightest star in seventeenth-century French theatre, writing plays that lived on long after his time, some of them in the form of operas. In all, 17 of Molière's plays have been turned into 75 operas since 1706, over

half of them in the twentieth century. Jean-Baptiste Lully provided music for plays by Molière. So did Marc-Antoine Charpentier towards the end of Molière's life, when he wrote music for *Le mariage forcé* and *Le malade imaginaire*. Molière came from a wealthy background. He was attracted to the theatre as a very young man, embarking on his first theatrical venture in 1643, when he was only 21. Ultimately, Molière's plays and his actors came to the attention of King Louis XIV, who absorbed the entire company into his household in 1665.

QUINAULT, PHILIPPE
(1635–88, FRENCH)

Philippe Quinault was a well-known playwright when he decided to switch to the writing of opera libretti. The techniques of plays and operas – spoken and sung drama – diverged considerably, but Quinault succeeded in transferring his skills from one genre to the other. Risk had been involved, but the star prize was collaboration with Jean-Baptiste Lully, the progenitor of French opera and protégé of the mighty Louis XIV. Although Quinault developed the *tragédie lyrique* for

LIBRETTISTS

COMMEDIA DELL'ARTE

The *commedia dell'arte*, which originated in Italy in the sixteenth century, was a forerunner of opera. The influence of *commedia dell'arte* was evident in both the cast lists and the plots of operas. There were, for example, slapstick sequences called *zanni* and comic servants, an elderly parent or guardian, usually named Pantalone, and his faithful sidekick *Il dottore Gratiano*. The beautiful but despairing heroine was usually involved in an unsuitable love match with an impoverished, but romantic, young man. On hand to help solve the dilemma was her maid, who acted as her confidante. Likewise, *commedia dell'arte* plots had ready-made features, such as disguise, mistaken identity, confusion over twins, lovers pretending to be servants and girls trapped in betrothals to rich old men. These ingredients are found in several operas written by composers from Mozart (1756–1791) to Giuseppe Verdi (1819–1901), among many others.

Commedia dell'arte was popular all over Europe and influenced such playwrights as William Shakespeare, Molière and Beaumarchais, all of whom wrote plays with plots that lent themselves easily to operatic treatment and were later turned into operas. The *commedia* characters and type of plot were directly translated to opera in *I pagliacci* ('The Clowns', 1892) by Ruggero Leoncavallo (1857–1919).

Lully and so later influenced French *grand opéra*, there were certain restraints. Libretti had to contain formal scenes, stereotyped sentiments and the required references to royal glory and eminence. Emotion was always under control, heroes attained their objectives without undue strain and love was idyllic rather than passionate. Pantomime, dance and spectacle were regular ingredients. King Louis had to approve of everything, so that both Quinault and Lully planned their operas with royal tastes in mind.

RINUCCINI, OTTAVIO
(1562–1621, ITALIAN)

Ottavio Rinuccini, a member of the Bardi Camerata, wrote his first libretti for sophisticated Florentine entertainments. In 1598, Rinuccini produced the first opera libretto, Peri's *Dafne* (1598). A musical setting of *Dafne* composed by Heinrich Shütz in 1627 may have been the first German opera. Rinuccini's libretto *Euridice* was set to music by both Peri (1600) and Caccini (1602) and in 1608, Rinuccini wrote his most famous text, for Monteverdi's *Arianna*. However, although he considered him to be the best librettist of his time, Monteverdi turned down Rinuccini's next text, *Narciso ed Ecco* ('Narcissus and Echo'), because of its unhappy ending. The sources for Rinuccini's libretti were the Roman poet Ovid and the lyrical pastoral legend. His verse, which was well suited to the natural delivery of words, set the style for many librettists after him.

ROSPIGLIOSI, GIULIO
(POPE CLEMENT IX)
(1600–69, ITALIAN)

Priest and librettist Giulio Rospigliosi served the opera-loving Barberini pope Urban VIII. Urban's family provided Rospigliosi with a magnificent setting for his libretto for *Il Sant'Alessio* (1632) by Stefano Landi which was performed at the opening of the opera house in the Barberini palace in 1632. Three more libretti in the next decade included Rossi's *Il palazzo incantato*. Rospigliosi borrowed from *commedia dell'arte* to make his comic characters more lifelike and produced the first thoroughly comic opera libretto for *Chi suffre, speri* ('Who Suffers May Hope', 1639) with music by Domenico Mazzocch and Marco Marazzoli. Rospigliosi continued in the same genre with libretti for two comic operas by Antonio Maria Abbatini: *Dal male il bene* ('Good from Bad', 1653) and *La Baltesara* ('The Girl from Balthesar', 1668). The latter was performed two years after Rospigliosi was elected pope, as Clement IX.

BELOW LEFT: French playwright Jean-Baptiste Molière (1622–73) was a favourite of Louis XIV and wrote 17 plays over his lifetime.
LEFT: An engraving showing a scene from Molière's comedy ballet Le mariage forcé, *written in 1664.*
BELOW: Before he became Pope Clement IX, librettist Giulio Rospigliosi was patronized by the opera-loving Pope Urban VIII.

Singers

CACCINI, FRANCESCA
(1587–c. 1637, ITALIAN)

Francesca Caccini was the daughter of composer and singer Giulio Caccini. She sang at lavish musical entertainments staged in Florence and also performed in Paris with her mother and sister in 1604–5. Francesca, known as *La Cecchina* ('The Little Fairy'), was extremely versatile: she was not only a singer, but a talented performer on the harpsichord, guitar and lute and a composer in her own right. Her first compositions were festive ballets, such as *Il ballo delle zigane* ('The Ballet of the Gypsies', 1615). She then graduated to monody in her *Primo libro della musiche* ('First Book of Music', 1618). From there, Caccini collaborated with Marco di Gagliano on the sacred work *Il martirio di Sant'Agata* ('The Martyrdom of Saint Agatha', 1622) and wrote the opera *La liberazione di Ruggiero dall'isola d'Alcina* ('Ruggiero's Liberation from Alcina Island', 1625). This was the first opera known to be composed by a woman.

RASI, FRANCESCO
(1574–1620, ITALIAN)

Composer and tenor Francesco Rasi took part in the first performances of Peri's *Euridice* and Caccini's *Rapimento di Cefalo* in Florence in 1600. By then he was already an experienced and much-admired performer, after 10 years in the service of aristocratic patrons, including Duke Fernando I of Tuscany before 1594, and, after 1598 the Gonzaga family, who ruled Mantua between 1328 and 1708 and were important patrons of music. Rasi was still in Mantua in 1607, when he is believed to have created the title role in Monteverdi's *Orfeo*. He also took part in the first version of *Dafne* composed by Marco di Gagliano (1582–1643), performed in Mantua in 1608. In 1617 Rasi doubled as composer and librettist for *Cibele ed Ati*, an opera written to celebrate the marriage of Ferdinando Gonzaga. The music, unfortunately, has been lost, though Rasi's text has survived.

RENZI, ANNA
(c. 1620–c. 1660, ITALIAN)

Anna Renzi created the part of Ottavia, the neglected wife of Emperor Nero in Monteverdi's *L'incoronazione de Poppea*, in 1642, and she sang many other operatic roles in Venice. Renzi was one of the first female opera singers and also one of the first, if not the first, singers to achieve the status of a prima donna. She was an impressive actress, possessed a fine "treble" voice and, it appears, had a fan following. In 1642 the librettist and poet Giulio Strozzi (1583–1652) wrote a book about her, *Le glorie della Signora Anna Renzi romana* ('The Glory of the Roman [singer] Signora Anna Renzi'), in which he described her in glowing terms: "Our Signora Anna," wrote Strozzi, "was endowed with such lifelike expression that her responses and speeches seem not memorized but born at the very moment. In sum," Strozzi concluded, "she transforms herself completely into the person she represents."

LE ROCHOIS, MARTHE
(c. 1658–1728, FRENCH)

Soprano Marthe Le Rochois, who was born in Caen in northern France, may have been a pupil of the French composer and singer Michel Lambert and afterwards of Lambert's son-in-law, Jean-Baptiste Lully. Lully greatly admired Le Rochois, who made her debut at the Paris Opéra in 1678 and remained a performer there for the next 20 years. Le Rochois created several roles in Lully's operas, including parts in *Proserpine* (1680), *Persée* (1682), *Amadis de Gaule* (1684) and *Roland* (1685). In 1686, she was also the first soprano to sing the title role in *Armide et Rénaud*, Lully's opera set at the time of the Crusades. Rochois appears to have been one of those stage performers who lack obvious physical attractions yet exercise a certain fascination over their audiences. In Le Rochois' case, her

RIGHT: Engraving of Marthe Le Rochois (1658–1728) in the title role of the opera Armide *by Jean-Baptiste Lully.*

advantages were vivacity and a sensual aura, which enabled her to outclass the many more obviously beautiful singers of her day.

SIFACE, GIOVANNI
FRANCESCO GROSSI
(1653–97, ITALIAN)

Castrato Giovanni Siface made his debut in Rome in 1672. He enjoyed considerable early success in Italy and created a sensation in Venice as Syphax in Cavalli's *Sciopine affricano* ('Scipio Africanus', 1685). Siface became so identified with the part that "Syphax" became his nickname. Siface was taken up by many important personalities, including ex-Queen Christina of Sweden and by Henry Purcell in England; Purcell wrote a piece for harpsichord entitled 'Sefauci's Farewell' when the singer left England in 1687. Siface, praised as the finest

living musician, received an almost hysterical reception in 1688 when he sang in Modena, Naples, Parma and Bologna. Unfortunately, Siface developed an ego to match his talents and his arrogance led to his murder near Ferrara by thugs hired by the family of a girl with whom he had been having a love affair.

SINGERS

BAROQUE OPERA IN NAPLES

Opera first reached Naples when Venetian companies brought their productions to the city after 1648. At that time, the city was recovering from the spate of murders and massacres that had taken place during the revolt against Spanish rule led by the fisherman Tommaso Aniello Masaniello. Masaniello was killed in 1647 by agents working for the Spanish Viceroy Count d'Onate. The introduction of opera in Naples was part of the Count's subsequent attempts to calm the populace. What d'Onate actually accomplished was the establishment of a tradition of opera in Naples that has lasted to the present day. Among the first operas to be seen there were *Ciro* (1653–54) by Francesco Provenzale and *Orontea* (1654) by Francesco Cirillo. Subsequently, the Venetian repertory gave operatic performances at the Teatro San Bartolomeo. After 1676, operas were produced at the Teatro for royal occasions, a task taken over in 1684 by Alessandro Scarlatti. The energetic, inventive Scarlatti was a great boon to the cause of Neapolitan opera. The San Bartolomeo was enlarged to hold bigger audiences, and while he remained in Naples, Scarlatti claimed to have written 80 operas for the Teatro, though half that number was more likely.

RIGHT: The Castillo Nova at Naples, once the residence of the Sicilian king and queen. Naples has a long history of opera appreciation.

STROZZI, BARBARA
(1619–67, ITALIAN)

Venetian-born Barbara Caterina Strozzi, singer and composer, was the daughter of the poet and librettist Giulio Strozzi by one of his servants. Although she was the principal singer at the Accademia degli Unisoni in Perugia, which had been founded by her father in 1634, her most important contribution to music was as one of the principal women composers of the Baroque era. In 1644 Barbara Strozzi composed her *Il primo libro de madrigali* ("First Book of Madrigals"), and by 1664 no fewer than 125 songs and other pieces of vocal music by Strozzi had been published. This included eight books of music, containing 100 songs for solo voice. The last of her published works, *Arie* ('Melodies'), consisted of six arias, five cantatas and one serenade for soprano. Music for the solo voice dominated the work of Strozzi, although some of her books contain songs with orchestral accompaniment.

LEFT: A seventeenth-century painted panel showing fire in Syphax's camp. Syphax was Italian singer Siface's most well-known role.

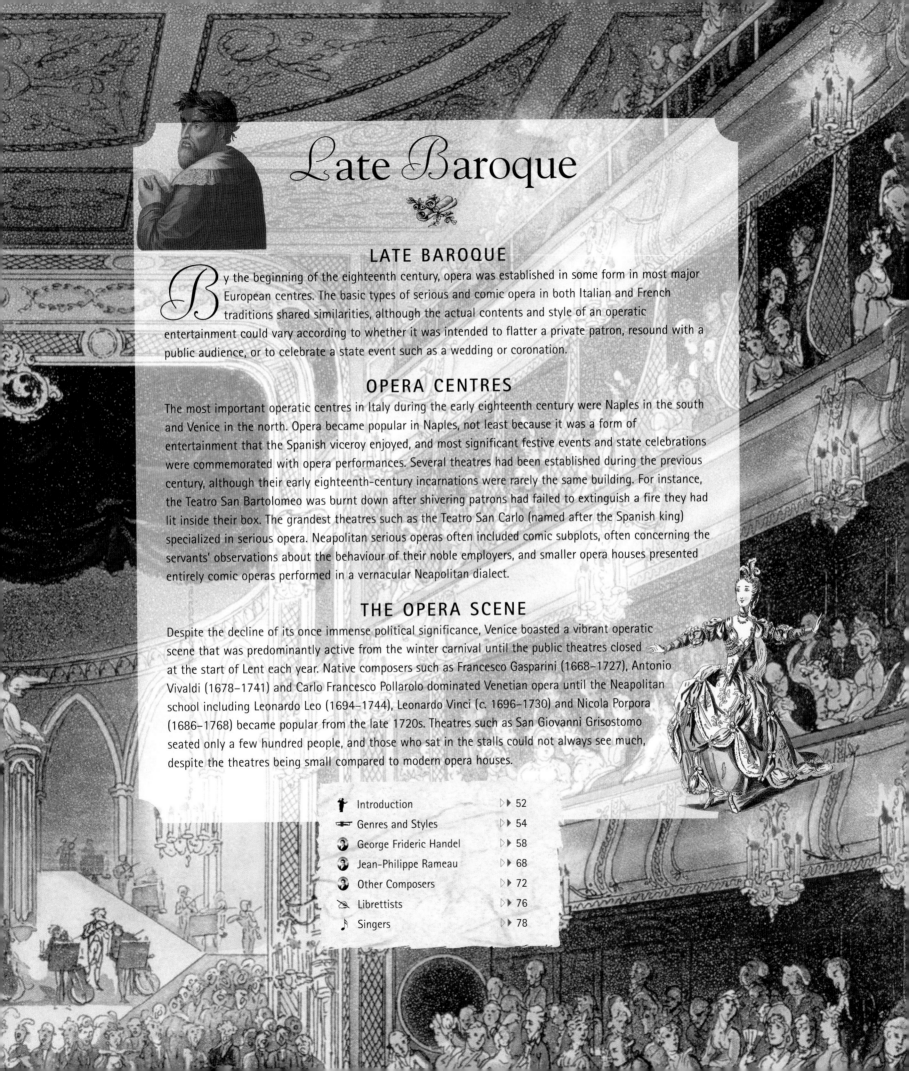

Late Baroque

LATE BAROQUE

By the beginning of the eighteenth century, opera was established in some form in most major European centres. The basic types of serious and comic opera in both Italian and French traditions shared similarities, although the actual contents and style of an operatic entertainment could vary according to whether it was intended to flatter a private patron, resound with a public audience, or to celebrate a state event such as a wedding or coronation.

OPERA CENTRES

The most important operatic centres in Italy during the early eighteenth century were Naples in the south and Venice in the north. Opera became popular in Naples, not least because it was a form of entertainment that the Spanish viceroy enjoyed, and most significant festive events and state celebrations were commemorated with opera performances. Several theatres had been established during the previous century, although their early eighteenth-century incarnations were rarely the same building. For instance, the Teatro San Bartolomeo was burnt down after shivering patrons had failed to extinguish a fire they had lit inside their box. The grandest theatres such as the Teatro San Carlo (named after the Spanish king) specialized in serious opera. Neapolitan serious operas often included comic subplots, often concerning the servants' observations about the behaviour of their noble employers, and smaller opera houses presented entirely comic operas performed in a vernacular Neapolitan dialect.

THE OPERA SCENE

Despite the decline of its once immense political significance, Venice boasted a vibrant operatic scene that was predominantly active from the winter carnival until the public theatres closed at the start of Lent each year. Native composers such as Francesco Gasparini (1668–1727), Antonio Vivaldi (1678–1741) and Carlo Francesco Pollarolo dominated Venetian opera until the Neapolitan school including Leonardo Leo (1694–1744), Leonardo Vinci (c. 1696–1730) and Nicola Porpora (1686–1768) became popular from the late 1720s. Theatres such as San Giovanni Grisostomo seated only a few hundred people, and those who sat in the stalls could not always see much, despite the theatres being small compared to modern opera houses.

LATE BAROQUE

Introduction

The traditions and styles of opera from Venice and Naples also dominated operatic life in Rome, although for a short time public opera performances were forbidden in the papal city. The influence of Italian opera also stretched much further, and companies were established outside Italy, most notably the Dresden opera house at the court of the Elector of Saxony, and in London by the Royal Academy of Music. It was only in France that a distinct national school of opera flourished without being substantially indebted towards Italian singers, librettists and musical style.

THE IDOLIZATION OF SINGERS

Opera audiences in London were primarily aristocratic or the well-educated upper-middle class, but in Italy and France opera was relatively more accessible to the wider public, especially the less serious forms of opera in Naples and Paris. Opera performances were undeniably a social event where prominent members of society could meet publicly or, indeed, illicitly, and it is easy to underestimate the fascination audiences had about discussing the merits and foibles of the most famous singers.

CASTRATO STATUS

In addition to the usual gossip and adulation that surrounded the *prima donna*, audiences were equally passionate about the leading man, the *primo uomo*. He was almost always a castrato ◆ p. 28, a singer who had shown musical potential while a boy that was enough to justify his parents authorizing his castration in order to preserve his voice and enable him to train as a professional singer. Castration for this purpose was technically forbidden, but the financial rewards and popularity for a successful castrato were enormous enough to tempt many parents to find ways to ensure that their son

ABOVE: Stefano Dionisi plays the legendary castrato in Gérard Corbiau's successful 1995 film Farinelli.
PREVIOUS PAGE: Interior of the Covent Garden Theatre, London in 1808.

needed the operation for alleged medical reasons. We do not know exactly what the castrati sounded like in their early eighteenth-century prime, but they were reputed to be tall and possessed a powerful stage presence that complemented their casting in godlike or majestic roles, which promoted ideas of heroism and dignity.

However, the concept of the castrated hero was not universally admired: it was never widely accepted in London despite George Frideric Handel's (1685–1759) successful operas starring Senesino (c. 1680–c. 1759) and Giovanni Carestini (c. 1704–c. 1760), and it was openly

ridiculed and scorned in France, where they instead preferred youthful lovers and heroes to be sung by high-tenors (*haute-contre*). By the end of Handel's career, he rarely used castrati in his English oratorios, and had instead trained native English singers such as the tenor John Beard. The voice fell out of fashion, although the castrato Crescentini was reputed to have been Napoleon's favourite singer, and both Wolfgang Amadeus Mozart (1756–91) and Gioachino Rossini (1792–1868) composed castrato roles.

ABOVE: A programme for Apollo's Feast – songs from Handel's operas.

DEVELOPMENT OF THE OPERA HOUSE ORCHESTRA

Most early eighteenth-century opera houses were small, and could not accommodate anything larger than a chamber orchestra. Thus, opera-house orchestras during the period were smaller than their nineteenth-century successors. The modern orchestra pit did not then exist, and the orchestra were usually seated on the floor at the front of the stalls, level with the first row of the audience. Most operas were scored for a band of strings, oboes and *continuo*, but the exact constitution of an opera orchestra could vary according to local traditions, the preferences of the composer, and the availability of less common instruments such as recorders, flutes, trumpets and horns. Several eyewitness accounts reveal that Handel's opera orchestra tended to have over 20 violins (including violas), three or four cellos, two double basses, between two and four oboes, up to four bassoons and the *continuo* section. The *continuo* section played in recitatives and formed the foundations upon which the orchestrations were based, and Handel's *continuo* section almost certainly comprised two harpsichords, one cello and a theorbo. The *continuo* section could occasionally be enhanced by exotic instruments such as the addition of viols and harp in Cleopatra's 'V'*adoro pupille*' in Handel's *Giulio Cesare in Egitto* ('Julius Caesar in Egypt', 1724) ➼ **p. 62**. Porpora's *Flavio Anicio Olibrio* (1711) requires lute, theorbo, viola da gamba, cello, double bass and harpsichord to contribute towards the *continuo* line, although it is unlikely that they all played together in every aria.

THE VISUAL ASPECT

Although early eighteenth-century operas were unashamedly designed for exploiting the virtuosity of expensive singers, they were also regarded as an opportunity to fuse all the arts together, in which the librettist's poetry and the composer's music were complemented by sumptuous costumes and scenery painted by master craftsmen. The mechanical wings in a Baroque theatre allowed swift scene changes that could surprise and entertain an audience visually, and inventive designers produced astonishing mechanical stage effects such as moving clouds, shipwrecks and even chariots that could allow a godlike character to descend and instigate the reconciliation of opposing parties at the end of an opera. New costumes and scenery were major attractions of a new opera, although materials were frequently recycled so the environments of a medieval crusader could look suspiciously identical to Alexander the Great in Persia.

ABOVE: The mechanics of Baroque opera productions could allow characters to descend from the sky, such as Jupiter in Handel's Semele.

STANDARDIZATION OF OPERA FORMS

Each operatic tradition had within it different types of opera. Serious operas were the highest regarded form of music dramas, Italian *opéra seria* and French *tragédie en musique*. Comic opera also developed within both cultures, and *opéra-ballet* also became popular in France. In Italy the comic *intermezzo* performed between the acts of an *opéra seria* rapidly gave birth to fully developed *opéra buffa*. Serious opera was certainly a forum for composers and librettists to create allegories that their audience could identify with. However, it was unwise to produce operas that contained unflattering parallels with contemporary events or satirical attacks during an age when both court and public opera houses alike depended on the patronage and support of the nobility and royal family.

PEDAGOGICAL AND POLITICAL ASPECTS OF OPERA

Instead, most commentaries concealed within late Baroque operas were intended to elevate and instruct audiences. For example, the righteous indignation or bravery of a hero could represent how a decent citizen ought to react against murderous injustice or even carnal temptation. Recurring themes, such as the tribulation of lovers overcome by notable fidelity, or a tyrant demonstrating clemency or restoring the throne to its rightful occupant, were intended to resonate with audiences and show an example of how true nobility should be achieved through behaviour rather than be a simple property of birthright. While the political content of opera tended to be generalized and concentrated on promoting enlightened principles, the most important political function of opera was certainly its role as an ostentatious public celebration of state events.

Genres and Styles

In the late Baroque era, opera was the most widely cultivated musical form. It had its own social and economic subculture and engaged many of the finest composers. By the early eighteenth century, most of the principal cities in Europe had imported opera from Italy and modified it to suit the local audiences' taste. In France, opera remained closely linked with the traditions of courtly entertainment established by Lully, whose *tragédie-lyriques* had developed into *opera-ballet*.

ITALY

Early eighteenth-century Italian opera was governed by conventions, but, within those rules, imaginative composers invented an enormous variety of musical moods and first-rate dramas. The most notable dominant convention was the *da capo* aria, which constructed opportunities for expensive singers to show off their skill, but could also effectively communicate the intensity of a dramatic moment. *Da capo* arias revealed the emotions of characters, but they rarely carried the plot forward. This was instead achieved through simple recitative, composed in a conversational manner and usually accompanied only by the harpsichord and cello. Recitative was closer to speech in its rhythms, and text tended to be more direct and less contemplative than arias. However, particularly important dramatic moments, such as a pivotal event for an individual character that has immense impact on their destiny, could be set to orchestral recitative for special effect. These were usually powerful recitatives accompanied by the entire string section of the orchestra. Several of the most celebrated examples were created for the castrato Senesino in Handel's London operas.

THE DA CAPO ARIA

A *da capo* aria is a simple formula dictated by the two-part organization of an aria's libretto text. Its mood could vary between rage, jealousy, despair or joy, according to the demands of the location of the plot. The singer's text can either directly describe their predicament, or take the form of a simile that has allegorical relevance to the course they must pursue. The first section in which a character expresses a particular emotion has an orchestral introduction (a *ritornello*), a dynamic opening vocal statement, and then subsequent development of that theme before a closing *ritornello*.

Then, in a shorter middle section, usually in a different but related key, the character clarifies, contradicts, or explores a wider context for their emotion, before consolidating his or her emotional response to events with an entire repeat of the first section. In this repeat of the entire first section, known as the da capo, the singer was expected to embellish the vocal line with difficult ornaments and to conclude the aria with an extempore cadenza.

OPERA SERIA, OPERA BUFFA AND INTERMEZZO

There were three basic types of operatic entertainments: *opera seria*, *opera buffa* and the *intermezzo*. The most highly esteemed of these forms was *opera seria*, which tended to focus on admirable behaviour such as clemency, heroism and fidelity. Naturally, in order to establish those principles, *opera seria* also explored the opposing emotions of rage, treachery and illicit lust. Only a minority were uncompromisingly serious and tragic, and most concluded with a

ABOVE: *Francesco Bernardi, known as Senesino, was one of the most popular castrati of his day and Handel wrote several roles for him.*

lieto fine ("happy ending"). It is a fallacy that *opera seria* was without humanism or humour, but resolutions usually portrayed morally uplifting reconciliation or the restoration of the correct and natural order of things. The comic style of *opera buffa* developed in Naples, and could ridicule its more aristocratic sibling with its focus on the foolish or ridiculous behaviour of common folk, often set in a vernacular Neapolitan dialect instead of the highbrow literary style of *opera seria* libretti. Similarly, the plots of *intermezzi* were more concerned about everyday life than promoting paragons of virtue, and featured a comic plot contained within a few short scenes that featured only two or three characters. However, these were usually designed as an intermediary entertainment between the acts of an *opera seria*.

FRANCE

France maintained an operatic tradition distinct from the rest of Europe. Italian operas tended to be structured into three long acts and rarely featured a chorus or dancers. In contrast, French operas frequently featured a prominent chorus, plenty of ballets and followed Jean-Baptiste Lully's (1632–87) model that contained five shorter acts. A unique genre was *opéra-ballet*, which grew out of Lully's *ballet de cour* and could contain a different exotically located story within each act, with the overall whole connected only by a tenuous theme. Unlike the imported Italian fashion that seemed exotic in London, Dresden, Vienna and Hamburg, Parisian audiences reacted with hostility to anything that attempted to increase Italian

influence in their operas, and the spectre of Lully remained potent even towards the end of the eighteenth century. However, as in Italy, the popular *opéra comique* was artistically overshadowed by the grandest genre *tragédie en musique*, which often depicted powerful stories taken from classical mythology.

RECIT

French recit could shift metre unpredictably, and there was the additional form of "measured" recitative that inclined towards greater expressive flexibility by emphasizing important moments with repeated figures or by elaborating the singer's declamation. Accompanied recitatives were an integral part of the action in French operas, and no Italian composer created more astonishingly vivid examples than Jean-Philippe Rameau (1683–1764).

An air was usually in binary form, but not always discernible from recit. An *ariette*, despite its misleading title, was the equivalent of the Italian *aria di bravura*, and Rameau's preference for *ariette* form was one of the most controversial aspects of his *Hippolyte et Aricie* (1733) ◆ **p. 70** that enraged the guardians of Lully's musical temple.

LEFT: Mademoiselle Arnould in the role of Psyche in Cupid and Psyche, *an opéra-ballet by Mondonville, first given on 9 May 1758.*
ABOVE: The harpsichord formed the accompaniment for recitative passages. This is a seventeenth-century Italian instrument by Zenti.

GENRES AND STYLES

1700—1750 LATE BAROQUE

ABOVE: Georg Philipp Telemann, who composed operas in German and Italian for audiences in Hamburg.

'RULE BRITANNIA'

'Rule Britannia' has become famous as a patriotic British anthem that is traditionally performed as an encore at the Last Night of the Proms. Its original version is the conclusion to Thomas Augustine Arne's masque *Alfred* (1740), and is an aria for the tenor title-hero that also features chorus, trumpets and drums.

POPULAR MELODY

GERMANY

An independent German style of opera did not flourish during the late Baroque period, and the many attempts made to produce vernacular German operas remain obscurities. The most widely respected German-born opera composers were Handel and Johann Hasse (1699–1783), who both acquired their mastery and reputation after they travelled south of the Alps to Italy. Hasse later enjoyed a long relationship with the Elector of Saxony's court at Dresden, but the operas produced there were essentially Italian in all respects. Handel only composed his first few operas in Germany, of which only *Almira* (1705) survives: its odd mixture of German recitative, Italian arias and French ballets were tailored for the peculiar tradition that had been established by Reinhard Keiser (1674–1739), the prolific, yet inconsistent, music director of the Hamburg opera house. Georg Philipp Telemann (1681–1767) also subsequently mixed Italian and German styles for Hamburg, although the consequent products of this mixture seem uneven and unsatisfying today despite frequent moments of musical brilliance. It was only in the later eighteenth century that a German school of operatic style began to be firmly established.

ENGLAND

Attempts to establish a native school of English opera were perpetually frustrated, not least because Henry Purcell's (1659–95) premature death had robbed him of the opportunity to develop beyond the theatrical limitations of semi-opera. The musician Thomas Clayton and author Joseph Addison's *Rosamund* (1707) was a pioneering attempt at English opera but it failed, and John Eccles' opera *Semele* (1707), composed to a libretto by William Congreve and later set as an oratorio by Handel, was cancelled by an anxious management before it could be publicly performed. Attempts to mix the Italian and English language together could not sustain popularity in London, despite a similar compromise becoming popular in Germany. During the early years of the eighteenth century, Italian opera became fashionable, perhaps because English gentlemen had enjoyed experiences of it while on the grand tour (an extended trip to experience the civilization of Italy that was believed to crown the education of every young aristocratic Englishman). The production of *Pyrrhus and Demetrius* (1709) at the Queen's Theatre on the Haymarket successfully presented music by Alessandro Scarlatti (1660–1725), and such events paved the way for Handel's *Rinaldo* (1711) ➛ p. 60, the first opera composed entirely in Italian specifically for a London audience.

THE BEGGAR'S OPERA

Although endeavours to formulate a native style of English opera were all doomed to long-term failure, John Gay's spoof *The Beggar's Opera* was tremendously successful. Gay chose existing popular tunes, but Johann Christoph Pepusch provided the musical substance of the arrangements. Like Handel, Pepusch was an immigrant composer from Germany who had worked for James Brydges, the Earl of Carnarvon, during the 1710s. In fact, the so-called "ballad opera" is hardly an opera at all, and contains over 60 short songs, based on country dances, folk tunes from Scotland and France, and an occasional slither of Purcell and Handel. Unlike the Royal Academy of Music's expensive Italian singers, Gay and Pepusch's entertainment featured actors who were not trained singers. The alleged influence of *The Beggar's Opera* on Handel's increasingly difficult career, composing Italian operas for London, has often been overstated. It was primarily a satire directed at the Whig government, although it incidentally pokes a little fun at the loftier world of Italian opera during the process. We can imagine that the Prime Minister Sir Robert Walpole, who attended the first performance, was not amused by the Tory Gay's frequent references to the low moral standards and corruption of politicians.

RIGHT: A contemporary publication depicting John Gay's popular satirical work The Beggar's Opera.

GENRES AND STYLES

AN EYEWITNESS ACCOUNT

Pierre-Jacques Fougeroux visited London and attended Handel's operas *Tolomeo*, *Siroe* and *Admeto* during the Royal Academy of Music's final season in 1727–28. His account of what he saw and heard is invaluable:

The Opera, which was once negligible, has become a spectacle of some importance in the last three years. They have sent for the best voices [and] the most skilled instrumentalists from Italy ... the orchestra consisted of 24 violins led by the Castrucci brothers, two harpsichords (one of which was played by the German Indel [Handel], a great player and great composer), one archlute, three cellos, two double basses, three bassoons and sometimes flutes and trumpets. This orchestra makes a very loud noise. As there is no middle part in the harmony, the 24 violins usually divide only into firsts and seconds, which sounds extremely brilliant and is beautifully played. The two harpsichords [and] the archlute fill in the middle of the harmony. They use only a cello, the two harpsichords and the archlute to accompany the recitatives. The music is good and thoroughly in the Italian style, although there are some tender pieces in the French style ... The auditorium is small and in very poor taste; the stage is quite large, with poor scenery. There is no amphitheatre, only a pit, with large curved benches uncomfortably together ... The sides of the stage are decorated with columns, which have mirrors fixed along them with brackets and several candles; ... Instead of chandeliers there are ugly wooden candlesticks suspended by strings like those used by tightrope walkers. Nothing could look more wretched, yet there are candles everywhere.

[English translation of Fougeroux's letter "*Voiage d'Angleterre*" is taken from Donald Burrows: *Handel*, Oxford, 1994, pp. 460–2]

ITALIAN IMPORT OPERA

Thereafter imported Italian opera dominated the London stage, although in the 1710s composers Johann Christoph Pepusch, Johann Ernest Galliard and Eccles turned their attention towards masques, which were like short one-act English operas. These could be performed as interludes in spoken plays, but Handel's masque *Acis and Galatea* (1718) ◄► **p. 61** was composed for a private performance. The most talented native composers did not successfully compete directly with Handel's Italian operas, and instead devoted most of their efforts to providing masques and incidental theatre music, although Thomas Arne (1710–78) produced English opera during the 1730s. Meanwhile, the poet John Gay (1685–1732) invented the genre of "ballad opera" with his popular *The Beggar's Opera* (1728) ◄► **p. 56**, which made prominent use of adopted popular tunes, but it was essentially a political vehicle rather than a credible music drama. When Handel eventually gave up composing Italian operas for dwindling English audiences, he continued to dominate serious music theatre in London with his oratorios. Despite the varying degrees of success generated by Arne's renewed attempts to establish English opera following Handel's death, there were few talented opera composers active between Purcell's death and the emergence of Benjamin Britten (1913–76) in the twentieth century.

RIGHT: The Baroque oratorio was similar in many ways to an opera, but tended to be more serious and sedate. The subject matter was always sacred and oratorios were often performed semi-staged. This engraving shows a rehearsal of the 1761 oratorio Judith *by Thomas Arne.*

GENRES AND STYLES

KEY COMPOSERS

George Frideric Handel

George Frideric Handel (1685–1759) composed 42 operas between 1704 and 1740, but most of these were neglected and seldom performed after his lifetime. In the twentieth century Handel's music dramas and, in particular, his operas underwent a renaissance that has established him as the definitive theatre composer of the late Baroque period. Handel was a maverick composer who pursued his own personal artistic direction, which was at times perceived by some of his London audience as old-fashioned compared to newer Italian composers Leo and Vinci. His eventual abandonment of Italian opera in favour of composing works in English allowed him to continue using his extraordinary gifts as a musical dramatist while establishing English oratorio as a distinctive and distinguished art form.

ABOVE: George Frideric Handel, painted by French artist Philippe Mercier in around 1730.

'NON LO DIRÒ COL LABBRO'
Taken from Handel's last Royal Academy opera *Tolomeo*, this depicts Alessandro's nervous admiration and feelings of first love for the lady Elisa. It has become famous as the song 'Silent Worship', arranged by Arthur Somervell, which was memorably sung by Ewan McGregor and Gwyneth Paltrow in the 1996 film adaptation of Jane Austen's *Emma*.
POPULAR MELODY

Operas

1705	Almira; Nero (lost)
1707	Florindo e Dafne (lost); Rodrigo
1709	Agrippina
1711	Rinaldo
1712	Il pastor fido; Teseo
1713	Silla
1715	Amadigi di Gaula
1718	Acis and Galatea
1720	Radamisto
1721	Muzio Scevola; Floridante
1722	Ottone
1723	Flavio
1724	Giulio Cesare in Egitto; Tamerlano
1725	Rodelinda
1726	Admeto; Riccardo I
1728	Siroe; Tolomeo
1729	Lotario
1730	Partenope
1731	Poro
1732	Ezio; Sosarme
1733	Orlando
1734	Arianna
1735	Ariodante; Alcina
1736	Atalanta
1737	Arminio; Giustino; Berenice
1738	Faramondo; Serse
1740	Imeneo; Deidamia
1743	Semele

FROM ORGAN LOFT TO OPERA HOUSE

Handel was born on 23 February 1685 in the provincial Saxon city of Halle. It is reputed that the Duke of Saxe-Weissenfels persuaded Handel's unsympathetic father to allow the boy to study music with the organist Friedrich Wilhelm Zachow. The young Handel presumably gained a thorough education in counterpoint and theory, but it is likely he yearned to escape Halle's devoutly Pietist atmosphere. In 1703 he arrived in Hamburg, where a chance meeting with Johann

Timeline

1685	George Frideric Handel born in Halle, Germany (as Georg Freidrich Händel)
1704	First experiences opera while playing in Hamburg Opera House orchestra, and composes first opera *Almira*
1709	Travels to Italy, and absorbs culture of Alessandro Scarlatti and Corelli
1709	Composes *Agrippina* for Venice
1711	*Rinaldo* premieres in London
1718	Composes masque *Acis and Galatea* and first English oratorio *Esther* for the Earl of Carnarvon.
1719	Formation of Royal Academy of Music
1724	*Giulio Cesare* premieres at King's Theatre
1727	Becomes a naturalized British citizen
1728	The Royal Academy of Music dissolves
1729	Handel begins partnership with Heidegger
1733	*Orlando* premieres at the King's Theatre
1734	Establishes independent opera company at Covent Garden
1735	*Alcina* is a massive success
1737	Peak of rivalry between Handel's company and the "Opera of the Nobility"; Handel becomes seriously ill
1738	*Serse* premieres but is a failure
1741	Handel's last Italian opera *Deidamia* is poorly received at Lincoln's Inn Fields Theatre
1742	A concert version of *Imeneo* in Dublin is Handel's final opera performance; first performance of *Messiah*
1743	Composes *Semele*
1752	Premiere of his last original oratorio *Jephtha* at Covent Garden
1759	Handel dies

Matteson (1681–1764) in an organ loft drew Handel into working his way up through the ranks of opera house orchestra until he composed his first opera *Almira* at the age of 19.

PAPAL ORATORIOS AND A PROTESTANT PATRON

Having exhausted his career possibilities in Hamburg, Handel resolved to visit Italy in 1706, where his first major undertaking was *Rodrigo* (1707), for Duke Ferdinando de' Medici at Florence. In Rome, where opera was forbidden by papal decree, Handel produced magnificent church music, dramatic oratorios and cantatas. His massively successful Venetian masterpiece *Agrippina* (1709) is the only opera that Handel

LATE BAROQUE

1700 —1750

HANDEL AND HIS SINGERS

Handel was notoriously tough on singers who caused him problems. While rehearsing *Flavio* (1723), the tenor Alexander Gordon became exasperated with Handel's method of *continuo* accompaniment, and threatened to jump on the composer's harpsichord. It is said that Handel retorted "Oh! Let me know when you will do that, and I will advertise it. For I am sure more people will come to see you jump, than to hear you sing". Handel was required to discipline petulant singers who wanted to sacrifice the drama in order to have something flashier to sing. The soprano Cuzzoni refused to sing the aria 'Falsa imagine' in *Ottone* (1722), perhaps because she did not care for its simplicity. Handel's first biographer, John Mainwaring, reports that the outraged composer exclaimed, in French, "*Madam, I know you are a veritable devil, but I would have you know that I am Beelzebub, chief of the Devils*". Without warning, Handel grasped her around the waist, and threatened to fling her out of the window.

set to a libretto written especially for him. Handel resisted attempts to convert him to Catholicism while in Italy, and preferred to accept the position of *Kapellmeister* at the Protestant court of the Elector of Hanover. Nevertheless, he soon composed *Rinaldo*, the first Italian opera performed in London. It was enormously popular and he deserted his post in Hanover and relocated permanently to London, where he seems to have overcome any diplomatic problems that might have arisen when his erstwhile employer became George I in 1714.

DIRECTOR OF THE ROYAL ACADEMY OF MUSIC

For a short period Handel provided music for James Brydges, the Earl of Carnarvon, including the masque *Acis and Galatea* that indicated a fertile future in composing English works. However, in 1719 Handel was appointed musical director of the Royal Academy of Music, an aristocratic company that funded performances of Italian opera at the King's Theatre on the Haymarket. This rivalled any opera house in Europe, starring the famous singers Francesca Cuzzoni (1696–1778) and Senesino, for whom Handel created *Giulio Cesare in Egitto*. The following season, the arrival of the tenor Francesco Borosini influenced *Tamerlano* (1724) and *Rodelinda* (1725) ➡ **p. 63**. The addition of a second

prima donna, the soprano Faustina (1697–1781), heralded the Royal Academy's last phase known as the "Rival Queens" era, and in operas such as *Admeto* (1727) and *Tolomeo* (1728), Handel was careful to feature two equally prominent female characters.

CONFLICTING OPERA TRENDS AND TENSIONS

Italian opera became increasingly difficult to sustain on the London stage. In 1729 Handel took over management in partnership with the King's Theatre impresario Heidegger. During the next five years, this semi-independent company (sometimes called the "Second Academy") allowed Handel to pursue a flexible choice of libretti that reveal a greater degree of variety than the conventional heroic subjects that the Royal Academy had preferred. In 1732 Handel introduced English works into his theatre seasons. For the 1734–35 season Handel established an independent opera company at John Rich's new Covent Garden Theatre, but, despite the successes of *Ariodante* (1735) ➡ **p. 65** and *Alcina* (1735) ➡ **p. 66**, Handel struggled against competition from the "Opera of the Nobility", who had replaced him at the King's Theatre. The rivalry did not benefit either faction, and by the end of the 1736–37 season Handel suffered a massive stroke, signalling the end of his most active years as an opera composer. Thereafter he produced *Serse* (1738) ➡ **p. 66** and *Imeneo* (1740) that present wittier subject matter, and reveal a more concise economical musical style. After nearly 30 years trying to make a success of Italian opera in London, Handel dedicated the rest of his career to non-staged theatrical works set to English texts, although *Semele* (1743) ➡ **p. 67**, *Hercules* (1744), and even some biblical oratorios, are fundamentally operatic in nature.

LEFT: A performance of Handel's music for King George at St George's Church, Hanover Square, London.
BELOW: Covent Garden Theatre, built for John Rich in 1732. Here, Rich makes his triumphal entry at the theatre's opening.

Rinaldo

Rinaldo by Handel

Composed	1711
Premiered	1711, London
Libretto	by Aaron Hill and Giacomo Rossi, after Torquato Tasso

A small number of Handel's dramatic works are known as the "magic operas", including *Rinaldo*, *Teseo* (1712), *Amadigi* (1715), *Orlando* (1733) and *Alcina*. These operas feature protagonists who use sorcery to manipulate love, usually for evil ends.

Most common among these operas is the prima donna sorceress figure that attempts to compel a castrato hero away from his true love and military duty. The wicked women's plans to entice the hero are always doomed to failure: in these operas, the hero's eventual disillusionment and disenchantment are considered in literal and favourable terms.

Rinaldo was Handel's first Italian opera composed for London and is notable for its flamboyant music and exotically devised libretto. It is not generally thought to be among Handel's best dramas, but instead seems to have impressed the London public by combining his most technically demanding arias with lavish spectacle.

The glories of Handel's score include the heroic aria 'Or la tromba' (featuring four trumpets) and the lament 'Cara sposa', both composed for the castrato Nicolini (1673–1732). However, the dominant character in the opera is the villainous enchantress Armida, whose conclusion to Act II, 'Vo far guerra', afforded Handel an opportunity to dazzle his audiences, both at the time and in the future, with stunningly intricate harpsichord solos.

Rinaldo, **Academy of Ancient Music**
Christopher Hogwood, **conductor**
Decca 467 087–2OHO3
Soloists: Luba Orgonasova (Armida), Cecilia Bartoli (Almirena), Bernarda Fink (Goffredo), David Daniels (Rinaldo), Gerald Finley (Argante)

RECOMMENDED RECORDING

Synopsis
Rinaldo by Handel

ACT I

During the first crusade, in the Christian camp, Goffredo delivers words of encouragement. To the young knight Rinaldo he promises his daughter Almirena's hand in marriage, if the army is successful in capturing Jerusalem. The Saracen king Argante appears and demands a three-day truce, to which Goffredo agrees. Argante then consults his lover, the sorceress Armida, who reveals that without Rinaldo the Christians will never succeed. Rinaldo and Almirena are in a garden exchanging lovers' vows when Armida, using her magic powers, abducts Almirena. Rinaldo runs to Goffredo and his brother Eustazio for advice; they suggest paying a visit to a Christian sorcerer. Rinaldo calls on the elements to assist him in retrieving his love.

ACT II

On their way to visit the sorcerer, Goffredo, Eustazio and Rinaldo arrive at the seashore, where sirens, sent by Armida, are singing to them. Despite the efforts of the others, Rinaldo is enchanted by the sirens; he goes to join them and sails off aboard a magic boat. Rinaldo is taken to Armida's palace, where Almirena is also being held prisoner. Argante has fallen in love with Almirena and is forcing his unwanted attentions on her. Likewise, Armida falls for Rinaldo; after he rejects her she uses her magic to make herself look like Almirena, and tries again to seduce him. Rinaldo sees through her disguise, but Argante fails to and continues his wooing of "Almirena". Armida, discovering Argante's treachery, swears she will have vengeance.

ACT III

Goffredo and Eustazio reach the home of the sorcerer, who lives at the base of the mountain on which Armida's palace is situated. They try to climb the mountain but are forced back by evil spirits; the sorcerer provides them with magic wands and they make a successful ascent. As Armida attempts to kill Almirena, Goffredo and Eustazio use their wands to destroy the palace and the setting once again becomes the countryside near Jerusalem. The

Christian soldiers, led by Rinaldo, storm the city and capture Argante; Eustazio captures Armida. Rinaldo and Almirena are reunited amidst much joy and celebration, while Argante and Armida agree to convert to the Christian faith.

ABOVE: Emma Bell as Almirena in Grange Park Opera's 2000 production of Handel's Rinaldo.

KEY COMPOSERS

THE FIRST PERFORMANCES OF RINALDO

The elaborate attempt to stage Rinaldo in London aroused interest from satirists Joseph Addison and Richard Steele in the *Spectator*. Addison, after examining the printed wordbook, reported:

The Opera of Rinaldo is filled with Thunder and Lightning, Illuminations, and Fireworks; which the Audience may look upon without catching Cold, and indeed without much danger of being burnt; for there are several Engines filled with Water, and ready to play at a Minute's Warning, in case any such Accident should happen. However, as I have a very great Friendship for the Owner of this Theatre, I hope that he has been wise enough to insure his House before he would let this Opera be acted in it.

After seeing the opera, Steele commented: *The Undertakers of the Hay-Market, having raised too great an Expectation in their printed Opera, very much disappoint their Audience on the stage. The King of Jerusalem is obliged to come from the City on foot, instead of being drawn in a triumphant Chariot by white Horses, as my Opera-Book had promised me; ... We had also but a very short Allowance of Thunder and Lightning; th' I cannot in this Place omit doing Justice to the Boy who had the Direction of the Two painted Dragons, and made them spit Fire and Smoke ... I saw indeed but Two things wanting to render his whole Action compleat, I mean the keeping his Head a little lower, and hiding his Candle.*

Acis and Galatea

Acis and Galatea by Handel
Composed   1718
Premiered   1718, Edgware
Libretto by   John Gay and others, after Ovid

While composing for the Earl of Carnarvon at Cannons, Handel was the musical contributor to a distinguished literary circle including the poets John Gay (later the author of *The Beggar's Opera*), Alexander Pope (1688–1744) and John Hughes. It is believed that all three authors contributed to the libretto of *Acis and Galatea*, which was given a private staged performance that probably required only a dozen performers. One observer noted in his diary that it was "a little opera". Its pastoral subject and chamber scoring are far removed from the spectacle and high drama of *opera seria*.

Synopsis
Acis and Galatea by Handel

ACT I

In an idyllic, pastoral setting, Galatea, a semi-divine sea-nymph, has fallen in love with Acis, a shepherd. She appeals to another shepherd, Damon, for assistance; with his help the two lovers are united and sing of their love for one another, accompanied by various nymphs and shepherds.

ACT II

Act II begins with a more sinister atmosphere, as the chorus warns Acis and Galatea of the approach of Polyphemus, a sea monster. Inflamed by jealousy, Polyphemus threatens to force his love upon Galatea. Acis, ignoring Damon's warnings, prepares to do battle with the fearsome monster. Acis and Galatea swear their eternal love, but their duet becomes a trio as they are interrupted by Polyphemus, who kills Acis. Galatea is heartbroken, but at this point is reminded by the chorus of her divine powers. She then transforms Acis into a beautiful fountain; everyone mourns Acis and sings of his immortality.

TOP LEFT: *Joseph Addison, a leading satirical author who wrote scathingly about Handel's opera* Rinaldo *in the* Spectator.

ABOVE: *Polyphemus surprises the lovers Acis and Galatea in a nineteenth-century statue from Paris, France.*

Giulio Cesare in Egitto
('*Julius Caesar in Egypt*')

Giulio Cesare in Egitto by Handel

Composed	1724
Premiered	1724, London
Libretto	by Nicola Francesco Haym, after Giacomo Francesco Bussani

Handel's operas principally revolve around the voices and particular gifts of the singers that were available to him. *Giulio Cesare* was created as a vehicle for Senesino and Cuzzoni, although the characteristic trademark of Handel's best operas is that the emotions and experience of the characters are not sacrificed to the virtuosity of the singers. We have come to appreciate in recent times that, although Handel's arias are an opportunity for the singer to impress his audience, they also function as engaging indications of the character's dramatic motivation and thoughts. Handel's ability to portray character often results in an organically evolving personality. In Act I of *Giulio Cesare*, the title-hero's arias show progress from pompous arrogance, '*Presti omai l'egizia terra*'; anger, '*Empio, dirò tu sei*'; to a realization of his own mortality, '*Alma del gran Pompeo*'. Likewise, Cleopatra is transformed from a flirtatious stereotype into a genuinely seductive lover in '*V'adoro pupille*', which features a lush onstage continuo band, before her sincere hopelessness demands our pity in '*Piangerò la sorte mia*'. The secondary roles of the grieving Cornelia and her vengeful son Sesto are also compellingly brought to life, especially in their sublime duet '*Son nata a lagrimar*'.

ABOVE: Bejun Mehta as Tolomeo with dancers in the 2000 Los Angeles Opera production of Handel's Giulio Cesare in Egitto.

RIGHT: A poster for Handel's Giulio Cesare in Egitto.

Synopsis
Giulio Cesare in Egitto by Handel

ACT I

Giulio Cesare is in Egypt and has promised a reconciliation with his old enemy Pompeo, if Pompeo shows himself personally. Achilla, commander of the Egyptian army under King Tolomeo, arrives with Pompeo's head; Cesare is angered by this. Pompeo's wife Cornelia and son Sesto are also present; they are distraught and Sesto swears vengeance. Cleopatra, who rules Egypt jointly with her brother, decides to seduce Cesare, while Achilla tells Tolomeo that he will murder Cesare in return for Cornelia's hand. Cesare, in his camp, is introduced to "Lidia", who is in fact Cleopatra in disguise. Cesare falls in love with her. Cornelia enters and tries to kill herself, but Sesto prevents her. "Lidia" offers the services of Nireno, an Egyptian courtier, to help them find Tolomeo, Pompeo's murderer. Cesare arrives at Tolomeo's palace, avoiding ambush. Tolomeo falls for Cornelia when they are introduced, but continues to pretend that Achilla can expect to win her. Cornelia spurns Achilla's advances towards her; Achilla in his anger imprisons Sesto.

ACT II

Cleopatra, as "Lidia", summons Cesare to her rooms; with the assistance of Nireno, he arrives. Meanwhile, both Achilla and Tolomeo try unsuccessfully to woo Cornelia. Guards approach "Lidia" and Cesare; Cleopatra reveals her true identity and prays for Cesare as he leaves to face the enemy. Cornelia sits among the people in Tolomeo's harem. Sesto rushes in and attempts to kill the king but is prevented by Achilla, who reveals

that Cesare has leapt from a castle window into the sea and cannot have survived. He requests his prize, i.e. Cornelia, but Tolomeo refuses. Sesto now tries to commit suicide but Cornelia stops him. The angry Achilla changes sides, joining the Romans and Cleopatra.

ACT III

A fierce battle rages on the shores of the Mediterranean. Tolomeo's army triumphs and he takes Cleopatra prisoner. Cesare is still alive and rises from the sea. Meanwhile Sesto and Nireno go in search of Tolomeo, but come across Achilla, who is dying. He gives Sesto a seal, which will give him command over a number of soldiers nearby. As Achilla dies, Cesare enters and takes the seal, vowing to save Cleopatra and Cornelia. Cesare saves Cleopatra from where she is being held prisoner. Sesto finds Tolomeo, who is still trying to court Cornelia, and slays him. They are all reunited; Cesare and Cleopatra declare their love for each other and the people rejoice that their land is at peace.

KEY COMPOSERS

Rodelinda

Rodelinda by Handel

Composed	1725
Premiered	1725, London
Libretto	by Nicola Francesco Haym, after Antonio Salvi and Pierre Corneille

Rodelinda is also remarkable for its quality. Handel composed many exceptional accompanied recitatives for Senesino throughout their collaborations, and in this opera the dethroned King Bertarido, believed dead by his steadfast wife, laments his misfortune in an accompanied recitative and aria, '*Pompe vane di morte! … Dove sei amato bene*', which shows Handel as a supreme master of his craft. Bertarido's eventual confrontation with his usurper Grimoaldo,

> **'OMBRA MAI FÙ'**
> '*Ombra mai fù*', known as 'Handel's Largo', has become popular as an arrangement for strings and an organ voluntary, which is frequently performed at weddings. In fact, Handel's arioso is marked *larghetto*. Handel based its simple melody, suspended over a gentle pulsating string accompaniment, on a previous setting by Giovanni Bononcini (1670–1747).
> **POPULAR MELODY**

in '*Vivi tiranno!*', is a thrilling example of how Handel's arias can be both technically spectacular and emotionally astute: the *coloratura* is bright and ferocious, but the sentimental tone of the aria brilliantly captures Bertarido's indignant defiance, giving him a full characterization.

BELOW: Anna Caterina Antonacci in Glyndebourne Festival Opera's 2002 production of Rodelinda.
RIGHT: Jean Rigby and Artur Stafanowicz perform in the same production.

𝒮*ynopsis*
Rodelinda by Handel

BACKGROUND

The kingdom of Lombardy was split between two brothers, Bertarido and Gundeberto, who then fought over the inheritance. Gundeberto called upon Duke Grimoaldo to help him, offering his sister Eduige's hand in return. Gundeberto met his death, probably through Grimoaldo's doing. Grimoaldo, while betrothed to Eduige, fell in love with Bertarido's wife, Rodelinda, and seized the Milanese throne. Bertarido left his wife and son and fled to Hungary, spreading the news of his death.

ACT I

As Rodelinda weeps for Bertarido, Grimoaldo offers to marry her; she rejects him. Duke Garibaldo persuades Grimoaldo to break his engagement to Eduige. Garibaldo then proposes to Eduige himself. Garibaldo, when alone, reveals that he does not love Eduige but hopes to gain the throne.

Bertarido has returned and is visiting his tomb. Unulfo, a courtier who has retained his loyalty to Bertarido, advises him to hide. Rodelinda and Flavio arrive, followed by Garibaldo, who threatens to kill Flavio unless Rodelinda marries Grimoaldo. She agrees, stipulating that her first act as queen will be to execute Garibaldo. Bertarido is dismayed at Rodelinda's apparent willingness to marry Grimoaldo.

ACT II

Eduige agrees to marry Garibaldo. Rodelinda asks Grimoaldo to murder Flavio in front of her, as she cannot marry a usurper and be the mother of the rightful king. Garibaldo encourages Grimoaldo to do just this; both Unulfo and Grimoaldo are horrified by the idea. As Bertarido laments his fate, Eduige hears him and is reunited with her brother. Bertarido admits that he is not interested in the throne and only wishes to be with his family; this pleases Eduige, who still hopes for power. Unulfo arrives and

reassures Bertarido of Rodelinda's continuing fidelity; he then brings her to him and the lovers are reunited. Grimoaldo finds them together and declares that he will kill Bertarido.

ACT III

Eduige, remorseful for coveting the throne, gives Unulfo the key to a secret passage through which Bertarido can escape. Garibaldo tries to persuade Grimoaldo to kill Bertarido. In the dungeon, Bertarido is thrown a sword. He uses it to attack the intruder, who turns out to be Unulfo. They hear footsteps approaching and exit, leaving behind a bloodied cloak. Eduige, Rodelinda and Flavio enter, find the garment and believe Bertarido to be dead. Unulfo leaves to fetch the others, while Bertarido conceals himself. Grimoaldo arrives, tortured by guilt, jealousy and love, and falls asleep. Garibaldo attempts to kill him, but is instead killed himself by Bertarido. Grateful for his life, Grimoaldo returns the kingdom of Milan to Bertarido, declaring that he will marry Eduige and they will rule Pavia together.

page 56 ... page 82   page 49 ... page 68

Orlando

Orlando by Handel

Composed	1732
Premiered	1733, London
Librettist	unknown, after Carlo Sigismondo and Lodovico Ariosto

The mid-1730s operas *Orlando, Ariodante* and *Alcina* represent the artistic peak of Handel's operatic career. Their stories all originate in the epic poem *Orlando Furioso* by the playwright and poet Ariosto, who was born and bred at the Ferrara court in the late fifteenth century. *Orlando* portrays the destructive insanity of its title-hero who ignores his destiny by pursuing the love of the unkind Angelica rather than glory in war. The climax of this madness, at the end of Act II, was brilliantly conveyed by Handel's use of eccentric time signatures within striking accompanied recitatives, paradoxically followed by the lyrical yet slightly disturbed aria 'Vaghe pupille'. Orlando's

Synopsis
Orlando by Handel

BACKGROUND ❧

Prince Medoro has been wounded in battle and is being nursed back to health by Dorinda, a shepherdess, and Angelica, Queen of Cathay, who is being courted by Orlando, a knight. Dorinda and Angelica have both fallen in love with Medoro.

ACT I ❧

Zoroastro, a magician, consults the stars and, seeing that Orlando has strayed from his destiny in his pursuit of Angelica, tries to persuade the knight to abandon his love and dedicate himself to noble deeds. Orlando maintains that he can reconcile his destiny and his love for Angelica. At Dorinda's house, the shepherdess muses on love, while Angelica and Medoro declare their feelings for

each other. Dorinda sees Angelica leaving, but Medoro pretends that she is a relative.

Zoroastro warns Angelica that if Orlando learns of her love for Medoro, the knight will wreak his revenge. To confirm that Orlando loves her, Angelica taunts him by accusing him of loving another. Orlando denies it and offers to prove his love for her by killing fearsome monsters. Angelica then joins Medoro and the two embrace; Dorinda enters and is inconsolable at discovering Medoro does not return her affections. Angelica gives her a jewel.

ACT II ❧

Orlando bursts in upon the grieving Dorinda and accuses her of telling Angelica that he has been unfaithful. Dorinda reveals the truth about Angelica and Medoro, showing Orlando the jewel, which, it turns out, was given to Angelica by Orlando. Consumed by rage, Orlando swears revenge and leaves. Zoroastro, scolding Angelica and Medoro for incurring Orlando's wrath, advises them to flee. They pause in the woods, where Medoro declares his love for Angelica, carving their names on a tree. Orlando finds this evidence and, eventually reaching the lovers, attempts to kill them. Zoroastro protects them and Orlando, tormented by love, fury, grief and his inner conflict, loses his mind.

ACT III ❧

Medoro, who has lost Angelica in the pursuit, returns to Dorinda's house and confesses his love for Angelica. Orlando arrives and declares his love for Dorinda, but he is obviously mad and leaves, guided by his raving fantasies. Dorinda tells Angelica that Orlando has killed Medoro. Orlando confronts Angelica and she defies him; he throws her in a cave. Zoroastro now decides to return Orlando's sanity. Dorinda tells him that he has killed Medoro and he attempts to kill himself, but is prevented by Angelica. With the help of Zoroastro, Orlando accepts Angelica and Medoro's love for each other and rejoices in his own destiny and triumph over love and his own madness.

LEFT: Kathleen Kuhlmann and Kevin Langan in a 1989 production of Orlando *by the San Francisco Opera.*

KEY COMPOSERS

Orlando, **Les Arts Florissants**
William Christie, **conductor**
Erato CD 0630–14636–2
Soloists: Rosemary Joshua (Angelica), Rosa Mannion (Dorinda), Patricia Bardon (Orlando), Hilary Summers (Medoro), Harry van der Kamp (Zoroastro)

RECOMMENDED RECORDING

magnificent arias also include 'Non fu già men forte Alcide', featuring Handel's typically robust yet melodic use of horns, in which the deluded warrior compares himself to Hercules. This was the last role Handel ever composed for his star castrato Senesino, and it is the most astonishing and innovative. Handel's music for Angelica, the shepherdess Dorinda and the Prince Medoro is also superb, and their trio 'Consolati o bella' that concludes Act I confirms that Handel's dramatic ensembles exploring the emotions of different characters can hold their own alongside Mozart's. The wise magician Zoroastro, composed for the remarkably agile bass Antonio Montagnana, is an antecedent of Mozart and Emmanuel Schikaneder's (1751–1812) Sarastro, and is the only magical character in Handel's operas who uses his power for good rather than evil.

Ariodante

Ariodante by Handel

Composed	1735
Premiered	1735, London
Librettist	unknown, after Antonio Salvi and Lodovico Ariosto

Ariodante also derives from Ariosto, but it is a serious opera. Thanks to a fine text, adapted from an old Italian libretto by Antonio Salvi, Handel was able to explore potent tragic situations, such as the King of Scotland being forced to contemplate executing his much-loved daughter Ginvera. The opera is best known for 'Scherza infida', an aria composed for Carestini that explores the anguish of a broken heart. Ariodante also featured a full chorus and several fine dances for Marie Sallé's ballet company.

RIGHT: Handel based several of his operas on the epic poem Orlando Furioso by Italian playwright and poet Lodovico Ariosto.

Synopsis
Ariodante by Handel

ACT I

Ginevra, daughter of the Scottish king, is in her chamber preparing to meet her betrothed. She reveals to her confidante Dalinda that her father approves of her engagement. Duke Polinesso enters, declaring his love for Ginevra. She rejects him harshly. Dalinda, herself in love with Polinesso, explains to him that Ginevra is betrothed to Ariodante, a knight. Polinesso then devises a plot by which he can use Dalinda's love for him to win Ginevra's heart. In the garden, Ginevra and Ariodante sing of their love for each other. The king gives them his blessing and orders Odoardo to begin the wedding preparations. Meanwhile, Polinesso appeals to Dalinda to help him by dressing up as Ginevra and inviting him into Ginevra's room. He offers her his love in return. Flattered,

Dalinda agrees. When Polinesso has left, Ariodante's brother, Lurcanio, enters and declares his love for Dalinda; she rejects him. Alone, she sings that she will always love Polinesso. There is a dance, in which Ginevra and Ariodante mingle with shepherds and shepherdesses.

ACT II

Polinesso encounters Ariodante and feigns surprise at the news he is to be married to Ginevra, explaining that he and Ginevra are in love. Ariodante demands proof, upon which Dalinda, dressed as Ginevra, welcomes Polinesso into Ginevra's chamber. Ariodante is shocked and tries to kill himself, but is stopped by Lurcanio. Polinesso continues to pretend that he loves Dalinda.

The king is informed that Ariodante has leapt into the sea and is drowned. Ginevra faints at the news. Lurcanio explains Ginevra's apparent treachery to her father, who disowns her. There is a dance in which we see Ginevra's feverish dreams.

ACT III

Contrary to the rumours, Ariodante is alive, and alone in the woods. He hears the frightened cries of Dalinda; she is running from Polinesso, who wants to kill her to buy her silence. Ariodante saves Dalinda, who then confesses the deception. Back at the palace, the king asks for a knight to defend Ginevra's honour in a jousting match against Lurcanio. Polinesso, hoping to win favour with the king, accepts. The jousting begins and Polinesso is mortally wounded. Lurcanio offers to fight anyone else who will defend Ginevra; an unknown knight responds. It is revealed to be Ariodante, who offers to tell all if Dalinda receives a Royal pardon.

Odoardo enters with the news that Polinesso has confessed to his crimes. Dalinda agrees to marry Lurcanio, while Ginevra, in her cell, is reunited with both her father and Ariodante. The opera closes with a courtly dance involving all the couples.

Alcina

Alcina by Handel
Composed   1735
Premiered   London, 1735
Librettist   unknown, after Antonio Fanzaglia
              and Lodovico Ariosto

Alcina is the most celebrated of Handel's "magic" operas. Its dynamic situations are compelling and poignant: Handel's portrayal of an enchanted hero, his brave true love and their evil enemy inspired him to create a particularly fine score that examines intense emotional experiences such as loss, guilt, lust, nostalgia and the restoration of memory. Handel's version is based on an anonymous adaptation of *Ariosto* that had been set to music by Riccardo Broschi, Farinelli's (1705–82) brother, for Rome in 1728.

The title role, composed for Anna Maria Strada del Pó (active 1719–40), is an especially fascinating and complex woman, although all the characters in the opera reveal complicated emotions and relationships that are examined by some of Handel's finest operatic music.

LEFT: Lisa Milne as Alcina in the English National Opera's 2003 production.

$\mathcal{S}ynopsis$
Alcina by Handel

ACT I

Bradamante, disguised as her brother Ricciardo, has arrived with her confidant Melisso in the realm of Alcina, an enchantress. They hope to rescue Bradamante's lover Ruggiero, who has been bewitched by Alcina. Pretending to have lost their way, the pair are welcomed by Alcina's sister, Morgana, who falls in love with "Ricciardo" (Bradamante). Alcina, who is in love with Ruggiero, welcomes "Ricciardo" and Melisso to her palace. Bradamante and Melisso try to rescue Ruggiero, but he does not recognize them.

Oronte, betrothed to Morgana, challenges "Ricciardo" to a duel; Morgana protects "Ricciardo". Oronte tells Ruggiero that Alcina loves "Ricciardo". Ruggiero confronts Alcina and she denies it.

Alcina vows to turn "Ricciardo" into a wild beast to prove her love for Ruggiero; Morgana urges "him" to flee. "He" asks her to tell Alcina that "his" heart belongs to another; Morgana is overjoyed.

ACT II

Disguised as Ruggiero's old tutor, Melisso manages to persuade Ruggiero of his true identity. He advises Ruggiero to tell Alcina he is going out hunting and then escape. Ruggiero again meets Bradamante, but

is mistrustful in case it is Alcina in disguise. As Alcina prepares to turn "Ricciardo" into a beast, Morgana enters, followed by Ruggiero. He persuades Alcina that she does not need to perform the spell in order to prove her love for him, and tells her that he is going out hunting. Oronte reveals that Melisso, "Ricciardo" and Ruggiero are preparing to flee and mocks Morgana for believing that "Ricciardo" loves her. Bradamante reassures Oberto that they will find his father. Bradamante and Ruggiero are finally reunited but are overheard by Morgana, who now knows about Bradamante's disguise and Ruggiero's betrayal. Alcina summons spirits to impede the lovers' escape, but her powers are weakening.

ACT III

Morgana and Oronte are reunited. Ruggiero encounters Alcina and explains that he is betrothed to Bradamante; Alcina swears vengeance. Melisso and Ruggiero prepare to destroy Alcina's powers, with the help of the magic ring; Oronte reveals to Alcina that her powers are no longer working properly. Ruggiero and Bradamante destroy the source of Alcina's powers, despite her protestations that she has no evil intentions. Alcina and Morgana lament their fate; their powers have been removed and the spell has been lifted from the land; the castle lies in ruins and Alcina's captives turn back into humans. Everyone rejoices in love and freedom.

Serse

Serse by Handel
Composed   1737–38
Premiered   1738, London
Librettist   unknown, after Silvio Stampiglia
              and Nicolò Minato

Although popular now, *Serse* was one of Handel's worst failures. It was only performed five times during its first run and Handel never revived it. Unusually among Handel's operas, its libretto by Silvio Stampiglia (1664–1725) is warmly light-hearted and does not seriously concern itself with tragic events or heroic actions. The most famous aria, 'Ombra mai fù', portrays the King of Persia eloquently expressing love to a tree. The opera's arias feature imaginative use of limited resources. As with *Imeneo* and *Deidamia*, the score shows that Handel's genius remained vibrant even towards the unhappy end of his operatic career.

$\mathcal{S}ynopsis$
Serse by Handel

ACT I

Serse, King of Persia, sings in his garden, watched by his brother Arsemene and his servant, Elviro. Romilda, Arsemene's secret lover, sings nearby; Serse is enchanted. He orders Arsemene to tell Romilda of his love. This interests Romilda's sister, Atlanta, who loves Arsemene. Romilda rejects Serse's love; Serse banishes Arsemene. Meanwhile, Serse's abandoned fiancée Amastre arrives in disguise and swearing vengeance. Ariodate, Romilda's father, brings news of victory; Serse promises him that his daughter will marry a royal. Arsemene gives Elviro a letter for Romilda, describing his grief. Atlanta taunts Romilda and says that Arsemene has been unfaithful.

ACT II

In disguise, Elviro tries to deliver Arsemene's letter. He meets Amastre and reveals that Serse is to marry Romilda. Atlanta intercepts Elviro and takes the letter to Serse, claiming that it was intended for her. Serse shows it to Romilda, who continues to reject his advances. Alone, Romilda confesses her jealousy,

KEY COMPOSERS

Semele

Semele by Handel

Composed	1743
Premiered	1744, London
Librettist	by William Congreve, after Ovid

Semele was first performed at Covent Garden on 10 February 1744 in the manner of an oratorio, without action or scenery. Nevertheless, Handel's occasional collaborator Charles Jennens regarded it as "a bawdy opera". Congreve's libretto, based on a story from Ovid, had originally been set as an opera by John Eccles in 1707 but it was never performed. However the libretto came to Handel's attention, it inspired him to compose a rich work in which the foolish and gullible Semele steals the show with her florid songs 'Endless pleasure' and 'Myself I shall adore'. Handel's music fits each character perfectly, whether it is the malicious venom of the jealous Juno, or the sweet and simple Athamus. The Arcadian music, especially

that for Jupiter ('Where'er you walk') and a sleep scene for Somnus, ranks among his finest achievements, but, despite its quality, Semele was not a success: it was performed only six times during Handel's lifetime. Several recent productions have proved that his secular "oratorio" is ideal for the modern opera house.

RIGHT: *Robert Tear as Jupiter with Valerie Masterson as Semele in Handel's* Semele *at Covent Garden in 1982.*

Synopsis
Semele by Handel

ACT I

In the temple of Juno the people of Thebes celebrate the marriage of Semele, daughter of Cadmus, King of Thebes, to Athamas. The goddess is seen to approve of the match. Semele is unwilling to go ahead with the wedding and prays to Jupiter, whom she is in love with, for guidance. Semele's sister Ino is also in a state of distress, for she loves Athamas. Jupiter expresses his disapproval of the marriage with a clap of thunder. The flame on the altar is extinguished and the people, with the exception of Athamas and Ino, flee. Ino tries to express her love for Athamas but he misconstrues her words. Cadmus returns and relates that Semele has been borne up to the heavens by a giant eagle. The priests return, not mourning but celebrating Semele's departure, as she can be heard in the distance singing of endless pleasure and love.

ACT II

Juno, wife of Jupiter, is enraged when Iris tells her of the house that Jupiter has built for Semele, and swears vengeance. Iris warns her of the dragons that guard the gates, and Juno decides to employ Somnus, god of sleep, to help her. Semele sleeps in her new home. On awakening, she feels lonely and ignored by Jupiter and wishes for sleep to reclaim her. Jupiter tries to reassure her but she maintains that while she remains mortal she cannot help but be dissatisfied. Jupiter is concerned that Semele has aspirations to immortality and attempts to distract her. He sends for Ino and transforms the surroundings into Arcadia, encouraging Semele to enjoy the pleasures of nature. Ino arrives, telling excitedly of her journey to the heavens and the beautiful music she has heard. Everyone celebrates the joy of music.

ACT III

Juno tries to persuade Somnus to help her carry out her plans. He is unenthusiastic until she promises him his favourite nymph, Pasithea. Somnus is to bring sleep upon Ino and the dragons at the palace, so that Juno can disguise herself as Ino and reach Semele's room. He is also instructed to send Jupiter an erotic dream, so that when he awakes he will be willing to do anything Semele asks of him. Semele is unhappy and alone when Juno, disguised as Ino, enters her room. Juno asks Semele about her hopes for immortality and shows her a mirror, in which Semele appears to have the perfection of a goddess. Juno then advises Semele that when Jupiter comes to her, she should insist on him appearing in his unmasked, godlike form instead of appearing as a man. In this way, Juno assures her, Semele will become immortal. Semele thanks Juno, who retires.

Jupiter, inflamed by desire following his dream, enters Semele's chamber and goes to embrace her. Semele hesitates, so Jupiter swears to give her anything she desires. She asks to see him in his godlike form. Jupiter, knowing that the force of this will kill Semele, is angry with himself for having sworn to grant her wish. He tries to warn her against it, but Semele assumes that he simply wants to deny her immortality. Juno revels in her victory. Jupiter then descends in a cloud with thunder and lightning. Semele is consumed by his fire and dies. Ino is returned to Thebes and, along with Athamas, Cadmus and the priests, witnesses Semele's death as a storm of fire.

Ino reveals that Jupiter has commanded that she and Athamas wed. Apollo descends with the news that from Semele's ashes will rise Bacchus, god of wine. Everyone celebrates the joyful news.

while Amastre attempts suicide; Elviro prevents her. Elviro relates all to Arsemene. By their new bridge, Serse and Ariodate sing of conquests. Arsemene arrives; Serse pardons him and gives him permission to marry Atlanta, but he explains that he loves Romilda. Serse encourages Atlanta to forget Arsemene. A storm destroys the bridge. Amastre, calling Serse a traitor, is arrested; Romilda secures her release and then sings of her love for Arsemene.

ACT III

Reunited, Romilda and Arsemene extract the truth from Atlanta. Romilda consents to marry Serse, if her father agrees, but she reveals that she will kill herself should the union go ahead. Serse asks Ariodate if he will allow Romilda to marry a royal man equal in status to Serse. Ariodate, assuming that he means Arsemene, consents. Romilda suggests to Serse that she and Arsemene have consummated their love; he orders Arsemene's execution. Serse is given a letter supposedly from Romilda (written by Amastre) chiding him for his betrayal. He orders Arsemene to kill Romilda, but Amastre reveals her identity and declares that if the treacherous must die, the sword should turn on Serse. Serse pleads for forgiveness and offers Romilda and Arsemene his blessing.

KEY COMPOSERS

KEY COMPOSERS

Jean-Philippe Rameau

A respected theorist and composer of keyboard music, Rameau (1683–1764) did not compose his first opera until he was 50 years old. Consistently adventurous in his operas, Rameau equally inspired passionate admiration and hostility from Parisian audiences and was a comparably powerful figure between the 1730s and 1750s.

ABOVE: Jean-Philippe Rameau, who wrote a wealth of instrumental music before turning his hand to opera.

THE WANDERLUST YEARS

Rameau was born at Dijon in 1683. Little is known about his early life, but he was presumably taught music by his organist father, and attended a Jesuit college in his teens. He visited northern Italy when he was about 18 years old. Rameau's first musical job was as a violinist with a theatrical troupe that performed throughout Provence and Languedoc. In January 1702 he was appointed temporary *maître de musique* at the Cathedral of Notre Dame des Doms in Avignon, but he quickly found a longer-term job at Clermont Cathedral. Rameau's wanderlust continued, and by 1706 he arrived in Paris, where his *Premier livre de pieces de clavecin* was published in the same year.

Rameau succeeded his father as organist at Dijon's Notre Dame in 1709, but probably moved to Lyons before 1713, where he provided church music for several establishments. In 1715 Rameau returned to his old job at Clermont Cathedral, where he stayed for seven years before settling in Paris in the summer of 1722. Rameau was at first unknown in Paris, but, when he was almost 40 years old, he won acclaim as a writer due to his *Traité de l'harmonie* ('Treatise on Harmony', 1722). This was followed by *Nouveau systéme de musique théorique* ('New System of Music Theory', 1726), and more controversially received theoretical writings about music throughout his life.

FIRST OPERA COMPOSED
IN HIS FIFTIES

By the late 1720s Rameau had provided incidental music for several Parisian plays, although most of his notable compositional activities up to this point were devoted to keyboard music. From at least 1727 it was Rameau's expressed ambition to compose

THE LULLISTES V. THE RAMISTES

The extended polemic between Lullistes and Ramistes was provoked by the former group's disgust for the Italianate elements in Rameau's *Hippolyte et Aricie*, and their arising concern that the repertory and tradition established by Lully was under threat. In contrast, Rameau's supporters championed his innovative music that included more elaborate solo songs and increasingly complex use of the orchestra. One venomous Lulliste complained that he was racked, flayed and dislocated by Rameau's *Les indes galantes*. Similar divisions between opposing opera-loving factions were common during the eighteenth century and Handel and the "Opera of the Nobility" had distinct camps of supporters in London during the mid-1730s. However, Parisian opera audiences took such matters to unusually passionate extremes. The derogatory attitude towards Rameau's pioneering work extended to jealous composers, librettists and disgruntled performers at the Paris Opéra, and at one point Rameau was involved in a physical brawl with one of his main detractors, after which friends advised him to stop wearing a sword. Each new Rameau opera during the 1730s intensified the feelings of both sides, but Rameau had considerable support when 1,000 Ramistes pledged to support every performance of *Dardanus*. They did not quite live up to that pledge, but afterwards the Lulliste dissent diminished.

operas. Performances of Michel Pignolet de Montéclair's *Jepthé* (1732) had a profound effect on him, and he was subsequently spurred into creating *Hippolyte et Aricie* (1733) → **p. 70** when he was 50 years old. Rameau's first opera caused a controversial storm, with reactions sharply divided between excited admiration and conservative disgust. For decades French opera had remained firmly under the influence of the late Lully, and *Hippolyte et Aricie* generated a passionate public dispute between the so-called Lullistes and Ramistes. The debate was heightened by Rameau's masterpieces *Les indes galantes* ('The Gallant Indians', 1735) → **p. 71**, *Castor et Pollux* (1737) → **p. 71** and *Dardanus* (1739). Nevertheless, most of Rameau's operas during this period were tremendously successful.

A CONTROVERSIAL CAREER
Voltaire claimed that Rameau said, "Lully needs actors but I need singers", and this emphasis on the musical content in his operas was ably supported by fine singers including his wife Marie-Louise Mangot, the high-tenor Pierre de Jélyotte and soprano Marie Fel (1713–94). While Rameau concentrated

Timeline

1683	Born in Dijon
1702	First appointments as organist at Avignon and Clermont
1706	Moves to Paris, where his first collection of keyboard pieces is published
1709	Appointed organist in Dijon
1713	Moves to Lyons
1715	Reappointed organist at Clermont Cathedral
1722	Settles in Paris, where his first scholarly treatise on music theory is published
1733	Composes first opera *Hippolyte et Aricie*
1735	Composes opéra-ballet *Les indes galantes*
1745	Writes comic opera *Platée* and collaborates with Voltaire on several projects
1754	Revises and improves 1737 opera *Castor et Pollux*
1763	His last opera *Les boréades* is abandoned after rehearsals
1764	Dies at home

increasingly on his operatic career, he worked less on writing theoretical works, but controversy surrounded this aspect of his career in 1735 when his former pupil Louis-Bertrand Castel published a letter in the Jesuit *Journal de Trévoux* accusing Rameau of failing to acknowledge his indebtedness to previous

Operas

1733	*Hippolyte et Aricie*
1735	*Les indes galantes*
1737	*Castor et Pollux*
1739	*Les fêtes d'Hebe; Dardanus*
1745	*Les fêtes de Polymnie; La Princesse de Navarre; Le temple de la gloire; Platée*
1747	*Les fêtes de l'hymen et de l'amour*
1748	*Nais; Les surprises de l'amour; Pygmalion; Zais*
1749	*Zoroastre*
1751	*Acante et Céphise; La guirlande*
1753	*Daphne et Eglé*
1754	*Lysius et Delia; La naissance d'Osiris*
1757	*Zéphire; Nélée et Mithis; Le retour d'Astré; Anacréon*
1760	*Les Sybarites; Les Paladins*
1763	*Les boréades*

scholars. Rameau's response was sufficiently sarcastic and devastating that the journal refused to print it, so it was instead published independently. Rameau was not prolific during the early 1740s, but a flurry of activity in 1745 produced *La princesse de Navarre* ('The Princess of Navarre') and *Le temple de la gloire* ('The Temple of Glory'), both of which were collaborations with Voltaire, and the comic opera *Platée*.

HIS BLOSSOMING POPULARITY
Despite the hostility of enemies including Jean-Jacques Rousseau, Rameau's popularity blossomed to the extent that the Marquis D'Argenson forbade the theatre management to stage more than two of Rameau's operas in any one year. But Rameau's newest operas frequently confused his audience, and were often more popular when revised and revived in later years. *Zoroastre* (1749) and *Les boréades* ('The Sons of Boreas', 1763) were both astonishingly original, although the latter was abandoned after rehearsals and never staged until the twentieth century. Rameau died at his home on 12 September 1764, and nearly 180 musicians performed in his honour at his funeral.

FAR LEFT: The Gothic church of Notre Dame in Dijon, France. Rameau succeeded his father as organist here in 1709.
LEFT: Les boréades, unstaged until the twentieth century, is performed at the 1999 Salzburg Festival under Simon Rattle.

LATE BAROQUE

1700—1750

KEY COMPOSERS

Hippolyte et Aricie

Hippolyte et Aricie by Rameau

Composed   1733
Premiered 1733, Paris
Libretto   by Simon-Joseph Pellegrin

Rameau's magnificent *Hippolyte et Aricie* is a rare example of a major composer's first attempt at opera also being one of his greatest achievements. However, Rameau was nearly 50 years old and already a respected and experienced musician when he composed it, and had evidently been contemplating the project for several years. The impressive literary quality of Simon-Joseph Pellegrin's (1663–1745) libretto possesses a plot derived from Euripides, Seneca and Racine. The tragic figures Thésée and Phédre, whose fatal errors of judgement inspired Rameau to tremendous musical achievements, overshadow the youthful lovers Hippolyte and Aricie. In particular, Phédre's remorse over the apparent death of her stepson is one of the outstanding soliloquies in Baroque opera. Rameau's music retains its ability to astonish and impress audiences today, not least due to many intense accompanied recitatives and dynamic choruses. In this opera more than any other, Rameau depicts pastoral beauty, emotional pathos and brutal cruelty with unfailing genius. Although the opera created controversy and acclaim alike for its composer, it was heavily abridged prior to its premiere in 1733, and was not considered one of Rameau's finest works during his own lifetime.

BELOW: A 1720 Turkish miniature. The exotic Middle East fascinated Europe in this period, as shown in works such as Rameau's Les indes galantes.
OPPOSITE: Celestial twins Castor and Pollux, the protagonists of Rameau's opera of the same name, are shown here at the fountain of youth.

Synopsis
Hippolyte et Aricie by Rameau

PROLOGUE

Diane and l'Amour dispute who holds more power over the forest's inhabitants. Jupiter explains that l'Amour is supported by le Destin (Fate). Diane resolves to protect Hippolyte and Aricie.

ACT I

Thésée, King of Athens, has vanquished his rivals, with the exception of Aricie. She has been ordered to make a vow of chastity but is in love with Hippolyte, the king's son. The king's second wife, Phèdre, also loves Hippolyte. Aricie prepares to make her vows. Hippolyte enters and they call on Diane for protection. During a procession, Phèdre accuses Aricie of not making her vows; she is defiant and the priestesses protect her. Diane confirms she will look after the lovers. The news arrives that Thésée has descended to the underworld and can therefore be considered dead. Phèdre is convinced that this means she is free to pursue Hippolyte.

ACT II

Thésée was promised three favours from his father, Neptune. His descent to the underworld is the first of these; he wishes to rescue his friend Pirithoüs, who is attempting to abduct Proserpine, wife of Pluton who rules the underworld. Thésée tries to persuade Pluton to let him join his friend. Eventually, a tribunal is called, but Thésée's wish to be reunited with Pirithoüs is not granted. Thésée calls upon his second favour from Neptune: to be released from the underworld. The gods tell him that it is not easy to leave the underworld, but Mercure intervenes and saves him. Thésée is told by spirits that he will find a similar hell at his home when he returns.

ACT III

Phèdre is trying to make Hippolyte return her affections. She offers him power and the crown as well as her love. Hippolyte is appalled and calls on the gods to punish her. Phèdre, ashamed, asks Hippolyte to kill her; he refuses and prevents her from killing herself. Thésée returns from the underworld and is led to believe that Hippolyte has been forcing his affections on Phèdre. A group of townsfolk come to welcome Thésée home. He dismisses them and requests his third favour from Neptune: the punishment of Hippolyte.

ACT IV

Hippolyte laments his fate and is joined by Aricie, who vows she will follow him into exile. A storm breaks out and a sea monster attacks Hippolyte. There is a fight, in which Hippolyte is consumed by the creature's flames and disappears. Phèdre arrives and accepts the blame for Hippolyte's death. She prays for his innocence to be revealed to Thésée.

ACT V

Phèdre tells Thésée the truth and he resolves to throw himself in the sea. Neptune prevents him, delivering the news that Hippolyte, saved by Diane, is alive. The king's joy, however, is short-lived; Neptune informs him that his lack of trust in Hippolyte means that he will never see him again. Diane tells Aricie that Hippolyte is alive. The lovers are reunited and everyone rejoices.

Synopsis
Les indes galantes by Rameau

BACKGROUND

Hébé, goddess of youth, calls upon the young people of Europe to sing, but the goddess of war, Bellone, convinces them to fight for glory instead. Hébé calls upon l'Amour, who descends from the heavens; they decide to concentrate on other parts of the world.

FIRST ENTRÉE

Osman, the pasha of a Turkish island, is in love with Emilie, who arrived on his shores after being kidnapped by pirates. She rejects his advances, explaining that she remains faithful to the naval officer Valère. After a violent storm, a ship is wrecked on the coast of the island and Valère is on board. As the lovers are reunited, Osman interrupts them. He recognizes Valère and confesses that he himself was once a slave but was liberated by Valère. He gives the two lovers his blessing.

SECOND ENTRÉE

A young Inca woman, Phani, and Don Carlos, a Spanish conquistador, are in love. The high priest of the Sun, Huascar, is also in love with Phani. He tells her that the gods have ordered him to find her a husband, and proposes himself as a suitable match.

KEY COMPOSERS

LATE BAROQUE

1700–1750

Les indes galantes

Les indes galantes by Rameau

Composed 1735
Premiered 1735, Paris
Libretto by Louis Fuzelier

Les indes galantes is an *opéra-ballet* in which each act has its own setting and self-contained plot. Its four entrées include a scene set in a Turkish garden, Incas worshipping the sun in a Peruvian desert, a flower festival at a Persian market and a village ceremony in a North American forest. The librettist Louis Fuzelier used these exotic elements to draw comparisons between "savage"

During a festival celebrating the Sun, there is a volcanic eruption. Huascar tries to persuade Phani that she has caused this by angering the gods, and that she must marry him to appease them. Don Carlos intervenes and reveals that Huascar caused the eruption by throwing rocks into the volcano. The volcano erupts again and kills Huascar.

THIRD ENTRÉE ❧

Prince Tacmas loves Zaïre, the slave of Ali, a courtesan. On the day of the flower festival, in Ali's garden, he prepares to win her love. Meanwhile, Tacmas's slave Fatima is in love with Ali. Disguised as a man, she too enters the garden. Tacmas, taking Fatima for a rival, goes to attack her, but recognizes her in time. In a joyous conclusion, the masters swap their slaves and join the flower festival.

FOURTH ENTRÉE ❧

In a North American forest, Ardario, an Indian chief, hides as he prepares to make peace with two officers – Damon, a Frenchman and Don Alvar, a Spaniard. Damon and Don Alvar are both in love with Zima, a young Indian woman. When she arrives, they try to make her choose between them by outlining how each will love her. Zima replies that the Spaniard is too fiery, the Frenchman too cold. Ardario appears and Zima reveals that she prefers him to either of the others. The two are united, along with the European and North American cultures, at a feast of peace.

---

rituals and European culture, often to the detriment of the latter. Rameau's witty music made this one of his most popular theatre works, and he revived it during every decade until his death.

Castor et Pollux

Castor et Pollux by Rameau

Composed 1737; rev. 1754
Premiered 1737, Paris
Libretto by Pierre–Joseph Bernard (Gentil–Bernard)

Castor et Pollux was considered Rameau's greatest achievement after he revised it in 1754. The storyline revolves around the generosity of one twin brother willing to forsake his unique immortality so that the other may live, but their complex situation creates strong portraits of inner conflict and tension between other characters. Rameau conveys the magical forces of Hades, the Elysian fields and the tempting celestial pleasures Pollux must forsake if he takes Castor's place in death. The famous lament '*Que tout gémisse*', a chorus in which the Spartans mourn at Castor's tomb, was performed at Rameau's own funeral in 1764.

Synopsis
Castor et Pollux by Rameau

BACKGROUND ❧
Minèrve and l'Amour persuade Venus to seduce Mars, bringing peace to the world.

ACT I ❧
In Sparte, the people are mourning the death of their king Castor, mortal twin of the immortal Pollux. Télaïre, Castor's lover, is consoled by Phébé. Pollux offers his love to Télaïre, but she resolves to remain faithful to Castor. She requests that Pollux convince Jupiter to let him descend to the underworld and retrieve Castor.

ACT II ❧
Upset at being rejected by Télaïre, as well as grieving for the death of his brother, Pollux asks Jupiter whether he may do as Télaïre requested. Jupiter agrees, but only on the condition that Pollux takes Castor's place in the underworld. Hébé, the goddess of youth, reminds Pollux of what he will be deprived of if he goes ahead, but Pollux remains determined.

ACT III ❧
At the entrance of the underworld, Phébé, who loves Pollux, begs him not to continue. Pollux explains that he loves Télaïre. Mercure, sent by Jupiter, arrives and helps Pollux to overcome the flames and demons and enter the underworld. Phébé is heartbroken.

ACT IV ❧
In the underworld, the Ombres Heureuses (joyful spirits) cannot bring cheer to Castor, who pines for Télaïre. Pollux arrives and breaks the news to him that he may return to the world of the living. Castor, learning of Pollux's love for Télaïre and the pact with Jupiter, at first refuses, but eventually agrees to exchange places with Pollux for one day.

ACT V ❧
In Sparte, Télaïre and Castor are reunited. Phébé descends to the underworld. Castor, to the distress of Télaïre and the people of Sparte, prepares to return to the underworld to release Pollux. Jupiter is impressed by the twins' loyalty and strength of character and descends from the heavens. He calls off the pact and rewards Castor, Pollux and Télaïre with places in the firmament.

KEY COMPOSERS

Other Composers

ARNE, THOMAS AUGUSTINE
(1710–78, ENGLISH)

Arne was born in Covent Garden, so it is not surprising that he spent most of his life providing music for the theatre. In 1732 he formed an English opera company with Lampe and Carey, and their first production *Amelia* (1732) featured his sister Susanna (later Mrs Cibber, for whom Handel composed 'He was despised'). Arne performed Handel's *Acis and Galatea* for the public in a London theatre in 1732 before Handel had considered the possibility of doing so himself, having composed it for a private performance 14 years previously. He subsequently created English comic operas at Lincoln's Inn Fields Theatre, including *Rosamond* (1733). In 1737 Arne married Cecilia Young, who was a renowned soprano who had performed in Handel's operas *Ariodante* and *Alcina*. Arne was invited to compose a musical setting of Milton's *Comus* (1738), which established his reputation as a serious composer, and he then composed the masque *Alfred* (1740), which became popular in London due to the final number 'Rule, Britannia', and he triumphed with his serious English opera *Artaxerxes* (1762). His only attempt at Italian opera, *L'Olimpiade* ('The Olympiad', 1765), was lost, probably with most of his music, in a fire at Covent Garden in 1808. Arne, more than any native English composer, had a knack of blending Italianate *coloratura* with English idioms, but even today he remains in the shadow of Handel.

BONONCINI, GIOVANNI
(1670–1747, ITALIAN)

Bononcini was orphaned at the age of eight, and moved to Bologna, where he studied music and was accepted into the Accademia Filarmonica in 1686. By 1692 Bononcini had moved to Rome, where he met Silvio Stampiglia. They collaborated on several operas, including *Il trionfo di Camilla* ('The Triumph of Camilla', 1696), which was an enormous success in Naples. It was revived in 19 other Italian cities, and was produced in an adapted version in London by Nicolini and Swiney in 1706. Bononcini was the favourite composer of Emperor Joseph I, and was based in Vienna between 1697 and 1712. In 1719 the Earl of Burlington secured Bononcini's services for the Royal Academy of Music in London, where the composer enjoyed tremendous popularity for several seasons. His last opera *Astianatte* (1727) was blighted by the repercussions of the rivalry between Faustina and Cuzzoni, and he did compose for the stage again. Bononcini directed private performances of his own music for the Duchess of Marlborough until 1731, and he was a prominent member of the Academy of Ancient Musick in London until he was discredited in the early 1730s for plagiarizing a madrigal composed by Antonio Lotti (*c.* 1667–1740). Bononcini's melodic style was considered agreeable and pleasant, and he was admired for his expressive setting of Italian texts.

BOYCE, WILLIAM
(1711–79, ENGLISH)

Boyce trained as a choirboy at St Paul's Cathedral, and between 1734 and 1768 he held organist posts. He is most regarded for his symphonies, trio sonatas and church anthems. Although the composition of music for the theatre was not a dominant part of his career, Boyce was a skilful composer who was more consistent than Arne and closer to the legacy of

Purcell than Handel. His earliest dramatic works were initially conceived as concert works, although *The Secular Masque* (1746) was performed at Drury Lane in 1750 with contributions by the famous theatre singers Kitty Clive and John Beard, who both sang for Handel. Boyce regularly provided music for the actor David Garrick's Drury Lane theatre company between 1749 and 1751, including a pastoral masque for Moses Mendez's *The Chaplet*

ABOVE: English composer William Boyce.
OPPOSITE: Leonardo Leo, whose operas were performed in Naples and across northern Italy.
RIGHT: Italian composer Antonio Caldara, who worked as maestro di cappella for various royal and noble patrons.

COMPOSERS AND THEIR LIBRETTISTS

During the early eighteenth century a few composers enjoyed regular close collaboration with a favourite librettist, such as Fux with Pariati, or both Vinci and Porpora with the young Metastasio. However, such examples were rare, and instead it was common for a popular libretto created for one major Italian opera centre to be adapted for the needs of other composers working all over Europe. Some texts were consequently used many times across several decades, such as the Florentine librettist Antonio Salvi's *Arminio*, which was first set by Alessandro Scarlatti (1703), but it was also set by Caldara (1705), Hasse (1730), Handel (1737) and Baldassare Galuppi (1747). In fact, all of Handel's London opera libretti were adapted from Italian sources. Although some were recent revisions of relatively new texts by Metastasio, most were surprisingly old during an era that craved newness in its fashionable entertainments, and several were modelled on operas that Handel probably encountered while he was in Italy, either during his youth or on his later travels recruiting singers for London. Many composers set the same opera, each with their own variations in arias and alterations to recitative, and often even with the same title!

OTHER COMPOSERS

(1749) that was his biggest theatrical success. *The Rehearsal* (1750) was a satire on contemporary *opera buffa* that featured several fine songs, and Boyce contributed music for Garrick's production of *Romeo and Juliet* (1750) that was blatant competition against Arne's similar production at Covent Garden. Boyce seems to have lost enthusiasm for the theatre during the 1750s, although the song 'Heart of oak' from Garrick's *Harlequin's Invasion* (1759) was a popular hit.

CALDARA, ANTONIO
(c. 1670–1736, ITALIAN)

Caldara was probably taught by Giovanni Legrenzi (1626–90) and was a choirboy at St Mark's in Venice. His earliest operas were composed for Venice, while he was working as a cellist at St Mark's. He was appointed *maestro di cappella* at Mantua to the last Gonzaga duke until about 1707, and then worked at Rome for Prince Ruspoli until about 1716. His most fertile years were spent in Vienna, where he was vice-*Kapellmeister* to Emperor Charles VI, and produced more than 35 dramatic works at the Habsburg court across 20 years. Meanwhile, the prolific Caldara also composed several operas for Salzburg. He was the first composer regularly to set libretti by reformers Apostolo Zeno (1669–1750) and Pietro Metastasio (1698–1782).

Caldara was one of the few composers of the era who regularly used choral forces in his operas, although his musical style for Vienna was required to be more conservative than it had been in Venice and Rome. Other composers must have admired Caldara's work: his lost setting of Stampiglia's *La partenope* (1708) for Venice probably impressed Handel, who was in Venice at the time, and composed his

own setting for London many years later. Many of Caldara's operas have survived, but have not yet been adequately explored.

FUX, JOHANN JOSEPH
(1660–1741, GERMAN)

Fux studied music at Graz, and became a talented organist and church musician. He probably travelled to Italy during the 1680s, and his *a capella* Masses influenced by Giovanni Pierluigi de Palestrina (c. 1525–94) attracted the admiring attention of Emperor Leopold I in 1698. Based in Vienna for the remainder of his life, Fux was a respected composer of church music, but his visit to Rome in 1700 attracted him to composing operas and oratorios. Most of Fux's 18 operas are settings of libretti by Pietro Pariati (1665–1733), although he also set some texts by Stampiglia, Zeno and Metastasio. His greatest triumph was *Costanza e Fortezza* (1723), performed in Prague to celebrate his patron Charles VI's coronation as King of Bohemia, although, owing to ill health, Fux's able assistant Caldara conducted the performances. However, Fux is most remembered for his scholarly book *Gradus ad Parnassum* (1725), which was a treatise on counterpoint that influenced the greatest Viennese choral composers of the late eighteenth century, including Mozart and Joseph Haydn (1732–1809). Fux was a respected teacher who trained Gottlieb Muffat and Jan Dismas Zelenka (1679–1745), and in his frail later years was assisted by Caldara.

LEO, LEONARDO
(1694–1744, ITALIAN)

Leo was born near Brindisi, studied music in Naples at the Conservatorio San Maria della Pietà dei Turchini, and spent most of the rest of his life in the city. He held various organist and church music positions, and his first opera *Il pisistrato* (1714) was staged before he was 20 years old. In 1723 he composed his first opera for Venice, but soon started to develop the new genre of Neapolitan comic opera. He was promoted to organist of the vice-regal chapel at Naples in 1725, but it was only after the death of Vinci and departure of Hasse from Naples that

Leo became a leading opera composer. In addition to Naples, Leo provided operas for Turin, Milan and Bologna, and acquired a reputation as an oratorio composer. Leo's music was considered to be cerebral and more grounded in counterpoint than that of his more liberal Neapolitan contemporaries, and his operatic style was more conservative than Hasse, Vinci and Porpora. In 1737 Leo set Metastasio's *L'Olimpiade*, but he mostly devoted his talents towards comic opera, and was one of the first to establish it as a respected art form.

MATTHESON, JOHANN
(1681–1764, GERMAN)

Born into a wealthy family, Mattheson received a gentleman's education in languages and the arts, and studied law before becoming immersed in Hamburg's operatic scene. He made his debut as a soprano in 1696, but his voice broke soon after and he sang tenor roles until 1705. He took part in more than 60 new operas, including some composed by Keiser, and soon began to compose and conduct his own. Mattheson is best remembered for his friendship with the young Handel, who arrived in Hamburg in 1703 and was encouraged by Mattheson to pursue a career in opera. Their friendship suffered when Handel refused to relinquish the harpsichord to Mattheson during a performance of the latter's *Cleopatra* (1704), and only a button saved Handel's life during the ensuing duel. Mattheson was a respected organist, but instead preferred to continue composing for the Hamburg opera house. In 1715 he became director of music at the city's cathedral, but by 1728 he was increasingly afflicted with deafness and gave up the post. Mattheson continued to compose until the last years of his life, but today he is less well known for his operas than for his several scholarly treatises about music theory and his relationship with Handel.

OTHER COMPOSERS

PERGOLESI, GIOVANNI BATTISTA (1710–36, ITALIAN)

Pergolesi died at a tragically young age, but he produced a substantial corpus of works during his brief yet intense six-year career. In the 1720s he studied in Naples with teachers including Francesco Durante (1684–1755) and Vinci, but his first opera, *La Salustia* (1732), was a failure due to the death of the star castrato Nicolini. Undeterred, Pergolesi produced his first comic opera *Lo frate 'nnamorato* ('The Brother in Love', 1732), which was enthusiastically received at Naples. Pergolesi specialized in comic works, although *Adriano in Siria* (1734) and *L'Olimpiade* were both serious operas that featured libretti by Metastasio. Pergolesi's last stage work *Il flaminio* ('Flaminio', 1735) was a very popular *opera buffa* that was still performed in Naples in 1750. However, success came too late for Pergolesi, whose international reputation was rapidly formed posthumously. Pergolesi is best known today for his *Stabat mater*, composed while he was suffering from the illness that eventually killed him, but his historical significance derives from the comic *intermezzo La serva padrona* ('The Maid as Boss', 1734), which was intended to be merely a short companion piece to his full opera *Il prigionier superbo* ('The Haughty Prisoner', 1733).

'ALTO GIOVE'

Porpora's *'Alto giove'* was powerfully used in the 1994 film *Farinelli, il castrato*. Director Gérard Corbiau invented a troubled history between the castrato and his composer brother Riccardo Broschi. Broschi, feeling remorse over his responsibility for his brother's castration, attempts suicide during a solar eclipse, accompanied by Porpora's ravishing music.

POPULAR MELODY

PORPORA, NICOLA ANTONIO (1686–1768, ITALIAN)

Porpora was born and trained in Naples, where he also taught and worked for much of his career. His first opera was *Agrippina* (1708), and a few years later he composed *Arianna e Teseo* (1714) using a new libretto by Pariati. Between 1715 and 1721 Porpora worked at the Conservatorio di St Onofrio, where he became a widely respected singing teacher. His pupils included Farinelli and Caffarelli, and he also taught Hasse composition. Porpora was one of Metastasio's first musical collaborators, resulting in *Angelica* (1720) and his operas were performed in Vienna and Rome. In 1726 he moved to Venice, but in 1733 he became the music director of the "Opera of the Nobility" in London, which opened with his *Arianna in Nasso* (1733). Some of Porpora's finest works,

ABOVE: Nicola Antonio Porpora, composer and teacher, with his pupils.

including five operas, were composed for London before the company ceased its activities in 1737. Porpora returned to providing operas for Venice and Naples, and in the late 1740s was employed at the Dresden court, where his *Filandro* (1747) was performed under the direction of Hasse. He retired to Vienna, where he met the young Haydn, before spending his final years back at Naples but in poverty.

TELEMANN, GEORG PHILIPP (1681–1767, GERMAN)

Telemann was born in Magdeburg, and created his first opera at the age of 12, in which he sang the title role and organized its informal

ABOVE: Giovanni Battista Pergolesi, who died tragically at the age of 26 but left behind some beautiful compositions.

𝒮ynopsis

La serva padrona ('The Maid as Boss')
by Pergolesi
Composed 1734
Premiered 1734, Naples
Libretto by Gennarantonio Federico

INTERMEZZO I ♪

Uberto, a rich bachelor, is at his wits' end regarding his servant, Serpina. She acts as though she is the mistress of the house and is disobedient, indecisive and opinionated. He decides to extricate himself from Serpina's tyranny by taking a wife who will suppress her capricious nature. He expresses this idea to his mute valet, Vespone. Serpina, who knows that Uberto, deep down, has a soft spot for her, decides that she should be his bride and sets about persuading Uberto to marry her.

INTERMEZZO II ♪

The cunning Serpina, along with Vespone, devises a plan to trick Uberto. She announces that she is to be married to a certain Capitan Tempesta and gives a terrifying description of him that causes Uberto to fear for her future. He demands to meet Capitan Tempesta, who arrives (in fact, it is Vespone in disguise). Serpina explains to Uberto that the capitan has demanded an enormous sum of money as her dowry. Uberto is horrified by the sinister capitan and his threats. Serpina then tells him that the capitan has explained that if he does not receive the dowry immediately, he will refuse to marry Serpina and Uberto must marry her instead. Uberto is not alogether displeased at this suggestion. Serpina reveals the capitan's true identity and the couple thank Vespone for his help in bringing them together. The happy couple then rejoice.

OTHER COMPOSERS

LATE BAROQUE

1700–1750

performance in the street. Telemann was influenced by the operas he heard at the Brunswick court and Berlin. He attended university in Leipzig, and became the director of the local opera house, while he also provided several operas for the court at Weissenfels. Telemann claimed to have composed more than 50 operas, but only nine of these are extant. The earliest of these is *Die Satyren in Arcadien* ('The Satyrs of Arcadia', 1719, revised for Hamburg 1724). After holding various positions in Sorau, Eisenach and Frankfurt, Telemann became director of music at Hamburg's five principal churches in 1721. The following year he became musical director at the Gänsemarkt opera house (where Handel and Mattheson had worked in the early years of the century). Seven of Telemann's alleged 35 Hamburg operas have survived. Most of these date from the 1720s, and demonstrate the bizarre mixture of German and Italian texts that was popular in Hamburg. By default this makes Telemann an innovative pioneer of German opera, although his musical style was essentially Italianate, and he also adapted operas by Handel, Porpora and André Campra (1660–1744) for the Hamburg stage.

VINCI, LEONARDO
(c. 1696–1730, ITALIAN)

Vinci studied at the Conservatorio dei Poveri di Gesù Cristo in Naples between 1708 and 1718, and afterwards made his operatic debut with *Lo cecato fauzo* ('The False Blind Man', 1719). He proceeded to dominate operatic life in Naples, and his *Li zite 'ngalera* ('The Lovers on the Galley', 1722) is the earliest extant comic opera of its kind. However, after the enormous success of *Publio Cornelio Scipione* ('Scipio', 1722), Vinci turned his attention primarily to *opera seria*. One of Vinci's greatest triumphs was *Farnace* (Rome, 1724), which initiated a busy period of activity in Rome and Venice. *Didone abbandonata* ('Dido Abandoned' Rome, January 1726) and *Siroe* (Venice, 1726) were both highly acclaimed collaborations with Metastasio. Vinci composed two operas every remaining year of his life, and his partnership with Metastasio produced *Alessandro dell'Indie* ('Alexander in India') and

Artaserse (both 1730). Vinci's music was a massive influence on the new generation of composers including Pergolesi and Hasse. Vinci's work also influenced Handel's later operas, and the older composer appreciated Vinci's operas enough to adapt several into *pasticcios* for London. It was rumoured that Vinci was poisoned as an act of revenge for an illicit love affair.

VIVALDI, ANTONIO
(1678–1741, ITALIAN)

Vivaldi's father was a talented violinist who was employed at St Mark's in Venice, and it is likely that his father was also involved in managing operas in that city during the late seventeenth century. Although Vivaldi was nominally a Catholic priest by profession, he did not have to say Mass for most of his life, and he followed his father's example by becoming a professional musician. Vivaldi enjoyed a fine reputation as a

composer of orchestral concertos, and taught music at the *Pio Ospedale della Pietà* (an orphanage for musically talented girls). Vivaldi's first known opera *Ottone in villa* (1713) was swiftly followed by *Orlando finto pazzo* ('Orlando Plays Mad', 1714), and he subsequently attempted to cultivate a dual career as an opera composer and impresario for most of the rest of his life. Vivaldi's endeavours were directed towards Venice, although he also produced operas for Mantua, *Teuzzone* and *Tito Manlio*, (both 1719); Rome, *Giustino* (1724); Verona, *Bajazet* (1735) and *Catone in Utica* (1737); and Florence, *Ginevra* (1736). In 1739 Vivaldi claimed to have written 94 operas, but this was probably an exaggeration: over 50 printed libretti and about 20 musical scores have survived, although several exist only in an incomplete form.

ABOVE: Antonio Vivaldi, who is best-known for his orchestral works but also wrote a substantial number of operas.

OTHER COMPOSERS

Librettists

DANCHET, ANTOINE
(1671–1748, FRENCH)

Danchet was born on 7 September 1671 at Riom in Auvergne. Danchet's first theatrical text *Vénus* (1698) was privately performed at Paris. This was also his first collaboration with composer André Campra. Between 1698 and 1735 Danchet and Campra produced several pastorals, ballets and *opéra ballets*, and 11 *tragedies lyriques* including *Hésione* (1700), *Cariselli* (1702, using fragments of music by Lully), *Tancrède* (1702), *Télémaque* (1704) and *Idomonée* (1712). From 1727 Danchet was director of the Académie Française. Voltaire commented that Danchet's operas were less bad than his spoken plays. He is best known for having written the French libretto upon which Mozart's *Idomeneo* is based, although his original contained a much stronger supernatural element.

GAY, JOHN
(1685–1732, ENGLISH)

A friend and collaborator of Alexander Pope and Jonathan Swift (1667–1745), John Gay invented the genre of ballad opera with *The Beggar's Opera*. It was premiered on 29 January 1728 at Lincoln's Inn Fields, and performed 62 times in its first season. The popular perception that *The Beggar's Opera* was an attack on Italian opera is untrue. It contains a mocking parody of the rivalry between Faustina and Cuzzoni, but Gay had previously contributed to Handel's *Acis and Galatea*, and the success of *The Beggar's Opera* cannot be securely attributed to the same audience that supported Italian operas at the King's Theatre. The target of the satire was intended to be Walpole's government, and censors suppressed the intended sequel *Polly*. Gay never repeated the success of *The Beggar's Opera*, and died one year before his last ballad opera *Achilles* was popularly received at Covent Garden in 1733.

ABOVE RIGHT: Sir Robert Walpole (far left) in the House of Commons. Walpole's government was mocked in John Gay's The Beggar's Opera.

HAYM, NICOLA FRANCESCO
(1678–1729, ITALIAN)

Haym was the skilful literary adaptor who prepared several of Handel's best opera libretti, including *Radamisto* (1720), *Giulio Cesare*, *Tamerlano* and *Rodelinda*. Rather than writing new texts for Handel, Haym's talent was at reorganizing old Italian texts so that they were adequately dramatic and balanced while also reducing the amount of simple recitative for the English-speaking audience. He also adapted the French dramas *Teseo* and *Amadigi* into Italian for Handel. Haym was an antiquarian and book-collector, but was also Handel's *continuo* cellist, and had been a member of Cardinal Ottoboni's orchestra in Rome for six years before coming to London in 1701. Although he died in 1729, it has been supposed that traces of his unfinished work could be evident in some of Handel's later operas.

BELOW: Bronze medal of Queen Christina of Sweden, patron of the arts.

THE ARCADIAN ACADEMY

Literary clubs that were established in seventeenth-century Italy were commonly known as "academies", taking their name from the Athenian garden where Plato was thought to have met with his followers. One of the most important such groups in the early eighteenth century was the Roman "Arcadian Academy". It was formally established in 1690 to honour the late Queen Christina of Sweden, who had been a keen supporter of the literary arts and was composer Arcangelo Corelli's (1653–1713) first patron. The "Arcadian Academy" principally constituted the artistic circle that had already regularly met under the patronage of the queen, although it expanded into a network that spread across Europe. All of the Academy's members adopted nicknames suitable for shepherds and nymphs, in an attempt to recreate the fabled pastoral paradise Arcadia, described in Greek mythology. Founder members included the librettist Silvio Stampiglia and Gian Vincenzo Gravina (the adoptive father of Metastasio). The Marcello brothers, Corelli and Alessandro Scarlatti were also granted membership, and Apostolo Zeno was the founder of an affiliated group in Venice. Handel's patrons Cardinal Ottoboni, Cardinal Pamphili and Prince Ruspoli were all members, but although Handel composed some chamber cantatas and duets using Arcadian texts and was closely involved with the Academy's circle of members, he never became a member himself.

PARIATI, PIETRO
(1665–1733, ITALIAN)

Pariati was born in Reggio Emilia, and was secretary to the Duke of Modena. He spent time in Madrid, wrote works for Barcelona and spent three years in an Italian prison. He lived in Venice for 15 years, until he was appointed a court poet at Vienna in 1714. While in Venice he worked with Zeno on several libretti, specialized in adapting recent tragedies into opera libretti and updated old seventeenth-century libretti. He gained celebrity for writing comic scenes and *intermezzi*, and drew on influences such as Moliére and Cervantes. Pariati wrote texts for 13 oratorios and 14 theatrical dramas for the imperial family in Vienna, the most famous of which was *Costanza e Fortezza*, set to music by Fux (1723). Pariati developed a new style of comic fantasy in his libretti, and used his texts as opportunities to provoke satire, not least against conventional *opera seria*.

PELLEGRIN, SIMON-JOSEPH
(1663–1745, FRENCH)

Pellegrin was a monk who sailed twice with the French fleet to the Orient, and who versified Biblical texts that were sung to music by Lully and Campra at the royal convent at St Cyr. Pellegrin provided libretti for many composers, including Campra and Desmarets, but his best known works are *Jephté*, set to music by Montéclair in 1732, and *Hippolyte et Aricie*, composed by Rameau in 1733. Pellegrin seemed content to mingle the domestic benefits of religious life with the pleasures of the theatre, and was granted a papal dispensation to continue live at the Cluny Monastery while providing texts for the Parisian comedies and tragedies, until he was eventually excommunicated.

SILVANI, FRANCESCO
(c. 1660–c. 1728–44, ITALIAN)

Little is known about Silvani's life, but he was an abbot who issued his earliest works under the anagram "Frencasco Valsini". Silvani regularly produced libretti for Venice between

ABOVE: Sixteenth-century Italian poet Torquato Tasso, on whose works composers such as Handel and Francesco Silvani based their operas.

1691 and 1716, and the title-pages of the printed wordbooks state that he served the Duke of Mantua between 1699 and 1705. Silvani identified with the "reform" librettists such as Zeno and Pariati, and his texts feature clearly motivated plots, elevated language and extensive recitatives. He occasionally based his libretti on literary sources such as Tasso, Seneca and Corneille. Silvani was sensitive to accusations of plagiarism, and he did not include his name on the title-page of libretti that had been collaborations with other writers. During an age when the literary credibility of librettists was often questioned, Silvani was esteemed enough to have a collection of 24 libretti published posthumously.

STAMPIGLIA, SILVIO
(1664–1725, ITALIAN)

Stampiglia was one of the 14 founding members of the Accademia dell'Arcadia (The Arcadian Academy) •• p. 76. Although a Roman by birth, for many years Stampiglia was associated with operas in Naples, and did not always conform to Arcadian ideals despite being part of their circle. Stampiglia's libretti are often ironic comedies in which conventional heroism is regarded with more affection than sincerity, and the ludicrous behaviour of aristocratic characters is often regarded with disbelief by comparatively sensible servants. *Il trionfo di Camilla* and *La partenope* were his most popular libretti, and set many times during the early eighteenth century. Stampiglia's final work was the serenata *Imeneo*, set to music by Porpora in 1723. His lively and witty examinations of courtly love inspired Handel to great artistic heights in his settings of *Il partenope*, *Serse* and *Imeneo*, although none of these were successful in London.

ZENO, APOSTOLO
(1669–1750, ITALIAN)

The Venetian librettist Zeno was a librarian and historian, who sought to establish opera libretti as a recognized literary form. His first opera libretto *Lucio Vero* was a huge success at Venice in 1695. Zeno continued to write more libretti, although he had reservations about it affecting his scholarly credibility. In 1718 Zeno replaced Stampiglia as imperial poet to the Viennese court of Emperor Charles VI, where he was also appointed imperial historiographer. Zeno wrote 35 opera libretti, including many in collaboration with Pariati, and he was especially proud of his 17 oratorio texts produced for Vienna. Zeno is credited with introducing historical subjects into opera, and he sought to represent the idealistic code of honour for real sovereigns in uncompromisingly serious operas influenced by the French dramatist Racine. Composers including Tomaso Albinoni (1671–1751), Caldara and Gasparini set his libretti to music. Alessandro Scarlatti and Handel both set versions of Zeno's libretti that were adapted for them by other authors. Zeno was a major influence on the young Metastasio, who in turn supplanted his predecessor as both court poet in Vienna and the most respected librettist of his generation.

Singers

BORDONI, FAUSTINA
(1697–1781, ITALIAN)

Venetian mezzo-soprano Faustina was brought up by the composers Alessandro (1669–1750) and Benedetto Marcello (1686–1739). She made her debut in Pollarolo's *Ariodante* in 1716, and was based in her home city until 1725, singing in operas by her teacher Gasparini, as well as Albinoni and Lotti. Between 1726 and 1728 she performed in London alongside Senesino and Cuzzoni in Handel's "Rival Queens" operas. The legendary enmity between Faustina and Cuzzoni culminated in 1727 when they came to blows on stage in a performance of Bononcini's *Astianatte*. Faustina married the composer Hasse in 1730, and the librettist Metastasio described them as "truly an exquisite couple". Faustina appeared in many of her husband's *opera seria* composed for Dresden, and eventually retired in 1751. In 1773 she and her husband settled in Venice, where both of their daughters trained as singers.

CARESTINI, GIOVANNI
(c. 1704–c. 1760, ITALIAN)

Carestini studied in Milan from the age of 12, and gave his debut there in 1719. He studied with Antonio Maria Bernacchi, and sang alongside his teacher in his Roman debut of Alessandro Scarlatti's *La Griselda* (1721). He spent most of the 1720s singing in operas by Vinci, Porpora and Hasse at Rome, Naples and Venice. Initially a soprano, when he arrived in London in 1733 his voice had settled as a mezzo-soprano. During two seasons Handel created impressive new roles for Carestini in *Arianna*, *Ariodante* and *Alcina*. Carestini returned to Italy, and during the remainder of his career he also sang at Dresden, Berlin and St Petersburg. Hasse commented that "He who has

not heard Carestini is not acquainted with the most perfect style of singing".

CUZZONI, FRANCESCA
(1696–1778, ITALIAN)

Cuzzoni was born and trained in Parma, where she gave her first performance in 1714. She first appeared with Faustina Bordoni in Venice in 1718, and they sang together several times during the early 1720s. Her London debut in Handel's *Ottone* (1722) was a sensation. Handel composed notable roles for her including Cleopatra (*Giulio Cesare*), Asteria (*Tamerlano*), and the title role in *Rodelinda*. Cuzzoni sang in every Royal Academy opera until its closure in 1728, although this almost ended prematurely when only the intervention of the king could prevent the academy from dismissing her after the notorious on-stage brawl with Faustina. She returned to Italy and performed in several operas by Hasse, before joining the "Opera of the Nobility" in 1734. In the late 1730s she sang for Leo and Caldara, but afterwards her career faded and she died in poverty.

DURASTANTI, MARGHERITA
(FL. 1700–34, ITALIAN)

The soprano Durastanti's first known appearance was at Venice in 1700. By 1707 she was employed by the Marquis Ruspoli in Rome, where she first met Handel, who composed several superb cantatas

LEFT: *Faustina Bordoni, a leading prima donna of Handel's operas.*

for her. Durastanti worked in Venice from 1709 until 1712, where she sang in nine operas by Lotti and the title role in Handel's *Agrippina*. She sang in Lotti's *Teofane* (1729) in Dresden, where Handel heard her and engaged her to join the Royal Academy of Music in London. Handel composed prominent roles for her in *Radamisto*, *Ottone* and *Giulio Cesare*. A second brief spell working for Handel in 1733–34 meant that she had a longer working relationship with the composer than any other musician, but the alterations Handel made to Arianna suggest that her stamina and range had diminished.

FARINELLI
(1705–82, ITALIAN)

Carlo Broschi, known as "Farinelli", studied with Porpora, and made his stage debut in Naples when he was only 15 years old. By 1723 he was taking lead roles in his teacher's operas. Farinelli was remarkably successful across Europe, and in 1734 he reunited with Porpora to work in London for the "Opera of the Nobility". While at the peak of his fame, Farinelli suddenly quit in 1737 and spent over two decades in the service of Philip V of Spain, where his duties were not all directly associated with music and opera. He retired to Bologna in 1759, and became a respected figure

LEFT: *Italian soprano Francesca Cuzzoni.*

visited by Mozart, Casanova and Emperor Joseph II. Today Farinelli is known as the most famous castrato, largely due to Gérard Corbiau's controversial and mostly fictional film *Farinelli, il castrato* (1994).

FEL, MARIE
(1713–94, FRENCH)

The daughter of a Bordeaux organist, Marie Fel studied singing with Mme Van Loo, and gave her operatic debut in October 1734. Mentioned in Rousseau's *Confessions*, Marie Fel was one of the most famous singers of the Académie Royale de Musique, and was a regular soloist at the Concert Spirituel and the Concerts chez la Reine. From 1739 she performed in many productions, including most of Rameau's operas: she created leading roles in *Castor et Pollux*, *Dardanus*, *Les indes galantes*, *Platée* and *Zoroastre*. The technique and quality of Fel's singing, along with that of other singers such as her pupil Sophie Arnould, allowed Rameau to compose a more

prominent number of demanding *ariettes* in his later operas. Fel also sang in works by Lully, Campra and Mondonville. She retired in 1758.

NICOLINI OR NICOLO GRIMALDI
(1673–1732, ITALIAN)

Nicolo Grimaldi, known as "Nicolini", studied singing in Naples with the composer Provenzale, and made his debut at the age of 12. Nicolini sang in the cathedral and royal chapel as a soprano, but soon became associated with operas by Alessandro Scarlatti. He also sang for Bononcini, Lotti, Leo, Porpora and Vinci. Nicolini visited London in 1708, and received great acclaim for performances of Scarlatti's *Pirro e Demetrio* (1708). With the theatre manager Owen Swiney, Nicolini made Italian opera fashionable with adaptations of works such as Bononcini's *Camilla* (1709). He created the title roles in Handel's *Rinaldo* and *Amadigi*. Nicolini left London in 1717, although during the mid-1720s Swiney repeatedly attempted to

influence the Royal Academy into engaging him once more. He remained active until his death, which occurred in Naples during the rehearsals of Pergolesi's first opera *La Salustia* (1732).

SENESINO OR
FRANCESCO BERNARDI
(c. 1680–c. 1759, ITALIAN)

Francesco Bernardi was nicknamed *"Senesino"* after his birthplace Siena. His first known performance was at Venice in 1707–08, and he sang for Caldara at Bologna in 1709. He was dismissed from Dresden in 1720 because he refused to sing an aria during rehearsals for Johan David Heinichen's (1683–1729) *Flavio Crespo* (1720). He joined the Royal Academy of Music in London in 1720, and remained with the company until its dissolution in 1728, during which time he sang in operas by Bononcini, Ariosti and Handel. Senesino was popular in London, which explains why Handel re-engaged him in 1730 despite their often-troubled working relationship. Senesino defected to the "Opera of the Nobility" in 1733. After he left London in 1736 he sang at Florence and Naples, but his singing had fallen out of fashion by the end of the decade.

STRADA DEL PÒ, ANNA MARIA
(ACTIVE 1719–40, ITALIAN)

The exceptional soprano Strada is known to have sung in Vivaldi's *La verità in cimento* ('The Truth Tested', 1720) in Venice in 1721. Between 1724 and 1726 she sang for Vinci, Porpora and Leo at Naples, where she also married the theatre manager Aurelio del Pò. She arrived in London in 1729, where she was Handel's prima donna in all his opera performances until 1737. Handel's arias for Strada in *Il partenope*, *Poro* and *Sosarme* indicate a superbly talented singer who had a high range, remarkable agility and dramatic conviction. Strada was the only member of Handel's company who did not defect to the "Opera of the Nobility" in 1733, and was amply rewarded by the roles Ginevra, in *Ariodante*, and Alcina. She returned to Italy in 1738, and retired two years later.

LEFT: The most famous castrato of all time, Carlo Broschi, known to his audiences as Farinelli.

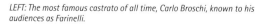

SINGERS

Classical

The Enlightenment was a natural, if late, consequence of the sixteenth-century Renaissance and Reformation. Also known as the Age of Reason, the Enlightenment advanced to be recognized in the late seventeenth and early eighteenth centuries and brought with it new, controversial beliefs that upended the absolutisms on which European society had long been based.

EMANCIPATION OF THE MASSES

Absolute monarchy, with its reliance on the Divine Right of Kings, and the Church, with its demand for unthinking obedience to doctrine, were major casualties of this great intellectual upheaval. In Enlightenment terms, their supremacy now belonged to the power of reason and a sense of individual worth. These new imperatives would promote social progress and education as a means of freeing the masses from ignorance and superstition. If Martin Luther opened the door to the Reformation as a challenge to the status quo, the Enlightenment flung it wide open.

PRIMACY OF THE PUBLIC

An important effect of Enlightenment ideas was to promote the public as a force in its own right, with its own tastes and preferences. This involved profound changes in opera and music generally. Until now, composers and performers, who were essentially servants to royal or noble employers, had been required to cater for the demands and whims of a privileged elite at the royal, ducal and other noble courts. Now, in the Age of Reason, a well-to-do middle class with the money to afford the price of tickets was flocking to public concerts and opera houses, where the music was tailored to catch and hold their attention. For the "old guard" in music, this looked very much like what today would be called the "dumbing-down" of opera. To adherents of the Enlightenment, the new style meant that opera acquired a wider appeal and mirrored the concerns of real people in the real, everyday world.

CLASSICAL

Introduction

The humanist principles of the Enlightenment removed opera from the extravagant world of baroque and landed it in entirely new territory. Baroque still flourished in the early eighteenth century, but after 1720 it became a target for changes initiated by the scholar Gian Vincenzo Gravina of the Arcadian Academy in Rome. Baroque operas based on classical myths had developed exaggerated, extravagant and ultimately ludicrous forms. Under the Enlightenment principles which influenced Gravina and the Arcadians, these fripperies, the convoluted plots, the outlandish characterization, were all pared away. In their place, operas assumed the spare, ascetic features of ancient Greek theatre and the stark human drama of its tragedies. The result was *opera seria* – serious opera.

METASTASIO AND OPERA SERIA

The protagonists of *opera seria* were not composers, but two Italian librettists – Apostolo Zeno (1668–1750) and Pietro Metastasio (1698–1782). Metastasio was Italy's most famous poet and, among composers, soon became its most popular librettist. This was how opera libretti acquired a new adjective – Metastasian. *Opera seria* with the Metastasian libretto which

became the main operatic genre of the early eighteenth century, was certainly a long move away from the intricacies of baroque. This, though, was not good enough for the German composer Christoph Willibald Gluck (1714–87) who spied too much clutter even in this new, slenderized form of opera.

GLUCK AND THE REFORM OF OPERA

Gluck thought *opera seria* was too formal, its plots overly restrictive and its structure excessively regulated. In his prologue to *Alceste* (1767) ◆ **p. 90**, which he may have written with the help of his librettist, Raniero de'Calzabigi (1714–95), Gluck poured particular scorn on the prominence of arias in *opera seria* and the chances they gave singers to show off: "I do not wish to arrest an actor in the greatest heat of dialogue in order to wait for a tiresome ritornello [repeat], nor make display of the agility of his fine voice in some long-drawn passage, nor wait until the orchestra gives him time to recover his breath for a cadenza. I did not think it my duty to pass quickly over the second section of an aria of which the words are perhaps the most impassioned and important, in order to repeat regularly four times over those of the first part ... for the convenience of the singer who wishes to show that he can capriciously vary a passage in a number of guises..."

Like his *Orfeo ed Euridice* ('Orpheus and Eurydice', 1762) ◆ **p. 89**, *Alceste* exemplified the "beautiful simplicity" Gluck believed opera should have. It also planted the seeds of the *Gesamtkunstwerk*, the 'total work of art' later championed by Richard Wagner (1813–83) which merged all elements in opera – singing, acting, orchestration, drama, poetry, lighting, stage design. Gluck's reforms never went that far, but they did exert strong influence, for instance on Wolfgang Amadeus Mozart's (1755–91) *Idomeneo* (1781) ◆ **p. 94** or *L'anima del filosofo*, 'The Soul of Philosophy', 1791) by Joseph Haydn (1732–1809). In the event, *opera seria* was overtaken less by Gluck's reforms, more

---

PASTICCIO OPERA

The eighteenth-century *pasticcio*, a rather uncomplimentary term meaning "hotch-potch", was an opera written by several composers. One example was *Muzio Scevola* (1721) which was based on the story of an early Roman hero who burned his hand to ashes in a fire rather than assist the Etruscan enemies of Rome. Filippo Amadei, Giovanni Bononcini and George Frideric Handel (1685–1759) composed one act each, in that order. Normally, though, the *pasticcio* did not result from such a neat division of labour. It was more of an assembly of choruses, airs, dances and other music taken from various composers. A *pasticcio* could start out as a conventional opera but then acquire extra text or music or arias grafted onto it from other works by other composers. Although this appears to justify the description of "hotch-potch", the additions were carefully selected from items which had already proved their popularity in performance, so that the pasticcio could be said to represent an eighteenth-century version of *Top of the Pops*. The *pasticcio* proved extremely popular, especially in mid-eighteenth century London, and some highly respected operas, including Gluck's *Orfeo ed Euridice* were first seen there as *pasticcios* rather than in their proper form.

ABOVE: A box at the Opera House in Parma, Italy in the mid-eighteenth century.

by two other developments which replaced *seria* and brought its eminence to an end. One was the German *Singspiel* ('song-play') p. 84 which evolved after about 1750 into comic opera with spoken dialogue. The other was the Italian *opera buffa*, a slightly different type of comic opera which began a separate life on stage after comic roles were deemed contrary to the solemn nature of *opera seria* and were eliminated from the main action.

THE RISE OF OPERA BUFFA

Instead, after around 1740, comic characters were consigned to the one-act *intermezzi* – interludes staged between the acts of *opera seria*. Comedy was not relegated for long. The *intermezzo* developed as a genre in its own right – the *opera buffa*, which in time proved more vivacious and more expressive and emotionally appealing than *opera seria*. When popular taste demanded more substance than comic opera provided on its own, Carlo Goldoni (1707–93), originator of the *opera buffa* libretto, introduced *parte serie* – serious roles – to give the genre the required mixture of comedy and tragedy. *Seria* and *buffa* were effectively re-united in a new genre, *dramma giocoso* ('jocular drama'), and reached their finest joint expression in Mozart's *Le nozze di Figaro* ('The Marriage of Figaro', 1786) p. 96.

THE FIGARO CONTROVERSY

Figaro was much more than another stage in the evolution of opera. By the time it was first performed, both opera and theatre had become highly politicized as Enlightenment philosophy made itself felt onstage. Opera, in fact, already tended to replace the pulpit as a place where new and radical ideas were expressed and new beliefs fortified. As early as 1735, *Les indes*

galantes p. 71 by Jean-Philippe Rameau (1683–1764) had mirrored the rejection of class divisions and religious and racial prejudice and the promotion of the 'Brotherhood of Man' by French philosophers such as Jean-Jacques Rousseau (1712–78). Mozart's *Figaro* was much closer to the French Revolution of 1789 which expressed the ideals of the Enlightenment in bloodthirsty violence. Consequently, it was controversial, even though Mozart's librettist, Lorenzo Da Ponte (1749–1838) had foreseen the problems and removed the inflammatory politics contained in the original play by the French dramatist Pierre Beaumarchais (1732–99). However, neutering the libretto in this way did not quieten fears that it encouraged social upheaval. For the reactionary powers-that-be, *Figaro* was alarming because a servant was given the central role while his master, Count Almaviva, was sidelined. Servants had previously occupied their "proper" place in the social hierarchy of opera when they appeared as stupid, clumsy or comic characters. It was, therefore, subversive for Mozart and Da Ponte to make one of them the centre of attention.

LEFT: Mozart's librettist Abbé Lorenzo Da Ponte in an engraving by M. Pettenino.
BELOW: A performance of Mozart's Marriage of Figaro *at Glyndebourne, featuring Peter Mattei and Marina Comparato.*

CLASSICAL

1750—1820

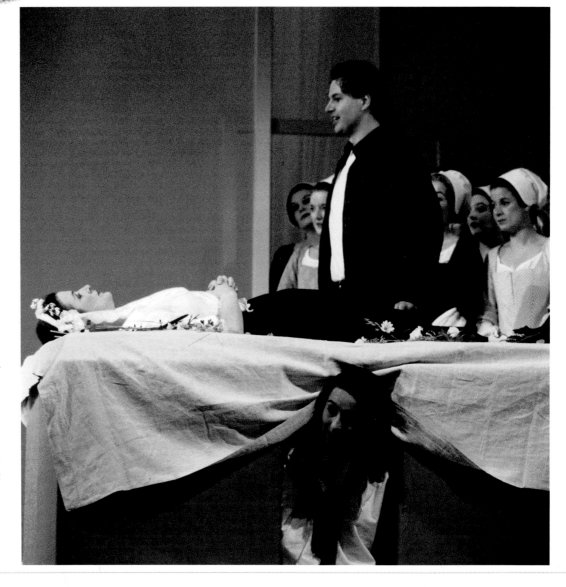

Genres and Styles

There was a certain mathematical precision about *opera seria*, which was very much in keeping with the ethos of the Enlightenment, in which the most startling advances were made in the sciences. "Mathematical" also applied to the Metastasian libretto which firmly reinforced *seria*'s somewhat inflexible and predictable principles. Almost invariably, the story of an *opera seria* was told in three acts. Each act was structured around alternating arias and recitatives, with occasional, though rare, duets and ensembles. Where ensembles occurred they were often placed at the end of the opera. There were generally six main characters, and the plot had to contain an element of tragedy or heroism.

THE METASTASIAN LIBRETTO

The first aim of the Metastasian libretto in *opera seria* was to provide elegant verse along lines that followed the doctrine of affections, such as hope, hate, love, despair. The other was to showcase the gifts of solo singers, especially castrati, who were by now developing into star performers with a fanatical following. It was for them that the *da capo* aria was developed to display the splendours of the individual voice and also to provide a means by which a

DEVELOPMENT OF THE DA CAPO ARIA

The *da capo* aria became an integral part of *opera seria* in the first half of the eighteenth century before it declined around 1750 as composers felt its limitations. In truth, the *da capo* aria was something of a musical straitjacket, with a set-piece structure consisting of three sections in which the third repeated the first. There was also a lack of action which rendered the aria somewhat static. The repeats and their ornamentation increased the aria's length, so that ultimately, forms like the *del segno* aria which cut the repeats came to be preferred. There were, however, opportunities for the solo singer to ornament the vocal line and put on thrilling displays of technique. The fame of the solo singer and the reverence and adulation they still attract dated from this time. Though without its later name, the *da capo* aria first appeared in 1607 in Claudio Monteverdi's (1567–1643) ground-breaking *L'Orfeo, favola in musica* ('Orpheus, a Legend in Music') ➡ p. 28 and was used again by the same composer in *L'incoronazione di Poppea* ('The Coronation of Poppea', 1642) ➡ p. 29. Its heyday, however, came a century later when the *da capo* aria was a universal ingredient in early eighteenth-century opera.

character could confide his innermost feelings to the audience. The *da capo* form of the aria eventually became indispensable to the *opera seria* and virtually synonymous with it. Metastasian texts were so arranged that an aria normally ended most of the scenes.

In the musical division of labour built into *opera seria*, arias and recitatives took the stage turn by turn, and it fell to the recitatives to deal with the workings of the plot and serve as the chief point of contact between the various characters. These recitatives were most often in *secco* form, that is, with *continuo* rather than orchestral accompaniment, although the full orchestra could step in to reinforce particularly dramatic moments. The dialogue of the recitative in *opera seria* was generally written to the strict pattern known as *versi sciolti* or blank verse, comprising a mixture of seven- and eleven-syllable lines, without rhyme.

RIGHT: Italian writer Pietro Metastasio, after whom the Metastasian libretto is named. This aimed to showcase the talents of solo singers.

JL SIGNOR ABATI PIETRO METASTASIO ROMA POETA CESAREO.

THE VIRTUES OF OPERA SERIA

Although *opera seria* eschewed the excessive decoration and complexities which baroque opera had acquired over the years, the source used for its plots– ancient classical myth and legend – remained the same. The difference was, however, that in *opera seria*, the plots were made to serve Enlightenment purposes. Characters were more credibly human, the music was less

SINGSPIEL

The *Singspiel*, or song-play, was a German form of opera in which songs and other music alternated with dialogue. Although the *Singspiel* originated in the seventeenth century, the term was not generally used until the eighteenth. *Croesus* (1711) by Reinhard Keiser (1674–1739) was an early example of *Singspiel*. Towards the middle of the eighteenth century other forms of opera - the French *opéra comique* and the English ballad opera - exerted their influence on *Singspiel* so that it developed into a type of comic opera with spoken words. One of the most eminent *Singspiel* composers was Johann Adam Hiller (1728–1804) who helped establish the German national form of the genre, and another was the Czech Georg Benda (1722–95) who was based in Berlin. *Opéra comique* provided *Singspiel* with its lyrical, comic and sentimental content and promoted its use of folk harmonies and rhythms. By contrast, in Vienna, the *Singspiel* developed in a rather different way, absorbing the lively melodies of *opera buffa*, with plenty of sharp wit and farce to spice up the action. For example, Mozart's *Die Entführung aus dem Serail* ('The Abduction from the Seraglio', 1782) was written as a Viennese-style *Singspiel* with the folk element represented by its Turkish flavour.

cluttered and better able to express emotion, and audiences had a greater chance to identify and sympathize with the sufferings being depicted onstage.

SERIA VERSUS BUFFA

Even so, by its very nature – stereotyped, restrictive, and with scant outlet or none for the odd amusing moment – *opera seria* could not appeal to audiences in the same warm way as its opposite, the *opera buffa*. *Opera buffa* did several things which *opera seria* did not do. The genre promoted the bass voice, where *seria* gave the best parts and the best music to castrati. In *opera buffa* – unlike in *Singspiel* – there was no spoken dialogue, which made for greater musical continuity than the straitjacket structure of *opera seria* allowed. The aria was retained in *buffa*, but it was no longer the same star turn it was in *seria*. *Buffa*, which was a more "democratic" form of opera than *seria*, majored instead in duets, trios, quartets and ensembles. This helped to create onstage an atmosphere of sociability that had the effect of drawing the audience into the action. This was particularly true of the *buffa* finale which, once again, was basically different from its equivalent in *opera seria*. In *seria*, the last act normally finished with a simple ensemble in which all the principal singers took part. In the ensemble finale of *opera buffa*, the last act went out with much more punch. All or the greater part of the cast was on stage for the occasion, and as each new figure entered, the music typified the character by a change of mood or style. In effect, the *buffa* finale resembled a synopsis in music of the plot and the characters featured in it.

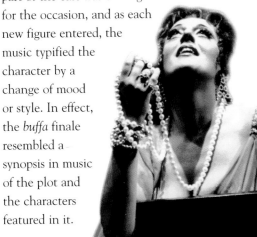

ABOVE: Tatiana Troyanos in the title role of L'incoronazione di Poppea, one of the first operas to employ the da capo aria.
RIGHT: A performance of Die Entführung aus dem Serail, an example of a Viennese Singspiel opera. Christine Schäfer plays Konstanze.

GENRES AND STYLES

GOLDONI AND THE BUFFA PLOT

Buffa plots played a major role in popularizing the genre. They were simpler, more down to earth and bore greater resemblance to real, everyday life, while emphasizing its more amusing elements. There were stereotyped characters but they were easily recognizable, coming as they did from the real rather than the legendary world: one was *Il dottore*, a stuffy lawyer from Bologna, another was Pantalone, a womanizer, and there were any number of comic servants, most notably Figaro. Like *opera seria*, the creation of *opera buffa* revolved around a dominant Italian librettist, in this case Goldoni. The earthiness and realism of his texts, their witty dialogue and touches of sentimentality were not only in complete contrast to the artificiality of *opera seria*, but allowed room for the genre to evolve. This was why it proved comparatively easy for Goldoni to respond to the change in public taste which demanded more serious content. In response, Goldoni introduced dramatic characters into *buffa* alongside the established comic roles and the

GUERRE DES BOUFFONS

Opposing tastes in opera have often provoked minor wars. One of them was the *guerre des bouffons* which took place in Paris between 1752 and 1754 and ranged the supporters of French serious opera against the advocates of Italian *opera buffa*. On the French side were King Louis, his influential mistress Madame de Pompadour, his court and the aristocracy. Louis' Polish queen, Mary, the philosopher Denis Diderot and other French intellectuals and connoisseurs of opera were ranged against them on the "Italian" side. Within the opera houses, battle lines were drawn by the "French" supporters who gathered around the king's box, and the "Italians" who were deployed before the queen's. The confrontation was originally sparked off in 1752 when the intermezzo *La serva padrona* by Giovanni Battista Pergolesi (1710–36) was performed in Paris by Italian comic actors, or *bouffons*. Ultimately, though, there was no clear victory for either side. French serious opera appeared to have won, but before long, French musicians began to play music in the Italian *buffa* style. This prompted the introduction of the *comédie mêlée d'ariettes*, a kind of comic miscellany, which took its cue more from the Italian than the French side of the argument.

resultant works were renamed *opera semiseria* ('semi-serious opera') and later, *dramma giocoso* ('jocular drama').

OPERA SEMISERIA AND OTHER DRAMAS

The sentimentality and melodrama implicit in *opera semiseria* or *dramma giocoso* had originated in the French *comédie larmoyante* ('tearful comedy') and later filtered into *semiseria* through works classified as *dramma disentimento* ('sentimental drama'), *dramma eroicomico* ('heroic-comic drama') and *drama tragicomico* ('tragicomic drama'). The term *opera semiseria* was apparently first used to describe the opera *Nina* (1789) by Giovanni Paisiello (1740–1816) which illustrated how a happy ending was essential to this form of opera, no matter what had gone before. In *Nina*, the eponymous heroine goes mad after her lover, Lindoro, is shot in a duel with a rival. All ends happily, however. Lindoro recovers, Nina regains her sanity and the two are married. It seems, though, that *semiseria* arose somewhat earlier than 1789, when *Nina* received its first performance at the royal palace in Caserta, near Naples. After 1748, for example, Goldoni was already describing his works as *dramma giocoso*. In addition, *La buona figliuola* ('The Good-Natured Girl') ➔ **p. 108** by Niccolò Piccinni (1728–1800) which was given its first performance in Rome in 1760, later came to be regarded as the first *opera semiseria*.

THE RONDO ARIA

Like Goldoni, his librettist for *La buona figliuola*, Piccinni was himself an innovator, as an important exponent of the rondo aria. This was a straightforward form, related to the instrumental or keyboard rondos used, for instance, in symphonies, sonatas and concertos.

Goldoni e la riforma della Commedia italiana.

LEFT: Six scenes celebrate Carlo Goldoni's reform of Italian comedy in the style of Molière. This superseded the older commedia dell'arte style.
RIGHT TOP: A fashionable tea party in the Prince de Conti's salon in 1766 depicts President Henault and the young Mozart, among others.
RIGHT: The Bourbon Royal Palace at Caserta, near Naples. It was here that Paisiello's Nina had its first performance.

Quite simple, but appealing in structure, the rondo aria featured one slow section and one fast section, each of them repeated twice. The rondo became a very popular form of aria in the eighteenth century, replacing the more elaborate, more showy *da capo* form of aria which was abandoned in *buffa* in about 1750. The rondo also had its own part to play in the evolution of the ensemble finale. Initially, the finale was somewhat atrophied by too great a devotion to established but inflexible musical forms. What was needed was a looser, freeform musical structure which allowed for rapid changes of tempo and simple melodies, and it was on this last count that the rondo made its contribution.

'DOVE SONO'

In this soprano aria from Act III of *Le nozze di Figaro*, set in a hall in the Almaviva castle, the Countess sings of her longing to have a happy marriage once again. She laments that she has lost the love of the Count, regretting the fatal comedown imposed on her by her cruel husband.

POPULAR MELODY

1750–1820   CLASSICAL

GENRES AND STYLES

KEY COMPOSERS

Christoph Willibald von Gluck

Famous above all as the composer of *Orfeo ed Euridice,* Christoph Willibald von Gluck (1714–87) was more than anyone responsible for purging opera of what he dubbed the "abuses" of *opera seria* in favour of "beautiful simplicity", emotional directness and dramatic truth.

FROM BOHEMIA TO VIENNA

Born in the small town of Erasbach in the Upper Palatinate on 2 July 1714, Gluck was determined to become a musician despite opposition from his father, a forester. At 13 he ran away to Prague, eking out a living by singing and playing the jew's-harp. In his early twenties he went to Milan, where he played in the orchestra of Prince Melzi and composed his earliest opera, *Artaserse* (1741). Its success led to several more works in the then fashionable genre of *opera seria*. After visiting London, where he met Handel, in 1745, and directing performances of his operas in other European

Operas

1762	*Orfeo ed Euridice* (revised 1774 as *Orphée*)
1767	*Alceste* (revised 1776)
1770	*Paride ed Elena*
1774	*Iphigénie en Aulide*
1777	*Armide*
1779	*Iphigénie en Tauride*
1779	*Echo et Narcisse*

centres, Gluck settled in Vienna in 1752. That year he composed his most boldly inventive *opera seria* to date, *La clemenza di Tito* ('Titus' Clemency', 1752), to a libretto by Metastasio, which Mozart was to use nearly 40 years later.

NEW DIRECTIONS

During the 1750s and early 1760s Gluck wrote, besides *opere serie*, celebratory works on mythological themes for the imperial court (such as *L'innocenza giustificata* ('Innocence Vindicated', 1755)) and several light, tuneful *opéras comiques* – a genre that became popular after the Viennese imperial chancellor Count Kaunitz brought a French troupe to the court. These culminated in *La rencontre imprévue* ('The Unforeseen Meeting', 1764), a delightful work whose plot and Turkish harem setting (then all the rage in Vienna) were reused by Joseph Haydn (1732–1809) in *L'incontro improvviso* ('The Unforeseen Meeting', 1775) and influenced Mozart's *Die Entführung aus dem Serail* <small>◆◆</small> **p. 95**. However, the two decisive events of these years were the revolutionary dramatic ballet *Don Juan* (1761) and the first of Gluck's so-called "reform" operas, *Orfeo ed Euridice*, on which he collaborated with the poet and librettist Calzabigi.

THE FRENCH CONNECTION

Orfeo's success prompted two further operas whose simple classical plots and close integration of solos, chorus and ballet consolidated Gluck's and Calzabigi's new dramatic principles: *Alceste*, and the less well-received *Paride ed Elena* ('Paris and Helen', 1770). Two years later Gluck was given an adaptation of Racine's tragedy *Iphigénie en Aulide* ('Iphigenia in Aulis', 1774) by the attaché to

the French embassy in Vienna. And between 1774, when this new opera was successfully premiered at the Académie Royale in Paris, and 1779 Gluck applied his revolutionary principles of music drama – themselves influenced by French opera, especially the *tragédies lyriques* of Jean-Philippe Rameau (1683–1764) – to further works for the Parisian stage: an expanded version of *Orfeo* as *Orphée et Euridice* (1774), and an even more radical reworking of *Alceste* (1776). This was followed by the romantically coloured *Armide* (1777), which Gluck pronounced "perhaps the best of all my works", and then by the opera many regard as his supreme masterpiece, *Iphigénie en Tauride* ('Iphigenia in Tauris', 1779) <small>◆◆</small> **p. 91**.

Gluck's final French opera, the delicately pastoral *Echo et Narcisse* ('Echo and Narcissus', 1779), was a failure. This was partly because of squabbling Parisian claques; a dispute had long raged between supporters of Gluck and those of rival composer Niccolò Piccinni. It was also partly because the composer's French operas had accustomed his audiences to sterner stuff. Gluck left Paris for the last time in October 1779 and spent his remaining years enjoying his wealth and fame in Vienna. He died, aged 73, on 15 November 1787.

LEFT: Christoph Willibald von Gluck was a great proponent of simplicity, emotional directness and dramatic truth in the operas he wrote.

Timeline

1714	Born in Erasbach
1745–6	Travels to London
1752	Settles in Vienna
1759	Holds salaried position at court theatre in Vienna
1762	Premiere of *Orfeo ed Euridice*, Vienna
1767	Premiere of *Alceste*, Vienna
1770	Premiere of *Paride ed Elena*, Vienna
1774	Premieres of *Iphigénie en Aulide* and revised *Orphée*, Paris
1776	Premiere of revised version of *Alceste*, Paris
1777	Premiere of *Armide*, Paris
1779	Premieres of *Iphigénie en Tauride* and *Echo et Narcisse*, Paris, the latter unsuccessful; Gluck returns to Vienna
1787	Dies in Vienna

Orfeo ed Euridice
('Orpheus and Eurydice')

Orfeo ed Euridice by Gluck

Composed	1762; revised 1774
Premiered	1762, Vienna (revised version 1774, Paris)
Libretto	by Raniero de' Calzabigi (revised version Pierre-Louis Moline)

When the Emperor Franz I and his retinue attended the premiere of *Orfeo ed Euridice* at the Burgtheater in Vienna on 5 October 1762, they were doubtless expecting a lightweight pastoral entertainment. The occasion – the emperor's name-day – and the opera's billing as an *azione teatrale* (literally "theatrical action") promised as much. What they got was a work of startling originality that integrated chorus, soloists and ballet in dramatic complexes, abandoned the

strict *da capo* aria, and broke down the clear-cut division between recitative and aria.

Raniero de' Calzabigi, the librettist, was a disciple of the French Enlightenment, and a passionate opponent of the artifices and excesses of Italian opera. His ideas chimed perfectly with Gluck's. Calzabigi took the archetypal story of Orpheus's descent to Hades to rescue his wife Eurydice and pared it down to essentials. And from the solemn opening chorus of mourning, through the elementally moving contrast between Stygian darkness and dazzling light in

ABOVE: An illustration from Orfeo ed Euridice. *Orpheus is shown holding a lyre, with Eurydice in flowing robes close behind him.*
RIGHT: Gillian Keith as Amor in Orfeo ed Euridice. *This 2002 production was performed by the Scottish Opera at the Theatre Royal, Glasgow.*

Synopsis
Orfeo ed Euridice by Gluck

ACT I
Orpheus mourns the death of his beloved wife Eurydice, who suffered a deadly snakebite. As he pleads with the gods either to bring her back to life or let him die so that he can be with her, Cupid descends from the heavens. He brings news that the gods have been moved by Orpheus's pleas and have agreed that he can descend to the underworld to try to retrieve Eurydice. To succeed, he must placate first the Furies and then Pluto with the power of his music. There is also one condition that he must observe: he must not look back towards Eurydice as she follows him out of the underworld, and he may not explain his reasons. Realizing that this may make Eurydice doubt his love and doom his quest to failure, Orpheus puts his trust into Cupid and the power of his love for Eurydice.

ACT II
At the entrance to the underworld, Orpheus encounters the terrifying Furies. He pleads with

Orfeo ed Euridice, **Freiburg Baroque Orchestra**
René Jacobs, **conductor**
Soloists: Harmonia Mundi HMC 901742
Bernarda Fink (Orfeo), Veronica Cangemi (Euridice),
Maria Cristina Kiehr (Amore)

RECOMMENDED RECORDING

Act II, to Orpheus's famous climactic lament, '*Che farò*' (What shall I do without Eurydice?), Gluck's music makes its effects with swift, shattering economy.

In 1774 he revised the opera as *Orphée et Euridice*, adding new arias and ballet numbers (including the thrilling 'Dance of the Furies' taken from *Don Juan* and the otherworldly flute solo in the 'Dance of the Blessed Spirits') for dance-mad Paris, but diffusing the dramatic force of the original. In Vienna the hero had been sung by the castrato Gaetano Guadagni. The French deemed castrati an offence against nature, and Gluck duly reworked the role for the celebrated *haute-contre* (high tenor) Joseph Legros.

them to be allowed entry but is repeatedly rebuffed as they try to frighten him into returning to the land of the living. Eventually, he charms them with his beautiful singing and they let him pass. Guided by his love for Eurydice, he reaches the Elysian Fields and finds her among other blessed spirits. They bring her to him and the lovers are reunited.

ACT III
Orpheus tries to persuade Eurydice to follow him out of the underworld but she is bewildered and is at first reluctant to leave. She grows more concerned when Orpheus refuses to look at her, crying out that he is cold and unfeeling, and that she would rather die if he no longer loves her. Unable to ignore her words, Orpheus turns around and embraces Eurydice, who dies. Orpheus is inconsolable and resolves to kill himself, but he is stopped by Cupid, who is moved by Orpheus's determination and enduring love for Eurydice. He then returns Eurydice to life. The lovers are reunited once again and everyone rejoices.

CLASSICAL

1750—1820

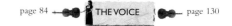

Alceste

Alceste by Gluck

Composed	1767 (revised 1776)
Premiered	1767, Vienna (revised version 1776)
Libretto	by Raniero de' Calzabigi (French version by Roullet)

Triumphantly premiered in Vienna's Burgtheater on 26 December 1767, *Alceste* was the second of the three collaborations between Gluck and Calzabigi. Today it is probably more famous for the reforming manifesto of its preface than for its magnificent music.

Like *Orfeo*, *Alceste* cultivates Gluck's ideal of noble simplicity, with the whole opera based essentially on a single situation – Alcestis's sacrifice for her dying husband. From the powerful overture – which, as Gluck said in the preface, should "apprise the spectators of the action to be represented" – *Alceste* is the most monumental and unrelievedly sombre of all eighteenth-century operas. In the defiant, self-sacrificing heroine, whose music includes the

ABOVE: Robert Tear plays the role of Admetus for the Royal Opera.

Synopsis
Alceste by Gluck

ACT I

A herald tells the grieving crowd gathered in the square next to the palace of Admetus, King of Thessaly, that the king is near to death. His queen, Alcestis, enters and beseeches the gods to relent and have pity on her and her children. She then invites the crowd to join her in the temple of Apollo and offer a sacrifice to the god. Inside the temple Alcestis asks Apollo to accept the offerings. The High Priest urges them all to listen to the words of the Oracle, which pronounces that Admetus can only live if another dies in his place. The terrified people flee from the temple, leaving Alcestis alone. Believing that the good of the people is more important than her own life, she offers herself in her husband's place, even if it means leaving her children. Life without Admetus would be meaningless. The High Priest tells her that Apollo has accepted her sacrifice and that the messengers of death will be waiting for her at the gates of Hades by sunset. Alcestis defiantly declares that she has no fear of what is to come.

ACT II

Admetus has recovered and the people are celebrating in the palace. Barely able to believe his recovery, he announces that he would have given his own life for any of his subjects, but he does not ask to whom he owes his life. Admetus and Alcestis are reunited as the people continue their celebrations. Alcestis, however, cannot hide her tears of sorrow for what is to come. At first Admetus urges her to be happy for his good fortune, but he eventually becomes disturbed and asks why she turns her eyes away from him. She says that she would willingly lay down her life for him a hundred times, but it is only under repeated questioning that she finally confesses what she has done. Admetus is horrified and cannot understand why she should choose to leave him, subjecting him to far greater pains than his own death could bring. The gods must reclaim their original victim. Alcestis calls on the gods to acknowledge that it is her duty to carry out the vow. She must abandon all she loves and be strong in the face of death.

ACT III

In the palace courtyard the people are preparing for the deaths of Alcestis and Admetus, who does not intend to live without her. The hero Hercules arrives to see his friend Admetus. On hearing the news, he declares that he will go to Hades and bring back Alcestis. Alcestis arrives at the gates of Hades, terrified but determined to go forward. The gods of the underworld call to her and she asks them to hasten her end. Admetus has followed her, seeking his own death, but Alcestis orders him to remember his children and his people. Both of them call on the gods, demanding the right to be the only one to be taken. Thanatos, a god of the underworld, replies that the choice is Alcestis's. As she moves towards the gates, and her death, Admetus tries to follow but is stopped as Hercules bursts in. He attacks the gods and brings Alcestis back from Hades. Apollo appears and grants Hercules immortality for his deeds.

As the gates of Hades disappear the scene returns to the palace, where Apollo calls on the people to renew their vows of loyalty to Admetus and Alcestis, now restored to life.

awesome invocation to the underworld '*Ombre, larve*', or, in the French version, '*Divinités du Styx*', Gluck surely created his greatest soprano role.

Although the opera excited the composer "to frenzy", he acknowledged its monolithic nature when he reworked it for Paris. The French *Alceste* is in effect a different opera: musically richer, dramatically tauter and more human than the Italian original, with a touch of comedy in the *deus ex machina* figure of Hercules. The librettist Roullet summed up the enthusiasm *Alceste* aroused when he described it as "the most passionate, the most energetic, the most theatrical music ever heard in Europe".

Alceste, **English Baroque Soloists**
John Eliot Gardiner, **conductor**
Philips 470 293–2PH2
Soloists: Anne Sofie von Otter (Alceste), Paul Groves (Admète), Yann Beuron (Evandre), Ludovic Tezier (Herald, Apollon), Dietrich Henschel (High Priest, Hercule), Nicolas Testé (Oracle, Thanatos)

RECOMMENDED RECORDING

Iphigénie en Tauride
('*Iphigenia in Tauris*')

Iphigénie en Tauride by Gluck

Composed	1779
Premiered	1779, Paris
Libretto	by Nicolas-François Guillard, after Guymond de la Touche and Euripides

Gluck's final *tragédie* for Paris, *Iphigénie en Tauride*, was his greatest success and is arguably his supreme achievement. With a tautly constructed libretto (by Nicolas-François Guillard, drawing on the play by Euripides), it represents the climax of Gluck's efforts to "purify" opera of dramatically superfluous decoration and display. The action moves forward swiftly and remorselessly. Not a note is wasted. In addition, the flexible musical structures, with many ensembles and a fluid intermingling of recitative and *arioso*, powerfully enhance the development of the drama.

Iphigénie and her tormented brother Oreste drew from Gluck some of his most intense and anguished music – say, the heroine's grieving aria '*O malheureuse Iphigénie*', with its forlorn oboe solo

THE PURSUIT OF DRAMATIC TRUTH

Two crucial figures in Gluck's operatic career were the controller of the Viennese theatres Count Durazzo and the Francophile poet and librettist Raniero de' Calzabigi. Both were intent on the reform and revitalization of Italian opera. In Gluck they found their perfect musical collaborator.

Some of Gluck's Italian stage works before *Orfeo* had already begun to integrate solos and chorus. Two leading Italian composers, Niccolò Jommelli (1714–74) and Tommaso Traetta (1727–79), were also cultivating a fusion of Italian *opera seria*, dominated by star sopranos and castratos, and French *tragédie lyrique*, with its important roles for chorus and dancers and its emphasis on *grands tableaux* rather than solo arias.

But it was in his three Italian "reform" operas – *Orfeo*, *Alceste* and *Paride ed Elena* – that Gluck broke most boldly with tradition. In the famous preface to *Alceste*, probably co-written with Calzabigi, the composer resolved to divest music of "all those abuses, introduced by the misguided vanity of singers or the excessive complaisance of composers that have so long disfigured Italian opera". The Byzantine plots and sub-plots and "useless superfluity of ornaments" of *opera seria* were ditched in favour of concentration, classical simplicity and the direct expression of profound emotion.

Gluck could, however, occasionally backslide. The Italian *Alceste* contains dramatically dispensable roles for two confidants (Evandro and Ismene) and stretches of "dry" recitative, while for the French *Orphée* he pandered to the "misguided vanity" of the star tenor, Joseph Legros, and gave him a brilliant *coloratura* showpiece to end the first act.

and agitated syncopated accompaniment (a favourite Gluckian combination); or the scene for Oreste in Act II culminating in the haunting arioso '*Le calme rentre dans mon coeur*', where his imagined peace is disturbingly contradicted by the orchestra. There are raucously barbaric numbers, in the fashionable "Turkish style", for

RIGHT: Jeanne Raunay as Iphigenia at the Théâtre Lyrique, Paris, in 1900.

King Thoas and his Scythian followers, while the serene, luminous choruses for Iphigénie's priestesses are the quintessence of Gluck's "beautiful simplicity" and left their mark on Mozart's *Idomeneo* (1781) •• **p. 94** and *Die Zauberflöte* (1791) •• **p. 100**.

$\mathscr{S}$*ynopsis*
Iphigénie en Tauride by Gluck

BACKGROUND ••

Iphigénie, daughter of Agamemnon and Clytemnestre, is a priestess of Diana on the island of Tauride. Clytemnestre killed Agamemnon and was killed in turn by Iphigénie's brother, Oreste. Oreste has travelled to Tauride with his friend Pylade.

ACT I ••

A storm rages on Tauride. Iphigénie and the priestesses appeal to the gods to calm the elements. Iphigénie tells of a terrible dream she has had, in which she was about to kill her brother Oreste. Desperate, Iphigénie prays for Diana to end her life. Thoas, King of Tauride, enters. He announces that Iphigénie must sacrifice every foreigner that arrives in Tauride; otherwise, say the oracles, he will die. He tells her of the capture of two young Greeks – in fact Oreste and Pylade – and orders their deaths.

ACT II ••

In a cellar, Oreste laments his responsibility for his friend's death and calls upon the gods to end his life. The loyal Pylade reassures him, telling him that he is happy to die if they are together. Pylade is then taken away. Oreste prays again for death and falls asleep, but is tormented by the Furies over his matricide. Iphigénie enters to find out more about the prisoners. They do not recognize one another, and although Oreste tells her of Agamemnon and Clytemnestre's fates, he does not reveal his own identity and claims Oreste to be dead. Iphigénie mourns the deaths of her parents and brother.

ACT III ••

Iphigénie tells the priestesses of her decision to save one of the prisoners. She has difficulty choosing, but eventually selects Oreste, as she feels an inexplicable tenderness towards him. When she tells the prisoners, however, Oreste will not accept the decision. He was hoping for death to release him from his torments and declares that if he is

freed, he will kill himself. Iphigénie reluctantly sets Pylade free instead, entrusting him with a letter to deliver to her sister Electre. Pylade and Oreste bid each other farewell; Pylade resolves to save Oreste.

ACT IV ••

Iphigénie prepares to sacrifice Oreste, praying to Diana for strength. Oreste offers words of encouragement; he wants to die. However, just as Iphigénie is about to plunge the dagger into Oreste, he cries out that his sister, Iphigénie, died in the same way. Finally realizing each other's true identities, the joyful siblings are reunited. A woman enters with the news that Thoas is approaching, enraged by the liberation of Pylade. When Thoas arrives, he orders the sacrifice of Oreste and, when Iphigénie refuses, attempts to carry it out himself. He also wants to kill Iphigénie, but at that moment Pylade arrives and kills Thoas. A battle follows but is halted by Diana, who frees Oreste from his torments and announces that he will rule Greece. Everyone celebrates the gods and the restoration of peace throughout the land.

KEY COMPOSERS

Wolfgang Amadeus Mozart

Alone of the great Viennese classical "trinity" – Haydn, Mozart and Beethoven – Mozart (1756–91) was a born theatre animal. From boyhood, opera was his greatest passion and he built on existing conventions to enrich and deepen three distinct types of opera: *opera seria*, *opera buffa* and German *Singspiel*.

THE CHILD PRODIGY

Wolfgang Amadeus Mozart was born in Salzburg on 27 January 1756, the son of Leopold Mozart, violinist and composer at the Salzburg court. From early childhood Wolfgang displayed what one contemporary called "premature and almost supernatural talents"; and Leopold was quick to promote his son's gifts in a series of concert tours. On a visit to London Wolfgang astonished the philosopher Daines Barrington by improvizing recitatives. At nine he had already absorbed the language of *opera seria*.

His own earliest operas, though, were both comedies: the ingenuous *La finta semplice* ('The Feigned Simpleton', 1768); and the little pastoral

---

'SOAVE SIA IL VENTO'

In *Così fan tutte* the two sisters and the cynical bachelor Don Alfonso bid farewell to the officers in a trio of serene, timeless enchantment, *'Soave sia il vento'*. This ravishing music has become one of Mozart's most famous pieces through its use in John Schlesinger's elegiac 1971 film *Sunday, Bloody Sunday*.

POPULAR MELODY

Singspiel Bastien und Bastienne (1768), performed at the home of Franz Anton Mesmer, the famous Viennese experimenter in magnetism.

THE CONQUEST OF ITALY

Two years later, on his first trip to Italy, Mozart landed his first major commission: an *opera seria* for the Milan carnival season of 1770–71. He plunged himself excitedly into the new work, *Mitridate, rè di Ponto* ('Mithridates, King of Pontus', 1770); and though preparations were dogged by malevolent intrigue, Leopold Mozart wrote that the first night "met with unanimous approval". The *Wunderkind* had "arrived" as an

---

international operatic composer with a work whose brilliance and mastery prompted a commission for another *opera seria*. Premiered in Milan, *Lucio Silla* (1772) is, if anything, an even finer work, with strong Gluckian resonances, especially in the darkly coloured music for Junia.

In the meantime Mozart had composed two slighter allegorical works: for Milan, *Ascanio in Alba* ('Ascanius in Alba', 1771), and for Salzburg, *Il sogno di Scipione* ('Scipio's Dream', 1772). Then, after a two-year hiatus, came the *opera buffa*, *La finta giardiniera* ('The Pretend Gardener Girl', 1774–5) staged at the Munich carnival in January 1775. Lavish in its invention, *La finta giardiniera* foreshadows *Figaro* in the multi-movement ensembles of chaos and bewilderment that end the first two acts. Three months later a royal visit prompted the last opera Mozart completed in Salzburg: *Il rè pastore* ('The Shepherd King', 1775), a static, *serenata*-type piece in the pastoral tradition.

TRIUMPH IN MUNICH

After his fateful journey to Mannheim and Paris in 1777–78, Mozart began a *Singspiel* with a fashionable oriental setting, *Zaide* (unfinished, 1779). Its many beauties include a glorious quartet and, uniquely in Mozart's works, passages of melodrama – declamation accompanied by highly charged orchestral music. However, there was no opportunity of performing *Zaide* in opera-starved Salzburg; and Mozart abandoned the score just before the final denouement. In the summer of 1780, though, his frustrated operatic ambitions were finally fulfilled when he received a commission to write an *opera seria* for Munich. The opera in question, *Idomeneo*, was a work of unique power and splendour and Mozart's first unqualified stage masterpiece.

Following his dismissal from the Archbishop of Salzburg's service in 1781, Mozart quickly became absorbed in another *Singspiel* on a Turkish theme: *Die Entführung aus dem Serail*, whose composition, like that of *Idomeneo*, is vividly documented in a series of letters between Mozart and his father.

ABOVE LEFT: Wolfgang Amadeus Mozart had a passion for opera from an early age. His extraordinary gifts enriched both comic and serious opera.

THE SONATA PRINCIPLE

One of Mozart's most brilliant achievements in his mature operas is the way he harnesses the symphonic energies and key structures of the Classical sonata style to reveal character and propel the action forward. The sextet from *Figaro* is a famous example: here the sonata design is a perfect musical equivalent of the stage action as the initial situation spawns confusion, discord (in the central "development") and, with the restoration of the original key of F major, eventual reconciliation.

Another sextet, in Act II of *Don Giovanni* (1787), is an equally inspired manipulation of the sonata principle. It

begins in E flat as Elvira and Leporello (disguised as Don Giovanni) grope their way in the darkness, and modulates to the "tensing" dominant, B flat, as Leporello becomes ever more agitated. Then, with a breathtaking shift to D major (enhanced by the solemn new sonority of trumpets and drums), Donna Anna and Don Ottavio enter. The tonality darkens to D minor (the opera's key of death and retribution) when Anna remembers her dead father; and a far-ranging development culminates in the glorious comic-dramatic moment of Leporello's "unmasking". Confusion yields to unanimous denunciation of Don Giovanni. The accumulated harmonic tensions are released in a long E flat Molto Allegro that emphasizes the basic chords of tonic and dominant.

CLASSICAL

1750–1820

ENTER DA PONTE

After the triumphant premiere of *Die Entführung* in 1782, Mozart flirted with two more operatic projects: *L'oca del Cairo* ('The Goose of Cairo', 1783), and *Lo sposo deluso* ('The Deceived Husband', also 1783), the former to a libretto by the maverick poet and man of the theatre Lorenzo Da Ponte. Both remained fragments. Then, in 1785, Mozart suggested that Da Ponte base a libretto on Beaumarchais' *succès de scandale* of the previous year, *Le mariage de Figaro*. Da Ponte duly obliged, purging the play of much of its subversive political sentiment. The result was *Le nozze di Figaro*, an *opera buffa* of revolutionary complexity and human insight. *Figaro* was a qualified success in Vienna but caused a sensation in Prague, where the impresario Pasquale Bondini commissioned a second Mozart–Da Ponte collaboration, *Don Giovanni* (1787) ➥ **p. 98**. This was still a comedy but one with unprecedented sombre, demonic overtones. The libretto for Mozart's third Da Ponte opera, *Così fan tutte* ('That's Women For You', 1790) ➥ **p. 99** has a brittle, typically eighteenth-century cynicism – a quality transmuted by the sensuous beauty and tenderness of Mozart's music.

THE FINAL YEAR

Mozart's fortunes were at a low ebb in 1790, the year of *Così fan tutte*'s premiere. However, they picked up in 1791, when he worked on two very different operatic projects. The first was *Die Zauberflöte*, a seemingly improbable mix of fairy tale, Viennese slapstick and high-minded Masonic allegory composed for a Viennese suburban theatre. Before rehearsals of *Die Zauberflöte* had begun, Mozart received a lucrative commission for an *opera seria* for the coronation of Leopold II as King of Bohemia. The upshot was the hastily composed *La clemenza di Tito* (1791) ➥ **p. 101**, long considered "cold" and old-fashioned, but now valued for its distinctive elegiac beauty.

Mozart lived just long enough to witness the ever-growing success of *Die Zauberflöte*. A week or so after its premiere, on 30 September, he began work on the *Requiem*. On 20 November he took to his bed; and on 5 December he died, aged 35, of acute rheumatic fever. His greatest operas soon became central to the European repertoire, touchstones of grace, humanity and dramatic truth. Their influence on later composers, from Ludwig van Beethoven (1770–1827) to Richard Strauss (1864–1949) and Igor Stravinsky (1882–1971), remains incalculable.

Timeline

1756	Wolfgang Amadeus Mozart born, Salzburg
1762	Performs at the Vienna court
1763	Tour of western Europe begins, including Paris and London
1770	*Mitridate, rè di Ponto* commissioned, written and premiered in Milan, with the young Mozart directing
1772	Premiere of *Lucio Silla*, Milan
1778	Visits to Mannheim and Paris
1781	Premiere of *Idomeneo*, Munich; Mozart settles in Vienna
1782	Premiere of *Die Entführung aus dem Serail*, Vienna; marries Constanze Weber
1784	Joins the Freemasons, which was to influence his writing, most notably in *Die Zauberflöte*
1786	Premiere of *Le nozze di Figaro*, Vienna; *Idomeneo* revived, Vienna
1787	Premiere of *Don Giovanni*, Prague; Mozart receives position of Chamber Composer to the court at Vienna
1789	Travels to Dresden, Leipzig and Berlin
1790	Premiere of *Così fan tutte*, Vienna
1791	Premieres of *Die Zauberflöte*, Vienna and *La clemenza di Tito*, Prague (allegedly written in just 18 days); *Requiem* composed; death of Mozart

Operas

1770	*Mitridate, rè di Ponto* K87/74a
1772	*Lucio Silla* K135
1775	*La finta giardiniera* K196
1775	*Il rè pastore* K208
1780–1	*Idomeneo* K366, revised 1786
1781–2	*Die Entführung aus dem Serail* K384
1786	*Le nozze di Figaro* K492
1787	*Don Giovanni* K527
1789–90	*Così fan tutte* K588
1791	*Die Zauberflöte* K620
1791	*La clemenza di Tito* K621

ABOVE: *Salzburg, in Austria. Mozart was born here on 27 January 1756, the son of a violinist and composer at the Salzburg court.*
BELOW: *Mozart worked on his* Requiem *while suffering from rheumatic fever, from which he later died aged just 35.*

KEY COMPOSERS

Idomeneo

Idomeneo by Mozart

Composed	1780–81
Premiered	1781, Munich
Libretto	by Gianbattista Varesco, after Antoine Danchet and Crébillon

Mozart had long admired the inspired synthesis of French and Italian opera in Gluck's "reform" works. His greatest *opera seria*, *Idomeneo*, premiered in Munich on 29 January 1781, draws much from Gluck, especially the hieratic scenes of *Alceste* (another opera concerned with human sacrifice). Yet its harmonic daring, orchestral richness and lyrical expansiveness are entirely Mozart's own. Combining the sophistication of maturity with the reckless abundance of youth, *Idomeneo* constantly challenges and expands the boundaries of *opera seria*. Its prodigious musical invention throws up problems in performance – something Mozart himself acknowledged when at the last minute he drastically pruned the recitatives and cut several arias. Even so, none of Mozart's other operas has such a grand, heroic sweep, or explores emotional extremes so searchingly as this allegory of the passage of power from age to youth.

The characters are drawn with subtlety and compassion, especially the tormented king, played in Munich by the 66-year-old tenor Anton Raaff; the raging, ultimately unhinged Electra; and the Trojan Princess Ilia. They grow from sorrow, in a piercing G-minor lament, through acceptance to radiance. In addition, the writing for the chorus – inextricably bound up in the fate of King Idomeneus and his son Idamantes – has a unique magnificence and dramatic force, above all in the thrilling storm scene that forms the climax of the second act.

Synopsis
Idomeneo by Mozart
ACT I

In the royal dungeons, Ilia, daughter of King Priam of Troy, is being held prisoner. Her hatred of the enemy is confused by her growing love for Idamantes, Idomeneus's son, who frees the prisoners and declares his love for her. Thinking that he is being courted by Electra, Ilia hides her feelings. The news arrives that Idomeneus has been killed at sea; Electra laments that he can now not bless her wedding to Idamantes and is perturbed to witness Idamantes and Ilia's feelings for each other. Meanwhile, Idomeneus arrives on the shore of Crete while Idamantes searches for his body among the wreckage. The two men meet but do not at first know each other, but as the truth of their identities dawns, Idomeneus is horrified to realize that the sacrifice he must make to Neptune is his only son. He rejects the bewildered Idamantes and runs off.

ACT II

Back at the palace, Idomeneus explains his predicament to Arbaces, his confidant, who feels that Neptune is more likely to spare Idamantes if he is exiled. The two plan for Idamantes to escort Electra back to Argos, her homeland, and stay there until the arrangement with Neptune has been resolved. Ilia encounters Idomeneus; the king, while reassuring and comforting her, realizes that she is in love with Idamantes and laments the fact that she too will suffer if he is exiled. Electra is pleased at the prospect of leaving with Idamantes, certain that she can win his love.

At the port, Idomeneus waits to see off Idamantes and Electra, but before the ship can sail a terrible storm brews up and a giant serpent rises from the sea. Taking this as a symbol of Neptune's anger, the people of Crete are terrified. Idomeneus admits that it is his fault, but does not reveal the dreadful bargain he has made.

ACT III

Idamantes goes to Ilia and announces that he is going to fight the serpent, which is wreaking havoc on the island. Finally, Ilia confesses her love for him. Idomeneo and Elettra interrupt them and Idamante asks his father why he is so cold towards him. Idomeneus cannot explain and urges him to leave. Arbaces arrives, bringing news that there has been an uprising and the Cretans are clamouring for the king. Idomeneus faces the people and is told by the High Priest that the serpent is killing the citizens and destroying the island. The High Priest demands to know the intended victim of the sacrifice and everyone is horrified when the king reveals that it is Idamantes. Idomeneus and the priests pray to Neptune at the temple, where they are preparing for the sacrificial ceremony. Arbaces arrives with the news that Idamantes has succeeded in killing the serpent and then Idamantes himself enters. Having discovered that his father was merely trying to protect him, he now offers himself gladly to be sacrificed in order to placate Neptune. As a despairing Idomeneus raises his weapon to strike the fatal blow, Ilia intervenes and offers to die in Idamantes' place. Suddenly, Neptune's great voice is heard, declaring that love has triumphed and that Idomeneus must now give up his throne to Idamantes, who will rule along with Ilia. Everyone rejoices, with the exception of Electra, and Idomeneus gives a farewell speech to the jubilant people of Crete.

Idomeneo, **Scottish Chamber Orchestra**
Charles Mackerras, **conductor**
EMI Classics 5 57260 2
Soloists: Lisa Milne (Ilia), Barbara Frittoli (Elettra), Lorraine Hunt Lieberson (Idamante), Ian Bostridge (Idomeneo), Anthony Rolfe Johnson (Arbace)

RECOMMENDED RECORDING

LEFT: A 1977 production of Idomeneo *by the San Francisco Opera.*
BELOW LEFT: The Act III ballet suite from Idomeneo *at Glyndebourne.*

KEY COMPOSERS

CLASSICAL

1750–1820

Die Entführung aus dem Serail

('The Abduction from the Seraglio')

Die Entführung aus dem Serail by Mozart

Composed	1781–82
Premiered	1782, Vienna
Libretto	by Johann Gottlieb Stephanie the younger, after Christoph Friedrich Bretzner

Premiered on 16 July 1782, two weeks before Mozart's wedding, *Die Entführung* quickly became his most popular work and sealed the composer's operatic reputation in German-speaking lands. The Viennese expected plenty of laughs from a *Singspiel*. Mozart obliged with his first great comic creation: the "foolish, coarse and spiteful" (Mozart's words) harem overseer Osmin, a larger-than-life compound of sullen irascibility, prejudice, lechery and (in his show-stopping final aria 'Ha, *wie will ich triumphieren*') gloating sadism. Mozart exploited, to wonderfully grotesque effect, the subterranean notes of the original Osmin, Johann Ludwig Fischer. Through his music, the jangling, crashing Turkish style of the overture becomes a unifying feature of the whole opera, not least in the rollicking drinking duet '*Vivat Bacchus*' – an instant hit in Vienna.

Die Entführung, though, is no mere oriental romp, and the music for the two "noble" Europeans, Belmonte and Konstanze, has a power, poignancy and lyrical beauty unprecedented in a *Singspiel*. As in *Idomeneo* the sheer richness of musical invention occasionally threatens the drama, above all in the gargantuan introduction to Konstanze's aria of heroic defiance, '*Martern aller Arten*' – magnificent as music, but famous as a producer's nightmare.

Synopsis

Die Entführung aus dem Serail by Mozart

ACT I

The beautiful Konstanze, her maid Blonde and Pedrillo, the servant of Belmonte, Konstanze's betrothed, have been bought by Pasha Selim from pirates. Konstanze lives in the Pasha's palace as his favourite and Pedrillo works as his gardener, while Blonde has been given as a gift to Osmin, the Pasha's overseer.

Belmonte has arrived at the seaside near the palace in search of Konstanze and the others. He encounters Osmin, who confirms that he is in the right place but becomes angry when Belmonte mentions Pedrillo; Osmin is in love with Blonde and Pedrillo is his rival for her affections. Belmonte then meets Pedrillo, who tells him that he is one of the Pasha's favourites and that, although the Pasha loves Konstanze, he will not force his affections on her. The two men devise a plan to rescue their loves and escape.

There is a chorus of Turkish guards and Belmonte, concealed, watches as Konstanze arrives with the Pasha. He asks her why she cannot accept his love and she explains to him that she is still in love with Belmonte. She then leaves, and Pedrillo takes the opportunity to introduce Belmonte to the Pasha, as a visiting architect. The Pasha is welcoming but then Osmin tries to deny the two men access to the castle; outwitting him, they go inside.

ACT II

In the garden, Blonde rejects Osmin's advances, confusing him with her fiery intelligence and promising him pain and violence if he does not leave her alone. Meanwhile, Konstanze laments her fate. Why has Belmonte not come to rescue her? The Pasha, beginning to grow impatient, tries to convince Konstanze to marry him. She refuses and, when threatened with torture, says that she would rather die than marry him. Pedrillo then tells Blonde the good news of Belmonte's arrival and reveals that they will rescue the two women from the *seraglio* [the area in the palace where the women reside] that evening, before escaping by boat. They plan to keep Osmin out of the way by plying him with alcohol.

Later on, Pedrillo takes his chance and does not have much trouble persuading Osmin to partake of some wine, even though it is against Osmin's religion. He falls asleep and is dragged out of the way. Belmonte and Konstanze are reunited and are joined by Pedrillo and Blonde; the men are at first unsure of the women's fidelity, but they are quickly reassured and the four sing of their love.

ACT III

Belmonte and Pedrillo arrive at the walls of the *seraglio* with ladders and the rescue operation begins. Belmonte rescues Konstanze, but before Pedrillo and Blonde can escape, the jealous and evil Osmin awakes and intercepts them. Palace guards bring the four lovers before the angry Pasha. When Belmonte suggests that the Pasha take a ransom from his family, the Pasha realizes that Belmonte's father is an old enemy, who instigated the Pasha's exile. As he considers the lovers' fate, Belmonte and Konstanze sing of their love for each other. Surprisingly though, the Pasha decides to be merciful rather than vengeful and releases the two couples, giving them his blessing and allowing them to set sail for Spain. Osmin is enraged, but the Pasha promises him rewards to make up for his losing Blonde. As the joyful lovers leave, the chorus praises the Pasha's generosity.

LEFT: Mozart's Die Entführung aus dem Serail *performed at the Royal Opera House, Covent Garden in 2001.*

Die Entführung aus dem Serail, **Orchestra del Maggio Musicale Fiorentino**
Zubin Mehta, **conductor**
TDK DV–OPEADS (DVD Region 0)
Soloists: Eva Mei (Konstanze), Patrizia Ciofi (Blonde), Rainer Trost (Belmonte), Mehrzad Montazeri (Pedrillo), Kurt Rydl (Osmin), Markus John (Pasha)

RECOMMENDED RECORDING

KEY COMPOSERS

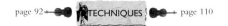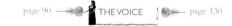
Le nozze di Figaro
('The Marriage of Figaro')

Le nozze di Figaro by Mozart

Composed	1786
Premiered	1786, Vienna
Libretto	by Lorenzo Da Ponte, after Pierre-Augustin Caron de Beaumarchais

The librettist Lorenzo Da Ponte wrote that *Le nozze di Figaro* offered "a new kind of spectacle ... to a public of such assured taste and refined understanding", and it would be fair to say that after Figaro's premiere on 1 May 1786, *opera buffa* was never quite the same again. There were precedents, of course, for the opera's social and sexual tensions, and for its extended "chain" finales – not least in Paisiello's recent "Figaro" opera, *Il barbiere di Siviglia* ('The Barber of Seville', 1782) ↔ **p. 106** and Mozart's own *La finta giardiniera*. Still, *Figaro* far eclipses all predecessors in its structural mastery, owing much to Da Ponte's ingenious adaptation of Beaumarchais' play, as well as its mingled comic brio and profound human insight, and the way Mozart's music simultaneously illuminates character and sweeps the drama forward. No opera unfolds at such a scintillating pace – indeed, the Countess's lament that opens Act II is all the more moving for being the first slow music in the work.

see p. 106

'NON PIÙ ANDRAI'

One of *Figaro's* many sure-fire hits was '*Non più andrai*', in which Figaro regales the disgraced Cherubino with the glories of battle. Mozart himself quoted the aria in *Don Giovanni* ("That's a tune I have heard once too often," mutters Leporello). Two centuries later, in the play and film *Amadeus* by Peter Schaffer, the composer evolves his irresistible melody out of a banal march by his rival Antonio Salieri.

POPULAR MELODY

Le nozze di Figaro, **Glyndebourne Festival Opera**
Bernard Haitink, **conductor**
Kultur 2039
Warner Music Vision 0630–14013–2
Soloists: Renée Fleming (Countess), Alison Hagley (Susanna), Marie-Ange Todorovitch (Cherubino), Andreas Schmidt (Count), Gerald Finley (Figaro)

RECOMMENDED RECORDING

RECONCILIATION AND REDEMPTION

All of Mozart's operas from *Idomeneo* to *La clemenza di Tito* are touched by a Shakespearean wisdom and compassion. In the spirit of the eighteenth-century Enlightenment, tolerance, forgiveness and reconciliation lie at the heart of each of these works, sometimes encapsulated in music of sublime, transfiguring stillness. The hushed reflections on forgiveness in the two finales of *Die Entführung*, and the Countess's pardon of her errant husband at the climax of *Figaro* are all the more poignant for the animation that surrounds them. Equally, the final union of Pamina and Tamino in *Die Zauberflöte*, initiated by a magical change of key, is a moment of rarefied loveliness that confirms the depth and truth of the opera's central message.

In the outwardly cynical, worldly *Così fan tutte*, such numbers as the "farewell" quintet and trio in Act I transform the potentially ridiculous into transcendent beauty. Donna Elvira in *Don Giovanni* begins as an object of mockery. But Mozart infuses her music in the second act, above all in the trio '*Ah taci, ingiusto core*' (Be still, unjust heart), with profound tenderness. His characters may be frail, self-centred and absurd, yet through Mozart's music they are ennobled and redeemed.

In this funniest and most humane of musical comedies, each of the characters is brilliantly drawn in their arias, with the servant pair Figaro and Susanna revealing a growing depth as the opera proceeds. But *Figaro's* greatest glories are its many ensembles, far more intricate than anything the Viennese had heard before. Here Mozart uses his symphonic and contrapuntal mastery to weave together contrasted musical lines for dramatic ends, as in the "recognition" sextet in Act III, the composer's own favourite number.

ABOVE: A programme from the first performance of Mozart's Le nozze di Figaro in 1786. The extraordinary pace, drama and structural mastery of this work meant that opera buffa would never be the same again.
RIGHT: A set design for a salon in Le nozze di Figaro.
LEFT: A performance of Le nozze di Figaro for the Garsington Opera, England in 2000.

Synopsis
Le nozze di Figaro by Mozart

ACT I

Figaro, the Count's valet, and Susanna, the Countess's maid, prepare for their wedding. Susanna reveals that the Count has designs on her; Figaro angrily resolves to outwit his master.

Dr Bartolo enters with his housekeeper Marcellina. They plan to force Figaro to marry Marcellina, as repayment for a debt he owes her. The Count's page, Cherubino, arrives and announces that the Count has caught him with Barbarina, the gardener's daughter. He professes his love for the Countess, and all the other women in the palace, but then hears the Count approaching and hides behind a chair. The Count makes advances towards Susanna, but also hides when Don Basilio, the music master, enters. Don Basilio mentions Cherubino's love for the Countess, at which the Count reveals himself, discovering Cherubino at the same time. The Count is furious, and orders Cherubino to join his regiment. Figaro returns with other servants; they praise the Count for renouncing the old right of the master to replace his valet on his wedding night. Figaro then advises Cherubino on military life.

ACT II

The Countess, in her bedroom, laments her husband's waning affection. Together with Susanna and Figaro, she hatches a plot to trick the Count: they will send Cherubino, dressed as Susanna, to meet the Count in the garden and then denounce his infidelity. Cherubino enters and the others begin to dress him. Susanna leaves to fetch a ribbon and suddenly the Count enters; Cherubino hides in the dressing room. Suspicious, the Count leaves with the Countess to fetch some tools, with which to open the dressing room door. Susanna returns and takes Cherubino's place, while he jumps out of the window. The Count and Countess open the door to reveal Susanna.

Figaro enters to announce that everything is ready for the wedding. Antonio, the gardener, arrives, furious that someone has jumped into his flowerbed beneath the window. Faking a limp, Figaro pretends that it was he who jumped. Bartolo, Marcellina and Basilio arrive to tell Figaro he must marry Marcellina to cancel his debt.

ACT III

Susanna offers to meet the Count in the garden that evening if he gives her the dowry he promised. However, the Count then sees her talking to Figaro and is suspicious. As Figaro tries to avoid marrying Marcellina by protesting that his parents are not present, it transpires that he is the son of Marcellina and Bartolo. Susanna enters and misconstrues Figaro and Marcellina's embrace, but all is explained. Susanna, with the help of the Countess, composes a note inviting the Count to meet her. The wedding ceremony then begins, during which Susanna slips the note to the Count. Figaro sees him receive the love letter.

ACT IV

Figaro and Marcellina encounter Barbarina, who unwittingly reveals that Susanna sent the note to the Count. Ignoring Marcellina's reassurances, Figaro plans to get revenge on his new wife for her supposed infidelity, and invites Basilio and Bartolo along as witnesses. Susanna and the Countess have swapped clothes. Susanna sings of her love for Figaro but he, overhearing, thinks she is referring to the Count. Cherubino arrives and begins to court the Countess – thinking she is Susanna – until the Count intervenes and begins seducing "Susanna" himself. Figaro tells the "Countess" (actually Susanna) about their respective partners' infidelities, but is quick to recognize Susanna's voice and joins in the joke. Figaro and the "Countess" loudly declare their love for one another; the Count arrives and is horrified. He calls everyone to the garden and denounces his unfaithful wife. The real Countess then reveals herself and the deception is explained. The Count begs forgiveness, the Countess relents and everyone rejoices.

CLASSICAL

1750–1820

Don Giovanni

Don Giovanni by Mozart

Composed	1787
Premiered	1787, Prague
Libretto	by Lorenzo Da Ponte, after Giovanni Bertati

Triumphantly premiered in Prague on 29 October 1787, *Don Giovanni* reworks the old legend of the serial seducer, drawing on the Spanish play by Tirso de Molina (1630) and Molière's *Don Juan* (1665). The opera revolves around the tensions of class and sex that were so central to *Figaro*. Ensembles and propulsive "chain" finales remain crucial, although the structure is more episodic than *Figaro*'s. The roles are likewise a mixture of the serious and the comic, with the chameleon Don Giovanni and the scorned but devoted Donna Elvira of so-called "mixed type" (*mezzo carattere*).

Mozart called *Don Giovanni* an *opera buffa*. However, from the awesome D minor introduction of the overture – foreshadowing the chilling appearance of the "stone guest" who drags the hero to his doom – it is a very different work from *Figaro*. The main section of the overture

is a tense, brilliant D major Allegro, leading directly to a wry *buffo* aria for the comic servant Leporello. Typically, though, comedy is immediately juxtaposed with tragedy as Don Giovanni emerges from Donna Anna's bedroom, fights a duel with her father

---

Don Giovanni, **Philharmonia Orchestra**
Carlo Maria Giulini, **conductor**
EMI Classics CDS 7 47260 8
Soloists: Joan Sutherland (Donna Anna), Elisabeth Schwarzkopf (Donna Elvira), Graziella Sciutti (Zerlina), Luigi Alva (Don Ottavio), Eberhard Wächter (Don Giovanni), Giuseppe Taddei (Leporello), Piero Cappuccilli (Masetto), Gottlob Frick (Commendatore)

RECOMMENDED RECORDING

Synopsis
Don Giovanni by Mozart

ACT I

Leporello awaits his master outside the Commendatore's house, where Don Giovanni is in Donna Anna's room. He comes out, pursued by Anna. Anna's father, the Commendatore, challenges Giovanni; they fight and the Commendatore falls, mortally wounded. Anna demands that her betrothed, Don Ottavio, avenge the murder. Giovanni scents a woman. Donna Elvira enters, seeking the man (Giovanni) who seduced her. He steps out to "comfort" her, then recognizes her and slips away, leaving Leporello to explain that she is but one entry in his catalogue of conquests.

Country folk are celebrating the wedding of Zerlina and Masetto. Giovanni, attracted by the bride, sends everyone else off to be wined and dined. Telling Zerlina she is too good for that peasant, he promises marriage and invites her to his villa. As she agrees, Elvira enters, denounces Giovanni and sends Zerlina off. Anna and Ottavio enter, and greet their neighbour Giovanni. Elvira claims that Giovanni is a betrayer but Giovanni assures them that she is mad. Anna recognizes Giovanni as the man who invaded her room and tells Don Ottario that after a struggle she freed herself. She again demands vengeance. Ottavio determines to bring her comfort.

Giovanni hopes for a successful party that evening, with many additions to his catalogue. Zerlina tries to calm Masetto and they go off to the ball. Anna, Elvira and Ottavio enter, masked, solemnly stating their intention of confronting Giovanni. The music starts, with different dances for the different social groups. Giovanni manoeuvres Zerlina to an anteroom; she screams and all make to rescue her. Giovanni re-enters, and the act ends in general confusion and confrontation.

ACT II

Giovanni has noticed Elvira's maid and to improve his chances with her exchanges cloaks with Leporello. Leporello is deputed to get Elvira out of the way: on her balcony, she hears Giovanni singing of love and repentance, descends and goes off – with the disguised Leporello.

Giovanni serenades the maid, but Masetto arrives, armed, with friends. Giovanni (disguised as Leporello) greets them, offers to help and sends them off in different directions, then giving Masetto a beating. Zerlina finds Masetto and offers the ultimate in comforts.

Leporello wants to free himself from Elvira. Anna and Ottavio arrive, then Zerlina and Masetto; they take him for Giovanni. He discards his disguise and slips off. Ottavio sings lovingly of Anna.

Giovanni and Leporello meet in the cemetery. A solemn voice is heard saying: Giovanni's laughter will be silent by dawn. It was the statue of the slain Commendatore. Invite him to supper, Giovanni commands, and the terrified Leporello does so. The statue nods its head in acceptance.

In Anna's house, Ottavio offers to marry her immediately. She asks for a period of mourning. Giovanni, in his banqueting hall, awaits a meal. Leporello serves, with a band in attendance. Elvira bursts in and begs Giovanni to mend his ways. She emits a piercing scream as she leaves. When Giovanni sends Leporello to investigate he too screams and tells Giovanni that the statue is there. The stone guest enters. Giovanni commands that another place is set for dinner. But the statue refuses and asks Giovanni to be his guest instead; Giovanni accepts. The statue seizes his hand in his chill grasp and demands repentance; Giovanni, refusing, is consigned to the flames of hell.

Leporello emerges from hiding and Elvira, Anna, Ottavio, Zerlina and Masetto enter, with police, for Giovanni. When Leporello describes what has happened they announce their plans for the future, and recite the moral – that evildoers come to a sticky end.

---

and kills him. In the second-act finale tragedy and comedy are not only juxtaposed but superimposed, with the terrifying statue commanding Don Giovanni to repent, while Leporello, cowed under a table, provides a chattering counterpoint. The demonic, supernatural elements of *Don Giovanni* and the enduring fascination of its convention-flouting hero made *Don Giovanni* beloved by the Romantics, at a time when much of Mozart's music was patronized for its supposed Dresden china prettiness.

LEFT: Wolfgang Brendel as Don Giovanni.

Così fan tutte
('That's Women For You')

Così fan tutte by Mozart
Composed   1789–90
Premiered   1790, Vienna
Libretto   by Lorenzo Da Ponte

While *Don Giovanni* was the nineteenth century's favourite Mozart opera, *Così fan tutte*, premiered on 26 January 1790, was widely considered frivolous, immoral and (not least by Beethoven) an insult to women. Today we can see it as perhaps the most ambivalent and disturbing of Mozart's three Da Ponte comedies. In the composer's hands the "laboratory experiment" of the elegant, geometrically structured libretto becomes an unsettling commentary on the unpredictability and alarming power of human feelings, and on the need for mature self-knowledge, cloaked in the most sensuously beautiful music Mozart ever wrote.

Of the quartet of lovers it is Fiordiligi who makes the most far-reaching journey to self-discovery. Both her arias exploit the virtuosity of the original singer of the role, Adriana Ferrarese. '*Come scoglio*' in the first act is at once serious and parodistic in its extravagant leaps and heroic posturing. But her Act II rondò '*Per pietà*' uses wide vocal leaps and the singer's rich low register to express the deep disquiet of a woman torn between her passion for the "Albanian" and the mingled guilt and tenderness she feels towards

Così fan tutte, **English Baroque Soloists**
John Eliot Gardiner, **conductor**
Deutsche Grammophon 073 026–9AH2
Soloists: Amanda Roocroft (Fiordiligi), Rosa Mannion (Dorabella), Eirian James (Despina), Rainer Trost (Ferrando), Rodney Gilfry (Guglielmo), Claudio Nicolai (Don Alfonso)

RECOMMENDED RECORDING

her fiancé Guglielmo. Fiordiligi then reveals a newly awakened understanding of her sexuality in her duet with Ferrando. Convention demanded that the original pairings should be restored. However, the emotional journeys undertaken by Fiordiligi and, to a lesser degree, Ferrando make this an unconvincing "happy end", a feeling reinforced by the finale's hollow burst of C major.

LEFT: Diana Montague as Dorabella and Etelka Csavlek as Fiordiligi.

Synopsis
Così fan tutte by Mozart

ACT I

Don Alfonso discusses women with his two friends, the young officers Ferrando and Guglielmo. The young men profess the virtue and constancy of their sweethearts, but Don Alfonso maintains that all women are fickle. He lays a wager that if the officers do everything he asks of them, he can prove it to them by the end of the day. Meanwhile, their sweethearts, the sisters Dorabella and Fiordiligi, proclaim their love for Ferrando and Guglielmo as they gaze upon their portraits. Alfonso enters, with the news that the young men must leave to join their regiment. Sure enough, the officers arrive and the lovers sing a heartfelt farewell. Alfonso remains sure of his impending victory.

The sisters' maid, Despina, tells them that all men are fickle and suggests that they find solace in courting others; she is scolded by the indignant sisters. Alfonso then persuades Despina to introduce the sisters to his two "Albanian" acquaintances; she does not realize that they are in fact Ferrando and Guglielmo in disguise. The two "foreigners" attempt to woo the sisters, each taking the other's sweetheart, but Fiordiligi and Dorabella declare their fidelity to their lovers and leave. The officers boast of their lovers' constancy but Alfonso warns them that there is still plenty of time. Ferrando sings of his love for Dorabella while Despina helps Alfonso devise a plan to make the sisters fall for the "strangers".

Fiordiligi and Dorabella mourn Ferrando and Guglielmo's absence when the "foreigners" stagger in, declaring that they have poisoned themselves in despair. Fiordiligi and Dorabella begin to soften towards the unfortunate men; Alfonso and Despina go to find a doctor who then appears – it is actually Despina in disguise. The "doctor" draws the poison from the men with a special magnet and bids Fiordiligi and Dorabella to nurse then back to health. As the men "recover", their passion for the sisters is renewed but they are again rejected.

ACT II

Despina scolds Fiordiligi and Dorabella for their stubbornness and advises them on dealing with men. She persuades them to indulge in a little harmless flirtation and the sisters decide which of the men to court, each choosing the other's original lover. A serenade is arranged in the garden. Guglielmo successfully courts Dorabella, persuading her to relinquish her portrait of Ferrando. Meanwhile, Ferrando courts Fiordiligi with less success, although when alone she confesses that she has feelings for him.

The young men compare their progress. Guglielmo, relieved that Fiordiligi appears to be faithful, reluctantly shows Ferrando his portrait that Dorabella has surrendered and sings of the fickle nature of women. Ferrando laments Dorabella's betrayal and reveals that he still loves her. Guglielmo, thinking that he has won the wager, has to be reminded again by Alfonso that the day is not yet over.

Fiordiligi scolds Dorabella for her infidelity but eventually admits that she too has fallen for her "foreigner". Alone, Fiordiligi plans to run away and join Guglielmo, but Ferrando enters and manages to seduce her. Alfonso explains to a furious Guglielmo that this is the way of women.

A double wedding is arranged. As the sisters, at the instigation of the notary – Despina in another disguise – sign the marriage contracts, fanfares are heard in the distance signalling the return of the regiment. Fiordiligi and Dorabella panic and force their new husbands out of the room, who then return as Ferrando and Guglielmo. When they find out about the wedding, the officers appear enraged, but go on to reveal the true identities of the "foreigners". Alfonso then explains the deception and encourages everyone to learn from the experience.

Die Zauberflöte
('The Magic Flute')

Die Zauberflöte by Mozart

Composed 1791
Premiered 1791, Vienna
Libretto by Emanuel Schikaneder

The librettist of *Die Zauberflöte*, Emanuel Schikaneder, Mozart's old friend and fellow-freemason, drew on an eclectic variety of sources, including a French novel *Sethos*, Paul Wranitzky's magic opera *Oberon* (1789), and the oriental fairy tale *Lulu*. In the bird catcher Papageno, Schikaneder created for himself a character that could exploit his talent for milking an audience; and in early performances he predictably stole the show, abetted by Mozart's own antics on the glockenspiel.

Stylistically *Die Zauberflöte* is the most heterogeneous opera in the repertoire, juxtaposing pantomime and grave Masonic ritual, solemn fairy tale and earthy Viennese humour. Yet the power of Mozart's music ensures that there is no sense of incongruity. Among the "low" characters, the children of nature, Papageno and Papagena, contrast with the Moor Monostatos, who sings in a frenetic *buffo* style. The hard glitter of the Queen of Night's music is set against the grave nobility of the numbers for Sarastro and the priests. At the centre are the two lovers, Pamina and Tamino,

and it is they who, in the two extended finales, dominate the opera's crucial scenes. The spiritual climax is the trial scene in the second finale, beginning with the Lutheran chorale of the two Armed Men and culminating in the lovers' final union. Pamina's *'Tamino mein!'* is the most sublime moment in the work, and the inspiring embodiment of its central message of human enlightenment and redemption.

LEFT: The Queen of Night as played by Zdislawa Donat in a 1975 production of Die Zauberflöte *for the San Francisco Opera.*

Synopsis
Die Zauberflöte by Mozart

ACT I

Prince Tamino, trying to escape a serpent, faints. Three ladies-in-waiting to the Queen of Night, in whose realm the action takes place, appear, kill the serpent, and leave. Papageno, the Queen's feathered bird catcher, arrives and tells Tamino, who has regained consciousness, that it was he who saved him. The ladies then reappear, padlocking Papageno's mouth and showing Tamino a portrait of Pamina, the Queen of Night's daughter. Tamino falls in love with Pamina and is told that she has been imprisoned by the evil Sarastro. The Queen of Night appears, lamenting the loss of her daughter. She promises Pamina to Tamino if he and Papageno will rescue her. The ladies remove the padlock from Papageno's mouth and issue him with some magic chimes to ensure his safety; to Tamino they give a magic flute. They are also to be accompanied by three Genii.

In Sarastro's palace, the Moor Monostatos is forcing his attentions upon Pamina. Papageno appears, frightening Monostatos away. He recognizes Pamina, and tells her of Tamino's love for her and her imminent rescue. The three Genii lead Tamino to three temples. He enters one and

encounters a High Priest, who reveals that Sarastro is not evil, but a wise and noble man. Tamino plays the magic flute and charms the wild animals. He hears Papageno's panpipes and goes to find him.

Papageno enters with Pamina. They are almost captured by Monostatos, but Papageno uses his magic chimes to overcome the Moor. As Pamina and Papageno celebrate their escape, a chorus is heard in praise of Sarastro, who then enters in a procession. Pamina explains that they were running away from Monostatos. The Moor then appears with Tamino, expecting to be rewarded by Sarastro, but is instead punished. Pamina falls in love with Tamino. Papageno and Tamino are then taken into the temple to learn how to qualify for higher happiness.

ACT II

Sarastro announces his intentions. Papageno and Tamino are to undergo the initiation process in order to gain admission to the Temple of Light and thereby overpower the Queen of Night. Tamino is then free to wed Pamina, who is to be held in Sarastro's protection for the time being.

At the temple, Papageno and Tamino are preparing to undergo their first ordeal: a vow of silence. The ladies-in-waiting try unsuccessfully to trick them into speaking.

In the garden, Monostatos creeps up

on the sleeping Pamina. The Queen of Night appears, giving her daughter a dagger with which to kill Sarastro. Monostatos threatens Pamina, but Sarastro arrives and dismisses him. Tamino is still trying to keep his vow of silence. Papageno talks to himself, before entering into conversation with an old lady who claims to be a lover he has yet to meet. She vanishes and the Genii appear, arranging a feast. Pamina arrives and, not knowing of Tamino's vow of silence, is hurt by his apparent coldness.

Sarastro comforts Pamina. Papageno is visited again by the old lady, who makes him swear to be faithful to her. When he swears, she turns into Papagena, a beautiful young feathered woman, but Papageno is told that he is not yet ready. Pamina considers suicide, but is prevented by the Genii. Tamino enters for the final ordeals of his initiation: those of fire and water. Pamina accompanies him as he undergoes the tests; he can now speak again. In a parody of the previous events, Papageno too contemplates suicide, but changes his mind when Papagena is brought to him. At the Temple of Light, the Queen of Night, her ladies-in-waiting and Monostatos try to wreak revenge on Sarastro, but are destroyed. Tamino and Pamina, who have passed the ordeals, are accepted into the community.

LEFT: Alan Titus and Pam South play Papageno and Papagena.

La clemenza di Tito
('*Titus' Clemency*')

La clemenza di Tito by Mozart

Composed	1791
Premiered	1791, Prague
Libretto	by Caterino Tommaso Mazzolà, after Pietro Metastasio

Premiered in Prague on 6 September 1791, Mozart's last opera is based on an old Metastasio libretto, updated (with added ensembles and choruses) for contemporary taste. Popular in the early nineteenth century, it then went into eclipse. Nowadays, though, *La clemenza di Tito* is valued on its own terms rather than as a pale successor to the much more expansive *Idomeneo*. While the music for the enlightened Emperor Tito has a certain chilly formality, that for the vacillating Sesto and, especially, the manipulative, ultimately remorseful Vitellia is richly expressive. Two other highlights, in a score characterized by a neo-classical purity, economy and restraint, are the exquisite farewell duet for Annio and Servilia '*Ah perdona*' ('Ah, forgive') and the moving finale to the first act. This does the opposite of what we expect from an operatic finale, beginning in turmoil and ending with an elegiac *Andante*.

RIGHT: A scene from La clemenza di Tito, *Mozart's last opera.*

Synopsis
La clemenza di Tito by Mozart

ACT I

Vitellia, daughter of the deposed Roman emperor Vitellius, wants to become empress. She persuades Sesto, who loves her, to assassinate the emperor, Tito, if he marries Berenice, whom he loves. News comes that Tito is sending Berenice away, as he must marry a true Roman, and her hopes are revived. Annio, Sesto's friend, asks for his sister Servilia's hand. Sesto agrees and they swear eternal friendship.

Tito enters and the people pay homage. He declares his determination to rule by kindness and to reward virtue. He then tells Annio that he has decided to marry Servilia; Annio, crestfallen, goes to tell her and bid farewell to her and to his hopes. However, Servilia does not accept the situation and courageously goes to tell Tito of her and Annio's love; he commends her candour and releases her. Vitellia, learning that Tito has selected Servilia, is enraged. She despatches Sesto to set the assassination in train. Reluctantly, but blindly obedient to her wishes, he agrees. Then Annio arrives with Publio, head of the Praetorian Guard: they tell Vitellia that she is the chosen empress. She is shocked and bewildered but cannot now call off the plot. The Capitol is on fire: Sesto and his friends have set the plot in motion. He returns, believing Tito dead, and wracked by guilt. All gather to mourn the emperor's death; Sesto makes to confess his role but Vitellia silences him, while the Roman people bewail the treacherous act.

ACT II

Annio tells Sesto that Tito has survived. Sesto admits he initiated the plot but will not explain why; Annio urges him to confess to Tito. It is too late however: Publio comes to arrest him. Sesto bids Vitellia farewell. The people assemble to give thanks for Tito's survival. Tito learns that Sesto is implicated and has been arrested and condemned to death by the Senate. Annio pleads for him. Tito summons him: surely there must be some rational explanation. Sesto cannot face his former friend (and cannot betray Vitellia); before his dismissal, he begs Tito to remember their friendship. Tito ponders: should he be merciful? Servilia pleads to Vitellia to intercede. Vitellia faces up to her dilemma: can she wed Tito, and let Sesto die? No, she must confess her role. The people acclaim the emperor. Tito intends to spare Sesto, but before he announces the punishment Vitellia steps forward and owns her responsibility. The magnanimous Tito spares everyone, and all join to praise his clemency.

Other Composers

BACH, JOHANN CHRISTIAN (1735–82, GERMAN)

Johann Christian Bach, the youngest son of J.S. Bach (1685–1750), acquired a more thorough training in opera than most contemporary composers, studying first in Germany and afterwards in Italy. Consequently, his operas combined both styles. As a composer, Johann Christian concentrated initially on church music, but he soon transferred his talents to writing for the opera stage. He was 25 when he wrote his first opera, *Artaserse* (1760), for a Turin opera house. *Catone in Utica* ('Cato in Utica', 1761), written for opera audiences in Naples, followed the next year and *Alessandro nell'Indie* ('Alexander (the Great) in India', 1762) the year after that. Also in 1762, Johann Christian travelled to London, where in the following year, his opera *Orione* thrilled audiences, which included King George III and Queen Charlotte, with its delicate orchestration. Subsequently, Johann Christian was appointed music master to the queen. However, he continued to write for European opera houses, in Mannheim, Germany and Paris,

LEFT: A portrait of German composer Johann Christian Bach, son of the composer Johann Sebastian Bach.

which staged his last opera *Amadis de Gaule* (1779). His final London opera was *La clemenza di Scipio* ('Scipio's Mercy'), which was staged in 1778. While in London in 1764, Johann Christian met the eight-year-old prodigy Wolfgang Amadeus Mozart and his influence was later evident in Mozart's own operas *Idomeneo* and *La clemenza di Tito*.

BENDA, GEORG (1722–95, CZECH)

Georg Benda was a Czech composer who produced several stage dramas for the ducal court at Gotha, where he was *Kapellmeister*. His first – and only – Italian opera was *Xindo riconosciuto* ('Xindo Remembered', 1765). Subsequent works were distinctly innovative. In this phase of his career, Benda turned first to German "duodramas" also known as "melodramas". He wrote three on ancient Greek themes, *Ariadne auf Naxos* ('Ariadne on Naxos', 1775), *Medea* (1775) and *Pygmalion*

Synopsis

Il matrimonio segreto ('The Secret Marriage')
by Cimarosa
Composed 1792
Premiered 1792, Vienna
Libretto by Giovanni Bertati, after George Colman and David Garrick

ACT I

Carolina, Geronimo's daughter, is secretly married to Paolino, her father's clerk. The couple are trying to find a way to tell Geronimo of their marriage; he would not approve of such a lowly match. Paolino comes up with a plan. In order to win Geronimo's favour, while also addressing his social aspirations, Paolino will arrange a marriage between nobleman Count Robinson and Carolina's elder sister Elisetta. Paolino tells Geronimo of his idea; Geronimo is overjoyed at the prospect of the wedding. When the Count arrives, he first assumes Carolina is to be his wife, and then turns his attentions to Fidalma, the sister's widowed aunt. He is unimpressed with Elisetta and asks Carolina to marry him instead; Elisetta is enraged. The act ends in confusion, as the deaf Geronimo struggles to make sense of the situation.

ACT II

The Count explains to Geronimo that he wishes to marry Carolina instead of Elisetta. Geronimo hesitates, but the Count offers to take a smaller dowry; this appeals to Geronimo's greed and he consents. Paolino hears about the change of plan. He goes to Fidalma, hoping to confide in her, but she reveals that she is in love with him. Carolina then happens upon the pair and assumes the worst; a heated discussion ensues. Paolino suggests to Carolina that they run away together. Elisetta and Fidalma are furious with Carolina for ruining their hopes of love. They ask Geronimo to send Carolina to a convent; he agrees. Carolina laments her fate and the Count, unaware of her true dilemma, comforts her.

As Carolina and Paolino prepare to escape, Elisetta intervenes and they withdraw into Carolina's room. Elisetta is convinced that the man Carolina is with is the Count. She brings everyone to the door of the room; the couple are forced to show themselves and reveal that they are married. All ends happily as the Count agrees to marry Elisetta, and Geronimo, pleased that everything has turned out well, forgives Carolina and Paolino.

(1779), in which the music provided background accompaniment to dialogue spoken by two actors. Between *Medea* and *Pygmalion*, Benda composed *Singspiels*: these featured a different arrangement in which the music alternated with the dialogue. Benda's three *Singspiels* – *Der Dorfjahrmarkt* ('The Annual Village Market', 1775), *Romeo und Julie* ('Romeo and Juliet', 1776) and *Walder* (1776). – were markedly different from previous examples of the genre which comprised comedy, ballads or fantasy. By contrast, Benda's experience with melodrama developed his dramatic musical skills and this enabled him to give much more serious plots the *Singspiel* treatment for the first time. Benda's music reflected the tense and heightened atmosphere of these stories and in doing so, created a much more dramatic musical language. This was done by Benda's frequent changes of tempo and rhythm and vivid orchestration.

CIMAROSA, DOMENICO
(1749–1801, ITALIAN)

The prolific Italian composer Domenico Cimarosa, who was born near Naples, first attracted attention with his opera *Le stravaganze del conte* ('The Eccentricity of the Count', 1772). By 1787 Cimarosa had produced one success after another, with 15 operas written for opera houses in Rome and Naples. In 1787, however, Cimarosa accepted a post as *maestro di cappella* at St Petersburg. There he scored further success with *La vergine del sole* ('The Virgin of the Sun' 1788) and *Cleopatra* (1789) but he now had a dazzling international reputation and this made him constantly in demand outside Russia. In 1791 he became *Kapellmeister* to the imperial court in Vienna and, the following year, produced yet another success, *Il matrimonio segreto* ('The Secret Marriage', 1792) ➛ **p. 102**. The same year, though, the Austrian emperor died and Cimarosa's appointment in Vienna came to an end. He returned home to Naples and a post as *maestro di cappella* to the royal court. Then in 1799 Cimarosa was imprisoned after King Ferdinand fled in the face of invasion by the armies of Revolutionary France. On his release, Cimarosa headed back to St Petersburg, but died on the way, in Venice. His output of more than 60 operas (the latter of which survive) are noted for their melodic warmth, sparkle and vivacity.

DIBDIN, CHARLES
(1745–1814, ENGLISH)

In the late eighteenth century, Charles Dibdin, composer, actor and singer, catered for the English taste for *Singspiels* and afterpieces, which were short operas or pantomimes provided as extra entertainment after the main work had finished. Initially, Dibdin favoured the Italianate style, but after *The Waterman* (1774), he turned to a more English ballad kind of composition. Dibdin did not entirely abandon European influences. He was among the first to introduce English audiences to the ensemble finale in which the entire cast of an *opera buffa*, or comic opera, gradually gathered on the stage in the last scene of an act. Dibdin's life was crammed with difficulties, such as his severe financial problems and his inability to work amicably with others. Debts forced him to flee to France in 1776. After his quarrel with the manager of Covent Garden theatre in 1778, no other London management would employ him. He opened his own theatre, but mishandled it and ended up in debtors' prison. His plan to emigrate to India foundered because he was seasick and unable to make the journey. Eventually, Dibdin built a small theatre, ironically named the Sans Souci – 'without care' – where he gave shows called table entertainments.

GALUPPI, BALDASSARE
(1706–85, ITALIAN)

Baldassare Galuppi wrote his first opera *La fede nell'incostanza* ('Faith in Inconstancy', 1722) when he was 16. It failed. Undeterred, Galuppi studied with Antonio Lotti (1667–1740) to improve his technique. Eventually, in 1729, he achieved his first big success, in Venice, with *Dorinda*. This opened the door to a brilliant career in which Galuppi produced some 100 works. In 1741 he began writing operas for London, including *Scipione in Cartagine* ('Scipio (Africanus) in Carthage', 1742) and *Sirbace* (1743), which were regularly performed in subsequent years. Fanny Burney (1752–1840), the diarist and novelist, believed that, of all Italian composers, Galuppi had the most influence on English music. After returning to Venice in 1743 Galuppi divided his output between opera and church music and in 1762 was appointed *maestro di cappella* at St Mark's. He had already made a seminal contribution to opera in 1749 when he wrote the first full-length *opera buffa*, *L'Arcadia in Brenta*: he later gave this genre an expanded version of the "chain finale" where successive sections in different rhythm, tempo and texture respond to the dramatic situation and convey the flux of emotions which are portrayed. Galuppi preceded Cimarosa as *maestro di cappella* at St Petersburg, where his *Ifigenia in Tauride* ('Iphigenia in Tauris', 1768) was performed. Galuppi wrote his last opera, *La serva per amore* ('The Servant for Love') in 1773.

ABOVE: *Charles Dibdin was a composer, an actor and a singer. Here he plays the part of Mungo in* The Padlock.
ABOVE LEFT: *Italian composer Domenico Cimarosa wrote more than 60 operas in his lifetime. He died in Venice in 1801.*

CLASSICAL

1750—1820

CLASSICAL

1750–1820

GRÉTRY, ANDRÉ-ERNEST-MODESTE (1741–1813, FRENCH)

Grétry, who was born in Liège, composed two *intermezzi* before he headed for Paris and his preferred genre, the *opéra-comique*. His first success, *Le Huron* (1768), came a year after his arrival and was followed in 1769 by the equally well received *Lucile* and *Le tableau parlant* ('The Talking Picture'). Grétry charmed French audiences with his elegant, expressive melodies and their distinctly Italian grace. A string of successes encouraged Grétry to spread his musical wings with his composition of *Andromaque* ('Andromache', 1780), which was based on Racine's play about the Trojan War. This was a big, dramatic subject, with rather too much tragedy for Grétry's particular talent, which was somewhat overstretched by it. However, the opera considered to be Grétry's masterpiece, *Richard Coeur-de-Lion* ('Richard the Lionheart', 1784) lay ahead of him and received its first performance in Paris. This opera in three acts was based on the thirteenth-century fable telling the story of King Richard and his faithful minstrel Blondel. Blondel's air *'Une fèvre brûlante'* was an early example of the reminiscence motif, which is repeated throughout the opera as a reminder of a place, a person or other feature of the story.

HASSE, JOHANN ADOLF (1699–1783, GERMAN)

At age 22, John Adolf Hasse had his first opera, *Antioco* (1721), produced before being sent to Italy to study under Alessandro Scarlatti. In Naples, Hasse's "dialect comedies" *Sesostrate* (1726) and *La sorella amante* ('The Loving Sister', 1729) made him something of a local celebrity. Hasse's *Artaserse* (1730), staged

ABOVE: André E. M. Grétry enjoyed considerable success in the opéra-comique genre. His melodies were notable for their elegance and grace.
ABOVE RIGHT: By the age of 22, German composer Johann Adolf Hasse had written his first opera and was on his way to study under Scarlatti.

'UNE FÈVRE BRÛLANTE'
This is a song sung by the minstrel Blondel, which enables him to make contact with the imprisoned Richard Coeur-de-Lion – the English King Richard I – whom he afterwards rescues. In various guises and tempos, this melody appears nine times as Blondel searches for the one prison that holds the king.

POPULAR MELODY

---

in Venice, proved to be a milestone in the development of opera. Hasse's music gave the stylized conventions of contemporary opera a new slant, with greater contrast and expression and more chances for the singers to demonstrate the beauty and agility of their voices. Another opera in the same vein – *Dalisa* (1730) – appeared that year. In this same brilliant year of his career, Hasse was invited to the court of Saxony, where the heir to the electorate, Prince Frederick Augustus II, was keen to establish an Italian opera company in Dresden. The company, with Hasse as its director, was established in 1733, after

---

Synopsis
Richard Coeur-de-Lion
('Richard the Lionheart')
by Grétry
Composed 1784
Premiered 1784, Paris
Libretto by Michel-Jean Sedaine

PROLOGUE ⠦
Richard I has disappeared on his way home to England from the Third Crusade. Blondel, his squire and a troubadour, is trying to find his master.

ACT I ⠦
Peasants are returning in the evening to their homes near Linz Castle. A local boy, Antonio, leads on a blind man and tells him about the girl he will be seeing at a wedding tomorrow, before going to find lodgings for the night. When left alone the man, who is indeed Blondel, reveals that he is only pretending to be blind and that he believes Richard is a prisoner in the castle. Florestan, the castle governor, sends a love letter to Laurette, daughter of the Welsh knight Williams, who intercepts the letter. Blondel asks

---

Frederick Augustus succeeded to the electorate. Subsequently Dresden became a centre of opera in Germany that was second only to Berlin. Hasse himself was recognized as an

---

Antonio to read it aloud, including a reference to a very important prisoner. Laurette declares her love for Florestan, but Blondel warns her that Cupid wears a blindfold. Marguerite of Flanders, Richard's beloved, arrives with her entourage. Blondel plays a tune the king had written for her and, when questioned, says he learned it from a crusader. He then leads the servants in a drinking song.

ACT II ⠦
On the castle terrace Richard despairs of his life as a prisoner. Blondel and Antonio appear below the wall. Richard recognizes Blondel's voice and joins in the song. The soldiers threaten to arrest Blondel, who pretends to have a message from Laurette, inviting Florestan to a party tomorrow.

ACT III ⠦
In Williams' house, Blondel reveals his true identity to Marguerite and tells her about Richard. He outlines a plot he has formed in order to capture Florestan when he comes to visit Laurette. During the dancing Florestan is seized. Blondel leads the assault on the castle and Marguerite and Richard are reunited.

OTHER COMPOSERS

Synopsis
La fedeltà premiata ('Fidelity Rewarded')
by Haydn
Composed 1780
Premiered 1781, Eszterháza
Libretto by Giambattista Lorenzi

ACT I

Amaranta reads an inscription in the Temple of Diana describing how two lovers are to be offered to a sea monster every year until a hero sacrifices himself. Melibeo, the High Priest, chooses the victims and everyone has to be careful not to cross him. On his advice Lindoro abandons the nymph Nerina for Celia, but Amaranta makes the mistake of preferring Count Perrucchetto to Melibeo. Fileno believes his beloved Fillide is dead, unaware that she is actually Celia. When she sees Fileno, Celia tries to maintain the deception or give herself away to Melibeo. The Count's fleeting interest in Nerina makes Amaranta furious. Melibeo tells Celia she must either marry Lindoro or face the monster with Fileno; before she is forced to accept, she is abducted by satyrs.

ACT II

Melibeo plans to win Amaranta's love by pairing off Celia and the Count, and he persuades Nerina to seduce Fileno. Fileno succeeds in killing a wild boar that is chasing Amaranta, but the Count claims the kill.

Fileno contemplates suicide, but manages to break his arrow while carving his story on a tree. Celia finds the carving and the arrow and believes he is dead. On Melibeo's instructions the Count enters a cave where Celia is hiding. When the pair emerges Melibeo announces that they are to be this year's sacrifice.

ACT III

Fileno refuses to accept Celia's protestations of innocence. Fileno declares that, to save Celia, he will be the single sacrificial victim and hurls himself in front of the sea monster, which turns into a grotto from which Diana appears. She brings together Celia and Fileno, Nerina and Lindoro, and Amaranta and the Count. As a punishment for his scheming, Melibeo is taken as her victim, but the curse on Cumae has been lifted.

---

important influence on the development of *opera seria*, which acquired a new depth, a greater dramatic sweep and emotional appeal for audiences.

HAYDN, JOSEPH
(1732–1809, AUSTRIAN)

The operatic career of Joseph Haydn spanned four decades, from his lost German *Singspiel Der krumme Teufel* ('The Crooked Devil', 1753) to his Orpheus opera *L'anima del filosofo* ('The Philosopher's Soul') composed for London in 1791 but not performed there (or anywhere else) during the composer's lifetime. In between he composed some 20 operas (several lost) for the Esterházy court, ranging from comedies like *Il mondo della luna* ('The World on the Moon', 1777) through "mixed-genre" works like *La fedeltà premiata* ('Fidelity Rewarded', 1780) and *Orlando paladino* ('Knight Roland', 1782) to the "heroic drama" *Armida* (1783). Haydn himself valued his operas highly. Yet while most have been recorded, none has entered the regular repertoire.

In his operas, more than anywhere, Haydn has suffered for not being Mozart. Criticisms of far-fetched, slow-moving plots (Haydn never had a Da Ponte at his disposal) and fallible dramatic instinct cannot be dismissed out of hand. Where Mozart would have propelled things forward in an ensemble, Haydn is too often content to write an elegant, static aria in full sonata form. Nevertheless his operas abound in richly worked, vividly characterized music, sometimes of a sensuous beauty not readily associated with Haydn – say, the ravishing "dream" trio in the oriental opera *L'incontro improvviso* ('The Unexpected Meeting', 1775). In addition, among the stock-in-trade characters, there are memorable individual portraits: the "sentimental" heroine Rosina in *La vera costanza* ('True Constancy', 1778–89); the irrepressible, fast-talking Pasquale in *Orlando paladino*, first cousin to Mozart's Leporello; or, most richly imagined of all, the impassioned, vengeful, ultimately tragic sorceress Armida in Haydn's final opera for the Esterhazy court.

RIGHT: Joseph Haydn was trained as a choirboy and sang in the choir of St Stephen's Cathedral in Vienna for around ten years.

DOCTRINE OF THE AFFECTIONS

The principle of "doctrine of the affections" was the dominant theory for the design of opera in the eighteenth century. Its name was not coined by German musicologists until the twentieth century, but the ideas behind it were discussed in the writings of theorists such as the German composer Johann Mattheson (1681–1764). These ideas were put into practice on stage by the famous librettists Zeno and, in the following generation, Metastasio. The doctrine defined specific "affections" or emotions, such as love, hate, sorrow, despair or hope. Each of these "affections" was given exclusive rights to its own musical feature – a movement, aria or choral passage, for example. The arrangement may strike modern opera goers as artificial and repetitive and something of a "one-size-fits-all" device. However, the set pattern made it easy to identify which human feelings were going to be explored and prepared audiences – not all of whom would be experts in opera or even in music – for what they were about to hear. The "doctrine of the affections" also enabled arias to be easily moved from one work to the next where the actual music would change, but the mood and the emotion would remain the same.

HILLER, JOHANN ADAM
(1728–1804, GERMAN)

The German composer and writer Johann Adam Hiller was a keen admirer of Hasse. Although already an established songwriter, Hiller wanted to move into more operatic mode, with Hasse's style as his yardstick. Hiller joined forces with the librettist Daniel Schiebeler (1741–71) and together they produced a romantic comedy-opera *Lisuart und Dariolette* ('Lisart and Darioletta', 1766). A second opera, *Die Muse* ('The Muse', 1767), followed a year later, but neither was much of a success. Subsequently Hiller reverted to the rustic, sentimental pieces he had previously produced with another librettist Christian Felix Weisse (1726–1804). The first three results of their renewed collaboration were important in establishing *Singspiel* as a popular form in opera. Hiller has been cited as the founder of *Singspiel*, and, in his lifetime, this new style of musical writing was widely emulated. Hiller's work with Weisse mixed together a number of influences – the French *operas comiques*, German song traditions, the *bel canto* technique used in *opera seria*, or the chatty staccato style used in *opera buffa*. Hiller helped to popularize his own work by publishing scores of his music in simplified versions so that amateur singers could perform them. An added purpose was to encourage German singers to improve their standards.

JOMMELLI, NICCOLÒ
(1714–74, ITALIAN)

Niccolò Jommelli scored successes with his first operas, *L'errore amoroso* ('The Loving Mistake', 1737) and *Ricimero* (1740) and *Astianatte* (1741), and before long these and other operas had won him recognition as an eminent composer. Jommelli's services were eagerly sought and he wrote operas for Rome, where he was appointed *maestro di cappella* at St Peter's in 1749, and that same year composed works for Vienna. Four years later Jommelli was appointed *Kapellmeister* to the Duke of Württemberg in Stuttgart, where he composed some 33 operas, some of them for other

LEFT: Jommelli developed a more realistic style.

'O QUANTO UN SI BEL GIUBILO!'
Mozart reacted sardonically to the fact that *Una cosa rara* by Martín y Soler replaced his own opera *Figaro* in Vienna in 1786. When writing his *Don Giovanni*, he quoted an aria from *Una cosa rara* 'O quanto un si bel giubilo!', in the banquet scene which preceded the hero's descent into hell.

POPULAR MELODY

German courts or for Italian opera houses. However, his experience in Stuttgart marked his style so that by the time he returned to Italy, two new operas he produced were judged too German for Italian tastes. Jommelli had more success with four operas written for Portuguese audiences, but Italian audiences seemed to have turned against him. So many of the operas he wrote for the Italians were failures that the stress caused a fit of apoplexy, which, sadly, proved fatal. Nevertheless, Jomelli's contribution to the

development of opera was not in doubt: his *opera seria* style was more realistic and less stereotyped than that found in contemporary works.

MARTÍN Y SOLER, VINCENTE
(1754–1806, SPANISH)

The Spanish composer Martín y Soler wrote his first opera, entitled *La Madrilena* ('The Girl from Madrid', 1776), which was probably a *zarzuela*. Afterwards, Martín went to Italy, where he gained a reputation for writing both serious and comic operas that were performed in Lucca, Parma, Turin, Venice and Naples. Soon his gifts for beautiful melody, striking orchestration and diverting characterization were widely recognized and he was encouraged to visit Vienna. There, together with the renowned librettist Lorenzo Da Ponte (1749–1838), he produced three operas, *Il burbero di buon cuore*

Synopsis
Il barbiere di Siviglia ('The Barber of Seville')
by Paisiello
Composed 1782
Premiered 1782, St Petersburg
Giuseppe Petrosellini, after Pierre-Augustin
Caron de Beaumarchais

ACT I

Count Almaviva stands below the window of Rosina, ward of Dr Bartolo, serenading her. Figaro, a self-important barber, arrives. Rosina appears at the window and drops a note for the Count, asking him to introduce himself in song. Figaro tells the Count to gain entry to the house by disguising himself as a drunken soldier. Learning that Rosina will be forced to marry Bartolo tomorrow, the Count presents himself to her as "Lindoro". He offers Figaro money in exchange for his help.

ACT II

Figaro tells Rosina of Lindoro's love. She gives him a letter for Lindoro. Bartolo tries to obtain information from his servants, Lo Svegliato and Giovinetto, but Figaro has drugged them. Bartolo's friend Don Basilio enters with news that Count Almaviva is pursuing Rosina and suggests that they slander him.

Figaro warns Rosina of Bartolo's intentions. Bartolo and Basilio find Rosina's letter and forbid her to leave the house. The Count, disguised as a soldier, arrives demanding lodgings, but Bartolo refuses. In the confusion, the Count passes a note to Rosina; Bartolo sees this and demands to read it but Rosina hands him another paper.

ACT III

The disguised Count arrives, claiming to be a music teacher sent by Don Basilio, and gives Rosina her music lesson. Figaro enters and the lovers plan their escape; Don Basilio arrives, but leaves with a hefty bribe. Figaro decides to distract Bartolo, but the doctor then recognizes the fake music teacher as Rosina's lover.

ACT IV

Bartolo tells Rosina that her lover is merely an agent for Count Almaviva. Distraught, she agrees to marry Bartolo; he sends Basilio to fetch a notary. Figaro and the Count arrive, ready to flee through the window with Rosina. She refuses until the Count reveals his true identity. Bartolo steals their ladder, trapping them. Basilio enters with the notary and, after some bribery, Rosina and the Count are married. Bartolo arrives too late and is forced to accept the situation.

OTHER COMPOSERS

Synopsis

Ernelinde, princesse de Norvège
('Ernelinde, Princess of Norway')
by Philidor
Composed 1767
Premiered 1767, Paris
Libretto by Antonine Alexandre Henri
Poinsinet after Francesco Silvani's libretto *La
fede tradita, e vendicata*

PROLOGUE ❧

The brother of Ricimer, King of the Goths (Sweden), has been killed by Rodoald, King of Norway. In revenge Ricimer has attacked Rodoald's capital at Nidaros (now Trondheim). Sandomir, Prince of Denmark, is in alliance with Ricimer, even though he is betrothed to Rodoald's daughter Ernelinde.

ACT I ❧

Nidaros has fallen and Ernelinde is found as the town is being sacked. Sandomir promises to defend her against any harm. The victorious Ricimer, who also wants to marry Ernelinde, enters and has a violent quarrel with Sandomir. Even though he has been taken prisoner, Rodoald forbids Ernelinde to have anything to do with Ricimer.

ACT II ❧

In order to get rid of his rival, Ricimer orders Sandomir's arrest. He then tells Ernelinde that either her father or her lover must die: the choice is hers. Ernelinde is in torment, but eventually decides that she must save her father. After she has told Ricimer her decision and Rodoald has been released, however, she is stricken with remorse and sees a vision of her lover reproaching her for abandoning him to his fate.

ACT III ❧

Ernelinde visits Sandomir in prison and they resolve to die together before the altars of Odin and Frigga. Rodoald, meanwhile, has rallied his troops and the Danes loyal to Sandomir. He arrives just in time to prevent the double suicide. Ricimer is overthrown, but Sandomir spares his life. Through his marriage with Ernelinde, Sandomir will now inherit the kingdoms of Denmark, Norway and Sweden.

ABOVE: Autographed page of L'idolo cinese *by Giovanni Paisiello.*

('The Moaner with the Heart of Gold', 1786), *L'arbore di Diana* ('Diana's Tree', 1787) and *Una cosa rara* ('A Rare Thing', 1786), the most successful of the trio. It displaced Mozart's *La nozze di Figaro*, which had been played for the first time earlier the same year. In 1787 Martín y Soler received an invitation to St Petersburg, where he became court composer to the Empress Catherine II (the Great). In St Petersburg, Martín wrote two operas, directed several opera productions and, most significantly, helped lay the foundations of native Russian opera.

PAISIELLO, GIOVANNI (1740–1816, ITALIAN)

Giovanni Paisiello scored his first successes in *opera buffa*. Compositions such as *L'idolo cinese* ('The Chinese Idol', 1767) were performed to enthusiastic audiences all over Italy. Paisiello's talents rivalled those of other prominent composers, such as Cimarosa. Like Cimarosa and others, he caught the interest of Empress Catherine of Russia who invited Paisiello to St Petersburg in 1776. Paisiello established the Italian opera tradition at Catherine's court and wrote two operas in the same year *Lucinda ed Armidoro* and *Nitteti* (both 1777). He also wrote his own "Figaro" opera, *Il barbiere di Siviglia*. Opera audiences loved it, so much so that Gioachino Rossini (1792–1868) had considerable trouble breaking down popular prejudice against his own *Il barbiere* ·•→ **p. 127**, written in 1816, the year Paisiello died. Paisiello returned to Italy in 1784 and while on the way, in Vienna, he composed *Il re Teodoro in Venezia* ('King Theodore in Venice', 1784). Paisiello was appointed *maestro di cappella* to King Ferdinand IV in Naples in 1783, and it was here that he wrote one of his best-loved operas, *Nina* (1789). Paisiello wrote more than 80 operas, including several in the *opera buffa* genre that he converted from light, somewhat inconsequential, entertainment into something more dramatic and emotional.

PHILIDOR, FRANÇOIS-ANDRÉ DANICAN (1726–95, FRENCH)

Philidor was more or less forced into writing *operas comiques* once his earlier, Italian, style got him banned, in 1756, from the Paris Opéra, where such foreign imports were frowned on. Philidor adapted splendidly. He soon became a successful composer in this typically French genre, producing *Blaise le savetier* ('Blaise the Cobbler', 1759) and *Le Sorcier* ('The Sorcerer', 1764). At a performance of *Le Sorcier*, Philidor became the first composer to take a curtain call. However, like his later opera *Ernelinde, princesse de Norvège* ('Ernelinde, Princess of Norway', 1767), *Le Sorcier* sailed perhaps too close to plagiarism due to the influence exerted by the work of Gluck whom Philidor greatly admired. Nevertheless Philidor's contribution to *opera comique* was impressive: melodies acquired greater character and his deft use of modulation coloured the musical harmonies to significant effect. Philidor was innovative too, though this was not always welcome to audiences. The unaccompanied canon quartet for his opera *Tom Jones* (1765) taken from Henry Fielding's story of the same name was at first too much of a novelty for audiences and it was booed. Later the opera was recognized as Philidor's masterpiece. Philidor also included everyday sounds in his scores – a hammer striking metal or a donkey braying.

RIGHT: A scene from Tom Jones *by Henry Fielding, the novel which inspired the opera of the same name by Philidor.*

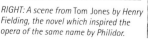

PICCINNI, NICCOLÒ
(1728–1800, ITALIAN)

Le donne dispettose ('The Spiteful Women', 1754) was Niccolò Piccinni's first opera and was received with great enthusiasm. Piccinni, the eventual composer of some 120 works, went on as he had begun, scoring several successes that climaxed with his masterpiece, *La buona figliuola*. Receiving its premiere in Naples, another of Piccinni's operas, *I viaggiatori* ('The Travellers', 1775) was particularly well liked. At around this time there was resistance in France to the reforms promulgated by Gluck, who had introduced a mixture of music, dance and mime into opera among other "unwelcome" innovations. Piccinni, unfortunately, became the stick with which this faction sought to beat Gluck. The Italian was invited to Paris in 1776, where he was obliged to enter a contest with Gluck, in which both of them wrote an opera, *Iphigénie en Tauride*. Piccinni lost out, and Gluck's 1779 version eclipsed Piccinni's, which was produced in 1781.

After Gluck, another rival for Piccinni – Antonio Sacchini (1730–86) – arrived in Paris. Although the success of Piccinni's *Didon* (1783) masked the truth, as a composer he was in decline. He has been mainly remembered for his *opere buffe*, his beautiful melodies and harmonies and his skilful orchestration.

SALIERI, ANTONIO
(1750–1825, ITALIAN)

When he was 16, Antonio Salieri was the protégé of the Bohemian composer Florian Gassmann (1729–74) who brought him to Vienna in 1766. Gassmann was influential at the imperial court and, as well as teaching Salieri composition, introduced him to some very high-ranking contacts. Salieri's first surviving opera, written when he was 20, was *Le donne letterate* ('The Cultured Ladies', 1770). It was a success, so much so that only four years later, Salieri, still only 24, was appointed court composer to the Austrian Emperor Joseph II. In 1784 he succeeded Gluck at the Paris Opéra, where he was

ABOVE: Niccolò Piccinni composed some 120 works.
ABOVE RIGHT: Antonio Salieri wrote his first opera aged 20.

Synopsis
La buona figliuola
('The Good-Natured Girl')
by Piccinni
Composed 1760
Premiered 1760, Rome
Libretto by Carlo Goldoni, after Samuel Richardson's novel *Pamela*

ACT I ◦

Cecchina, a servant girl, is secretly in love with the Marchese della Conchiglia. Believing that her dream will never come true, she runs away when he confesses his own affections for her. He asks one of the maids, Sandrina, to assure Cecchina of his intentions, but she also once had hopes of the Marchese and is now jealous that the servant Mengotto also loves Cecchina. Sandrina warns the Cavaliere Armidoro, who is engaged to the Marchese's sister Lucinda, that the Marchese is to marry a common gardener with no known parents, and a foreigner. To prevent this spoiling her own coming marriage, Lucinda arranges for Cecchina to leave the household. The Marchese discovers her in tears and

declares his love. Mengotto offers Cecchina his love again, but the Marchese surprises them together and rejects Cecchina.

ACT II ◦

The Marchese regrets his jealousy, but by now Cecchina has been arrested on Armidoro's orders. Mengotto rescues her from the armed escort, but the Marchese arrives and takes her away, leaving Mengotto ready to commit suicide. He is stopped by Tagliaferro, a German soldier looking for Mariandel, his colonel's daughter, who was lost there 20 years ago. Lucinda is made to believe that the worst is happening, but in fact Cecchina still refuses the Marchese. Tagliaferro tells the Marchese that Cecchina is indeed Mariandel. Together they come across Cecchina asleep, dreaming of her father.

ACT III ◦

To the satisfaction of Armidoro and Lucinda, the Marchese announces that he is to marry a German noblewoman and persuades Cecchina of her true identity, confirmed by a blue mark on her breast. Mengotto consoles himself with Sandrina.

---

regarded as Gluck's true successor. His exalted, original and rather austere post-Gluckian operas, *Les Danaïdes* ('The Danaids', 1784) ◦ **p. 109** and *Tarare* (1787), were his greatest accomplishments while in Paris. In 1788 he became *Kapellmeister* to the Austrian court, and in this post Salieri was in charge of Italian opera. Salieri's life

and work was now centred on Vienna, where he wrote some 30 operas, including both *opere serie* and *opere buffe*, including *La fiera di Venezia* ('The Fair of Venice', 1772) and *Falstaff* (1799), although he was interested in combining both elements in a single work. Most Salieri operas were produced in Vienna, but he also

---

A ROYAL PATRON OF OPERA: FREDERICK THE GREAT OF PRUSSIA

A composer, librettist or other musician who attracted a royal patron was "made" by the achievement and acquired personal influence as a result. In Germany this great good fortune devolved on anyone favoured by King Frederick II of Prussia, better known as Frederick the Great. Frederick was an immensely powerful and able ruler and a rigid disciplinarian and it was inevitable that he approached his great interest, *opera seria*, as a demanding martinet. His control over operas performed in Berlin was unprecedented, even in an age of royal despotism.

No libretto could reach Frederick's composers – Johann Adolf Hasse or Carl Heinrich Graun (1703–59) – unless the king had seen and approved it first. He also composed his own plots for operas and insisted on supervising the design of the stage sets and costumes. He was a constant, and daunting, presence at rehearsals where he halted proceedings if one of the singers deviated even slightly from the agreed score. However, Frederick's "reign" as master of Berlin opera was relatively brief. Military and political considerations intervened after the outbreak of the Seven Years' War in 1756, when all opera staff were dismissed and Berlin's influence on *opera seria* came to an end.

OTHER COMPOSERS

scored much success in Milan, Venice and Rome. Salieri's output observed the musical conventions of his era and show Gluck's influence, with accompanied recitative, dramatic choral writing and careful declamation. His popularity, considerable in his lifetime, failed to endure once that era was past.

SHIELD, WILLIAM
(1748–1829, ENGLISH)

William Shield, who was both composer and librettist, belonged to a trio of musicians – the others were Charles Dibdin and Stephen Storace – who dominated the English comic opera stage in the last two decades of the eighteenth century. Shield started out as an apprentice boat builder, but moved on to become a violinist. In 1772 he arrived in London from the north of England to take up a position of leader of the viola section of the Haymarket theatre orchestra. Shield's first work was an "afterpiece" called *The Flitch of Bacon* (1778). *The Flitch* was very successful and set up him as a popular composer, much-liked and admired by London audiences. Shield's output included more than 50 works, both full-length operas and afterpieces. Most of these were written for performance at Covent Garden, where Shield was the house composer for 13 years. As their titles indicate – *The Magic Cavern* (1784), *The Enchanted Castle* (1786) and *The Crusade* (1790) – a fair number of Shield's pieces dealt with exotic or magical themes and catered for the contemporary English taste for fantasy. In addition to writing his own works, Shield made adaptations of Grétry's *Richard Coeur-de-Lion*.

STORACE, STEPHEN
(1762–96, ENGLISH)

The English composer Stephen Storace wrote his first two operas *Gli sposi malcontenti* ('The Discontented Newlyweds', 1785) and *Gli equivoci* ('The Misunderstandings', 1786) for Vienna. His next two works, written for London after 1787, were not particularly successful, and subsequently Storace concentrated on English dialogue operas, either full-length or in the form of short afterpieces.

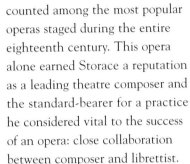

Storace's normal practice was to borrow music from other operas and sometimes from his own. Another of his methods was to rework operas written by other composers. This is what he did with, for example, *Doktor und Apotheker* ('Doctor and Apothecary', 1788) by Karl Ditters von Dittersdorf (1739–99). Success arrived at last with Storace's full-length opera *The Haunted Tower* (1789), which packed Drury Lane with enthusiastic audiences and counted among the most popular operas staged during the entire eighteenth century. This opera alone earned Storace a reputation as a leading theatre composer and the standard-bearer for a practice he considered vital to the success of an opera: close collaboration between composer and librettist. This, though, was no democratic arrangement: as Storace's own opera *The Pirates* (1792) indicates, the effect in practice was to increase the importance of the music, while the words were of lesser standing.

TRAETTA, TOMMASO
(1727–79, ITALIAN)

The Italian composer Tommaso Traetta reflected Gluck's ideals for opera, in which orchestration, choral scenes, dance and solo arias were combined. One example of these principles was Traetta's setting of an Italian translation of the text Rameau had used in his own *Hippolyte et Aricie* ('Hippolytus and Aricia', 1759) ➡ **p. 70**, which married the French and Italian opera styles. However, Traetta was much more than a copyist. He had a gift for impressive chorus work as shown in his *Ifigenia in Tauride* (1763). Just as admirable was his symphonic treatment of operatic themes and his ability to write graceful melody; this last was admirably displayed in his short solo songs known as *cavatinas* and in his *da capo* arias, a vocal form in which the first verse was repeated in the third. Traetta's early operas were written in the main for Naples and Parma, but in 1765 he moved to Venice where his output included two comic operas. In 1768 Traetta became another composer to be tempted from Western Europe to Russia, where the Empress Catherine the Great appointed him director of opera. For the Russian court, Traetta wrote *Antigona* (1772), which was based on an ancient Greek tragedy. However, life in Russia had a bad effect on his health and he departed in 1775. He died four years later in Venice.

LEFT: The Haymarket theatre in London where Shield led the violas.

Synopsis
Les Danaïdes ('The Danaids')
by Salieri
Composed 1784
Premiered 1784, Paris
Libretto by Marie François Louis Gand Leblanc Roullet, after Raniero de' Calzabigi

The opera is based on a Greek myth. Under the guise of an act of reconciliation, the daughters of Danaus (the Danaids) have been betrothed to the sons of Danaus's brother and enemy, now dead, Aegyptus. They swear an oath of friendship. Hypermnestra, the eldest daughter, loves Lynceus, the eldest son. However, Danaus tells his daughters that the marriages are a trick and part of his scheme to secure revenge. They must kill their husbands on their wedding night and, at his command, they take an oath to Nemesis, goddess of vengeance. All must conform or, the oracle has foretold, he himself will die. Hypermnestra does not take the oath, but her father demands that she too kill her husband. In her dilemma she prays for guidance and for death.

The wedding is celebrated with singing and dancing. Hypermnestra comes close to warning Lynceus of the plot. She pleads vainly to her father for mercy for Lynceus. After the wedding celebrations she tells Lynceus that they must part. Then they hear his brothers' cries, off stage, as they are attacked by their brides. Danaus tells them to pursue Lynceus, but he has fled: he returns to attack the palace and he slays the Danaids, finishing by burning down the palace. Hypermnestra faints. In the final scene the Danaids are seen in the underworld, with the Furies promising them eternal torment; Danaus is chained to a rock and a vulture attacks his entrails.

CLASSICAL

1750—1820

OTHER COMPOSERS

Librettists

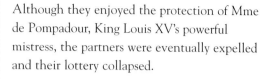

'MARTERN ALLER ARTEN'
Soprano aria from Act II of Mozart's opera *Die Entführung aus dem Serail*, which is set in Turkey. The aria is sung by the heroine Konstanze, who declares that nothing, not even torture and the threat of death is going to not make her give herself to her captor, Pasha Selim.

POPULAR MELODY

BEAUMARCHAIS, PIERRE-AUGUSTIN CARON DE (1732–99, FRENCH)

Pierre Beaumarchais, best known for two plays on the theme of "Figaro", was an amateur musician as well as a playwright. His first Figaro play, *Le barbier de Séville* (1775), was produced at the Comédie-Française and his second, *La folle journée, ou Le Mariage de Figaro* ('The Mad Day, or the Marriage of Figaro') was completed in 1781 and performed in 1784. The character of Figaro is said to have been a type of self-portrait of the playwright, who shared a colourful personality with the barber. At the time, just before the French Revolution, these plays were considered seditious, since they depicted an equality between servant and master. As operas, the music for the Figaro stories was written by Rossini and Mozart respectively. As a librettist, Beaumarchais was best known for the five-act opera *Tarare* (1787), produced in Paris. Gluck turned it down, and it was subsequently set to music by Salieri.

RIGHT: Beaumarchais was variously a clockmaker, a writer and a financier for the American colonies.

CALZABIGI, RANIERO DE' (1714–95, ITALIAN)

Calzabigi was best known for three libretti for Gluck – *Orfeo ed Euridice*, *Alceste* and *Paride ed Elena*, the last taking its eponymous characters, Paris and Helen, from the ancient Greek story of the Trojan War. In these libretti, Calzabigi moved away from the artificiality and limited conventions of *opera seria*, preferring simplicity and realistic drama. Calzabigi avoided stereotyping his characters. Rather, he drew them as real-life human beings and, although he gave them poetic words to sing, he made sure they followed natural speech patterns. In complete contrast to the intensive business of writing opera libretti, Calzabigi had his scallywag side. While in Paris, he and his brother opened a lottery and took as a partner the adventurer and lover Giacomo Casanova (1725–98).

Although they enjoyed the protection of Mme de Pompadour, King Louis XV's powerful mistress, the partners were eventually expelled and their lottery collapsed.

DA PONTE, LORENZO (1749–1838, ITALIAN)

Young Lorenzo Da Ponte's career as a priest came to an abrupt end when he was thrown out of his seminary for adultery. After settling in Vienna, he became poet to the imperial theatres without having written a single libretto. Nevertheless, Da Ponte produced an impressive adaptation of *Iphigénie en Tauride* (1783) by Nicolas-François Guillard (1752–1814). *Il rico d'un giorno* ('A Rich Man for a Day', 1784), which Da Ponte wrote for Antonio Salieri, was his first original libretto. Da Ponte was soon in demand in Vienna and of his total of 46 libretti, his most famous, written for Mozart, were *Le nozze di Figaro*, *Don Giovanni* and *Così fan tutte*. In 1791 Da Ponte fell out of favour in Vienna and left for London. Pursued by creditors, he moved on to the United States, where he established the Italian Opera House in New York in 1833.

FAVART, CHARLES SIMON (1710–92, FRENCH)

Charles Favart became director of the Comédie-Italienne in Paris in 1758. His 11-year term as director was evidently important in the theatre's history, for in 1871 it was renamed Salle Favart. As a librettist, Favart's output was prodigious: he wrote 150 libretti for composers such as Gluck, Philidor and Grétry. Favart's forte was the comic libretto, and he was the first really important writer in this genre. His early libretti were, among others, vaudevilles and *drames forains*, which were pieces meant to be performed at trade fairs. In the mid-eighteenth century Favart developed the *comédie mêlée d'ariettes*, a form of the libretto as a continuous story into which songs could be fitted. Favart also became known for his depictions of peasants, normally seen as lumpish oafs, but in his libretti they were treated more realistically and with greater respect. The realism of the later *opera comique* owed much to Favart's writing.

VAUDEVILLE

Vaudevilles, which took melodies from well-known operas, were popular tunes incorporated into works performed at popular venues such as the Comédie-Italienne in Paris. The vaudeville – taken from *voix de ville*, "voice of the town", had its own identifiable pattern. Its title was the same as the first line of the melody: this, in turn, was the first line as it appeared in the original opera. At the start, in the sixteenth century, "vaudeville" described a short song, usually on the subject of love. The melody was simple and made no serious demands on the singer. Repeated rhythms were a regular feature of the vaudeville. These tunes were sometimes called *fredons*, from the French verb *fredonner*, to hum, or *Pont du Neuf* melodies, after the broad bridge over the River Seine where minstrels gathered. When incorporated into opera, the mix of music and drama that resulted greatly influenced the development of *opéra comique*, which also included parodied versions of serious opera and other satirical material, some of it political. The vaudeville itself could be backed up by a vaudeville finale, in which the stanzas are shared out between each character and are then performed, ensemble-style, by the whole cast singing together.

GOLDONI, CARLO
(1707–93, ITALIAN)

By profession a lawyer in Pisa, Carlo Goldoni became resident poet at several Venetian opera houses. There he devised and specialized in the *opera buffa* libretto and wrote over 100, using pseudonyms for some of them. Goldoni left Venice for Paris in 1762 and for some years became well known and much admired for his work at the Comédie-Italienne. Goldoni's libretti had a seminal importance and exercised an influence over several major opera composers, including Mozart, Rossini and Gaetano Donizetti (1797–1848). Goldoni's influence was felt, too, in the peculiarly Italian genre, the *commedia dell'arte*, some of whose features found their way into comic opera. To these Goldoni added earthy characters and everyday situations that greatly humanized the genre and made it very popular in Italy. Goldoni himself classified his libretti as *drammi giocosi*, "dramas for fun", and was particularly known and appreciated for the opportunities he created for ensemble singing.

METASTASIO, PIETRO
(1698–1782, ITALIAN)

The Italian poet Pietro Metastasio wrote 27 large-scale opera libretti, some of which were set to music up to 100 times. He created a genre of opera – Metastasian opera – that not only bore his name, but set new patterns for libretti during the 50 years he spent in Vienna. Invited to the imperial court in 1729, Metastasio created a sensation the following year when Hasse used Metastasio's libretto for his *opera seria Artaserse* (1730). This introduced a new elegance into opera, which increased the prominence of solo singers. Metastasio became a particular favourite of performers, whose voices he allowed to be put on very effective display. Metastasio's libretti were faithful to the "doctrine of the affections", the dominant aesthetic theory of eighteenth-century opera. Although it restricted characterization and expression, Metastasio's use of the "doctrine" was tempered by his elegant verse, his vivid imagery and the sheer charm of his writing.

ROUSSEAU, JEAN-JACQUES
(1712–78, SWISS)

Best known as the Swiss political philosopher with a crucial influence on Romanticism and the French Revolution, Jean-Jacques Rousseau was also a composer, author and musicologist. In his most famous work, *Le devin du village* ('The Village Soothsayer', 1752), Rousseau's small talent confined him to simple melodies with simple accompaniments. What was really important was the way his liberal outlook in politics coloured his plot and its characters. *Le devin du village* demonstrated how simple, honest, virtuous, country folk overcame the corrupt, cynical aristocracy – an idealized, sentimental but recognizable metaphor for the Revolution of 1789. In addition to Rosseau's influence on the cast list of operas, in which simple folk were given more prominence, he was partly responsible for the increasing importance of the orchestra in early Romantic opera, where the instrumentalists were able to depict natural events – storm, rain, wind – when they were part of the plot.

SCHIKANEDER, EMANUEL
(1751–1812, AUSTRIAN)

Emanuel Schikaneder spent his early years as a nomadic musician, until he encountered a travelling theatrical troupe in Augsburg. He married the director's daughter and eventually took over the management of the troupe. However, Schikaneder was not just an opportunist with an eye for the boss's daughter and the boss's job. The eventual author of 50 libretti, including Mozart's last opera, *Die Zauberflöte*, Schikaneder ranked among the most talented comic singer-actors of his day. His meeting with Mozart, which took place in Salzburg in 1780, while the troupe was on tour, proved very fortuitous. Some years later, Schikaneder was in all sorts of trouble while running theatres in Regensburg and Vienna. He sank deep in debt, but was saved from financial ruin by the success of *Die Zauberflöte*. Subsequently, Schikaneder returned to theatrical management, but in 1806 he suddenly went mad and had to leave Vienna.

VERAZI, MATTIA
(c. 1730–94, ITALIAN)

The Italian librettist, Mattia Verazi, was the author of around 20 libretti. Among the first, most of them written for performances in Italy, was *Ifigenia in Aulide* (1751), which was set to music by Jommelli. Some 10 years later, Verazi was at the court in Mannheim, which later moved to Munich. Verazi went too. The most important libretti that he wrote while in Munich included *Sofonisba* (1762), written for music by Traetta, and an ancient Roman subject, *Lucio Silla* (1775), which Verazi wrote for Johann Christian Bach. Verazi did not confine himself to the Munich court, but wrote for other noble patrons, including *Fetonte* (1768) for the Duke of Württemberg. This, too, was set by Jommelli, who used it to write one of his most inventive scores.

Verazi and Jommelli frequently worked as a team and between them created several dramatic French-style operas for the ducal court at Stuttgart.

LEFT: An engraving showing Italian playwright Carlo Goldoni's home in Venice. Goldoni was also a trained lawyer who practised in Pisa.
BELOW: Emanuel Schikaneder became a friend of Mozart and was saved from poverty by being librettist for Die Zauberflöte.

Singers

BENUCCI, FRANCESCO
(c. 1745–1824, ITALIAN)

Francesco Benucci, an Italian bass, created the role of Figaro, in Mozart's *Le nozze di Figaro* in 1786. Benucci spent the first 13 years of his career as an opera singer, between 1769 and 1782, in Italy before joining the renowned Italian company in Vienna. Benucci remained in Vienna until 1795, with a short break in London in 1789. The London visit, which he made with the English soprano Nancy Storace – reputedly his mistress – was important for English opera audiences. Benucci and Storace introduced them to their first piece from a Mozart opera – 'Crudel! perchè?' from *Le nozze de Figaro*. Mozart himself admired Benucci's voice, calling it "especially good". It was deep, rounded and full, and despite the "weight" of the bass voice, Benucci was able to use it with delicacy. The Irish singer, Michael Kelly (1762–1826), observed that it had tenor-like qualities.

BERNACCHI, ANTONIO MARIA
(1690–1756, ITALIAN)

The Italian mezzo-soprano castrato Antonio Maria Bernacchi earned fame throughout Europe for his impressive technical virtuosity. Bernacchi performed in operas by most of the important composers of his time, including Handel. In 1716 and 1717, Bernacchi sang at the Haymarket, London in parts previously sung by women, including Goffredo in Handel's *Rinaldo*. However, Bernacchi was not popular with English audiences; the writer Charles Burney thought his singing "artificial". Bernacchi performed for the Elector of Bavaria in Munich between 1720 and 1735. During this period he won a singing contest in 1727 with the castrato Farinelli (1705–82), even though Farinelli was 20 years his junior and is now considered the most famous castrato. Nevertheless, Bernacchi was close to the end of his career and by 1736, when he founded a singing school in his native city, Bologna, his voice was in decline.

BERNASCONI, ANTONIA
(c. 1741 –c. 1803, GERMAN)

The soprano Antonia Bernasconi was the step-daughter of the Italian composer Andrea Bernasconi, *Kapellmeister* at the Munich court, and created the title role in Gluck's *Alceste* at its first performance in Vienna in 1767. Her father was in the service of the Duke of Württemberg, but after his death and her mother's remarriage, Antonia took her stepfather's name. She made her operatic debut in 1762, but seems to have had a somewhat "small" voice. Nevertheless, Antonia Bernasconi became prominent in Vienna in tragic roles. In 1770 she left Vienna for Milan, where she sang Aspasia in Mozart's *Mitridate*. Usually described as a "German" singer, Antonia Bernasconi became known for interpreting German-language roles in such operas as Gluck's *Iphigenie auf Tauris* in which she sang in Vienna in 1781.

CAVALIERI, KATHARINA
(1760–1801, AUSTRIAN)

Katharina Cavalieri, the Austrian soprano, was both the student and the mistress of the court composer Antonio Salieri. In 1775, when she was 15, she made her debut in Vienna in the role of Sandrina in *La finta giardiniera* by Pasquale Anfossi (1727–97). Her voice was expressive and "full" and she possessed a first-class singing technique. Though not beautiful, Cavalieri was graceful and Mozart was much impressed with

ABOVE: This engraving shows Katharina Cavalieri being accompanied on pianoforte by Mozart, who was much taken with the Austrian soprano.

her. He wrote for her the role of Konstanze in *Die Enteführung aus dem Serail*, and Elvira's aria 'Mi tradi' in the Vienna revival of *Don Giovanni*. Cavalieri complained that Elvira did not have sufficient music to sing and the special aria was Mozart's answer. In 1789 Cavalieri sang the role of the Countess Almaviva in a revival of *Le nozze di Figaro*. Considered one of the best among the very gifted singers in Vienna in the late eighteenth century, Cavalieri retired from the opera stage in 1793.

FERRARESE, ADRIANA
(c. 1759–c. 1803, ITALIAN)

Adriana Ferrarese was known as "La Ferrarese" from her birthplace, Ferrara. In 1785, in London, she sang in *Demetrio* by Luigi Cherubini (1760–1842). Lorenzo Da Ponte, her mentor, wrote libretti for operas by Martín y Soler and Salieri in which she took part. However, Mozart was not particularly impressed when she sang Susanna in a Vienna revival of *Le nozze di Figaro* in 1789: she failed to perform two arias he had specially written for her in the required "artless manner". Ferrarese was a difficult woman, described even by the faithful Da Ponte as a "troublemaker". The pair became the focus of scandals and they were made to leave Vienna in 1791. They went to Trieste, where Ferrarese sang in Mozart's *Così fan tutte* in 1797, having created the role in Vienna in 1790.

GUADAGNI, GAETANO
(1725–92, ITALIAN)

The castrato Gaetano Guadagni first sang as a contralto, but later retrained as a soprano. Although he had no early training, Handel hired him to sing in his oratorios *Messiah* and *Sampson*. In 1754–55 Guadagni made up for his lack of training by studying with Gioacchino Gizziello (1714–61) in

ABOVE: A Meissen teapot showing actor David Garrick as Richard III.

Lisbon and with the English actor David Garrick (1717–79) in London. After returning to mainland Europe in 1757 Guidagni sang in operas by Hasse and Traetta, and created the title roles in Gluck's *Orfeo ed Euridice* and *Telemaco*. In later years Guadagni performed in Munich and Potsdam before retiring to Padua in 1776. Charles Burney was a great admirer of Guadagni, praising him as an actor "without equal"'on stage and as an "impassioned and exquisite" singer. In retirement Guadagni continued to sing, notably in performances for the puppet opera house, which he built in his own home.

LEGROS, JOSEPH
(1739–93, FRENCH)

The French tenor and composer Joseph Legros made his debut at the Opéra in Paris, singing Titon in *Titon et Aurore* by Jean-Joseph Mondonville (1711–72). Subsequently he built up a considerable repertoire of roles in operas by Lully, Rameau, Grétry and Gluck, among others. One of his greatest roles was as Gluck's Orpheus, a role in which he was considered "a true to life actor, full of passion". Legros appeared in several other of Gluck's works, including roles as Achille in *Iphigénie en Aulide*, Cynire in *Echo et Narcisse* and Pylade in *Iphigénie en Tauride*. Legros' voice was flexible, with a brilliant high register, but on stage he was ungainly and awkward. He fought a running battle with his weight, but it eventually caught up with him. Legros became so fat that by 1783 he could not function properly on stage and had to retire.

LEVASSEUR, ROSALIE
(1749–1826, FRENCH)

For 10 years, between 1766 and 1775, Rosalie Levasseur, who appeared in cast lists as Mlle Rosalie, played minor roles, starting with Zäide in *L'Europe galante* by André Campra (1660–1744). In 1775, however, she caught the eye and the interest of the Austrian ambassador to Paris, Count Florimond Claude de Mercy-Argenteau, who decided to promote her talents. Mercy-Argenteau also made Rosalie Levasseur, as she once more became, his latest mistress. The ambassador's efforts on her behalf were brilliantly

successful. Levasseur became principal soprano at the Opéra and sang the title role in the first Paris performance of Gluck's *Alceste*. In addition, she created leading roles in *Armide* and in *Iphigénie en Aulide*. Levasseur had a powerful, but somewhat inflexible, voice, although it certainly suited the music of Gluck, who was both her teacher and her friend. As an actress, however, Rosalie Levasseur was considered the most outstanding of her time.

PACCHIEROTTI, GASPARO
(1740–1821, ITALIAN)

The Italian soprano castrato Gasparo Pacchierotti made his debut in Venice in 1766 in *Achille in Sciro* by Gassmann. He had joined the Teatro San Giovanni Grisostomo the previous year and after another six years he moved to the Teatro San Carlo in Naples. Pacchierotti made his first appearance at the King's Theatre, London in 1778 where he created a sensation. His triumphs in London were considered quite unparalleled. Also in 1778 he sang at the inauguration of the Teatro alla Scala in Milan. Pacchierotti's repertoire included Orpheus in Gluck's opera, and roles in operas by Jommelli. Haydn was impressed by Pacchierotti's beautiful voice, wide range, virtuosity and acting ability, and picked him to sing in his cantata *Arianna a Naxos*. Two years later, Pacchierotti sang at the inauguration of the Teatro la Fenice in Venice, but soon afterwards he retired to Padua.

RAAFF, ANTON
(1714–97, GERMAN)

The German tenor Anton Raaff studied in both Germany and Italy and made his debut in Munich in 1736. There followed performances in Italy in 1739, Bonn and Frankfurt in 1742 and in Vienna in 1749, where, according to Pietro Metastasio, he "sang like an angel". Raaff went on to perform in Madrid in 1755 and Naples in 1759. In 1770 he entered the service of Carl Theodor, the Elector Palatine. When Mozart first heard Raaff, he was not impressed, but changed his mind and wrote an aria especially for him. Raaff returned the

compliment and asked the elector to commission *Idomeneo* from Mozart. *Idomeneo* was produced in Munich in 1781, and Mozart wrote the title role with Raaff's vocal qualities in mind. One rare quality Raaff's voice possessed was longevity: it was still in top condition in 1787, when he was 73.

STORACE, NANCY
(1766–1817, ENGLISH)

The English soprano Nancy Storace was the sister of the composer Stephen Storace and sang in his operas at Drury Lane, London, from 1789 until his death in 1796. Nancy was only 10 years old when she made her debut as Cupid in *Le ali d'amore* by Venanzio Rauzzini (1746–1810). Five years later, in Florence, still only 15, Nancy Storace outmatched the great castrato soprano Luigi Marchesi (1755–1829). Marchesi was one of the greatest contemporary castrati, with a sizeable ego to match, and Storace had to go. In 1783 Storace's gift for comedy was earning her great popularity in Vienna, where Mozart was impressed by her. Mozart started to write a part for her, as Emilia in *La sposa deluso* ('The Deceived Bridegroom') but the opera was unfinished. However, Susanna in Mozart's *Le nozze di Figaro* was also written for Storace and was one of her greatest successes.

ABOVE: Nancy Storace, the eighteenth-century English singer.

Early Romantic

The early nineteenth century was a period of insurgence in Europe, beginning with the French Revolution in 1789 to the uprisings in around 1848. The Industrial Revolution, which began in Britain before spreading south to the rest of Europe, was also making its mark. These two strands of revolution brought transformations on society: growing awareness of national identity, social development, growth of cities and important technological advances, all of which were reflected in the arts.

INDIVIDUAL EXPRESSION

The first two decades of the nineteenth century also marked a rejection of the scientific certainty that had defined the Enlightenment: symmetry, classical balance and simplicity were replaced gradually by Romantic expressivity, individualism and grand gestures. Distinctive traits – many of which derived from French philosopher Jean-Jacques Rousseau's writings – included an interest in nature, the supernatural, the relatively recent past (the Middle Ages in particular) and individual and national identity. Closer links were forged between the arts and social and political reality. In literature, Goethe's *Faust* and Walter Scott's chivalric novels were seen as an embodiment of the age. Of all the arts, it was music that came to be seen as the ideal means of expression, partly because of its ambiguous, indefinable quality.

THE SHOCK OF THE NEW

Classical structures were retained in music, but were expanded upon, and new ways to shock or move were sought. Opera increasingly used realistic settings and historical events for its subjects; orchestral music was inspired by historial or literary themes, and virtuoso concertos and intimate mood pieces focused on the expression of the individual. The most influential developments in opera took place in Italy and France, and instrumental music flourished in German-speaking lands.

EARLY ROMANTIC

Introduction

The Romantic period in opera, music, literature and art lasted more than a century overall, from around 1790, the year after the French Revolution, to 1910, four years before the outbreak of the First World War. In this context, the meaning of "romantic" went far beyond the usual amorous connotations: it stood for the imaginative, the exotic, the fantastic, even the occult. This new ethos drew a line under the Classical era, which emphasized restraint and discipline, balance, good taste and expressiveness, but not the sort that spilled over into sentimentality or blurred too far the edges of musical convention.

NEW SOCIAL AND POLITICAL IDEAS

In time, Romantic music was revealed as a quantum leap away from the set-piece formulae of Baroque. It was, in its way, a metaphor for the French Revolution that caused a fundamental and ultimately fatal crack in the armour of absolute kingship in Europe. It was not simply a matter of exchanging a monarchy for a republic. The Revolution let loose new social and political ideas, which included the notion that a country belonged not to its king, but to its people. The slogan of the Revolution, "*liberté, egalité, fraternité*", and its defiant nationalistic anthem the '*Marseilleise*' were

only the start of an upheaval that made once-seditious ideas mainstream and one-time heresies respectable.

IDEALOGY AND MYTHOLOGY

Opera reflected the new situation, in which a particular *bête-noire* was the privilege once reserved for royalty and aristocracy. The ancient Greek and Roman myths, which now lost favour, had been the staple of Baroque opera plots; they were now identified with the unfair social advantages monarchs and nobles had once enjoyed and the exploitation of the peasantry for which their supremacy stood. Kings, queens, emperors and princes ceased to be the heroes or heroines of opera. Their place was taken by stories featuring ordinary people, mainly young men who had sacrificed themselves during the Revolution.

THE ORDINARY HEROES OF "RESCUE OPERA"

Several such men became the subjects of operas, such as *Le siège de Lille* ('The Siege of Lille', 1826) by Rodolphe Kreutzer, which was staged barely three months after the siege in question was lifted in October 1792. The new heroes also included victims of political and other persecution and this produced a new genre, the "rescue opera". In rescue opera, the plot included the saving of a hero, heroine or a persecuted group from prison or some other dangerous threat. The composer Henri-Monton Berton, for one, lost no time in getting the first of these rescue operas into production, with his *Les rigeurs du cloître* ('The Rigours of the Cloister'). The victims in this opera, which was staged in 1790, were monks persecuted by a vengeful authority bent on destroying their way of life.

OPÉRA-COMIQUE

The Opéra-Comique company was established in 1714 to offer French opera as an alternative to the Italian opera that dominated the continent at the time. After several misadventures, which included a bankruptcy, the Opéra-Comique settled at the Salle Feydeau in 1805. Here, its essentially radical approach to opera soon became clear. At this time, composers such as Etienne-Nicolas Méhul, François-Adrien Boieldieu (1775–1834) and Nicolo Isouard (1775–1818) were pioneering a new genre, the *opéra-comique*, which was not yet acceptable to the rather hidebound Paris Opéra. The Opéra-Comique, by contrast, gladly embraced the genre and its early practitioners, and its stage was the scene of sensational premieres that became the talk of Paris opera goers all season long. The Opéra-Comique, which moved to the Salle Favart in 1840, continued in the same vein, featuring unconventional, new or foreign works that were turned down by the more conservative management of the Paris Opéra. Unlike its rival, where spoken dialogue on stage was banned, the Opéra-Comique made itself a home for works that used this technique and included in its repertory operas by the "new wave" of composers such as Daniel-François-Esprit Auber (1782–1871), Adolphe Adam (1803–56) and, much later, Jules Massenet (1842–1912).

ABOVE: The Paris Opéra-Comique, shown here in a nineteenth century engraving, specialized in unconventional and controversial works.

ROLE OF OPERA AS ENTERTAINMENT

All this meant that opera was in danger of being politicized. If this trend went unchecked, opera could cease to be entertainment and become propaganda. However, the didactic approach did not prove popular even with the patriotic, nationalist audiences in France. They, at least, had not forgotten the role of opera as entertainment, and fortunately there were more subtle ways to inject into the action the social and psychological changes initiated by the Revolution. Four operas by Etienne-

Nicolas Méhul (1763–1817) typified this less blatant approach: *Euphrosine* 1790), *Stratonice* (1792), *Mélidore et Phrosine* (1794) and *Ariodant* (1799). These featured characters marooned in isolation by problems of jealousy, frustration, or anger, problems they were unable to resolve. Far from being secure, if limited, in the assigned social place as they existed pre-Revolution, these characters were cast adrift in the storm of their own emotions.

BELOW: Liberty Leading the People, Eugene Delacroix 's Romantic representation of the French uprising in July 1830. The artist has depicted himself (wearing a top hat) towards the left of the painting.

THE ESSENCE OF ROMANTICISM

This was the essence of Romanticism and the new ethos was reflected in Méhul's music. Unlike some Baroque composers, such as Antonio Salieri (1750–1825), Méhul was not afraid to experiment. He believed that expression in music did "not dwell in melody alone ... everything concurs either to create or destroy it – melody, harmony, modulation, rhythm, instrumentation, the choice of deep or high registers ... a quick or slow tempo".

EARLY ROMANTIC

1800—1845

MORTE OR DEATH OPERAS

Around this time, at the dawn of Romantic music, Italian as well as French opera was affected by the more realistic, more sober atmosphere that prevailed after the Revolution. This, after all, had been an appallingly bloodthirsty event, in which the fury of the disadvantaged had let loose a tide of manic vengeance, and Madame Guillotine made severed heads rolling into baskets a popular entertainment. As a mirror of its time, at least in the 1790s, opera could no longer countenance the regulation happy ending of *opéra seria* ➡ **p. 53**. *Opéra seria* had been welcomed in 1772 by the critic Antonio Planelli as a sign of society's "gentility, urbanity and clemency". However, these were qualities well and truly buried by the Revolution and from the last decade of the eighteenth century, a long series of morte or death operas was performed.

GOTHIC THEMES

This was not an entirely new genre, but had been prefigured by operas such as *La vendetta di Nino* ('Nino's Revenge', 1786) by Alessio Prati in which a son murdered his mother on stage, watched by the ghost of the husband whose death she had caused. Under the impetus of the Revolution and its fearful events, the death opera caught the imagination of audiences and began to create a new, somewhat morbid, taste in entertainment. In 1796 this development was praised in a review written after a performance at La Scala ➡ **p. 158**, Milan, of *Giulietta e Romeo*, composed by Niccolo Zingarelli and based on William Shakespeare's tragedy *Romeo and Juliet*.

   "The gloominess of the story ... appears somewhat weighty to those who ... are used to

RIGHT: The Scots author Sir Walter Scott, whose novels were worked into libretti for composers such as Donizetti, Bellini and Rossini.
BELOW: The grim events of the French Revolution and the constant presence of the guillotine inspired a new wave of death operas.

INTRODUCTION

going to the theatre to be entertained and not distressed. But if the action demands, if the music responds to the text, one cannot but praise the poetry and the composer who has dressed it with such beautiful and expressive notes."

A REPERTORY IS DEVELOPED

As soon became clear, the action did demand, the music did respond, and suitable stories were salted to provide opera plots. In this context, the writings of the prolific Scots novelist, Sir Walter Scott (1771–1832) proved a gold mine for librettists on the hunt for material. Scott was so successful in giving them what they were looking for that 19 of his novels were turned into a total of 63 operas; *Ivanhoe* (1819) was used 10 times and another novel, *Kenilworth* (1821), 11 times. The Scott operas were written by several composers, notably Gioachino Rossini (1792–1868), Gaetano Donizetti (1797–1848) and Vincenzo Bellini (1801–35), whose work scaled the pinnacle of the *bel canto* ➠ **p. 130** singing style.

EXOTIC INFLUENCE OF NOVELS

Some of Scott's novels, such as *Ivanhoe*, *Quentin Durward* (1823), or *The Talisman* (1825) catered for another new preference among opera audiences – their interest in operas with exotic locales, gothic story lines and medieval settings.

Others, such as *The Bride of Lammermoor* (1819), on which Donizetti based his opera *Lucia di Lammermoor* (1835) ➠ **p. 137**, amply fulfilled the requirements of the death opera; Walter Scott provided the chance for Donizetti to depict the heroine, Lucia, wandering the stage overtaken by madness and soaked in the blood of the husband she had just married – and murdered. As a genre, the death opera had a very long-term effect: throughout the nineteenth century and into the twentieth, the majority of operatic heroes and heroines routinely died on stage before the final curtain came down.

RIGHT: Andrea Rost as Lucia in the Royal Opera House's 2003 production of Donizetti's Lucia di Lammermoor, *based on a Sir Walter Scott novel.*

MASTERY OF STAGE DESIGN: PIERRE-LUC-CHARLES CICÉRI (1782–1868)

The artistry, ingenuity and creativity of Pierre Cicéri, the greatest designer in early nineteenth-century France, made him an almost legendary figure in the world of Romantic opera. Originally, Cicéri trained as a singer, but turned to painting and became an assistant at the Paris Opéra in 1806. When he graduated to stage design, he made use of the latest technological innovations, for example using gaslight for *Aladin, ou La lampe merveilleuse* ('Aladdin, or the Marvellous Lamp', 1822) by Nicolo Isouard (1775–1818). Cicéri's instinctive appreciation of architecture and sense of history enabled him to create on-stage panoramas wonderfully keyed into the grandiose drama of French *grand opéra*. For Auber's *La muette de Portici* ('The Dumb Girl of Portici', 1828) he constructed a view of Vesuvius and its surrounding countryside and used carefully controlled fireworks to simulate a volcanic eruption. Cicéri devised a mobile panorama, in which a backcloth was turned on a revolving drum, gradually unwinding a scene so that a boat, static on stage, looked as though it was sailing along a river. The same device, when used in Auber's *Le lac de fées* ('The Lake of Fairies', 1839) simulated a descent from the sky down to Earth.

INTRODUCTION

KEY COMPOSERS

Ludwig van Beethoven

Ludwig van Beethoven (1770–1827) was born in Bonn, Germany, to a musical family, on 16 December 1770. He started composing at the age of 11 and experienced opera from the inside when he joined the Bonn court orchestra as a viola player in 1789. His letters reveal that from his early years in Vienna, where he moved in 1792, he was eager to compose music for the stage. In the event, though, it was to be over a decade before he completed the first version of *Fidelio* ➼ p. 121.

AN ABORTED ROMAN OPERA

In 1803 Beethoven got as far as writing the first scene of a *grand opera*, *Vestas Feuer*, to a libretto by Emanuel Schikaneder (1751–1812), Mozart's collaborator on *Die Zauberflöte* ('The Magic Flute', 1791) ➼ p. 98. But the project foundered on the incongruity between the ancient Roman setting and what the composer called "language and verses that could only have come out of the mouths of our Viennese apple-women". Beethoven was, though, to rework a G major duet from the abandoned opera as the climactic love duet for Leonore and Florestan in *Fidelio*.

A TRUE STORY

Much more to Beethoven's taste was Jean-Nicholas Bouilly's *Léonore, ou L'amour conjugale* ('Leonore, or Conjugal love'), based on a true incident in the author's native Tours. Beethoven came across this libretto at the end of 1803 and gave it to the Viennese court secretary Joseph Sonnleithner to rework in German. *Fidelio* – the title was changed, apparently against Beethoven's wishes, to avoid confusion with operas by Pierre Gaveaux (1798) and Ferdinando Paer (1804) – finally saw the stage on 20 November 1805. It lasted for only three performances, partly because Beethoven's supporters had fled Vienna as Napoleon's troops advanced, and partly because it was deemed too repetitious and undramatic. Beethoven tightened the score for a revival in 1806, but this, too, failed. It was only in 1814, after wholesale revisions, that *Fidelio* finally triumphed.

HIS SEARCH FOR LIBRETTI

In 1807 Beethoven had offered to compose an opera each year in exchange for a fixed income. He continued to cast around for suitable libretti, making sketches for an opera on a German adaptation of *Macbeth* (1808–11) and around 1823–24, he was seriously contemplating a "fairy-tale" opera, *Melusine*, to a libretto by the Austrian poet Franz Grillparzer. But *Fidelio* remained Beethoven's sole opera, and the work he cherished above all others, yet of which he said shortly before his death: "Of all my children, this is the one that caused me the most painful birth-pangs and the most sorrows".

'IN DES LEBENS FRÜHLINGSTAGEN'

The generally lofty tone of *Fidelio* has precluded the kind of popular hit that gets piped into shopping malls. However, the nostalgic opening of Florestan's great aria '*In des Lebens Frühlingstagen*' inspired many nineteenth-century composers, notably Schubert.

POPULAR MELODY

Operas

1805; rev. 1806; 1814 *Fidelio*

Timeline

BEETHOVEN AND MOZART

Mozart was, with Handel, the composer Beethoven revered above all others. And *Fidelio* could hardly have been written without the example of Mozart's mature operas. Yet with his strongly ethical, idealistic outlook, even to the point of priggishness, Beethoven regarded works such as *Don Giovanni* (1787) and, especially, *Cosi fan tutte* (1790) as flippant and immoral. His favourite Mozart opera by far was *Die Zauberflöte*, though we can guess that he valued it more for its Masonic solemnity and portrayal of ideal love than for the Viennese pantomime antics of Papageno.

Beethoven may have been repelled by the "La donna è mobile" sentiments of *Cosi fan tutte*, but at least two of its numbers left their mark on *Fidelio*: the "canon" quartet in the second-act finale of *Cosi* surely lies behind the sublime quartet '*Mir ist so wunderbar*' (I feel so strange) in Act I, where the four characters voice their contrasting emotions in turn; and the opening of Leonore's '*Komm, Hoffnung*', with its elaborate *obbligato* for three horns, recalls Fiordiligi's second-act aria in the same key. Other numbers, including the trio '*Gut, Söhnchen gut*' (Good, my son, good), look back to *Die Zauberflöte*; while the quintet of transfigured stillness at the heart of the second finale, with its ethereal oboe melody, evokes such transcendent Mozartian moments as the final union of Pamina and Tamino and the Countess's forgiveness of her errant husband in *Figaro*.

ABOVE: A 2003 Holland Park Opera production of Beethoven's Fidelio, directed by Olivia Fuchs.
LEFT: Ludwig van Beethoven, whose compositions included only one opera.

Fidelio

Fidelio by Beethoven

Composed	1805; rev. 1806, 1814
Premiered	1805, Vienna (early version)/1814, Vienna (final version)
Libretto	by Joseph Sonnleithner (early version)/Friedrich Treitschke (final version), after Jean-Nicolas Bouilly

Premiered at Vienna's Kärntnertor Theater on 23 May 1814, the final version of *Fidelio* is a fundamentally different opera from the 1805 original. There is now much less emphasis on the gaoler's daughter Marzelline and her world of *Singspiel* domesticity. Although the fate of Florestan and Leonore remains central, the individual characterization becomes more idealized and stereotyped. The human element is now subordinate to the opera's moral message; and the prisoners, released from darkness into daylight, become archetypes of oppressed humanity. *Fidelio* in its final form is above all a celebration of abstract ideals dear to Beethoven: freedom, heroic courage in the face of tyranny, perfect womanhood and the brotherhood of man.

The insistent, emphatic tone of *Fidelio's* choral finale, drawing its power from massed forces and sheer reiteration, shows Beethoven's debt to Cherubini and the composers of the so-called French Revolutionary School. A more pervasive influence on the opera is Mozart, though a movement like the quartet in Act II has a dynamic force unique to Beethoven. The quartet encapsulates the opera's movement from oppression to liberation, and contains its most thrilling coups, above all the offstage trumpet call that heralds the final denouement. It is strokes like this, together with such moments as Leonore's aria of hope and resolve '*Komm, Hoffnung*' ('Come, hope'), and the dazed emergence of the prisoners into daylight in the first-act finale, that can make *Fidelio* the most elementally moving of all operas.

Synopsis

Fidelio by Beethoven

ACT I

In a Seville prison, Marzelline, daughter of Rocco the jailer, rejects the advances of Jacquino, her father's assistant and porter, whom she had previously agreed to marry. Although feeling pity for Jacquino, Marzelline is smitten by the conscientious new assistant, Fidelio. Fidelio is in reality the noblewoman Leonore; she has disguised herself as a boy and gained employment at the prison in the hope of finding her husband, Florestan, who disappeared two years previously under suspicious circumstances. Knowing that Pizarro, the prison governor, was an enemy of Florestan, she has high hopes of finding him here. Fidelio is understandably disturbed by Marzelline's affections, especially when Rocco blesses their union, but Leonore sees that she can use it to her advantage.

Leonore asks Rocco whether she can accompany him to the deepest dungeons, where the most closely guarded prisoners are kept. She learns of one prisoner that only Rocco is allowed to see; he has been there for about two years, is near death and is treated harshly by Pizarro. Believing it to be Florestan, Leonore again pleads to assist Rocco on his rounds; the jailer agrees to ask Pizarro.

Pizarro receives news that Don Fernando, the Minister for Justice, is coming to inspect the prison, after hearing reports of unjust imprisonment. Panicking, Pizarro organizes a watch and, paying Rocco, orders him to murder the prisoner. Rocco refuses, but is nevertheless charged with the task of digging the prisoner's grave. Pizarro resolves to kill the prisoner himself.

Leonore arranges for the prisoners to walk in the courtyard. They enjoy their brief moments of freedom before Pizarro orders them back to their cells. Rocco, having persuaded Pizarro to allow Fidelio in the deepest dungeons, asks Fidelio to help him dig the grave. Leonore is horrified, but follows him as he descends.

ACT II

In the deepest dungeon, Florestan languishes in chains. He has a vision of Leonore, in the form of an angel, coming to rescue him, and lies down in exhaustion. Rocco and Fidelio enter and begin to dig the grave. It is too dark for Leonore to distinguish Florestan in the cell, but when he speaks she knows it is indeed her husband. Florestan asks Rocco who is keeping him prisoner and, when told it is Pizarro, asks for a message to be sent to his wife. Rocco is afraid to tackle Pizarro, but he and Fidelio defy his orders by offering bread and water to the grateful prisoner.

Rocco signals to Pizarro that the grave is ready and the governor rushes in to kill Florestan. But as he raises the dagger Leonore, revealing her true identity, throws herself between them and threatens Pizarro with a pistol. A trumpet sounds in the distance, signalling the arrival of Don Fernando. Pizarro, furious at realizing it is too late for him to kill Florestan, is led away by Rocco. Leonore and Florestan enjoy an ecstatic reunion.

Outside the prison, Don Fernando announces that he has been sent to end Pizarro's tyranny and release all the prisoners that are being held unjustly. He is surprised and overjoyed to find his old friend Florestan alive; Rocco relates the fantastic events that have taken place. Marzelline realizes her misplaced love and Pizarro is arrested, while Leonore is given the keys for Florestan's chains. She releases him and everyone celebrates the virtues of love and fidelity.

KEY COMPOSERS

Carl Maria von Weber

Carl Maria von Weber (1786–1826) was a teenage prodigy who wrote his first opera aged 14. By 1804 Weber, still only 18, was musical director in Breslau. By the time he had moved on to Stuttgart, Weber had reworked his first opera, *Das Waldmädchen* ('The Forest Girl', 1810), and gave it the new title of *Silvana*. With *Silvana*, first performed in Frankfurt in 1810, Weber's music prefigured his masterpiece, *Der Freischütz* ('The Free-Shooter', 1821) ●▶ p. 123 and revealed an impressive sense of theatre.

INGENIOUS IDEAS

The composer made life difficult for himself by creating a heroine who was unable to talk, much less sing. Even so, he met the challenge with some ingenuity, making his orchestration "speak" for her and speak lyrically, too. Weber first came across the story of *Der Freischütz* in 1810, but his first attempt at writing an opera on the subject foundered when his librettist deserted him. Eleven years passed before the opera finally triumphed in Berlin. By that time, Weber had occupied posts at Prague and Dresden and in both cities set about reforming the management of opera. He hired performers as ensemble singers rather than as opera "stars".

RADICAL REHEARSALS

He formulated a new, radical schedule of rehearsals that began with the performers absorbing the drama of the opera before tackling the music. He rearranged both the chorus and the seating of the orchestra and, in Dresden, brought German opera to the fore as his answer to the rival Italian opera performing there. Weber was influential in promoting what Richard Wagner (1813–83) later termed *Gesamtkunstwerk* – "the total work of art" – in which all related arts are blended into a new creation. Tragically, time was short for the consumptive Weber, who died aged 39 in 1826.

LEFT: Carl Maria von Weber, who began writing operas at an early age.

'LEISE, LEISE FROMME WEISE' (QUIET, QUIET, PIOUS PROPHECY!)

In Act II, Scene One of *Der Freischütz*, the heroine Agathe prays to God for help, for herself and her lover, Max, who must win a shooting competition if he is to marry her. Then, she sings of her joy as he comes into sight.

POPULAR MELODY

Operas

1800	*Das Waldmädchen*
1801–02	*Peter Schmoll und seine Nachbarn*
1804–05	*Rübezahl*
1808–10	*Silvana*
1810–11	*Abu Hassan*
1817–21	*Der Freischütz*
1820–21	*Die drei Pintos*
1822–23	*Euryanthe*
1825–26	*Oberon*

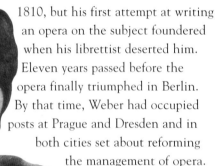

Timeline

1786	Carl Maria Weber born, Oldenburg, Germany
1798	Is taught by Michael Haydn in Salzburg
1800	Moves to Freiburg, and composes first opera, *Das Waldmädchen*
1803	Returns to Salzburg and completes *Peter Schmoll und seine Nachbarn*
1803	Begins to study under Abbé Vogler
1804	Weber appointed *Kappellmeister* at Breslau; begins work on *Rübezahl*
1806	Quits Breslau for Karlsruhe
1807	Is offered court secretarial post at Stuttgart
1808	Begins work on new version of *Das Waldmädchen*, called *Silvana*
1810	Falsely accused of embezzlement and banished from Stuttgart
1810	Moves to Darmstadt and takes lessons from Vogler once more; writes *Abu Hassan*
1810	Premiere of Silvana, Frankfurt
1813	Appointed director of Prague Opera
1817	Becomes Court *Kappellmeister* at Dresden, briefed to establish German national opera
1820	Begins work on *Die drei Pintos*, a comic opera which he never completes
1821	Completes *Der Freischütz*, which premieres in Berlin with great success
1822	Begins work on *Euryanthe* for Kärntnerthor Theatre, Vienna
1823	*Euryanthe* is produced, Vienna
1824	Commissioned by manager of Covent Garden to write an opera, *Oberon*
1826	Weber and family move to London, *Oberon* premieres at Covent Garden
1826	Weber dies, London

THE REMINISCENCE MOTIF

The reminiscence motif – *Reminiscenzmotiv* or *Errinerungsmotiv* in German – is an example of a dramatic technique that only opera and music can use to utmost effect. French *opéra-comique* ●▶ p. 116 made frequent use of the motif between the end of the eighteenth century and the beginning of the nineteenth. The motif is a short theme that is memorable, perhaps consisting of only a few notes, but which can be identified with some feature in the opera; this might be a person, a place, an object, an event occurring in the plot or simply an idea. Introduced at the first appearance of this feature, the motif can recall it to the minds of the audience when it is played again later on. The reminiscence motif was a forerunner of the leitmotif – the leading motif. However, the reminiscence motif was less expressive and was not designed to alter its form so as to indicate change in a situation that had taken place since it was last heard in the opera. One example of the reminiscence motif occurred in *Zampa* (1831) by Ferdinand Hérold, where the same sequence of chords is heard whenever a statue depicting Zampa, the Pirate's former bride, is involved in the action.

Der Freischütz
('The Free-Shooter')

Der Freischütz by Weber

Composed	1817–21
Premiered	1821, Berlin
Libretto	by Friedrich Kind, after Johann August Apel and Friedrich Laun

The Faustian theme, with its connotations of the black arts, was not new to opera when Weber wrote *Der Freischütz*. Since 1796 there had already been eight operas based on the sixteenth-century legend as composers responded to one of the most seductive themes of the early Romantic era: a pact with the devil for personal gain or, in the influential drama by Johann Wolfgang von Goethe (1749–1832), for the chance of immortality. Among these early Romantic operas, Weber's achieved much greater impact than most, as well as far greater popularity. His treatment of the theme was imaginative and his melodies were inspired by well-known German folk songs. There were echoes of the *Singspiel* tradition that originated in the sixteenth century, and a skilful recreation in music of the mysteries and supernatural feel of the forest. In this, *Der Freischütz* was the embodiment of German Romanticism, familiar in its traditional musical forms, yet eerie in its occult atmosphere. However, *Der Freischütz* was not just a work for German consumption. It had universal and international appeal and was among the most popular and successful operas ever written. The libretto, by Friedrich Kind (1768–1843) was translated into no less than 25 languages.

BELOW: Gidon Saks in English National Opera's 1999 production.

Synopsis
Der Freischütz by Weber

ACT I

Max, a forest ranger, is in love with Agathe, daughter of the head ranger Kuno. Her father agrees to the match, on the condition that Max passes a test of marksmanship. Max's shooting skills get worse as the day of the test draws near. A peasant, Kilian, beats him in a competition and the people mock him. Caspar, who also loves Agathe, offers to help Max win Prince Ottaker's shooting competition the next day. He reveals that seven magic bullets can be cast, which will automatically reach the marksman's intended target. Unbeknownst to Max, Caspar has sold his soul to the devil, represented by Samiel, the "Dark Huntsman", and is due to forfeit his life. Caspar hopes that he can arrange for another human life to be sacrificed in his place. To prove to Max the power of the bullets, Caspar hands him a loaded rifle. Max, discharging it in into the air, manages to shoot an eagle flying high above. Impressed, Max agrees to accompany Caspar to Wolf's Glen at midnight, in order to cast the magic bullets.

ACT II

In her room, Agathe is feeling uneasy. She tells her relative Aennchen that she has encountered a hermit, who warned her of danger and gave her flowers to offer her protection. A picture of one of Agathe's ancestors has also fallen from the wall, injuring her; she sees this as a bad omen; Aennchen tries to amuse her.

Agathe and Aennchen are horrified when Max arrives and tells them that he has shot a deer near Wolf's Glen and is going to retrieve it. They plead with him not to go, telling him the glen is haunted, but he is resolute.

At Wolf's Glen, Caspar summons up Samiel and they prepare to forge the magic bullets. Samiel agrees to allow Caspar three more years of life in exchange for a substitute human life. Samiel will be in control of the seventh bullet; Caspar suggests that it be aimed at Agathe. Max arrives and they begin to cast the bullets. Various fantastic and terrible visions appear to Max, including the ghost of his mother, who warns him of the danger he will face. There is also a ghostly hunt with fire-breathing animals, and a vision of Agathe dying.

ACT III

During the next day's hunt Max is, unsurprisingly, rather successful. He only has one magic bullet remaining – the one controlled by the "Dark Huntsman" – for the prince's shooting contest. Meanwhile, Agathe is filled with a sense of foreboding. She has had a bad dream, in which she took the form of a dove and was shot by Max. Aennchen again seeks to comfort her. The bridesmaids then arrive with her bridal wreath in a box, but she opens it to reveal a funeral wreath. Everyone is shocked. Agathe fashions a new bridal wreath from the flowers given to her by the hermit.

At the contest, a dove is selected as Max's target. Agathe, distraught, tries to stop him, crying out that she is the dove, but Max fires his gun. Both Agathe and Caspar fall to the ground. However, Agathe, protected by the hermit, survives; the bullet was deflected by the bridal wreath and she has merely fainted. Samiel chooses to take Caspar's life rather than Max's; Caspar dies, cursing the world.

Max offers an explanation of the events to Prince Ottaker, who at first decides to exile him. However, the hermit declares that shooting contests should be abolished and Max given another chance. The prince agrees to give Max a year to prove himself; after that time he is free to marry Agathe. Everyone rejoices in God's mercy.

BELOW: The Hunstmen's Chorus from Weber's Der Freischütz.

EARLY ROMANTIC

1800—1845

KEY COMPOSERS

KEY COMPOSERS

Gioachino Rossini

By the age of 14, Gioachino Rossini (1792–1868) could play the violin, cello, harpsichord and horn and had written a *buffo*-style *cavatina*, a short solo song. In 1806 Rossini was studying at the Bologna Conservatory and wrote his first opera, *Demetrio e Polibio*. The next year he produced his first professional work – *La cambiale di matrimonio* ('The Bill of Marriage').

A RUNAWAY SUCCESS

The lyrical charm of Rossini's music soon made him a run-away success. His *L'inganno felice* ('The Happy Deception', 1812) and a commission from La Scala, Milan, *La pietra del paragone* ('The Touchstone', 1812) entranced opera audiences, who loved their graceful melodies, amusing characters and ingenious plots. At barely 20 years of age, Gioachino Rossini was made.

LEFT: Gioachino Rossini, who wrote witty, lyrical operas with innovative orchestrations and catchy melodies.

A PROFUSION OF OPERAS

In the next 17 years, until he retired, a profusion of operas flowed from Rossini's pen. He produced four in the six months between November 1812 and May 1813. One of these, the darkly dramatic *Tancredi* (1813), made Rossini internationally famous. The opera's appeal owed much to his sensitive handling of heroic virtues, and innovative orchestration, most particularly his use of woodwind instruments to track the vocal line and give it added expressiveness. For Rossini, *Tancredi* was a venture into sombre territory, but with his next work, *L'italiana in Algeri* ('The Italian Girl in Algiers', 1813) ➡ **p. 126** he returned to the operatic romp, full of subterfuge, false identities and impudent ruses.

HIS LIVELY MASTERPIECE

Rossini was now in great demand not only by audiences, but also by opera-house managements. In around 1814 the composer accepted a six-year contract from Domenico Barbaia (1778–1841) as music director of the Teatro San Carlo and the

ROSSINI'S INNOVATIONS

Gioachino Rossini dominated opera in the first half of the nineteenth century and many of his innovations were used as models by later composers for their own works. Rossini was the first opera composer to do away with the unaccompanied recitative, which had the effect of "halting" the music and robbing it of homogeneity. Another of his innovations was the so-called "Rossini rocket". This gave the orchestra a gradual crescendo in which the same passage was repeated over and over again, with mounting drama and increasing excitement as more and more instruments joined in. Rossini used this device to considerable effect in the accompaniment to Don Basilio's aria '*La calunnia*' ('Calumny') in the first act of *Il barbiere di Siviglia*. The aria starts simply and quietly, but builds to a thrilling climax. Opera singers in Rossini's time were assuming a new, personal importance. Although it had been the custom to leave them to devise their own vocal ornamentation and cadenzas, Rossini did not trust them to handle it in a way that served his opera rather than their own egos. He therefore made a point of writing out his own ornamentations and cadenzas and making sure the singers performed them.

ABOVE: Rossini remained an extremely popular composer throughout his long retirement. His funeral, which took place at Santa Croce church in Florence in 1868, attracted more than 6, 000 mourners. Fittingly, the choir sang a prayer from one of his operas.

Operas

1809	*Demetrio e Polibio*
1810	*La cambiale di matrimonio*
1811	*L'equivoco stravagante*
1812	*L'inganno felice; Ciro in Babilonia; La scala di seta; La pietra del paragone; L'occasione fa il ladro*
1813	*L'italiana in Algeri; Aureliano in Palmira; Il Signor Bruschino; Tancredi*
1814	*Il turco in Italia; Sigismondo*
1815	*Elisabetta, regina d'Inghilterra; Torvaldo e Dorliska*
1816	*Il barbiere di Siviglia; La gazzetta; Otello*
1817	*La gazza ladra; Armida; Adelaide di Borgogna; La Cenerentola*
1818	*Mosè in Egitto; rev. 1827 as Moïse et Pharaon; Adina; Ricciardo e Zoraide*
1819	*Ermione; Eduardo e Cristina; La donna del lago; Bianca e Falliero*
1820	*Maometto II*
1821	*Matilde di Shabran*
1822	*Zelmira*
1823	*Semiramide*
1825	*Il viaggio a Reims*
1826	*Le Siège de Corinthe (rev. of Maometto II)*
1828	*Le Comte Ory*
1829	*Guillaume Tell*

Timeline

1792	Gioacchino Antonio Rossini born, Pasaro, Italy
1796	Moves with mother to Bologna
1805	Only appearance as singer in Ferdinando Paer's *Camilla* at Bologna's Teatro del Corso
1806	Enters Bologna Academy and writes fist opera, *Demetrio e polibio*
1810	First commission for opera, *La cambiale di matrimonio*
1812	*La pietra del paragone* produced at La Scala, Milan
1813	Has first international successes with his *opera seria Tancredi* and *opera buffa L'italiana in Algeri*
1815	Rossini moves to Naples to become director of Teatro San Carlo and Teatro del Fondo
1815	Premiere of *Elisabetta, regina d'Inghilterra*; leading part taken by Rossini's future wife Isabella Colbran
1816	*Otello* produced, and admired by composers including Verdi
1816	Writes *opera buffa Il barbiere di Siviglia*, reputedly in 2 weeks
1818	Premiere of *Mosè in Egitto*
1822	Marries Isabella Colbran
1823	Travels to London and meets Beethoven
1823	*Semiramide*, last of his Italian operas, premieres in Venice
1824	Becomes director of Théâtre Italien, Paris
1825	Appointed composer to King Charles X
1828	New opera *Le comte Ory* written for the Opéra
1829	Writes his last opera, *grand opéra Guillaume Tell*
1832	Begins work on his *Stabat mater*
1837	Returns to Italy; suffers from long illness
1845	Isabella dies
1846	Marries Olympe Pelissier and then leaves Bologna
1855	Settles in Paris
1857	Begins *Péchés de viellesse*
1863	*Petite messe solennelle* completed
1868	Rossini dies, Paris

Teatro del Fondo in Naples. It was in Naples that Rossini unveiled his great masterpiece, *Il barbiere di Siviglia* ('The Barber of Seville', 1816) ➡ **p. 127**. This was Rossini at his witty, vivacious best, in an opera full of fun, lively, inventive orchestration and catchy melodies.

A TRAGIC ALTERNATIVE

Yet this same year, Rossini unveiled a total contrast – his *Otello* (1816), a dark tale of love, jealousy and betrayal based on one of Shakespeare's four great tragedies. The part of the doomed heroine, Desdemona, was written for Rossini's wife, Isabella Colbran, who specialized in tragic roles. The violent ending of *Otello* in which Otello murders Desdemona was considered too disturbing for audiences, who preferred problems solved and happiness ever after. As a result, Rossini had to concoct a happy ending when *Otello* was premiered in Rome.

A PROLIFIC AND POPULAR COMPOSER

Nevertheless, Rossini was all the rage, the most popular opera composer of his day and the most prolific, with 25 operas to his credit in the 10 years since *Tancredi* won him international fame. He was still only 31 when he left Italy to take up a post in Paris as director of the Théâtre Italien. At this time, in the early 1820s, *grand opéra* was beginning to make an impact on French audiences. It was a change of mood that was going to upstage the charm and the light touch of which Rossini was such a consummate master. Ironically, Rossini himself helped to set the new-style opera on its way with his *Guillaume Tell* ('William Tell', 1829) ➡ **p. 129**. This had a length and scope that made it one of the masterpieces of early French *grand opéra*, but it was the last of Rossini's 40 works for the opera stage. Though his retirement lasted nearly 40 years, he was not forgotten and some 6,000

mourners attended his funeral at Santa Croce Church in Florence in 1868. A chorus 300-strong sang the prayer from his opera *Mosé in Egitto* ('Moses in Egypt', 1818). The performance was so compelling that the audience outside the church demanded an encore.

L'italiana in Algeri
('The Italian Girl in Algiers')

L'italiana in Algeri by Rossini

Composed	1813
Premiered	1813, Venice
Libretto	by Angelo Anelli

Despite its North African setting, Rossini's *L'italiana in Algeri* was a resolutely Italian opera. Unlike *Aida* (1871), in which Verdi took care to evoke the mysterious atmosphere of ancient Egypt, Rossini made no particular attempt to reflect the exotic nature of Algiers. However, given the good-natured harum-scarum fun of this two-act comic opera and the inventiveness of Rossini's music, none of this mattered a great deal to the audience at the opera's premiere at the Teatro San Benedetto in Venice on 22 May 1813. What mattered was Rossini's mastery of comedy in this first of what were to become his three masterpieces of *opéra buffa*.

RIGHT: Marylin Horne as Isabella in the Royal Opera House's 1993 production of Rossini's L'Italiana in Algeri.

Synopsis
L'italiana in Algeri by Rossini

ACT I

Elvira, wife of Mustafa, Bey (governor) of Algiers, is lamenting her husband's waning affection to her confidante, Zulma. Mustafa reveals to Captain Haly that he is tired of Elvira and wishes her to marry Lindoro, his Italian slave. He asks Haly to find him an Italian woman for his harem. Lindoro does not wish to marry Elvira; he still loves his lost Italian sweetheart Isabella.

Haly's pirates return with their captives – Isabella, who is searching for Lindoro, and Taddeo, her admirer. The pirates attempt to separate them, but they claim that Taddeo is her uncle and they must stay together. Haly rejoices in having found an Italian woman for Mustafa's harem. Isabella is annoyed by Taddeo's jealousy, but they determine to stick together.

Lindoro and Elvira eventually agree to marry, although neither is keen. Lindoro will be allowed to leave for Italy, but Elvira still loves Mustafa and has no desire to go. Mustafa meets Isabella and falls in love with her. She realizes that she can outwit him and plays along. Elvira, Lindoro and Zulma come to bid farewell to Mustafa; Lindoro and Isabella recognize each other. Isabella persuades Mustafa not to send his wife away, and insists on keeping Lindoro as her slave.

ACT II

Elvira still hopes to regain Mustafa's love. Isabella scolds Lindoro for agreeing to marry Elvira; he assures her of his fidelity and they decide to escape. Mustafa, meanwhile, employs Taddeo as his *Kaimakan*, to help gain Isabella's affection. Isabella advises Elvira on how to handle Mustafa. She then leaves and Isabella keeps Mustafa waiting outside.

She eventually invites him in, along with Taddeo, whom Mustafa has instructed to leave when the Bey sneezes. Taddeo refuses to leave and Mustafa is further frustrated when Isabella invites Elvira to join them for coffee.

As Lindoro and Taddeo plan their escape, Mustafa enters. Lindoro reassures him that Isabella is in love with him, to the extent that she wants him to join the exclusive Italian order of Pappataci. Mustafa is pleased at this honour; Lindoro and Taddeo explain that he must only eat, drink and sleep, oblivious to the world around him. Isabella prepares a ceremony of initiation. Mustafa is pronounced a Pappataci and is presented with food, while Isabella and Lindoro loudly declare their love, as a test. As Mustafa concentrates on remaining oblivious, the Italians prepare their ship for departure. By the time he realizes what is happening, they have set sail. Mustafa has learned his lesson and begs Elvira for forgiveness.

KEY COMPOSERS

Il barbiere di Siviglia
('The Barber of Seville')

Il barbiere di Siviglia by Rossini

Composed	1816
Premiered	1816, Rome
Libretto	by Cesare Sterbini, after Pierre-Augustin Caron de Beaumarchais

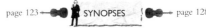
Rossini's opera was given its first performance, in Rome, on 20 February 1816, but not under the name by which it is now known. The reason was that Rossini's *Il barbiere* was faced with a rival, an opera on the same subject by Giovanni Paisiello, which had first been produced in St Petersburg in 1782. More than 30 years later, when the first performance of Rossini's opera was about to take place, Paisiello's *Il barbiere* was still enjoying great popularity among Italian opera audiences. Rossini was therefore obliged to resort to subterfuge: he changed his title to *Almaviva, ossia L'inutile precauzione* ('Almaviva or The Useless Precaution'). The title *Il barbiere di Siviglia* was not used until the opera was performed in Bologna later on in 1816. However, the opera illustrated Rossini's use of a common practice among nineteenth-century opera composers – borrowing from their own works as long as the reused music was not first performed in the town that had heard the original. This was how Rossini's overture for *Il barbiere* was the third run of this music: he had already used the overture in his *Aureliano in Palmira* (1813) and *Elisabetta, regina d'Inghilterra* ('Elizabeth, Queen of England', 1815).

Synopsis
Il barbiere di Siviglia by Rossini

ACT I

The beautiful Rosina, ward of Dr Bartolo, is confined in the doctor's house. Count Almaviva, disguised as a poor student, Lindoro, stands below her window with a group of musicians and serenades her. She does not come to the window, so the musicians, receiving payment from the count, depart. Figaro, the town barber, approaches, boasting of his skills and importance. The count offers him a reward, if he will assist the count in gaining entry to Bartolo's house and wooing Rosina. The count, as Lindoro, sings again to Rosina, who is entranced by his voice and drops him a note as Bartolo pulls her away from the window. Figaro suggests than the count should go to the house disguised as a drunken soldier and say that he has been billeted there.

Rosina recalls Lindoro's voice and decides to try and outwit Bartolo. Meanwhile Bartolo is warned by Don Basilio, the music master, that Count Almaviva has designs on Rosina. Bartolo hopes to marry Rosina himself and Basilio suggests slandering the count, to which Bartolo agrees. Figaro overhears and relates to Rosina that Bartolo plans to marry her the next day; she entrusts him with a note for Lindoro. The housekeeper, Berta, opens the door to a drunken soldier – the count in disguise – who is demanding lodging; Bartolo refuses him entry. The count manages to pass Rosina a love letter, but Bartolo is watching. When he demands to see it, Rosina hands him a laundry list. Figaro enters with the news that a crowd has gathered outside to see what the commotion is about. The police arrive and arrest the count, but he quietly informs them of his identity and is released.

ACT II

A young music teacher, Don Alonso – in fact the count in another disguise – arrives at the house, claiming to have been sent by Don Basilio, who is unwell. Rosina enters for her music lesson and recognizes Don Alonso as "Lindoro". As Bartolo sleeps in a chair, Rosina and Don Alonso sing of their love for one another. As a further distraction, Figaro arrives to shave Bartolo and manages to procure the key for the balcony window. Basilio arrives, in full health; he is bribed to become "ill" and leaves. As the lovers plan their escape, via the balcony window, Bartolo becomes aware of the conspiracy and sends Figaro and Lindoro away. Bartolo sends Basilio to fetch a notary and tells Rosina that Lindoro is probably working for Count Almaviva, who is known to be in pursuit of her.

Following a storm, Figaro and the count climb into the house through the balcony window. Rosina at first rejects Lindoro, believing what Bartolo has told her, but succumbs when the count reveals that he and Lindoro are one and the same. As they leave they realize that the cunning Bartolo has removed the ladder. Basilio enters with the notary and, after some bribery, the marriage ceremony is instead performed between Rosina and the count. Bartolo arrives too late and is forced to accept the new married couple. The count suggests that he keep Rosina's dowry in compensation for his loss.

LEFT: Susanne Mentzer as Rosina and Patrick Power as Almaviva in a 1987 production of Rossini's Il barbiere di Siviglia.

EARLY ROMANTIC 1800–1845

La Cenerentola
('Cinderella')

La Cenerentola by Rossini

Composed	1816–17
Premiered	1817, Rome
Libretto	by Jacopo Ferretti, after Charles Perraut

Rossini's two-act version of the Cinderella story, his twentieth opera and last Italian comic opera, received its first performance at the Teatro Valle in Rome on 25 January 1817. This was followed by performances in London (1820), Vienna (1822) and New York (1826). The Teatro Valle, which had commissioned Rossini to write the opera for the carnival in Rome, gave him a deadline of 26 December 1816. However, by 23 December, no

subject had yet been decided. The librettist, Jacopo Ferretti (1784–1852) suggested 20 possibilities to Rossini. The composer rejected them all. At last, though, Rossini agreed to the Cinderella theme. Ferretti stayed up all night, writing an outline. Just over three weeks later, the libretto was complete and Rossini composed the music for it in another 24 days. When the premiere of *La Cenerentola* ('Cinderella', 1817) took place, just over six weeks separated the initial idea from the first performance. Unfortunately, the opera was not well received and Ferretti became depressed. Rossini, however, assured him that audiences would eventually "fall in love" with *La Cenerentola*. He was right. In the last few days of the Rome Carnival, the opera was being applauded frenziedly by its audiences.

Synopsis
La Cenerentola by Rossini

ACT I

Don Magnifico's daughters Clorinda and Tisbe pamper themselves while his stepdaughter Cenerentola completes her chores. A beggar – in fact Prince Ramiro's tutor, Alidoro – comes to the door. The sisters send him away, but Cenerentola gives him food. He says her goodness will be rewarded. Prince Ramiro, who is holding a ball to find a bride, arrives. Don Magnifico hopes that he will marry one of his daughters.

Prince Ramiro arrives, disguised as his valet, Dandini. Alidoro has told him that one of Don Magnifico's daughters is a suitable bride. He meets Cenerentola and they fall in love. Ramiro announces the arrival of the "prince" – a disguised Dandini. Cenerentola pleads in vain to be allowed to attend the ball. Alidoro asks the whereabouts of Don Magnifico's third daughter and he declares that she is dead. Everyone leaves for the ball. Cenerentola encounters the "beggar", who reveals his identity and asks her to accompany him to the ball.

The "prince" escorts the sisters into the

palace and offers Don Magnifico the position of court vintner. Dandini tells Ramiro that the sisters are awful. Dandini offers his "valet" – Ramiro – to the sister he does not choose; they are unimpressed. Alidoro introduces a lady; all are struck by her resemblance to Cenerentola.

ACT II

Don Magnifico is worried and Ramiro bewildered by the mysterious guest. Ramiro hides as she enters with Dandini. She tells the "prince" that she is in love with his valet; Ramiro reveals himself. Cenerentola tells him that he must seek her out, and gives him one of two matching bracelets. She leaves; Ramiro and Dandini resume their identities. Don Magnifico demands to know which daughter Dandini is to marry; the valet admits the truth. He orders Don Magnifico and the sisters to leave.

Cenerentola tends the fire. The others return and demand their supper. A storm breaks out. Alidoro causes Prince Ramiro's carriage to break down outside Don Magnifico's castle. The prince and Dandini enter and the truth slowly dawns on Cenerentola. She begs Ramiro to forgive Don Magnifico and his daughters; eventually everyone is reconciled.

Le Comte Ory
('The Count of Ory')

Le Comte Ory by Rossini

Composed	1828
Premiered	1828, Paris
Libretto	by Eugène Scribe and Charles Gaspard Delestre-Poirson

Le Comte Ory (1828) was another of Rossini's bright, brilliant *operas buffa*. This one, based on an old Picardy legend, premiered at the Paris Opèra on 20 August 1828. The first performance in London took place at the Haymarket on 28 February 1829, and was possibly intended as a celebration for Rossini's thirty-seventh birthday, the best the theatre could do for a celebrity born on 29 February. However, *Le Comte Ory* was not entirely an original piece of work. Rossini had already used much of the music, including the overture, in his *Il viaggo a Reims* ('A Journey to Rheims', 1825).

Guillaume Tell
('William Tell')

Guillaume Tell by Rossini

Composed	1829
Premiered	1829, Paris
Libretto	by Etienne de Jouy and Hippolyte Louis-Florent Blis, after Johann Christoph Friedrich von Schiller

Rossini called the first performance of his *grand opéra Guillaume Tell* a "*quasi-fiasco*". The overture, he said, was fine, the first act had some interesting effects, and the second was a triumph, but the third and fourth were disappointing. However, the theatre director was more concerned with audience reaction at the Théâtre de l'Académie Royale de Musique in Paris, where the premiere took place on 3 August 1829; the reception had been distinctly cool. As a result, he told Rossini, he was going to cancel his contract for future works. Rossini, unfazed, offered to withdraw the contract himself, adding that he would never write another opera. He kept his word. In time, though, *Guillaume Tell* was appreciated for the colour and variety of its music and its brilliant special effects, such as the thunderstorm in the

KEY COMPOSERS

Synopsis
Le Comte Ory by Rossini

ACT I

While the men are away on a crusade, Countess Adèle renounces love. Count Ory has disguised himself as a hermit who gives the villagers potions for matters of the heart. He hopes to court the countess. The countess's confidante Ragonde arrives and informs the hermit that her mistress wishes to see him; he consents. The count's tutor and his page Isolier arrive in search of the count, and also hope to find the countess, whom Isolier loves. The tutor realizes the hermit's true identity. Isolier asks the hermit for advice and reveals his plan to gain entry to the castle by dressing up as a nun; the count resolves to use this idea himself. The countess arrives to consult the hermit, who tells her that falling in love will ease her pain. She admits that she is in love with Isolier, but the hermit advises her against the match. The tutor then reveals the count's deception. News arrives that the men are returning. The count resolves to enter the castle.

ACT II

While the women await the men's return, a storm breaks out. Hearing cries, the women discover several nuns (in fact the count, his tutor, Raimbaud, and associates), who plead for protection. They are admitted and the count insists on embracing the countess. The "nuns" celebrate. Isolier announces that the men will return that night, and reveals the true identities of the "nuns". The count insists on joining the countess in her bedroom, not realizing that Isolier is also there. In the darkness, he takes Isolier's hand. Trumpets announce the return of the crusaders and the count realizes that Isolier has tricked him. The count and his associates flee and the household rejoices in love's victory.

Synopsis
Guillaume Tell by Rossini

ACT I

As the villagers on the shores of Lake Lucerne celebrate the impending marriage celebrations, Guillaume Tell laments the rule of Gesler, an Austrian oppressor. The respected patriarch Melchthal advises his son Arnold to marry, but the youth is in love with Gesler's daughter Mathilde. The sound of horns signal that Gesler's hunt is near and Arnold prepares to meet Mathilde. Guillaume Tell tries to recruit him to his patriotic cause and

Arnold agrees, but he is torn between loyalty to his country and love for Mathilde.

Melchthal blesses the wedding couples and the festivities continue, with Tell's son Jemmy winning an archery contest. The celebrations are interrupted by the arrival of Leuthold, a shepherd. He announces that he has killed an Austrian soldier, who was attempting to rape his daughter. Tell ferries him to safety across the lake, much to the anger of the Austrian soldiers. Gesler's henchman Rodolphe demands to know the identity of the rescuer but the villagers remain silent in their loyalty towards Tell. Infuriated, Rodolphe takes Melchthal hostage.

ACT II

Mathilde is contemplating her love for Arnold when he appears and the couple sing a duet. Mathilde hears Guillaume Tell and Walter approaching and leaves, promising to meet Arnold the next day. Tell and Walter break the news to Arnold that Melchthal has been murdered. Arnold swears vengeance, allying himself to Tell's cause. Foresters join them and together the Swiss revolutionaries, with Tell as their leader, plan to overthrow the tyrannical Austrian rule.

ACT III

Arnold and Mathilde rendezvous in a ruined chapel. Arnold explains about the death of his father and the plans for an uprising. The lovers bid each other farewell, assuming they will not meet again.

Meanwhile, in the town square, Gesler has ordered a celebration marking 100 years of Austrian rule. The Austrian soldiers force the Swiss to dance, sing and bow down before their ruler. Guillaume Tell is alone in refusing to bow, enraging Gesler, and his fate is further sealed when Rodolphe recognizes him as the accomplice in Leuthold's escape. Gesler decrees that Tell can live only if he successfully shoots an apple from Jemmy's head. Thankfully, Tell's shot is accurate, but he then drops a second arrow which was meant for Gesler should he have failed in his task. To the horror of the Swiss people, Tell is sentenced to death and taken away by boat. Mathilde announces that she will protect Jemmy.

ACT IV

Arnold has returned to his family home. He is informed that Guillaume Tell has been taken prisoner and resolves to lead the uprising himself, showing his companions where Tell and Melchthal concealed the weapons in preparation for the revolt. Mathilde restores Jemmy to his mother, Tell's wife Hedwige, and offers herself as a hostage to ensure Tell's safety.

A storm breaks out and Tell, a skilful oarsman, is released from his chains to be given control of the boat. Tell steers back to the shore and escapes. Gesler follows, but Jemmy hands Tell a bow and arrow, with which he shoots the Austrian ruler dead. As the storm passes, Arnold and the other patriots capture the castle and everyone rejoices that peace and liberation have been restored to their country.

overture. However, the opera was immensely long, spreading its four acts over three hours and 45 minutes. Soon after the first performance, the theatre management began performing it one act at a time. Even this did not solve the problem, as Rossini was well aware. On being told that the second act was to be given, he remarked, sardonically: "What, the whole of it?"

EARLY ROMANTIC

1800–1845

KEY COMPOSERS

KEY COMPOSERS

Vincenzo Bellini

The musical abilities of Vincenzo Bellini (1801–35) were already well known in his home city of Catania in Sicily before he went to Naples at age 18 to study at the conservatory under Nicola Zingarelli (1752–1837). A competent pianist at age five, composer of his sacred music at six, the youthful Bellini's ariettas and instrumental works were performed in aristocratic salons and provided anthems for the churches in Catania.

VOCAL POWER IN ROMANTIC OPERA

The greater drama and intensity, the expanding orchestras and the trend for larger opera houses that marked the early Romantic era placed pressure on singers to increase their voice power to match. A larger opera house, seating more people and employing more orchestral musicians than before, meant a bigger space for voices to fill and greater competition from the accompaniment. The *bel canto* singing style of the eighteenth century, while undoubtedly beautiful and never out of fashion, even today, had neglected the "resonances" that could reinforce and prolong the sound of a voice. Jenny Lind (1820–87), the Swedish soprano who made her operatic debut in Stockholm in 1838, was one *bel canto* soprano who was able to project her voice sufficiently to make it fill a concert hall. However, this ability was not all that common. Singers, therefore, had to go into new, special training in order to acquire weightier timbre, more sonorous low notes and more brilliant top notes so as to cope with the more demanding requirements of Romantic opera. The result was the advent of new types of voice that underlined greater strength and volume, among them the *tenor robusto, tenor di forza* and dramatic soprano.

A SUCCESSFUL STUDENT

Like Rossini, whose admiring disciple he was, Bellini scored success with while still a student. His *opera semiseria, Adelson e Salvini* (1925), which was staged at the conservatory, showed such promise that both the Teatro San Carlo,

Timeline

1801	Vincenzo Bellini born, Sicily
1819	Moves to Naples to study at San Sebastiano Conservatory
1822	Begins to study under Conservatory's director, Nicola Zingarelli
1824	Attends the Naples performance of Rossini's *Semiramide*
1825	Premiere of first opera *Adelson e Salvini* leads to commission from Teatro San Carlo, Naples
1827	Begins partnership with librettist Felice Romani on *Il pirata*
1827	*Il pirata*, produced at La Scala, Milan, lays foundation for his career
1829	*Zaire* is inaugural opera at Parma's new Teatro Ducale
1830	*I Capuleti e i Montecchi* premieres in Venice, with soprano Giuditta Pasta
1831	Premiere of *La sonnambula* in Milan
1831	*Norma* is greeted coolly at its premiere in Milan, but soon becomes a hallmark of the *bel canto* style
1833	Bellini visits London; four of his operas are performed
1835	Commissioned to write *I Puritani* for Théâtre Italien, Paris
1835	Appointed *Chevalier de la Légion d'honneur* after *I Puritani*'s success
1835	Bellini dies, Paris

TOP RIGHT: The Teatro San Carlo in Naples, for which Bellini composed a number of commissioned works.
LEFT: Vincenzo Bellini, who developed the bel canto style of romantic vocal lines set to luscious melodies.
RIGHT: Italian soprano Giuditta Pasta, who sang in many of Bellini's operas.

Naples, and La Scala, Milan, commissioned work from him. For Naples, Bellini composed *Bianca e Fernando* (1826). He was obliged to change the latter name to *Gernando*, because Ferdinand I, the autocratic king of the Two Sicilies (Naples and Sicily) claimed a monopoly of his own name and any other too closely resembling it. The original name of the opera was restored, though, after Ferdinand died later in 1825.

THE OPERA TO MAKE HIS NAME

The opera that made Bellini's name was his work for Milan, *Il pirata* ('The Pirate', 1827) which had its first performance at La Scala on 27 October 1827. Though still only 26 at the time, Bellini had already demonstrated the basic elements of his personal style – creamy melody, graceful ornamentation, dramatic orchestration and touching, heartfelt sentiment. This was a winning combination that he carefully honed to reflect the emotions of his characters and the drama of their plight.

THE MASTER OF BEL CANTO

Bellini soon revealed himself as the master of *bel canto*, a style that had connotations beyond the world of opera: the nocturnes, preludes and other melodies of the Polish pianist and composer Frederic Chopin (1810–49) reproduced on the keyboard the long, lyrical musical lines Bellini wrote for the voice.

A FAVOURITE WITH THE LADIES

Like Chopin, whom he met when he visited London in 1833, Bellini had a strong appeal for women, with his slim figure, aristocratic looks and the delicate aspect that marked so many nineteenth-century musicians destined for short lives. While in Milan, where he remained for six years after the success of *Il pirata*, Bellini caught the eye of Giuditta Cantu, who was married to a wealthy landowner and silk manufacturer. The two embarked on a passionate love affair, which was later romanticized in literature, but caused a considerable scandal at the time. Gossip about it was all the more vigorous because in 1831, Bellini had become internationally famous after writing two more operas *La sonnambula* ('The Sleepwalker', 1830) and *Norma* (1833). Bellini's visit to London in 1833 removed him from the scene of scandal not long after the affair became public and divorce proceedings began.

AN EARLY END

Bellini disliked London, its audiences and its climate, although his *La sonnambula* was a great success there. In August 1833 Bellini travelled to Paris, which was much more to

his liking and where Rossini, now retired, was on hand to encourage him. In Paris Bellini wrote his tenth and last opera, *I puritani* ('The Puritans', 1835), which received its first performance on 25 January 1835. It was a tremendous success and Bellini was the toast of Paris.

He was, however, exhausted and later that year, he fell ill, first with dysentery and then with an inflamed intestine, complicated by a liver abscess. Years earlier, it was said, Bellini had heard 'Stabat Mater' by Giovanni Battista Pergolesi (1710–36) and afterwards remarked: "If I could write one melody as beautiful as that, I would not mind dying young like Pergolesi." He did write melodies as beautiful as that, and he did die young, aged 34.

Operas

1825	*Adelson e Salvini*
1826	*Bianca e Fernando*
1827	*Il pirata*
1829	*La straniera*
1829	*Zaira*
1830	*I Capuleti e i Montecchi*
1831	*La sonnambula*
1831	*Norma*
1833	*Beatrice di Tenda*
1835	*I puritani*

EARLY ROMANTIC

1800—1845

KEY COMPOSERS

La sonnambula
('The Sleepwalker')

La sonnambula by Bellini

Composed   1831
Premiered   1831, Milan
Libretto   by Felice Romani, after Eugène Scribe

Vincenzo Bellini's two-act opera *La sonnambula*, which had a pastoral background, was first produced at the Teatro Carcano in Milan on 6 March 1831. The story derived from a *comédie-vaudeville* of 1819 and a ballet-pantomime of 1827, both part-written by the French dramatist Augustin Eugene Scribe (1791–1861). The title role, Amina, was created by Giuditta Pasta (1797–1865) who, though essentially a mezzo, performed brilliantly in the soprano range. Pasta was regarded as the greatest tragic singing actress of her day. Subsequently, Her Majesty's Theatre in London, where the opera was performed in 1833, was the scene of one of the most talked-about stage effects of the early nineteenth century: a virtual high-wire act in which the sleepwalking Amina crossed the eaves of the mill-house roof, several feet above the characters watching in horror on the stage below. The bridge, it seems, was the idea of the Swedish soprano Jenny Lind (1820–87) who sang the role of Amina at Her Majesty's. When

La sonnambula premiered in New York in 1835, the role was sung by the Scottish soprano Mary Ann Paton, a beautiful singer, but one who acted her parts "like an inspired idiot", as one observer put it.

> *La sonnambula*, **Orchestra del Maggio Musicale Fiorentino**
> Richard Bonynge, **conductor**
> Decca 448 996-2DMO2
> Soloists: Joan Sutherland (Amina), Sylvia Stahlman (Lisa), Margreta Elkins (Teresa), Nicola Monti (Elvino), Giovanni Foiani (Alessio), Fernando Corena (Rodolfo)
>
> ## RECOMMENDED RECORDING

LEFT: Elena Kelessidi as Amina and Juan Diego Florez as Elvino (2002).

Synopsis
La sonnambula by Bellini

ACT I

The villagers celebrate the approaching wedding of Amina and Elvino, with the exception of Lisa, the innkeeper and Elvino's former lover. Consumed by jealousy, she rejects the advances of her new admirer, Alessio. Amina gives thanks to all of her friends, in particular Teresa, who owns the mill and who raised the orphaned Amina as her own child. Elvino returns from praying at his mother's grave and presents Amina with a ring, which belonged to his mother.

A stranger arrives in the village, with a curiously detailed knowledge of the local area. Unbeknownst to the villagers, he is in fact Count Rodolfo, the long-lost son of the recently deceased count, returning home. He shows a marked interest in Amina, much to Elvino's displeasure. Teresa and the villagers warn the stranger of a phantom who haunts the village by night. Realizing that the castle is a long way off, he agrees to stay at Lisa's inn. Amina assures a piqued Elvino that he has no need to be jealous.

Lisa is now aware of Rodolfo's true identity and flirts with him in his room. Amina then enters, sleepwalking and talking about Elvino. Lisa leaves, dropping a handkerchief as she does so, and goes to fetch Elvino. Rodolfo is tempted to take advantage of the vulnerable Amina, but is touched by her innocence and restrains himself. Rodolfo leaves as the villagers, who have learned of the stranger's identity, arrive to welcome their new lord. They find only a sleeping woman. Lisa and Elvino return, and the woman is revealed to be Amina; Elvino is furious and breaks off the engagement. Only Teresa remains to comfort Amina.

ACT II

The villagers remain fond of Amina and set off for the castle to ask Rodolfo for confirmation of her innocence. Amina and Teresa are also on their way to the castle, but Amina can go no further than Elvino's farm. Elvino continues to reject her, even when the villagers return with the joyful news that the count has declared Amina's innocence. Elvino takes back his mother's ring.

Alessio learns that Elvino has decided to marry Lisa instead of Amina. Rodolfo tries in vain to explain to Elvino that Amina is a sleepwalker and was unaware of her actions, but Elvino will not be persuaded. Teresa, meanwhile, bids the villagers remain quiet to let Amina sleep. She confronts Lisa with the handkerchief, proving that she too spent time alone with Rodolfo in his room. Elvino laments the fickleness of women. Rodolfo continues to plead Amina's innocence, when she appears, sleepwalking along the roof of the mill and mourning the loss of Elvino's love. Elvino goes to her and replaces the ring and she awakes in his arms. Everyone rejoices and the wedding plans resume.

KEY COMPOSERS

EARLY ROMANTIC

1800—1845

Norma

Norma by Bellini

Composed	1831
Premiered	1831, Milan
Libretto	by Felice Romani, after Alexandre Soumet

'CASTA DIVA' (CHASTE GODDESS)

'Casta diva' is sung by the Druid priestess Norma in Act I of the opera, which is set in the first century BC, during the conquest of Gaul by Rome. Addressing the goddess of the Moon, she prays for peace between her war-torn homeland, Gaul (France), and the Roman invaders.

POPULAR MELODY

Norma, Bellini's eighth opera and his masterpiece, followed hard on the heels of his *La sonnambula* when its first performance was given at La Scala, Milan, less than four months later, on 26 December 1831. Once again, Giuditta Pasta created the title role, although this time she had parts of the opera transposed down to the key of F where it catered more comfortably for her mezzo-soprano voice. The role has remained scored in F ever since. Pasta's problems – and Bellini's – did not end there, however. The singer declared that *'Casta diva'* was "ill-adapted to her vocal abilities" – in other words, the aria was to blame for being "impossible" to sing. Bellini deployed all his diplomatic gifts and told Pasta to practice the aria every morning for a week. Then, if she was still dissatisfied, he would change it. A week later, the composer received a gift from the singer and a confession of shame that she had been "little suited to performing your sublime harmonies". *Norma* was coolly received at first – "the audience was harsh" Bellini wrote in despair – but they gradually warmed to it. During the 1831–32 season, *Norma* was performed 39 times and was received with great enthusiasm.

Synopsis
Norma by Bellini

ACT I

The high priest Oroveso leads the druids to worship at the altar of Irminsul. They are preparing for moonrise, when Oroveso's daughter, Norma, will lead them in an uprising against the Romans. The Roman pro-consul Pollione enters with his friend Flavio and confesses that he no longer loves Norma, but has discovered a new passion for Adalgisa, a novice priestess. He plans to take her back to Rome and marry her. The druids return; Norma prays to the moon and laments the loss of Pollione's love. Adalgisa, meanwhile, prays to be released from the bonds of Pollione's ardour, but he eventually persuades her to flee to Rome with him.

Norma learns that Pollione must return to Rome and she is concerned for the future of the two children she has borne him. She confides in her companion Clotilde that Pollione has another lover, although she does not know her identity. Adalgisa enters, declaring that she is in love and asking Norma for guidance. Norma, bearing in mind her own conduct, is about to allow Adalgisa to revoke her chastity vows when Pollione enters and Norma, realizing he is the object of Adalgisa's affections, flies into a rage. Adalgisa is equally horrified to learn that Pollione is Norma's former lover and declares that she would rather die than take him from Norma. The temple gong sounds and Pollione is warned that his death is imminent.

ACT II

Norma watches over her sleeping children with a dagger in her hand, tormented by the choice of either killing them or letting Pollione take them to Rome as slaves. She cannot bring herself to carry out the murder and asks Adalgisa to take them to their father. Adalgisa pleads with Norma to pity her children, swearing that she will renounce Pollione's love and bring him back to Norma.

Oroveso announces to the druids that Pollione is departing, only to be replaced by an even crueller pro-consul. He laments the hardships of living under Roman rule, but promises that, with patience, the time will come to revolt.

At the temple of Irminsul, Clotilde informs Norma that Adalgisa's protestations to Pollione have made no difference to the pro-consul's plans. Enraged, Norma announces that the moment of revolution has arrived. Oroveso demands a victim to sacrifice to the gods and Pollione is brought in, having been arrested for breaking into the virgins' sanctuary. In private, Norma offers him his freedom if he will leave Adalgisa and return to her, but Pollione refuses. Norma then orders the druids to prepare a funeral pyre, confesses her affair and offers herself as the human sacrifice. Pollione, moved by her nobility, resolves to die with her. Oroveso is deeply ashamed by Norma's confessions, but she eventually persuades him to look after her children, following which Norma and Pollione are led to their deaths among the flames.

RIGHT: Ezio Flagello as the high priest Oroveso in a 1982 production of Bellini's Norma.

1800–1845 EARLY ROMANTIC

KEY COMPOSERS

Gaetano Donizetti

EARLY ROMANTIC

1800—1845

Gaetano Donizetti (1797–1848), who was born in Bergamo, Italy, wrote seven operas, some of them while still a student in Bologna, and several of them unproduced, before he scored his first success with *Zoraide di Granata* ('Zoraide of Granada', 1822), which was performed in Rome. *Zoraide* attracted the attention of impresario Domenico Barbaia, who offered Donizetti a contract to write for the Naples theatres. The result was a series of comic works, which, though successful, were clearly influenced by the compositional styles of Rossini and Bellini.

ARRIVAL OF
INTERNATIONAL FAME

Then Donizetti wrote *Anna Bolena* ('Anne Boleyn', 1830), an opera set in sixteenth-century England, dealing with the life and death of Anne Boleyn, the second wife of King Henry VIII. *Anna Bolena*, which revealed Donizetti's individual style for the first time, brought

international fame that enabled him to branch out beyond the confines of Naples and write for other opera houses. One of the first fruits of Donizetti's new artistic freedom was *L'elisir d'amore* ('The Elixir of Love', 1832) a sentimental comedy produced at the Teatro della Canobbiana in Milan.

A SINISTER AND
SOMBRE OPERA

After the great success of *L'elisir d'amore*, Donizetti turned in a new direction. He was anxious to explore the high emotion of tragic opera and found his ideal plot in the story of Lucrezia Borgia (1480–1519), the incestuous poisoner of lurid, though fanciful, popular history. The opera, based on a play by the

French writer Victor Hugo (1802–85), was strong stuff, so much so that it was not staged for two years, until 1833, when it was produced at La Scala, Milan, and ran for 33 performances. *Lucrezia* included several innovations, among them a sombre melody played by the orchestra as a sinister comment that reflected the plotting of two conspirators on stage.

HIS INFLUENCE ON VERDI

The dramatic effect was not lost on the 20-year-old Giuseppe Verdi (1813–1901), who was studying in Milan in 1833. Eighteen years later,

ABOVE: A watercolour of a stage set by Bagnara for Donizetti's most famous opera, Lucia di Lammermoor.
LEFT: Gaetano Donizetti wrote an incredible number of operas and enjoyed great success all over Europe.

Verdi used a similar device in his *Rigoletto* (1851), as musical background to the furtive meeting between Rigoletto and the assassin Sparafucile. In this and other ways, Donizetti was an important forerunner of Verdi, pioneering greater dramatic expression, richer orchestration and new combinations of voices for ensemble singing – and all of it without losing the beautiful melodic lines and harmonies that were his hallmarks.

THE INFLUENCE OF GRAND OPÉRA

In 1835 Donizetti returned to high-operatic drama, this time fortified by viewing French *grand opéra* during a visit to Paris. The result was his most famous opera, *Lucia di Lammermoor*, based on the novel *The Bride of Lammermoor* by Sir Walter Scott. *Lucia* was followed in 1837 by one of Donizetti's many ventures into English history, for another sinister tale of betrayal, despair and death in high, royal places with *Roberto Devereux*

ossia Il conte d'Essex ('Robert Devereux, or The Count (Earl) of Essex', 1837). Robert Devereux (c.1566–1601), the last favourite of Queen Elizabeth I, was executed for plotting against her.

A SLIGHTLY DISMAL END

After *Roberto Devereux* premiered in Naples on 29 October 1837, Donizetti left for Paris, where he returned to his former, light-hearted vein with *La fille du régiment* ('The Daughter of the Regiment', 1840). This was his first French opera and was well received, running for 44 performances in 1840. However, his time in Paris was not entirely successful. Audiences reacted coolly to his *grand opéra La favorite* ('The Favourite', 1840). Victor Hugo objected to changes in his plot

Timeline

1797	Gaetano Donizetti born, Bergamo, Italy
1806	Begins to study music with Mayr at Bergamo
1816	Composes opera, *Il pigmalione*
1818	While in Austrian Army, Donizetti writes *Enrico di Borgogna*
1822	*Zoraida di Granata* premieres in Rome; obtains release from army
1822	Establishes himself at Naples Conservatory with *La zingara*
1830	*Anna Bolena* premieres, bringing composer international fame
1832	Milan premiere of *L'elisir d'amore*
1835	*Lucia di Lammermoor* opens in Naples, including tenor Gilbert-Louis Duprez
1837	Becomes director of Naples Conservatory
1838	Donizetti moves to Paris
1840	*La fille de regiment* and *La favorite* premiere in Paris
1842	Conducts Rossini's *Stabat mater* in Bologna
1842	Becomes *Kapellmeister* to the Austrian court, Vienna
1843	Comic masterpiece *Don Pasquale* premieres in Paris
1844	Premiere of *Caterina Cornaro* in Naples
1844	Becomes paralysed and mentally unbalanced due to syphilis
1848	Donizetti dies, Bergamo

Operas

1816 *Il pigmalione* (comp.)
1817 *L'ira d'Achille*
1818 *Enrico di Borgogna*; *Una follia*
1819 *Il falegname di Livonia*; *Le nozze in villa*
1822 *Zoraida di Granata*; *La zingara*; *La lettera anonima*; *Chiara e Serafina*
1823 *Il fortunato inganno*; *Alfredo il Grande*
1824 *L'ajo nell'imbarazzo*; *Emilia di Liverpool*
1826 *Alahor in Granata*; *Gabriella di Vergy* (comp.; 2nd version 1838); *Elvida*
1827 *Otto mesi in due ore*
1828 *Alina, regina di Golconda*; *Gianni di Calais*; *L'esule di Roma*
1829 *Il giovedì grasso*; *Il paria*; *Elisabetta al castello di Kenilworth*
1830 *Il diluvio universale*; *I pazzi per progetto*; *Imelda de' Lambertazzi*; *Anna Bolena*
1831 *Olivo e Pasquale*; *Il borgomastro di Saardam*; *Le convenienze teatrali*; *Le convenienze ed inconvenienze teatrali*
1831 *Gianni di Parigi*; *Francesca di Foix*; *La romanziera e l'uomo nero*
1832 *Fausta*; *Ugo, conte di Parigi*; *L'elisir d'amore*; *Sancia di Castiglia*
1833 *Il furioso nell'isola di San Domingo*; *Parisina*; *Torquato Tasso*; *Lucrezia Borgia*
1834 *Rosmonda d'Inghilterra*; *Gemma di Vergy*
1835 *Marin Faliero*; *Lucia di Lammermoor*; *Maria Stuarda*
1836 *Belisario*; *Il campanello di notte*; *L'assedio di Calais*; *Betly*
1837 *Roberto Devereux*; *Pia de' Tolomei*
1838 *Poliuto* (comp.; 2nd version, *Les martyrs*, 1840); *Maria de Rudenz*; *Elisabetta di Siberia*
1839 *Le duc d'Albe* (incomplete)
1840 *La fille du regiment*; *La favorite*
1841 *Adelia*; *Rita, ou Le mari batt* (comp.); *Maria Padilla*
1842 *Linda di Chamounix*
1843 *Don Pasquale*; *Maria di Rohan*; *Dom Sébastien, roi de Portugal*
1844 *Caterina Cornaro*

for *Lucrezia*, which had to be withdrawn, and there were censorship problems in Milan. Worse was Donizetti's declining health, but even as his syphilis advanced, he produced his comic masterpiece, *Don Pasquale* (1843). Eventually, syphilis paralysed him and he died, aged 50, on 8 April 1848.

LEFT: Mary Stuart, also known as Mary, Queen of Scots, the protagonist of Donizetti's 1834 opera Maria Stuarda. *British history held a certain fascination for Donizetti and he also composed operas about Anne Boleyn and Elizabeth I's courtier Robert Devereux, Earl of Essex.*

KEY COMPOSERS

L'elisir d'amore
('The Elixir of Love')

L'elisir d'amore by Donizetti

Composed	1832
Premiered	1832, Milan
Libretto	by Felice Romani, after Eugène Scribe

Donizetti's prolific output owed a great deal to the speed with which he was able to compose. He could compose operas at the rate of three or four a year. However, even this rate of production was overtaken by the mere fortnight it took him to write the music for *L'elisir d'amore*. This pastoral comedy was his forty-first opera in 16 years, and premiered at the Teatro della Canobbiana in Milan on 12 May 1832. *L'elisir* owes much of its enduring popularity to *'Una furtiva lagrima'* (One Furtive Tear), the exceptionally beautiful tenor aria in Act II sung by the opera's hero, Nemorino.

'UNA FURTIVE LAGRIMA' (ONE FURTIVE TEAR)

Nemorino tries to win Adina with a love potion. In this tenor aria from Act II, he sings of a tear in her eye, showing she loves him, and believes the potion has worked; in fact Adina was jealous of the other girls.

POPULAR MELODY

Synopsis
L'elisir d'amore by Donizetti

ACT I

The wealthy Adina relaxes with her friend Giannetta and peasants, while Nemorino, her admirer, looks on. He is a poor villager and laments that he can offer her nothing but his love. Adina relates the story of Tristan, who drank a love potion to make Isolde return his love. A drum roll announces the arrival of Sergeant Belcore, who asks Adina to marry him. She refuses, but says she will consider it. Nemorino, wishing he had Belcore's confidence, shyly declares his love to Adina. She answers that she is fickle and enjoys her freedom, and that he would do better to leave for the city and tend to his rich, ailing uncle.

The travelling quack Dr Dulcamara arrives in the town square, selling his new medicine. Nemorido asks whether he has a love potion like the one in Adina's story. Dulcamara produces a bottle – which contains cheap wine – and tells Nemorino that it is just what he is looking for. Nemorino drinks the "love elixir" and ignores Adina when she arrives, trusting in the magic of the elixir to win her heart. Adina is annoyed by his coldness and flirts with Belcore, who announces that he must leave and that she should marry him immediately; she accepts. Nemorino begs for the wedding to be postponed, worried that it will be over before the elixir starts to take effect. Adina ignores his pleas and invites everyone to her wedding.

ACT II

Everyone, with the exception of Nemorino, celebrates the approaching marriage. Dr Dulcamara suggests that Adina and Belcore sing a duet about a girl who chooses a poor man over a rich suitor. The couple prepare to sign the marriage contract, but to Adina's annoyance Nemorino is not present; she postpones the wedding until nightfall. Nemorino pleads with Dulcamara for another bottle of the magic elixir, but he is refused as he has no money. Belcore intervenes, revealing that if Nemorino signs up to the army immediately he will be rewarded in cash. Nemorino agrees and leaves to sign up.

Giannetta spreads the news among the women that Nemorino's rich uncle has died, leaving him a fortune. Nemorino, dizzy after drinking another bottle of "elixir", does not yet know this. As the girls flock around him, he believes that the magic potion has finally taken effect. Adina sees Nemorino surrounded by girls and is enraged that he no longer loves her. Dulcamara explains that Nemorino's newfound popularity is a result of the love elixir and attempts to sell Adina a bottle; she refuses, saying that she will use her own charms. Nemorino sees tears in Adina's eyes and knows that she will soon be his, so he feigns indifference when they meet. Adina restores his enlistment papers to him, declaring her love. Belcore takes the rejection well, assuming that many other women await him. Dr Dulcamara alerts the villagers to the success of his love elixir and sells as many bottles as he can.

ABOVE: An ensemble scene from San Francisco Opera's 1984 production of Donizetti's L'elisir d'amore.
RIGHT: Barry McCauley in a 1986 production of Donizetti's dramatic opera Lucia di Lammermoor.

Lucia di Lammermoor

Lucia di Lammermoor by Donizetti

Composed	1835
Premiered	1835, Naples
Libretto	by Salvatore Cammarano, after Sir Walter Scott

While writing *Lucia di Lammermoor*, Donizetti observed a common custom of the 1830s; tailoring his music to the voices of the original cast. For example, Fanny Tacchinardi-Persiani (1812–67), who created the role of *Lucia*, was technically brilliant and Donizetti's writing reflected her outstanding abilities. Matching music to performers was a shrewd move: the formula increased the popularity of operas. In the case of *Lucia*, the effect on the first-night audience at the Teatro San Carlo, Naples on 26 September 1835 was startling. They became so caught up in the drama and in the plight of the lovers that many of them wept openly during Lucia's mad scene preceding her death and Edgardo's suicide. There was a French as well as an Italian version of *Lucia*, first performed at the Théâtre de la Renaissance in Paris on 6 August 1839. *Lucia* was given in opera houses all over Europe and in Cuba, Mexico, the United States and even Indonesia and Trinidad; *Lucia* was the first opera to be seen on the Caribbean island in 1844.

Synopsis

Lucia di Lammermoor by Donizetti

ACT I

In the grounds of Lammermoor Castle, Normanno leads a group of guards searching for an intruder. Enrico enters and laments his sister Lucia's refusal to marry Arturo, a match that would save him from his impending political and financial ruin. Normanno reveals that she has been secretly meeting a lover who saved her from a wild bull. After further questioning, Normanno confesses that the man in question is Edgardo, Enrico's bitter enemy, and he swears vengeance.

Near a ruined fountain, Lucia and her confidante Alisa await Edgardo. Lucia tells Alisa of a female ghost who haunts the fountain, and who has warned her that her secret affair will end in tragedy. Alisa pleads in vain with Lucia to end the relationship. Edgardo arrives and announces that he must depart for France on a political matter. He suggests that they tell Enrico of their affair and try to make amends, but Lucia, knowing Enrico will never allow it, begs him to keep it secret. Edgardo eventually relents. The lovers exchange rings and vows, and bid each other farewell.

ACT II

In the months since Edgardo's departure, Enrico and Normanno have continued to plan how to persuade Lucia to marry Arturo. They have been intercepting the lovers' letters and forge a letter to Lucia from Edgardo, declaring that he loves another. Enrico shows Lucia the forged letter and, distraught, she hopes for death. Enrico reminds her of the benefits to be gained from her marrying Arturo. Lucia's elderly tutor Raimondo, unaware of the deception and believing Edgardo to be faithless, gently persuades her to agree to the match.

At the wedding ceremony, Enrico explains to Arturo that their mother's recent death is the cause of his sister's melancholy demeanour. As soon as the bride and groom have signed the contract, Edgardo bursts in. He challenges his rival to a duel, but Raimondo dissuades them. Edgardo is shown Lucia's signature on the marriage contract and, cursing her faithlessness, removes his ring and leaves. Lucia, overcome by emotion and confusion, collapses.

ACT III

As a storm rages, Edgardo sits alone pondering on the day's events. Enrico enters and challenges him to a duel at dawn. Meanwhile, Raimondo interrupts the wedding celebrations to inform the guests that Lucia has gone mad and has stabbed and killed Arturo. Lucia enters, deranged and covered in blood, believing herself to be married to Edgardo. Enrico rushes in to berate her, but is filled with pity and remorse when he sees her condition. Lucia dies in Alisa's arms. By the tombs of his ancestors, Edgardo awaits Enrico and prepares for the duel. Filled with anger at Lucia's betrayal, he hopes to die. As the wedding guests leave, they inform him that the dying Lucia spoke of him. He rushes to be with her but it is too late; Raimondo brings news of her death. Realizing he has misjudged her, Edgardo stabs himself and dies.

La fille du régiment
('The Daughter of the Regiment')

La fille du régiment by Donizetti

Composed	1840
Premiered	1840, Paris
Libretto	by J. F. A. Bayard and Jules-Henri Vernoy de Saint-Georges

Donizetti's *opéra-comique La fille du régiment* acquired its French title because of its French librettists, Jules-Henri Vernoy, Marquis de Saint-Georges (1799–1875) and Jean-François-Alfred Bayard (1796–1853), and its first night was at the Opéra-Comique in Paris on 11 February 1840. *La fille*, which was set in the Tirol, in Austria during the Napoleonic Wars was Donizetti's first French opera

FRENCH VERSUS ITALIAN OPERA

At the start of the Romantic era, French and Italian opera were fighting it out for possession of the opera stage in Paris. However, in attempting to turn back the tide of Italian taste and vocal technique, which had "invaded" the opera in France, the French were at a severe disadvantage. As one contemporary English guidebook to the Paris opera commented: "Nothing can be worse than the style of singing which characterizes the French School." Worse still, the French style was fighting a losing battle when the Italian had the keen support of no less a personage than Napoleon Bonaparte, the effective ruler of France. Napoleon and his wife Josephine were enthusiastic patrons of the new Théâtre Italien, which opened in Paris in 1801. Here, Italian operas virtually monopolized the repertory and the great stars of the show were Italian singers – the contralto Giuseppina Grassini (1773–1850) and the castrato Girolamo Crescentini (1752–1846). Subsequently, the Italians grasped the management of the Théâtre Italien. Rossini was musical director from 1824 to 1826 and was officially named "Inspector General of Singing in France" by the government. Eventually, even the more chauvinistic Paris Opéra and Opéra-Comique had to bow to the vogue for Italian opera.

and one of his greatest successes. In 1840 it ran for 44 performances. The opera's Italian premiere took place at La Scala, Milan on 3 October, followed by New Orleans in 1843 and London in 1847.

Don Pasquale, **Opéra de Lyon**
Gabriele Ferro, **conductor**
Erato 2292-45487-2
Soloists: Barbara Hendricks (Norina), Luca Canonici (Ernesto), Gino Quilico(Malatesta), Gabriel Bacquier (Don Pasquale)

RECOMMENDED RECORDING

♪*ynopsis*
La fille du régiment by Donizetti

ACT I ⁊

As villagers pray for protection from the Napoleonic forces, the Marquise of Berkenfield, forced to take a detour on her way home, arrives at the village. Sergeant Sulpice of the 21st Regiment enters, with Marie, their *vivandière*. She was found on the battlefield as a baby and had been raised by the regiment. Sulpice questions her about a young man she has been seen with. She explains that the man, Tonio, saved her from falling off a cliff. Just then, soldiers enter with Tonio; he has been discovered in the camp and arrested as a spy. Marie explains that he is her rescuer and saves him from execution. Tonio is taken away, but manages to return and he and Marie sing of their love for each other.

The marquise asks Suplice to ensure her safe conduct to Berkenfield. The name Berkenfield reminds Suplice of Captain Robert, a former officer; it also appeared on the birth papers found with Marie. The marquise declares that her sister was married to Captain Robert and that Marie is her niece. She insists on taking her back to Berkenfield, to live a more ladylike existence.

Tonio has joined the regiment to be near Marie. The other soldiers accept him, having learned that she returns his love. However, Suplice enters with Marie and announces that she is to leave with the marquise. Marie is pleased that Tonio has joined the regiment. The soldiers express their sorrow at her departure and bid her farewell.

ACT II ⁊

The marquise has arranged for Marie to marry the Duke of Crakentorp, to which Marie has reluctantly agreed. The marquise summons Sulpice to encourage Marie; together they sing the regimental song, to the marquise's distaste. Although Marie has tried to please the marquise, she misses the military life to which she is accustomed and still loves Tonio. Suplice reminds her that she is the marquise's niece and must do as she says. Marie hears the sound of marching in the distance and the 21st Regiment appears, including Tonio, whose bravery has earned him the post of officer. He tells the marquise of his love for Marie, but she will not change her plans. She confesses to Sulpice that Marie is in fact her illegitimate daughter; marrying the duke will provide Marie with the wealth and nobility that the marquise cannot offer her. As the wedding guests arrive, the marquise reveals her real identity to Marie, who resigns herself to the proposed match. Tonio and the regiment enter and declare that Marie was their *vivandière*. The wedding guests are shocked, but are moved as Marie tells them of the regiment's kindness towards her. The marquise relents and allows her to marry Tonio.

ABOVE: A military scene from a 1974 production of Donizetti's opéra-comique La fille du régiment.
ABOVE LEFT: Swedish soprano Jenny Lind, known as 'the Swedish nightingale', as Maria in an early production of the opera.

Don Pasquale

Don Pasquale by Donizetti
Composed   1842, 1843, Paris
Premiered   1843, Paris
Libretto   by Giovanni Ruffini, after Angelo Anelli

Donizetti's three-act comic opera, *Don Pasquale*, full of fun and infectious humour, was first performed at the Théâtre Italien in Paris on 3 January 1843. There was no hint here of Donizetti's failing health, but as time proved, *Don Pasquale* was among the last of his remarkable total of 67 operas. The first performance was a tremendous success. Donizetti was there and, to judge from a letter he afterwards wrote to his music publisher, Giovanni Ricordi (1785–1853), he was lionized by the audience: "I was called out at the end of the second and third acts," he wrote, "and there was not one piece, from the overture on,

that was not applauded to a greater or lesser extent. I am very happy." Donizetti was not the only one to score a brilliant success. Luigi Lablache (1794–1858), who created the title role, sang at the London premiere at the Haymarket Theatre on 29 June 1843. Afterwards, a contemporary journal, *The Musical World of London*, raved about Lablache, calling him "one of the greatest ornaments of the Italian opera in this or any other age". Queen Victoria, the reigning monarch, was certainly impressed with him: she appointed Lablache as her singing teacher.

BELOW: Paolo Montarsolo in the title role and Diana Soviero as Norina in a 1984 production of Donizetti's Don Pasquale.

𝒮ynopsis
Don Pasquale by Donizetti

ACT I ❧

Don Pasquale, a bachelor, is angry with his nephew Ernesto for refusing to marry the woman of his choice. Ernesto is in love with the widow Norina, who is far from wealthy, and Don Pasquale has decided to punish him by taking a bride himself and disinheriting his nephew. His friend Dr Malatesta arrives to announce that he has found a suitable bride – his sister Sofronia, a shy convent girl. Don Pasquale is delighted.

Don Pasquale offers Ernesto one more chance to agree to the match, but Ernesto, declaring his love for Norina, refuses. His uncle then tells Ernesto about his own coming wedding. Ernesto is dismayed, realizing he will never marry Norina, and begs his uncle to talk it over with Malatesta. When Don Pasquale reveals that not only does Malatesta approve of the idea, but has offered his own sister as the bride, Ernesto feels betrayed.

Norina laughs over a romantic novel, declaring that she is more capable of manipulating men. She receives a letter from Ernesto, which she later shows to Malatesta; it explains that Malatesta has betrayed

them by arranging Don Pasquale's marriage, and that Ernesto, disinherited, is leaving Europe. Malatesta reassures Norina and explains his plan: she is to be Sofronia and a phoney notary will perform the marriage ceremony. As soon as she becomes Don Pasquale's bride, Sofronia will transform into the caricature of a nagging, extravagant wife.

ACT II ❧

A dejected Ernesto prepares for his departure. Malatesta arrives with "Sofronia" – Norina in disguise – who is as shy and innocent as Malatesta promised. She admits that her only real pleasure lies in sewing. When she is unveiled, Don Pasquale demands that they marry immediately. Malatesta fetches the "notary", who provides a pretend marriage contract. As they sign the contract, Ernesto is called in as a witness and is appalled to see that the bride is Norina. Malatesta takes him aside and explains the plan.

Sofronia, now that she is married to Don Pasquale, changes completely. She refuses to kiss her new husband and declares that nothing in the household is good enough – they must order new servants, furniture, and carriages. Poor Don Pasquale is in despair. Amid the confusion, Norina reassures Ernesto that everything is going to plan.

ACT III ❧

Don Pasquale laments the mounting bills, as servants deliver Sofronia's extravagant purchases. Sofronia enters, announcing that she is going to the opera. She slaps Don Pasquale when he tries to stop her, telling him that old men should be in bed. She drops a note as she leaves and Don Pasquale is enraged when he reads it – it is a letter from a mystery lover arranging a rendezvous in the garden. Malatesta feigns incredulity at Sofronia's dreadful conduct and advises Don Pasquale to go along to the garden and catch his wife red-handed.

In the garden Ernesto and Norina meet and sing a romantic duet. Ernesto then leaves, as Don Pasquale and Malatesta arrive. Sofronia feigns horror at being caught, but defiantly defends her right to meet people in her own garden. Malatesta suggests that he take control of the situation and tells Sofronia that, provided Don Pasquale approves, Ernesto is to marry Norina, so that her power in the household will be diminished. Sofronia objects, causing Don Pasquale to approve the match and promise Ernesto a generous allowance. Ernesto then shows himself, and Norina reveals her identity, while Malatesta explains the deception. Don Pasquale is furious at first, but his relief at not being married to Sofronia is greater and he gives the couple his blessing.

Other Composers

AUBER, DANIEL-FRANÇOIS-ESPRIT
(1782–1871, FRENCH)

The French composer Daniel Auber made a favourable impression on his teacher, Luigi Cherubini (1760–1842) with his first opera *L'erreur du moment* ('The Mistake of the Moment', 1805). However, he had to wait 15 years for popular appreciation until he established himself with two works: *La bergère châtelaine* ('The Lady Shepherdess', 1820) and *Emma* (1821). In 1823 Auber teamed up with the French playwright Eugene Scribe, his librettist for the Italian-style operas *Leicester* (1823) and *La neige* ('The Snow', 1823) and then the French-style *Léocadie* (1824). Auber

1800—1845   EARLY ROMANTIC

ABOVE: French composer Daniel-François-Esprit Auber, who studied under Luigi Cherubini.

was soon establishing himself as a master of *opéra-comique* and confirmed this status with *Le Maçon* (1825), again with a libretto by Scribe. Three years later, Auber changed course again and, with his *La muette de Portici*, produced a work that helped establish French *grand opéra* as a new and imposing genre. In this seminal work, Auber injected more power into the leading roles and the choruses, reflected in his music the vivid scenic effects produced on stage and increased the role of the orchestra in building up the drama. Auber's music was an important influence on the works of other composers, including Richard Wagner's *Lohengrin* (1850).

Les Troyens, **London Symphony Orchestra**
Colin Davis, **conductor**
LSO Live LSO0010
Soloists: Petra Lang (Cassandre), Michelle DeYoung (Didon), Sara Mingardo (Anna), Ben Heppner (Enée), Kenneth Tarver (Iopas), Toby Spence (Hylas), Peter Mattei (Chorèbe), Stephen Milling (Narbal)

RECOMMENDED RECORDING

BERLIOZ, HECTOR
(1803–69, FRENCH)

The French composer Hector Berlioz, who once wrote that the opera houses of his time were too large, did a splendid job of filling their auditoria with the mighty sound of epic opera. His opera

Synopsis

Benvenuto Cellini
by Berlioz
Composed 1834–37
Premiered 1838, Paris
Libretto by Léon de Wailly and Auguste Barbier, after Cellini

ACT I

The Pope has commissioned Cellini to make a statue of Perseus. Balducci, the treasurer, is annoyed; he wants the commission to go to Fieramosca, who he also wants to marry his daughter Teresa; she is in love with Cellini.

Masked revellers, Cellini among them, mock Balducci. Teresa watches, hoping to see her lover. Cellini and Teresa meet and he outlines a plan for their elopement: he and his apprentice Asciano, dressed as monks, will abduct Teresa at the theatre. Fieramosca overhears the plan but is discovered by a furious Balducci.

Cellini and the metalworkers drink and praise their art. Balducci's meagre payment for the statue arrives; they arrange for him to be mocked in a play. Fieramosca tells Pompeo of Cellini's plan; they decide to steal the idea.

At the theatre, Balducci is enraged by the play. He attacks the actors and the four "monks" make for Teresa. A fight breaks out, in which Cellini kills Pompeo. Cellini escapes, while Fieramosca is arrested.

ACT II

Teresa and Asciano pray for Cellini, who appears. They rejoice, until an angry Balducci arrives with Fieramosca. The Pope enters, demanding his statue. After being persuaded not to re-commission the work, the Pope promises Cellini a pardon and Teresa's hand if the statue is finished in a day; if not, Cellini will hang.

Cellini wishes for an easy life as he works on the statue. Fieramosca enters, challenging Cellini to a duel, and bribes the workers to leave. Teresa intervenes and Fieramosca is forced to join in the workforce.

The Pope and Balducci arrive to watch the casting. The metal runs out; Cellini orders his previous works to be melted down. The casting is successful. The Pope is pleased and Balducci allows Teresa to marry Cellini. Everyone rejoices in the triumph of the arts.

LEFT: Benvenuto Cellini's statue of Perseus, on which Berlioz based his opera.

FIRST PERFORMANCE OF LES TROYENS

Les troyens was such a monumental proposition that even Berlioz was daunted by it. An entry for 1854 in his memoirs read: "For the last three years I have been tormented by the idea of a vast opera for which I would write both the words and the music ... I am resisting the temptation of carrying out this project, and I hope I will resist to the end (Footnote: Alas, no, I have not been able to resist) ... The subject seems to me elevated, magnificent and deeply moving – sure proof that the Parisians will find it dull and boring." Be that as it may, *Les troyens* certainly made too many demands on performers and audience for a continuous performance, which is why it was divided into two parts. The first was entitled *La prise de Troie* ('The Capture of Troy'). The second, *Les Troyens à Carthage* ('The Trojans in Carthage') premiered at the Théâtre Lyrique in Paris on 4 November 1863. *La prise de Troie*, however, had to wait almost 30 years for its first performance, until 1890, when it was reunited with *Les troyens à Carthage* and both were played together at Karlsruhe in Germany on 6 December 1890.

output was small, consisting of only five completed works, but their impact transcended mere numbers. Berlioz' first surviving opera, *Benvenuto Cellini* (1837) based on the life of the famous goldsmith and engraver of Renaissance Italy, was a failure. However, a later work, the two-part *Les troyens* ('The Trojans', 1856–58 and 1860–63), for which Berlioz wrote both words and music, was an epic fully worthy of the name. *Les troyens*, set during the Trojan War in the twelfth century BC, combined impressive spectacle, lyricism and classical grandeur with heroic tragedy on the most monumental scale possible. Berlioz had a fascination for the ancient Roman poet Virgil (70–19 BC) whose account of the Trojan War in his *Aeneid* was used as the basis for *Les troyens*. Berlioz, however, was also capable of the delicate touch and demonstrated this in an opera which he himself described as "a caprice written with the point of a needle" – his *Béatrice et Bénédict* (1862), based on Shakespeare's *The Taming of the Shrew*.

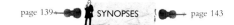

ABOVE: *The entry of the Greeks into Troy, shown here in an illustration from a fifteenth-century manuscript, inspired Berlioz'* Les Troyens.

Synopsis
Les troyens ('The Trojans')
by Berlioz
Composed 1856–58
Premiered 1846, Paris
Libretto by Almire Gandonnière and the composer, after Gérard de Nerval and Johann Wolfgang von Goethe

ACT I

The Trojans celebrate peace and admire the wooden horse left by the Greeks after the siege. Cassandre (Cassandra), King Priam's daughter, forsees the fall of Troy. Her husband Chorèbe (Coroebus) urges her to join the celebrations, but she begs him to flee. Énée (Aeneas) reveals that sea serpents have killed the priest Laocöon, after he suggested destroying the horse. Fearing the fury of the gods, the Trojans bring the horse into the city.

ACT II

Hector's ghost tells Énée to leave for Italy, where he will found a new Troy. Panthée, Énée's friend, enters with the news that Greeks have burst out of the horse and are sacking the city.

In the palace, Cassandre tells the Trojan women of Énée's quest. She prepares to kill herself, urging the others to do the same to save themselves from the Greeks. Some refuse and are driven away; the others declare their right to die free. The Greeks enter in search of the treasure, which Énée has taken; they are greeted by a mass suicide.

ACT III

In her palace, Didon (Dido) celebrates the anniversary of the founding of Carthage. Her sister Anna assures her she will find love again. The poet Iopas brings news of the shipwrecked Trojans and Didon welcomes them. Énée, hearing that Carthage is to be attacked by Numidians, offers to assist in battle; Didon falls in love with him.

ACT IV

The royal hunt is halted by a storm. Didon and Énée seek shelter in a cave.

Didon's advisor, Narbal, complains to Anna that since the Numidian battle the queen is neglecting her duties. He is also uneasy of Didon's affair, since Énée has to leave for Italy.

Didon enters with Énée, requesting tales of Troy and finding comfort in his words. They declare their love for each other until interrupted by Mercury, who reminds Énée of his destiny.

ACT V

The Trojans are besieged by omens and ghosts, urging them to leave for Italy. Énée reluctantly tells Didon that he must leave. She entreats him not to go, but he is resolved, especially when the Trojan ghosts appear. Didon curses him. Later she asks Anna to persuade Énée to stay, but the Trojans have set sail. Furious, she orders a pyre to be built.

Didon burns the relics of Énée's visit. A vision of the glory of Rome appears. Predicting that Hannibal will avenge her, Didon stabs herself. The Carthaginians swear vengeance on Énée and his race.

1800–1845 EARLY ROMANTIC

OTHER COMPOSERS

page 124 · page 150 · page 138 · page 158 · page 130 · page 184

'DIE LEIZTE ROSE' (THE LAST ROSE)

In this aria from Act II of *Martha*, Lady Harriet, disguised as Martha, is asked by her lover Lionel to sing a folk song. She responds with an old Irish air, originally named 'The Groves of Blarney', which von Flotow adapted into 'Last Rose of Summer'.

POPULAR MELODY

BOIELDIEU, FRANÇOIS-ADRIEN
(1775–1834, FRENCH)

Adrien Boieldieu wrote his first opera *La fille coupable* ('The Guilty Girl', 1793) when he was 18. Shortly afterwards, he left his home town of Rouen and settled in Paris. He scored quick success with his *opéras-comiques*, but his talent did not stop at the standard ingredients of the genre. He was also capable of writing, for example, the exotically oriental *Le calife de Bagdad* ('The Caliph of Baghdad', 1800). After five years as court composer in St Petersburg, Boieldieu returned to France in 1812 where his *Jean de Paris* ('John of Paris', 1812) was admired by Carl Weber for the "freedom and elegance of his vocal line ... and ... his careful and excellent use of the orchestra." Boieldieu's masterpiece, *La dame blanche* ('The White Lady', 1825), was judged one of the most important French Romantic operas written in the 1820s. By this time Boieldieu had spent the last 10 years as court composer to King Louis XVIII (1755–1824), who was restored to the throne after the downfall of Napoleon in 1815. However, his career effectively ended with the revolution of 1830, which swept away the old Bourbon monarchy – and everyone, even musicians, who had served it.

CHERUBINI, LUIGI
(1760–1842, ITALIAN)

The Italian composer Luigi Cherubini studied in Florence, Bologna and Milan, first writing church music, and then, in 1779, producing his first operas.

By 1787, when he settled in Paris, he had written 13 operas, but nothing, as yet, that was innovatory. This changed when his *Démophon* (1788) signalled a new direction, towards the pioneering of *opéra-comique* and *grand opéra*.

CABALETTA

The *cabaletta* or *cavaletta* came from the Italian word for "grasshopper". Originally, the *cabaletta* was a short popular aria with a simple, repetitive rhythm. However, by the nineteenth century the *cabaletta* had a more specialized meaning; now, it described the final, lively section of an aria or a duet, which followed a "smoothly sung" *cantabile* and so ignited the enthusiasm of the audience with an exciting ending. Unfortunately, the *cabaletta* – and especially its repeats – provided opportunities for singers prone to show off with a *bravura* vocal display and much ornamentation. This prolonged an aria or duet and held up the action of the opera. Both Rossini and Donizetti wrote *cabalettas* for their operas and so did Bellini, in the "sleepwalking aria" he wrote for Amina in Act III of his *La sonnambula*. However, the real master of the technique was Giovanni Pacini (1796–1867). Pacini, composer of some 40 operas, produced very energetic melodies with all the fire that made the *cabaletta* so rousing. Giuseppe Verdi also wrote *cabalettas* for arias in some of his operas, notably *La traviata* ('The Fallen Woman', 1853) and *Il trovatore* ('The Troubador', 1853). Even so, Verdi did not really approve of the *cabaletta*, and, under his influence, it eventually disappeared.

OTHER COMPOSERS

With his *Loidoïska* (1791), Luigi Cherubini introduced richer orchestration, more powerful ensemble music, stronger, more compelling drama, more realistic characters and a new ingredient – the contribution to the action made by natural forces, in this case a fire. Gradually, as more operas followed, Cherubini displayed more of the early symptoms of Romantic opera, with arias for subordinate characters or peasants depicted as simple but virtuous in accordance with the social principles of Rousseau. *Musique d'effet* – effect music – entered the equation, with Cherubini increasing the importance of the orchestra and accompanying the voice with horn or clarinet *obbligati*. These Romantic elements were poignantly on display in Cherubini's *Médée* ('Medea', 1797) – a tragedy of elemental passion based on Greek legend. However, Cherubini was just as sure-handed with the simpler characters of *opéra-comique* and the suspense of 'rescue operas', such as the work *Faniska* (1806).

FLOTOW, FRIEDRICH VON
(1813–83, GERMAN)

Though German-born, Friedrich von Flotow studied in Paris and became largely identified with French opera. His first operas in the French style were written for private salon performances. *Alessandro*

Stradella (1844), his first international success, revealed his penchant for building a work around one "hit tune", in this case '*Jung Frau Maria*'. After leaving Paris for Vienna, von Flotow scored his greatest and most enduring triumph with *Martha* (1847), which included the popular song 'The Last Rose of Summer'. Sadly, von Flotow never scaled these heights again, despite the charm of his *La veuve Grapin* ('The Widow Grapin', 1859). Nevertheless, von Flotow ensured his place in the development of opera with his cosmopolitan approach; he combined the influence of French *opéra-comique* with the Italian lyricism of his vocal writing and the orchestral style favoured in German Romantic opera. Though his light touch made his music less suited to the more weighty operatic subjects, it was ideal for comic arias, with just the right fluency, grace and charm. One secret of von Flotow's success in Paris was his skill in adapting the somewhat florid sentimental style of German Romantic opera to please the more cerebral French taste.

LEFT: German composer Friedrich von Flotow.
FAR LEFT: Luigi Cherubini, who wrote many Romantic operas.

Synopsis
Médée by Cherubini
Composed 1797
Premiered 1797, Paris
Libretto by François Benoit Hoffman, after Pierre Corneille

ACT I

At the palace of Corinth, Glaucé, daughter of King Créon, prepares for her approaching marriage to Jason. She fears the wrath of Médée, a sorceress who helped Jason to steal the Golden Fleece from Cholcis. Médée betrayed her family to help Jason and later bore him two children, who are now in Jason's care. Créon and Jason reassure Glaucé.

Médée arrives and orders Jason not to marry Glaucé, but he defies her, warning her against incurring Créon's wrath. She curses him and swears vengeance.

ACT II

Créon has banished Médée from the city, but she insists on seeing her children; he allows her to remain for one more day. She asks Jason to see them but he refuses. Realizing how much he loves the children, she resolves to kill them in order to spite him. He eventually allows Médée to look after the children until she leaves the city. Médée admits to her servant Néris that she considers the children to belong only to Jason, and that she does not love them. She gives Néris a cloak and diadem to deliver to Glaucé as wedding gifts and then gleefully looks on as the wedding guests arrive.

ACT III

Néris brings the children to Médée. Momentarily recovering her maternal instincts, she embraces them. Cries from the temple signify that Glaucé has been killed by Médée's gifts, which were steeped in poison. Remembering Jason's treachery, Médée resumes her path of revenge and takes the

ABOVE: A 530–510 BC Greek vase, showing the figure of Medea, the subject of Cherubini's opera, together with Dionysos.

children into the temple. Jason arrives with an angry crowd; Néris tries to tell him of Médée's plans but it is too late. Médée, having slaughtered her sons, emerges from the temple covered in blood and surrounded by Furies. As the temple burns, Médée vanishes into the air with the Furies, promising to meet Jason in the underworld.

EARLY ROMANTIC

1800–1845

GLINKA, MIKHAIL IVANOVICH (1804–57, RUSSIAN)

As the composer of *A Life for the Tsar* (1836), Mikhail Glinka became the founder of Russian historical opera. *A Life for the Tsar* told the story of Ivan Susanin, a popular Russian hero who, in 1612, saved the life of the future tsar and founder of the Romanov dynasty, Michael Romanov. Although French and Italian influences were present, Glinka's music was unmistakably Russian with its use of folk songs, balalaika music and recitative that conformed to the inflections of the Russian language. The opera made Glinka an overnight success and Russia's leading composer at its first performance in St Petersburg on 9 December 1836. He was already planning his next work, *Ruslan i Lyudmila* ('Ruslan and Ludmilla', 1842), but suffered problems with the text after Alexander Pushkin (1799–1837), who had written the poem on which the opera was based, was killed in a duel. Glinka had to make do with a less than satisfactory libretto, written by several people. His music, however, transcended this problem with its original rhythms, strong

harmonies, oriental content and dazzling orchestration. Like *A Life for the Tsar*, *Ruslan* was a seminal work, this time founding the genre of Russian magic opera.

HALÉVY, JACQUES-FRANÇOIS-FROMENTAL (1799–1862, FRENCH)

Jacques-François-Fromental Halévy, who was born in Paris, studied there with several composers of whom the most influential was Luigi Cherubini. Success at the opera house was rather long in coming, however, and Halévy had to endure rejections and failures before

scoring his first success with *Clari* (1828), which was written for the Spanish mezzo-soprano Maria Malibran (1808–36). Halévy's next significant work did not appear for another seven years, but when it did, it was his

BELOW LEFT: Mikhail Ivanovich Glinka, the founder of Russian historical opera and composer of works such as A Life for the Tsar.

'RACHEL'
In this tenor aria from Act IV of *La juive*, the Jewish goldsmith Eléazar sings of his fearful dilemma: should he let his daughter Rachel die at the hands of her persecutor Cardinal de Brogni, or should he save her by revealing that she is, in reality, de Brogni's daughter?

POPULAR MELODY

Synopsis
A Life for the Tsar
by Glinka
Premiered 1836, St Petersburg
Libretto by Baron Yegor Fyodorovich Rozen
and others

BACKGROUND ❧

The years of turmoil following the death of Tsar Fyodor I in 1598 might finally be coming to an end. The revolt of the "False Dmitri" in 1605 has led to Polish intervention. In 1613, after an interregnum of nearly three years, Mikhail Fyodorovich Romanov has been elected tsar, but has been forced to go into hiding in a monastery near Kostroma.

ACT I ❧

In the village of Domnino the peasants are affirming their devotion to the tsar. Antonida, daughter of the peasant Ivan Susanin, is preparing for her marriage to Sobinin, who arrives with news of Prince Pozharsky's victories against the Poles. He asks permission to marry Antonida, but Susanin says they must wait until there is a lawful Russian tsar on the throne. When told of Mikhail Romanov's election Susanin withdraws all objections to the marriage.

ACT II ❧

At the Polish court the nobility are celebrating their successes against the Russians in a series of national dances. A messenger brings news of the

election of a Russian tsar, to challenge their own claimant. Some soldiers set off to capture the new tsar before his coronation.

ACT III ❧

Susanin assures Vanya, his ward, that no one would betray the tsar. They are joined by Antonida and Sobinin, and Susanin blesses the couple. Polish soldiers burst into the hut and demand to know where the tsar is hiding. Susanin eventually agrees to show them the way, but whispers to Vanya that he will take them in the wrong direction, giving Vanya time to raise the alarm. Antonida begs him not to go, knowing the Poles will kill him. After they have left, Sobinin and the peasants swear vengeance.

ACT IV ❧

In the forest, Sobinin's men have lost their way. Vanya arrives at the monastery and warns them that the Poles are on their way. The Poles suspect that they have been tricked and pitch camp. While they sleep Susanin takes leave of his life, hoping that he can hold out until dawn. When they awake, he tells the Poles how he deliberately misled them. As they beat him to death he sees the first light of day. Sobinin and the peasants fall on the Poles.

EPILOGUE ❧

Among the crowds celebrating the tsar's coronation are Antonida, Sobinin and Vanya, who are told that the tsar will never forget Susanin's sacrifice.

OTHER COMPOSERS

masterpiece. The opera, *La juive* ('The Jewess', 1835) took its place among the fundamental works of French *grand opéra* and was praised at several levels by other composers. Hector Berlioz admired its vivid orchestration, while Richard Wagner lauded the "pathos of (its)

high lyric tragedy" and Halévy's skill at recreating the fifteenth-century background of religious persecution with a minimum of detail. Halévy went on to show remarkable versatility as a composer, moving easily between *opéra-comique* with *L'éclair* ('The Brief Meeting',

1835) or *Le lazzarone* ('The Vagabond', 1844) and *grand opéra* with *Guido et Ginevra* (1838) or *Charles VI* (1844). Although Hector Berlioz believed that he was at his best in light opera, Halévy was one of the most important proponents of French *grand opéra*.

Synopsis
Ruslan i Lyudmila ('Ruslan and Ludmilla')
by Glinka
Composed 1837–42
Premiered 1842, St Petersburg
Libretto by Konstantin Bakhturin, Valerina Shirov and various others, after Alexander Pushkin

ACT I
Everyone celebrates the marriage of Lyudmila to the knight Ruslan. Her rejected admirers Farlaf and Ratmir are also present. As Lyudmila's father Svyetozar blesses the couple, a thunderbolt is heard and darkness falls. When the light returns, Lyudmila has vanished. Her father offers half his kingdom and Lyudmila's hand in marriage to whoever saves her. Farlaf, Ratmir and Ruslan all pledge to find her.

ACT II
Ruslan meets Finn, a magician, who informs him that Lyudmila has been abducted by Chernomor, an evil dwarf. Finn warns him of Naina, a wicked sorceress. Meanwhile, Farlaf encounters Naina, who says she will help him to find Lyudmila. Ruslan arrives at a battlefield. He encounters an enormous head, which belongs to a sleeping giant. The giant, revealing a magic sword, explains that he is Chernomor's brother. This sword is the only weapon that can overcome the evil dwarf, whose strength lies in his beard.

ACT III
Naina arranges for her servants to seduce Ratmir, much to the distress of his companion and admirer, Gorislava. Ruslan is also drawn to the maidens, but is saved from temptation by Finn, who also frees Ratmir from the spell and makes him return Gorislava's love. Ratmir resolves to help Ruslan.

ACT IV
Lyudmila considers suicide and is not amused by the dwarf's attendants. Chernomor arrives, hoping to seduce her, and performs a dance. Ruslan challenges Chernomor to a duel. The dwarf sends Lyudmila to sleep and then consents. Ruslan cuts off Chernomor's beard, rendering him powerless, and sets off with the slumbering Lyudmila.

ACT V
Farlaf abducts Lyudmila, but Finn gives Ratmir a magic ring for Ruslan, which will awaken her. Farlaf arrives at the palace with Lyudmila to claim his reward, but cannot awaken her. The others arrive with the ring and Ruslan rouses Lyudmila. The wedding celebrations resume and everyone rejoices.

LEFT: The set for Naina's castle in Act III of Glinka's Ruslan i Lyudmila *by Boris Bilinsky, from a 1930* Opera Russe à Paris *programme.*

EARLY ROMANTIC

1800—1845

OTHER COMPOSERS

MARSCHNER, HEINRICH
(1795–1861, GERMAN)

Heinrich Marschner, the German composer, had the best possible backer for his first opera, *Heinrich IV und d'Aubigné* (1817–18), which was set around the turn of the seventeenth century. It featured King Henri IV of France and his follower the Huguenot poet Théodore d'Aubigné. Carl Maria von Weber, no less, staged the opera in Dresden, where Marschner became his assistant in 1824. However, their friendship faded when Weber became convinced that Marschner was imitating his style and using it, not for the advancement of German opera, but for his own commercial purposes. After Weber's death in 1826, Marschner was passed over as his successor and left Dresden. For a time Marschner's fortunes faltered, as he failed as music director in Danzig. However, after moving to Leipzig, Marschner began to work on *Der Vampyr* ('The Vampire', 1828), which scored a welcome success despite its resemblance to Weber's *Der Freischütz*. This was followed by his third and last success, *Hans Heiling* (1833). Although his work was uneven – none of his five other operas reached the same heights as his successful trio – Marschner pioneered the hero torn between good and evil, the real and supernatural worlds and showed how music could typify melodrama and emphasize its emotional effects.

MAYR, JOHANNES SIMON
(1763–1845, GERMAN)

The German-born composer Johannes Mayr was studying in Italy when the patron who supported him died and he faced an uncertain future. Niccolo Piccini encouraged him to write opera and Mayr took his advice. Mayr's first opera *Saffo* (1794) attracted several commissions. Mayr's great breakthrough came when his *Ginevra di Scozia* ('Geneva of Scotland', 1801) was performed at the Teatro Nuovo in Trieste. It made his name known all over Italy. Subsequently Mayr wrote operas for Naples, Rome, Milan and Venice and his work was performed internationally in Germany, London, St Petersburg, New York and several other places. Mayr's masterpiece, *Medea in Corinto* ('Medea in Corinth', 1813), was first performed in Naples in 1813, a year in which he wrote two other operas, but after that he produced no more. In his last years, he was blind. Mayr's output, however, made a significant mark on the evolution of opera, which influenced Rossini and his generation of Italian composers. Mayr increased the role of the chorus, characters acquired a greater range of expression, the orchestra was able to emulate storms and earthquakes, among other natural happenings, and in *Medea in Corinto* there was greater continuity between the arias.

MÉHUL, ETIENNE-NICOLAS
(1763–1817, FRENCH)

Euphrosine (1790), the second opera composed by Etienne Méhul, was an *opéra-comique* containing a duet that not only became instantly popular, but also used a comparatively

ABOVE: German composer Johannes Simon Mayr, painted by by Gaetano Birabini. Mayr's work was an influence on composers such as Rossini.

1800—1845   EARLY ROMANTIC

Synopsis
Hans Heiling
by Marschner
Premiered 1833, Berlin
Libretto by Eduard Devrient after a
Bohemian legend

PROLOGUE

Hans Heiling, the King of the Gnomes, announces that he wishes to marry Anna, a mortal. His mother tries to dissuade him, since he would lose his powers.

ACT I

Anna and her mother Gertrude come to Heiling's house above ground. While Anna still dreams of her lover Conrad, Gertrude insists on the match with Heiling. Anna makes Heiling burn the magic book that gives him his powers. He declares his love for Anna and agrees to go to the village festival with her, but forbids her to dance.

At the festival Conrad tells his friends that anyone who marries an earth spirit will meet with disaster. Heiling is jealous of the attention Anna pays to Conrad. She still wants to dance, saying that she will do as she pleases until she is married. Heiling storms out, realizing that she never loved him.

ACT II

Anna is alone in the forest. The Queen of the Gnomes appears and tells her of Heiling's true identity. Before sinking into the ground she urges Anna to send him back to his home. Conrad is surprised to find Anna here. On hearing that she will never marry Heiling, Conrad offers his protection.

As a storm rages, Conrad brings Anna to Gertrude's hut. Heiling appears and offers her a casket of jewels. Anna still refuses him and in a fight Conrad is wounded.

ACT III

Heiling resolves to return to his underground kingdom. The villagers process to the church for the wedding of Anna and Conrad. Heiling enters during the ceremony. Conrad challenges him, but his sword is shattered. As gnomes burst in and threaten the villagers, the queen appears to recall Heiling to his kingdom, never to be seen again.

OTHER COMPOSERS

new musical device, the reminiscence motif. In *Gardez-vous la jalousie* ('Beware of jealousy') Méhul wrote alternating thirds to represent "jealousy" and repeated it throughout the opera. This was only one way in which Méhul made his name as an innovative composer. In typical Romantic fashion, he made imaginative use of the orchestra, giving it a greater share in the drama on stage. In *Ariodant* (1799), set in the world of knightly adventures, Méhul provided dark, moody orchestration to add expressiveness to the music. Méhul's career coincided with the French Revolution and its aftermath and some of his work inevitably reflected contemporary politics. For example, he was commissioned, possibly by Napoleon, to write an opera – *La prise du pont de Lodi* ('The Capture of the Bridge at Lodi', 1797) – celebrating Napoleon's victory over the Austrians in Italy in 1796. Four years later, Méhul embarked on a series of comedies, but reverted to a biblical theme for his last

STAGE EFFECTS IN ROMANTIC OPERA

Spectacle and optical illusion were involved in opera stage settings from the start. Even the comparatively intimate Baroque operas, while musically "balanced" and "restrained", relied heavily on visuals and scenic effects. In Romantic opera, the music itself acquired more drama and more atmosphere so that stage settings had to increase their impact to match. In Italy, for example, cunning use of backdrops and receding arches made the stage appear deeper than it really was. In Paris, popular theatres were quick to modernize, adopting more elaborate lighting, scenery and stage effects, together with historically accurate costumes. Except for the introduction of gas lamps for stage and front-of-house lighting in 1822, the conservative Paris Opéra held back. Eventually, in 1827, a committee was formed to look into new ways of staging opera and in particular, *grand opéra*. Before long, the Opéra acquired extra changes of scenery, correctly dressed choruses and non-singing performers to fill out processions on stage and make it appear crammed with people. One important innovation was the method of double-painting scenery devised by the pioneer of photography Louis Jacques Mandé Daguerre (1789–1851). This made it possible to transform scenery as the audience watched, by lighting it from different angles.

successful opera *Joseph* (1807), which contained the graceful melody and realistic atmosphere that were his trademarks.

RIGHT: A photograph of Louis Daguerre, showing the effects of his unique process of image reversal. He also turned his hand to opera sets.
BELOW: The capture of the Bridge at Lodi, which became the subject of an opera by Méhul, possible commissioned by Napoleon.

OTHER COMPOSERS

MEYERBEER, GIACOMO
(1791–1864, GERMAN)

Neither Giacomo Meyerbeer's first oratorio, nor his first opera, written in 1812 and 1813, was successful and his *Singspiel Das Brandenburger Tor* (1814) came too late to achieve its purpose – to celebrate the return home of the victorious Prussian army. It was a poor start for Meyerbeer but his fortunes changed dramatically after he left his native Germany for Italy, where he wrote six operas. These were so successful that Meyerbeer was touted as the new Rossini. More success awaited in France with his *Robert le diable* ('Robert the Devil', 1831) – a *grand opéra* set in thirteenth-century Sicily when it was under the rule of the demi-devil Robert, Duke of Normandy. In this and his next, even more successful work – *Les Huguenots* ('The Huguenots', 1836) – Meyerbeer showed keen understanding of how to cope with the vast size and lavish staging of *grand opéra. Les Huguenots*, based on the history of the massacre suffered by the Protestants of France in the sixteenth century, established Meyerbeer as, arguably, the most important composer of *grand opéra*. In this context, he deployed many brilliant talents – his inventive orchestration, dazzling vocal music and his unerring ability to match imposing themes to major historical events.

NICOLAI, CARL
OTTO EHRENFRIED
(1810–49, GERMAN)

Although Carl Otto Ehrenfried Nicolai was born in Kaliningrad, northwest of Moscow, he is classed as a German composer. Between 1833 and 1836, Nicolai was organist at the Prussian Chapel in Rome where he became fascinated with opera. His first work for the opera stage, *Enrico II* ('Henry II', 1839) was enthusiastically received in Trieste. Best known as a conductor, Nicolai cleverly combined this career with the opera by becoming principle conductor at the Vienna Hofoper in 1841. One of his first tasks was to introduce the 'Leonora No. 3' overture as an *entr'acte* at a performance of Beethoven's opera, *Fidelio*. After six years in Vienna, Nicolai moved to Berlin, where he became opera *Kapellmeister* and cathedral choir director in 1848. In Berlin, Nicolai wrote his Romantic comic opera *Die lüstigen Weiber von Windsor* ('The Merry Wives of Windsor', 1849), which was based on Shakespeare's comedy of that name. *Die lüstigen*, Nicolai's masterpiece,

ABOVE: Giacomo Meyerbeer, who made an unpromising start but went on to compose the popular grand opéra Les Huguenots.

𝒮*ynopsis*
Les Huguenots ('The Huguenots')
by Meyerbeer
Premiered 1836, Paris
Libretto by Eugène Scribe, Emile Deschamps
and Gaetano Rossi

ACT I ⁊

Nevers, a Catholic, has invited the Huguenot Raoul to a feast, as the king desires peace between the two factions. The guests describe their experiences of love. Raoul has fallen for a lady whom he saved from some students. Marcel, Raoul's servant, arrives and sings a Huguenot song.

Nevers' page announces the arrival of a woman to see Nevers. The guests watch the encounter; Raoul is incensed to see it is the woman he loves. She is Valentine, Nevers' fiancée, and has come to break off the engagement as she now loves another. Urbain, a page, enters with a note for Raoul inviting him to a rendezvous, and to come blindfolded. The guests notice the seal of Marguérite de Valois.

ACT II ⁊

Marguérite is arranging for Raoul to marry Valentine, uniting the Catholics and Huguenots. Raoul is led in and his blindfold removed; he pledges loyalty to Marguérite. He agrees to the match, but when Valentine is brought in he recognizes her as his "faithless" lover and rejects her. Her father, Saint-Bris, is furious; the Catholics swear vengeance.

ACT III ⁊

The wedding of Nevers and Valentine begins. Marcel delivers Raoul's challenge of a duel to Saint-Bris, who plots an ambush. Valentine overhears and warns Marcel. Raoul rallies his companions but Marguérite intervenes and prevents the fight. Raoul learns the truth about Nevers and Valentine, but they are now married.

ACT IV ⁊

As Valentine laments losing Raoul, he appears. He hides as Saint-Bris enters and overhears the Catholics' plans for a slaughter of Huguenots that evening. He leaves to warn the others.

ACT V ⁊

As the Huguenots celebrate Marguérite's marriage to Henri de Navarre, a badly injured Raoul enters with news of the conflict. Raoul, Marcel and Valentine find each other among the fighting. Nevers is dead and they are free to marry. Saint-Bris and Catholics shoot at the Huguenots, realizing too late that they have killed Valentine.

premiered in Berlin on 9 March 1849 and only
just in time. Two months later, Nicolai was dead.
In *Die lüstigen*, which marked the apogee of
German comic opera, Nicolai skilfully married
German musical traditions with the fluent
melodic grace of the style he imbibed in Italy.

SCHUBERT, FRANZ
(1797–1828, AUSTRIAN)

Celebrated for his instrumental works and over
600 songs, Franz Schubert knew that musical fame
and fortune in Vienna lay above all in the opera
house. In his teens he completed several one-act
comedies and the 'magic opera', *Des Teufels
Lustschloss* ('The Devil's Pleasure Palace', 1814).
Thanks to his friend, the baritone Johann
Michael Vogl, his operetta *Die Zwillingsbrüder*
('The Twin Brothers', 1818–19) was professionally
staged in Vienna in June 1820. Though only
a moderate success, it was followed by the
melodrama *Die Zauberharfe* ('The Magic Harp',
1820). Though its often-delightful music did not
go unnoticed, *Die Zauberharfe*'s preposterous plot
doomed it to failure, setting the pattern for most
of Schubert's stage works over the next few years.
In any case German opera had little chance in a
Vienna intoxicated by Rossini. Schubert's
grandest, most ambitious operas, *Alfonso und
Estrella* (1821–22) and *Fierrabras* (1823) were

rejected by the
Court Theatre, and
remained unperformed
in his lifetime.

Both *Alfonso* and *Fierrabras* contain much
beautiful and characteristic music, especially in
nature descriptions such as the exquisite duet
'*Weit über Glanz und Erdenschimmer*' ('Far
above the shimmering earth') from *Fierrabras*.
Yet both suffer from creaky, diffuse plots and
unsure dramatic timing. Probably Schubert's
most successful opera in the theatre is the
ebullient one-act comedy *Die Verschworenen*
('The Conspirators', 1823), a nineteenth-
century take on Aristophanes' *Lysistrata*.

SPONTINI, GASPARE
(1774–1851, ITALIAN)

Gaspare Spontini's early career was blighted by
insecurity after the French, under Napoleon
Bonaparte, invaded Italy in 1796. Spontini, it
seems, decided that his future lay in France, but
after arriving in Paris in 1800 he found his
musical style was unsuited to the prevailing
genre, *opéra-
comique*. Spontini
turned instead to serious
themes and produced *Milton* (1804),
which dealt with the English Puritan poet John
Milton in old age. *Milton* was a success but *La
vestale* ('The Vestal Virgin', 1807) took success a
step further and marked out Spontini as one of
the leading composers of opera in his time.
Subsequently Spontini played a crucial role in
founding French *grand opéra*, pioneering the
genre's most imposing features – rituals,
processions, large choruses, stage bands and other
grandiose effects. These ingredients came
together in their greatest splendour in *Fernand
Cortez* (1809), Spontini's historical pageant on
the sixteenth-century Spanish conqueror of
Aztec Mexico. Among its sensational effects was
a full-scale cavalry charge on stage.
Unfortunately, Spontini was haughty and
overbearing and his later career was marked by
quarrels with colleagues in Paris and Berlin,
where his later work, *Agnes von Hohentaufen*, a
German *grand opéra*, was performed in 1827.

ABOVE: *Maria Callas and Ebe Stignani in a 1954 production of Spontini's*
La Vestale, *staged at La Scala Opera House, Milan, Italy.*
RIGHT: *Franz Schubert, best known for his beautiful songs and
instrumental compositions, also wrote some rarely performed operas.*

EARLY ROMANTIC

1800—1845

Librettists

CAMMARANO, SALVADORE (1801–52, ITALIAN)

Salvadore Cammarano wrote several plays before producing his first libretto in 1834. This so impressed the management at the Teatro San Carlo in Naples that Cammarano was appointed house poet in 1835. That same year, Cammarano wrote the libretto for *Lucia di Lammermoor*, composed by his friend Gaetano Donizetti. Cammarano and Donizetti worked on many more operas together, notably *Robert Devereux, ossia Il Conte d'Essex*. In 1845 Giuseppe Verdi asked Cammarano for a libretto for *Alzira*, a two-act opera based on a tragedy by Voltaire. This, unfortunately, was one of Verdi's – and Cammarano's – few failures. Disappointment did not deter Verdi from again working with Cammarano, who had an unusual talent for writing libretti acceptable to everyone – audience, composer, even the censor. Cammarano wrote the text for Verdi's *Luisa Miller* (1849) and *Il trovatore* but died six months before the latter premiered in Rome on 19 January 1853.

GOETHE, JOHANN WOLFGANG VON (1749–1832, GERMAN)

Johann von Goethe, greatest of all German poets and dramatists, created what became almost a genre in its own right with his *Faust* (1808). The

theme captured the imaginations of numerous composers and among the 122 operas based on Goethe's writings, the Faustian legend formed the plot for 20 of them. Goethe did more than provide texts for composers, however. He had a passion for music and wrote the libretti for eight *Singspiel* compositions. He was a great admirer of Mozart's *Die Zauberflöte* and, being a Freemason, recognized and appreciated its masonic content. Goethe wrote part of a sequel to *Die Zauberflöte*,

ABOVE: Johann Wolfgang von Goethe, whose works inspired a great many operas, and who wrote libretti in addition to poems and plays.
RIGHT: Friedrich von Schiller, whose plays provided inspiration for composers such as Verdi, Donizetti and Puccini.

FRENCH GRAND OPÉRA

In France audiences had a taste for imposing grandeur and the big canvas of elemental events that manifest itself in opera after about 1820 as French *grand opéra*. Everything about *grand opéra* was supersized and deliberately made so by its chief architects, the artist and set designer Pierre-Luc-Charles Cicéri (1782–1868), the lighting expert Louis Daguerre, the librettist Eugene Scribe and the co-ordinator of all their efforts Louis Véron (1798–1867), manager of the Paris Opéra. French *grand opéra* normally comprised four or five acts and included performances of ballet. Great care was taken to use only historically and geographically accurate sets that were changed for each act, and sometimes for each scene. Scenery was usually three-dimensional and was subtly varied by the use of lighting effects and moving backcloths. Stage machinery came into operation for the finale to depict some cataclysmic event such as an earthquake, volcanic eruption, avalanche, shipwreck, or other disaster. The cast list for *grand opéra* could be extensive, since the performers had to "populate" processions, battles, festivals, riots and other crowd scenes. The orchestra, too, increased in size and there were also on-stage bands, which played unusual instruments such as saxhorns, tuned bells and even anvils.

but unfortunately it was never set to music. Between 1791 and 1817, when Goethe was director of the Weimar Theater, the repertory included several operas and Mozart's music featured in 280 of the performances.

ROMANI, FELICE (1788–1865, ITALIAN)

Felice Romani was greatly admired by around 100 Italian composers who sought to enlist his instinct for operatic drama and his ability to write elegant verse. Among them were Rossini, for whom Romani wrote *Il turco in Italia* ('A Turk in Italy', 1814) and Verdi, whom he provided with the libretto for *Un giorno di regno* ('King for a Day', 1840). However, the name of Romani is most closely associated with Bellini and Donizetti. Romani supplied Donizetti with the libretti for *Anna Bolena* and *L'elisir d'amore*. For Bellini, Romani wrote the text for *La sonnambula* and *Norma*. Romani's collaboration with Bellini began with the opera that first made the

composer's name – *Il pirata* – and included a third member, the tenor Giovanni Battista Rubini (1794–1854) who created the title role at La Scala, Milan on 27 October 1827.

SCHILLER, FRIEDRICH VON (1759–1805, GERMAN)

Friedrich von Schiller, the great German poet, playwright and historian, trained for the Church, the army, the law and military medicine before he finally found his niche. It happened when, at his own expense, Schiller published his revolutionary drama *Die Raüber* ('The Robbers', 1781). When the play was staged in Mannheim in 1782, it was an encouraging success, but the playwright, who was still in the army, was arrested for attending the first night without the permission of his commanding officer. Over 50 years later, in 1836, the Italian composer Saverio Mercadente (1795–1870) wrote an opera based on Schiller's first play.

As an opera it was the first of an ultimate total of 56 by various composers. Among the most famous, Giuseppe Verdi based *Luisa Miller* and *Don Carlos* (1867) on Schiller's work, as did Donizetti for his *Maria Stuarda* and Giacomo Puccini for his *Turandot* (1926).

SCRIBE, EUGENE (1791–1861, FRENCH)

Eugene Scribe, the French librettist, scored his first success with Auber's *opéra-comique*, *La dame blanche* ('The White Lady', 1825). However, Scribe concentrated mainly on French *grand opéra*, with libretti that matched the genre's visual and musical grandeur and the dramatic on-stage action. Scribe formed a partnership with Auber, who set no less than 38 of his libretti to music. The central figures of French *grand opéra*, such as Halévy and Meyerbeer also recognized in Scribe an artist whose verse was capable of equalling the "size" of their music. A situation in which composer and librettist "thought big" was essential in *grand opéra* for which Scribe drew his plots from history at its most dramatic: he specialized in the clash of religions, as in Meyerbeer's *Les Huguenots*, or in political and national rivalries in which real life was entwined with the fate of characters caught up in epoch-making events.

ABOVE: French librettist Eugene Scribe, from a bust by David D'Angers.

Singers

CINTI-DAMOREAU, LAURE
(1801–63, FRENCH)

The French soprano Laure Cinti-Damoreau was only 15 when she made her debut at the Théâtre Italien in 1816 in Martín y Soler's 30-year-old opera *Una cosa rara* ('A Rare Thing', 1786). Ten years later, Cinti-Damoreau created several leading roles at the Paris Opéra, for example in Rossini's *La siège de Corinth* ('The Siege of Corinth') or in his last opera, *Guillaume Tell* ('William Tell'). Cinti-Damoreau's voice was classed as "exceptionally pure". She had the clear, controlled mastery of ornamentation that led the Belgian scholar, critic and composer François-Joseph Fétis (1784–1871) to write of her *"beau* talent" – "beautiful talent". The French writer Stendhal (Henri Marie Beyle) (1783–1842) apparently referring to her diminutive stature, wrote of Cinti-Damoreau as "that charming little singer". The soprano was certainly versatile, able to encompass both *grand opéra* and roles in Auber's works that were performed at the Opéra-Comique between 1837 and 1841.

COLBRAN, ISABELLA
(1785–1845, SPANISH)

Isabella Colbran, the Spanish soprano, married Gioachino Rossini in 1822 after a seven-year relationship, and sang a series of leading roles that he wrote for her. Colbran specialized in dramatic, tragic roles and having her on hand, as it were, enabled Rossini to write roles in this more serious genre. They included Elisabetta in *Elisabetta, regina d'Inghilterra*, Desdemona, the doomed wife in *Otello*, and Elena in *La donna del lago* ('The Lady of the Lake', 1819), based on a poem by Sir Walter Scott. Colbran, who was famous throughout Europe, was among the first operatic "divas", with a fiery temperament, an imposing physical presence on stage, impressive acting talent and a big, dramatic voice that had a range of some three octaves. Although her voice was already past its best in 1815, Colbran continued to sing for another nine years before she retired.

DAVIDE, GIOVANNI
(1790–1864, ITALIAN)

The tenor Giovanni Davide, son of another Italian tenor, Giacomo Davide (1750–1830), made his debut at 18 in Milan, in Mayr's *Adelaide di Guesclino* (1806) and six years later created the role of Narciso in Rossini's *Il turco in Italia*.

Rossini was impressed enough to write other parts for Davide in *Otello* and *La donna del lago*, among others. Davide was also in demand by Mayr, Donizetti and Giovanni Pacini the Sicilian composer; the tenor created roles in operas by all of them. Davide's voice was described as "full-toned and extremely flexible"; he was able to cover three octaves by skilful use of falsetto, in which the normal range of the tenor voice was extended upwards by partial use of the vocal chords. Davide retired from the opera stage in 1839, and then travelled to Russia, where he took up a position as manager of the St Petersburg Opera.

DUPREZ, GILBERT
(1806–96, FRENCH)

Gilbert Duprez, the French tenor, made his debut aged 19 as Count Almaviva in Rossini's *Il barbiere di Siviglia*. He went to Italy in 1829 to further his operatic studies, and remained there for six years. During this time, Duprez created the role of Edgardo in Donizetti's *Lucia di Lammermoor*. He had arrived as a youth with a beautiful, but small, light voice. By the time he returned to Paris, he was a mature 29 with much more vocal power. This enabled Duprez to become the leading tenor at the Paris Opéra where he performed for 12 years between 1837 and 1849. Duprez created the title role in

ABOVE: An engraving of Cornélie Falcon playing the role of Rachel in Ludovic Halévy's La Juivre *in 1835.*
BELOW LEFT: Isabella Colbran, the Spanish soprano who married composer Gioachino Rossini in 1822.

Berlioz' *Benvenuto Cellini* among others. Duprez created something of a sensation in Paris when he became the first tenor to produce a "chest voice" top C, an extraordinarily high note beyond the range of many tenors before and since.

FALCON, CORNÉLIE
(1814–97, FRENCH)

Cornélie Falcon's singing career was brief. At 18 she made her debut at the Paris Opéra in 1832, singing the role of Alice in Meyerbeer's *Robert le diable*. However, Falcon was a mezzo-soprano who wanted to be a soprano and ruined her full, resonant voice by forcing it too high. By 1838 her career was over and an attempt to return in 1840 was an embarrassing failure. Nevertheless, despite her few years on stage, Falcon achieved a great deal. She created Rachel, the tragic heroine of Halévy's *La juive* and Valentine in *Les Huguenots* by Meyerbeer among other important roles. Falcon was a fine actress, and together with the French tenor Adolphe Nourrit (1802–39) raised the artistic status of the Paris Opéra. Her voice came to typify the dramatic soprano roles in which she specialized, and its type is today called "Falcon soprano".

GARCIA, MANUEL
(1775–1832, SPANISH)

The Spanish tenor, composer and teacher Manuel Garcia founded a remarkable family of eight singers in four generations. He was best known for interpretations of Rossini – notably

SINGERS

Otello – and created the part of Norfolk in *Elisabetta, regina d'Inghilterra*. The role of Count Almaviva in *Il barbiere* was written for Garcia. After some six years performing in Paris and London between 1819 and 1825, Garcia went to New York, where he introduced American audiences to Italian opera. Performances of Rossini's *Il barbiere*, *La Cenerentola* ➦ **p. 128** and *Otello* and Mozart's *Don Giovanni* ➦ **p. 98** were Garcia family affairs, with casts that included Manuel's wife, son and 16-year-old daughter Maria, later the famous Malibran. Later, while touring Mexico, the scores of *Il barbiere*, *Otello* and *Giovanni* were stolen by bandits, but Garcia saved the day by rewriting them from memory. A handsome man of great vitality – Stendhal found his acting "full of fire and fury" – Garcia wrote several *zarzuelas* and popular Spanish songs.

GRISI, GIULIA
(1811–69, ITALIAN)

The Italian soprano Giulia Grisi made her debut at age 17 in Bologna, singing in Rossini's *Zelmira*. Three years later, in Milan in 1831, Grisi created the role of the priestess Adalgisa in Bellini's *Norma* ➦ **p. 133**, a part he wrote especially for her. Her Paris debut followed in 1832, when she sang the title role in Rossini's *Semiramide* at the Théâtre Italien. Grisi remained in Paris for the next 14 years. In the role of Elvira in Bellini's *I puritani*, which she created, the composer remarked that "she sang like an angel". Her subsequent career was peripatetic. Grisi sang at Covent Garden, London (1847–51), toured the United States (1854–55) and made a

ABOVE: Spanish tenor Manuel Garcia, painted by John Singer Sargent.

series of "final" performances (1854–66). These constant shifts meant that Grisi had a far-flung – and adoring – public, who appreciated her beauty as much as her rich, flexible voice and acting ability. Queen Victoria was among her numerous admirers.

LABLACHE, LUIGI
(1794–1858, ITALIAN)

The Italian bass Luigi Lablache enjoyed a career lasting over 40 years. He possessed a magnificent, sonorous voice with a wide range, impressive stage presence and the ability to sing both comic and tragic roles, many of which he created. His repertory was vast and included Figaro in Rossini's *Il barbiere di Siviglia*, King Henry VIII in Donizetti's *Anna Bolena* and the title role in Donizetti's *Don Pasquale* ➦ **p. 139**. Lablache also sang leading roles in works by Bellini, Mercadante and Pacini, among others. The English opera house manager Benjamin Lumley described Lablache as "the greatest dramatic singer of our time". Despite growing hugely fat, Lablache was physical strong and robust and his voice was still fresh and powerful when he was 60. Royalty figured among Lablache's numerous admirers, including Tsar Alexander I of Russia and Queen Victoria, and Franz Schubert (1797–1831) dedicated three Italian songs to him.

LIND, JENNY
(1820–87, SWEDISH)

The soprano Jenny Lind was nicknamed "the Swedish nightingale" because of her fresh, pure voice. She sang as a child performer before making her operatic debut in Stockholm in 1838 as Agathe in Weber's *Der Freischütz*. In the next three years, Lind sang several demanding roles, including Lucia di Lammermoor and Norma, and her voice began showing signs of strain. She retrained in Paris and returned to Stockholm in 1842, her voice restored. Her Norma in Bellini's masterpiece was highly praised, as was her Vielke in Meyerbeer's *Ein Feldlager in Schlesien* ('A Field Camp in Silesia', 1844) – a part that had been written for her. Jenny Lind went on to become a sensation in Germany, Austria and in England where she created the role of Amalia in Verdi's *I masnadieri* (1847). In 1850 she travelled to New York, where she made her name immortal. She remains one of the nineteenth century's most famous prima donnas.

MALIBRAN, MARIA
(1808–36, SPANISH)

The Spanish mezzo-soprano Maria Malibran was the elder daughter of Manuel Garcia and made her debut at age 17 singing in the chorus of the King's Theatre in London. Shortly afterwards, she replaced the indisposed Giuditta Pasta as Rosina in *Il barbiere*. Malibran was a brilliant, charismatic performer and was so successful as Rosina that she sang the part for the remainder of the season. In 1825, when the Garcia family was in America, Malibran sang the lead in eight operas performed over nine months. After returning to Europe in 1827, Malibran sang in London, Bologna, Naples and Milan, excelling in Norma, *La Cenerentola* and as Desdemona in Rossini's *Otello*. She appeared in London, Bologna, Naples and Milan, where she took the title role in Donizetti's *Maria Stuarda*. In 1836 she died aged 28 from injuries sustained in a riding accident.

MARIO, GIOVANNI
(1810–83, ITALIAN)

The Italian tenor and one-time army officer Giovanni Mario created the title role in Meyerbeer's *Robert le diable* at the Paris Opéra in 1838 and in 1843 was the first to sing Ernesto in Donizetti's *Don Pasquale* at the Théâtre Italien. Mario Cavaliere di Candia, to use his real, aristocratic, name, had good looks, elegance, an attractive stage presence and a voice of great sweetness and expressiveness. After his debut, Mario travelled the opera world receiving great acclaim for his extensive repertoire of roles: these included Rossini's Otello, Count Almaviva in Rossini's *Il barbiere* and Manrico in Verdi's *Il trovatore* ➦ **p. 169**. Mario sang in London at the Haymarket (1839–46) and Covent Garden (1847–71), in St Petersburg (1849–63 and 1858–70), in New York in 1854 and in Madrid in 1859 and 1864. His voice lasted and lasted, despite his fondness for cigars, and he did not retire until he was over 60.

EARLY ROMANTIC

1800–1845

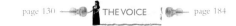
MARTIN, JEAN-BLAISE
(1768–1837, FRENCH)

The French baritone Jean-Blaise Martin gave his name to the voice type termed *baryton-Martin*, through his ability to extend his voice range into falsetto mode by an extra octave. This sort of voice, in which the baritone's normal top notes shade into the falsetto, is classed as a "high baritone" and enables singers to take on part of the tenor repertoire. Subsequently, these roles became a regular feature of the *opéra-comique* genre. Martin made his debut at the Théâtre de Monsieur in Paris at age 20 in 1788. Subsequently, he performed in *opéra-comique* at La Salle Favart between 1794 and 1801 and its successor theatre in Paris, the Opéra-Comique ➜ **p. 116**, from 1801 to 1823. He returned to the Opéra-Comique in 1826 and 1833. Jean-Blaise Martin created numerous roles for several composers, including Méhul, Boieldieu and Halévy. Martin simultaneously taught at the Paris Conservatoire.

MILDER-HAUPTMANN, PAULINE ANNA
(1785–1838, AUSTRIAN)

This Austrian soprano studied in Vienna with Antonio Salieri. In 1803 she made her debut in Vienna as Juno in *Der Spiegel von Arkadien* ('The Mirror of Arcadia', 1794) by Franz Xaver Süssmayr (1766–1803), a one-time pupil of Mozart. In 1805 Milder-Hauptmann created the role of Leonore in Beethoven's *Fidelio*. She was, however, dissatisfied with certain "unbeautiful, unsingable" passages in Leonore's aria and persuaded Beethoven to rewrite them in the later, 1814 version of his opera. Beethoven hoped to write another opera for Milder-Hauptmann, but it never transpired. Milder-Hauptmann, whose powerful voice was "like a house" according to the composer Josef Haydn (1732–1809), became identified with the role of Leonore. She sang in Berlin in 1812 and 1816–29 before appearing in Vienna. Milder-Hauptmann evinced great nobility on stage and her emotional intensity brought her acclaim in several roles, notably in Christophe Gluck's (1714–87) two "Iphigénie" operas, *Iphigénie en Aulide* (1774) and *Iphigénie en Tauride* ➜ **p. 91**.

NOURRIT, ADOLPHE
(1802–39, FRENCH)

Adolphe Nourrit, the French tenor, made his debut at the Paris Opéra in 1821, singing Pylade in *Iphigénie en Tauride* by Gluck. Nourrit remained at the Opéra until 1837, singing, among other roles, Mozart's Don Giovanni and Rossini's Otello.

Nourrit was a brilliant all-round performer, charming his audiences with his subtle, expressive voice and riveting them with his acting talent. Hector Berlioz, for one, found Nourrit "electrifying". In addition, Nourrit was a gifted writer; Meyerbeer found his help invaluable while composing *Les Huguenots* ➜ **p.148**, calling him the "second father" of the opera. After leaving the Paris Opéra in 1837, Nourrit successfully toured Belgium and France. Tragically, one asset Nourrit did not possess was mental stability, which left him vulnerable to melancholia. Problems with his voice, perhaps through over-use, exacerbated the problem and in Naples, in 1839, Nourrit, 37, committed suicide in a fit of depression.

NOZZARI, ANDREA
(1775–1832, ITALIAN)

Andrea Nozzari was one of the greatest tenors to sing in Rossini's operas, creating, among many others, the roles of the Earl of Leicester in *Elisabetta, regina d'Inghilterra* and the title role in *Otello*. Nozzari was the complete opera singer, with a strong voice and graceful stage presence. He probably made his debut at Pavia, Italy in 1794, afterwards moving on to La Scala, Milan where he performed in 1796–97, 1800 and 1811–12. Meanwhile, Nozzari performed at the Théâtre Italien in Paris in 1803 and 1804. His final berth was at the Teatro San Carlo in Naples (1811–25) where he was one of a group of tenors who set new standards of singing, including great technical facility, wide voice range and the ability to sing top notes in falsetto. Another member of the group was Giovanni Battista Rubini (1794–1854), a one-time pupil of Nozzari's.

PASTA, GIUDITTA
(1797–1865, ITALIAN)

Giuditta Pasta, who created the title role in Bellini's *Norma*, was classed as a soprano, but was probably closer to a mezzo-soprano. On stage, she was majestic, and her acting was so powerful that, according to Stendhal, she "electrified the soul". However, success did not come her way all that quickly. After her debut in Milan in 1815, she performed in Venice, Padua, Rome, Brescia and Turin before scoring her first substantial success at the Théâtre Italien in Paris in 1821. Three years later, Pasta appeared at London's Haymarket Theatre and continued to sing in both of these capital cities until 1837. She also appeared at the Teatro San Carlo, Naples (1826), in Vienna (1829), at La Scala, Milan (1831) and in St Petersburg (1840). In addition to Norma, Giuditta Pasta created many other title roles such as Donizetti's Anna Bolena and Amina in Bellini's *La sonnambula* ➜ **p. 132**.

RUBINI, GIOVANNI BATTISTA
(1794–1854, ITALIAN)

The Italian tenor Giovanni Battista Rubini was said to "enchant" listeners with his powerful yet sweet and subtle voice. He was also able to move his audiences to tears with his famous musical "sob". Bellini created several roles for Rubini, including Gualtiero in *Il pirata*, Elvino in *La sonnambula* and Arturo in *I puritani*. The qualities of Rubini's voice greatly influenced Italian Romantic opera, especially when it was showcased in Bellini's supremely smooth and tuneful operas. Rubini made his debut at 20 in 1814 in Pavia when he sang in *Lagrime di una vedova*

SINGERS

('A Widow's Tears', 1808) by Pietro Generali (1773–1832). He performed in Naples for 13 years, 1816–29, and also at La Scala, Milan in 1818 and 1825–31, the Théâtre Italien in Paris in 1825 and 1831–43, London 1831–43, and St Petersburg in 1843 and 1844.

SCHRÖDER-DEVRIENT, WILHELMINE
(1804–60, GERMAN)

Wilhelmine Schröder-Devrient was born into "show business". Her father was Friedrich Schröder (1744–1816), the first German Don Giovanni in Mozart's opera of that name, and her mother was the "Mrs Siddons of Germany", the actress Sophie Bürger (1781–1868). Wilhelmine was a child actress and ballet dancer before making her debut at the Kärnterthortheater in Vienna as Pamina in Mozart's *Die Zauberflöte* in 1821. She sang in Dresden for 25 years (1822–47), with excursions to Berlin (1828), Paris (1831–32), and the London Haymarket in 1832–33 and 1837. She retired in 1847. Schröder-Devrient was a highly emotional singer and actress who became known as the "Queen of Tears" for weeping on stage while performing the many powerful and tragic parts in her repertoire. She sang Bellini's Norma, Valentine in Meyerbeer's *Les Huguenots*, and, in what was termed the greatest interpretation of the role, Leonore in Beethoven's *Fidelio*.

SONTAG, HENRIETTE
(1806–54, GERMAN)

The German soprano Henriette Sontag made her debut in 1821 as the princess in Boieldieu's *Jean de Paris* (1812). In 1823, in Vienna, Weber asked Sontag to create the title role in his *Euryanthe* (1822–23) after seeing her in Rossini's *La donna del lago*. He was justified when her appearance in Berlin in 1825 caused an outbreak of "Sontag-fever". Sontag's voice was sweet, flexible, and she possessed a "brilliant, inventive and pleasing" freshness. She sang many top roles – Rossini's Semiramide, Donizetti's Lucrezia Borgia and Weber's Agathe in *Der Freischütz* among them. Sontag retired in 1830 after marrying a diplomat whose career might have been compromised by her fame, but returned to the opera stage after he retired. She was still at the peak of her powers and her fame when she died of cholera in 1854.

TACCHINARDI-PERSIANI, FANNY
(1812–67, ITALIAN)

The angelic-looking soprano Fanny Tacchinardi-Persiani was made to play the delicate, suffering heroines of early Romantic opera. Fanny Tacchinardi – as she was before marrying the composer Giuseppe Persiani in 1830 – made her debut in 1832 at Livorno and went on to great success in Venice, Naples and Milan. She sang at the Théâtre Italien in Paris (1837–48), in London at the Haymarket Theatre (1838–46) and Covent Garden (1847–49), in Vienna in 1837 and 1844, and St Petersburg (1850–52). Tacchinardi-Persiani created the title roles in Donizetti's *Rosmonda d'Inghilterra*, *Lucia di Lammermoor* and *Pia de' Tolomi* ('Pia of Tolomi', 1837). She was widely acclaimed for her Linda of Chamonix and Lucrezia Borgia. Giuseppe Persiani's operas benefited from his marriage to such a brilliant and popular singer. So did the London opera world, for in 1847, husband and wife helped establish the Royal Italian Opera at Covent Garden.

TAMBURINI, ANTONIO
(1800–76, ITALIAN)

Antonio Tamburini, the Italian baritone, was 18 when he made his debut at Cento in *Contessa di colle erboso* ('Countess of the Grassy Hill', 1814) by Pietro Generali. Tamburini went on to appear at La Scala, Milan in 1822 and 1827–30, in Naples in 1824 and 1828–32), the London Haymarket (1832–51) and Covent Garden (1847). He sang regularly at the Théâtre Italien in Paris between 1832 and 1854 and also appeared in Vienna, Genoa and St Petersburg. The handsome, popular Tamburini was personable, with a "rich, sweet and equal" voice, splendid coloratura technique and "sensational" falsetto. When he failed to appear at the Haymarket Theatre, London in 1840, the disappointed audience staged a riot. Tamburini performed in Mozart and Rossini operas and created roles in Bellini's *Il pirata* and *I puritani*. He sang in 10 operas by Donizetti, including *Lucia di Lammermoor* and *Don Pasquale*, in which he appeared as the doctor Malatesta.

VELLUTI, GIOVANNI BATTISTA
(1780–1861, ITALIAN)

Giovanni Battista Velluti, the Italian soprano castrato, created Gioachino Rossini's only castrato role, as Arsace in his *Aureliano in Palmira* (1813), but infuriated the composer with his pretentious and showy ornamentation. After that Rossini wrote his own ornamentation. Velluti also created the role of Armando in Meyerbeer's *Crociato in Egitto* ('Crusade in Egypt', 1824); Meyerbeer wrote the opera especially for him. Velluti made his debut at Forli in 1800. He went on to perform at the Teatro San Carlo, Naples (1803), Rome (1805–07), La Scala, Milan for most years between 1808 and 1814 and later in Vienna, St Petersburg and the Haymarket, London. Despite his good looks and what Stendhal called his "prodigious gifts", Velluti shocked London audiences who were no longer familiar with castrati or their voices. However, women found Velluti fascinating and he had numerous mistresses. Velluti, the last great castrato, retired in 1830, and became a farmer.

ABOVE: Antonio Tamburini in the role of Assur, from Rossini's opera Semiramide, *in an 1847 production.*
LEFT: Berlin prima donna Henriette Sontag *in 1828.*
FAR LEFT: Giovanni Battista Rubini in Donizetti's Anna Bolena *in 1842.*

1800—1845 EARLY ROMANTIC

SINGERS

155

High Romantic

In 1891, when the Irish playwright Oscar Wilde (1854–1900) wrote "Life imitates art far more than art imitates life", he had somehow managed to overlook the artistic realities of the late nineteenth century. By that time, after some 50 years of the High Romantic era, music and opera had brought real life on stage and had presented it in the raw, with all its disappointments, tragedies, insecurities, injustice and grief.

THE OPERA OF ORDINARY PEOPLE

In a foretaste of the Italian *verismo*, or "reality" opera, that crystallized after 1880, opera audiences were confronted with uncomfortable truths as they affected characters not unlike themselves. There were the agonies of jealousy endured by Verdi's (1813–1901) Otello or by Canio, the betrayed husband, in *I pagliacci* ('Clowns', 1892) by Ruggero Leoncavallo (1858–1919). Verdi's Rigoletto struggled to preserve his daughter from would-be rapists, the consumptive Violetta in Verdi's *La traviata* ('The Fallen Woman', 1853) was doomed to early death from a then-incurable disease. In *Carmen* by Georges Bizet (1838–75), the soldier, Don José, was ruined by a fascinating but promiscuous gypsy.

CONSEQUENCES OF POLITICAL CHANGES

In real life, these situations were nothing new. They and many others like them had been there for the suffering for hundreds, if not thousands, of years. What was new was a fundamental change of emphasis that was set in train by the French Revolution of 1789 and reverberated through the nineteenth century. The focus of attention shifted to ordinary people of no particular eminence or achievement, wealth or favoured status. Previously, their concerns had been subsumed in the priorities of their privileged rulers. Now, they had been brought to the fore by unprecedented events and, through those events, had recast the action on the opera stage.

THE HIGH ROMANTIC

Introduction

On the face of it, the French Revolution failed when the House of Bourbon returned to rule France after the defeat of Napoleon in 1815. The face of it, however, was deceptive. The forces of liberalism unleashed by the Revolution had simply made a strategic withdrawal. In France, liberals, socialists and republicans remained opposed to extreme right-wing royalists, a situation duplicated throughout Europe where the ruling elites and the formerly powerless masses were set for collision.

CONDUCTORS, COMPOSERS AND POLITICS

Richard Wagner (1813–83) was conductor of opera in Dresden when revolution broke out in the city in May of 1849. He joined in public demonstrations and was present when the street barricades went up. Twice, he opened his house for meetings designed to organize the distribution of arms to the citizens of Dresden, and, it appears, participated in the manufacture of hand-grenades. This was sedition and treason, punishable by death. A warrant was issued for Wagner's arrest but by then he had managed to escape to Switzerland.

In Italy, Wagner's close contemporary Giuseppe Verdi – they were born in the same year, 1813 – was less inclined to go to extremes. Nevertheless, there was little doubt about his liberal leanings and the way he identified himself with the man-in-the-street. When King Victor Emmanuel offered him a noble title, Verdi declined. He told the monarch: "*o son un paesano*" – "I am a peasant". Strictly speaking, this was not true – Verdi's parents were village innkeepers and shop owners – but he certainly looked for his audiences among ordinary people rather than the intellectual elite.

ABOVE: The world-renowned La Scala opera house in Milan, Italy. Many of the world's most famous singers have performed here and La Scala has been the scene of many opera premieres, including works by Rossini and Verdi.

LA SCALA, MILAN

The Teatro alla Scala – known outside Italy as La Scala, Milan – is one of the world's most famous opera houses and originally opened in the sixteenth century as the Salone Margherita in the Palazzo Ducale. Both this theatre and another built on its site, the Teatro Regio Ducale, burned down, in 1708 and 1776 respectively. After an appeal by 96 box holders to the Austrian Empress Maria Theresa, La Scala was built to replace the Ducale in 1778. The new opera house, which could hold an audience numbering 2,800, opened on 3 August 1778 with the premiere of Antonio Salieri's (1750–1825) *L'Europa riconosciuta* ('Europe Revisited'). The worldwide reputation of La Scala was established in the early nineteenth century, when it staged important premieres of works by Gioachino Rossini (1792–1868), Gaetano Donizetti (1797–1848), Giacomo Meyerbeer (1791–1864) and others. In two years alone – 1824 to 1826 – operas by Rossini were given some 250 performances at La Scala. Works were commissioned from Vincenzo Bellini (1801–35) and from Verdi, including his *Oberto, conte di San Bonifacio* ('Oberto, count of Saint Boniface', 1839) and *Nabucco* (1842). Towards the end of the High Romantic era, in 1898, the despotic but charismatic conductor Arturo Toscanini (1867–1957) became director of La Scala, and later attracted many of the world's greatest singers to its stage.

INTRODUCTION

POLITICAL OPERATIC PRODUCTIONS

Even before the revolutions of 1848, Verdi made what was taken as a political statement in support of the downtrodden masses: the Jews in exile in Babylon in his *Nabucco* were regarded by the people of Milan as a metaphor for their own servitude under the harsh rule of the Austrians. The following year Verdi was in trouble over the fiery, patriotic choruses in *I Lombardi alla prima Crociata* ('The Lombards at the First Crusade', 1843), which were considered politically dangerous and in 1851, his *Rigoletto* ➡ p. 168

ABOVE: *Programme from the first London performance of Verdi's Rigoletto at Covent Garden around 1853.*

was initially banned because of its unflattering portrait of a ruler, the licentious Duke of Mantua.

CENSORSHIP AND FEAR

These were not the only occasions when Verdi fell foul of the opera censorship, but they certainly established his progressive credentials. It has been suggested that Verdi's identity as a symbol of the *Risorgimento*, the movement to free and unite the states of Italy under the rule of Victor Emmanuel, may have reflected the view of later generations. However, Verdi's liberal contemporaries seemed to regard the composer as one of their own, so much so that the letters of his surname became a symbol of their struggle. V-e-r-d-i, by unusual coincidence, stood for "Vittorio Emmanuele re d'Italia"– "Victor Emmanuel, King of Italy" – and since it was seditious to proclaim the monarch's name in public, the cry of *Viva Verdi!* ('Long live Verdi!') was substituted.

The *Risorgimento* achieved its objective and acquired its chosen king in 1870. This development, and the unification of the German states in 1871, symbolized another

consequence of revolution – a new pride in the sovereign nation state, its culture and its traditions. This influence also made itself felt in opera, notably in the works of Wagner, with their mighty Teutonic heroes and elements taken from German and Norse Viking myths.

NATIONAL PRIDE AND NATIONALISTIC COMPOSERS

Similar influences were at work elsewhere. For example, in Russia, Nikolai Rimsky-Korsakov (1844–1908) devoted all but two of his 15 operas to Russian themes, infusing many of his scores with the seductive oriental harmonies that typified the Eurasian character of his vast country. In Czechoslovakia, Zdenek Fibich (1850–1900) promoted a Czech idiom in opera, and his work was furthered by the first of the country's great nationalist composers, Bedrich Smetana (1824–84). Traditions, national heroes and historical themes also marked the operas of Polish composer Stanislaw Moniuszko (1819–72) and the Hungarian Ferenc Erkel (1810–91). In the nineteenth century, Czechoslovakia and Hungary were under Austrian rule – although the latter had some autonomy – and Poland was part of Russia. Without independence, therefore, it was left to opera and the other arts to make a statement of national identity.

ABOVE: *Germany's unification gave a sense of national pride and led composers such as Wagner to draw inspiration from Nordic mythology.*

HIGH ROMANTIC

1845–1890

Genres and Styles

The Italian Giuseppe Verdi and the German Richard Wagner, the dominant composers of the High Romantic period, were totally disparate personalities who shared the same operatic aim. Both saw opera as Gesamtkunstwerk, the total work of art in which all elements – singing, acting, orchestration, drama, poetry, stage design – merged into a single homogeneous entity. This music-drama meant continuous on-stage action, in which none of the component parts was preponderant. In particular, there would be no arias to hold up the story or provide a platform for bravura displays by individual performers.

EMERGENCE OF MUSIC DRAMA

In the event, the total revolution in music and opera, which these changes implied, never fully transpired. The aria survived but the "democratic" concept of equal partners in performance foundered, as opera, including Wagner's total works of art, continued to be identified by its music. Nevertheless, neither Verdi nor Wagner left opera as they found it: music drama, or at least its most powerful elements, had seminal effects.

RIGHT: Cover of the vocal score of Oberto, Conte di San Bonifacio, *Verdi's 1839 opera, published by Ricordi.*

PARIGI, O CARA'
In *La traviata*, Alfredo returns to his lover, Violetta, whom he deserted. In this duet from Act III, he tells her their separation is at an end and they will soon leave the bustle of Paris behind and resume their life together. It is a pretence, as Alfredo knows that Violetta is dying.

POPULAR MELODY

EARLY ROMANTIC LEGACY

Of the two composers, Verdi was much more the heir of his early Romantic predecessors than Wagner. Verdi retained the *bel canto* ➡ p. 130 style of singing and lavished it on a long series of memorable melodies. Inevitably, this meant the show-stopping aria figured in most Verdi

EDIZIONE POPOLARE DELLE OPERE DI G·VERDI CANTO E PIANOFORTE OBERTO CONTE DI S. BONIFACIO G·RICORDI & C EDITORI·MILANO

ABOVE: Wager's 'music dramas', such as Das Rheingold, *altered the course of opera by moving away from conventions such as the aria.*

operas. Verdi's first two works – *Oberto* and the unsuccessful *Un giorno di regno* ('King for a Day', 1840) – were clearly influenced by the music of Rossini. However, with *Nabucco* ➡ **p. 166** Verdi's sense of drama, particularly human drama, had greatly heightened, and

---

END OF THE ARIA?

The demise of the aria, as suggested by Wagner and to a lesser extent by Verdi, never really happened. The aria, of course, had its disadvantages. To start with, it encouraged performers to show off and hog the stage for much longer than was justified. This was a real possibility as the fame of individual singers increased, and their egos expanded to match. However, even if this did not occur, arias interrupted the story and held up the action. There were, however, equally cogent arguments in favour of the aria. A well-written aria was a memorable melody that stuck easily in

the minds of audiences and so prolonged their enjoyment long after they had left the theatre. An opera's popularity, therefore, depended principally on its arias. Secondly, the aria served a dramatic purpose that nothing else in opera could do. Like the soliloquy in William Shakespeare's (1564–1616) plays, it provided a niche for a character's personal musings, fears or anxieties. It also acted like the theatrical "aside", enabling characters to confide to the audience thoughts or information kept secret from the rest of the cast. Ultimately, the aria survived and in the twentieth century achieved new prominence in the works of neo-classical composers.

of it on an unprecedented scale. The music drama, he planned, would grow out of the libretti which he himself wrote, and would undercut established ways of composing and using music. For example, Wagner eschewed the tonality and predictable harmony, which "told" an audience what the music was going to do next. Instead, he intended to write music that ebbed and flowed like the current of a river: it was much more continuous, with one melody barely finishing, or not finishing at all, before it melted into the next.

THE LEITMOTIF

The orchestra in the Wagner music drama did much more than accompany the singers on stage: it was an equal partner, so much louder than orchestras had ever been before that singers needed to undergo special training to acquire the lung-power to compete with it. This was the origin of the Wagnerian soprano and the *Heldentenor*, the heroic or Wagnerian tenor. Harmonies were richer and denser. Characters, events or ideas were associated with their own leitmotif – leading motive – which was played by the orchestra throughout the drama as a reminder to the audience. This was opera as *tour de force* and, like its composer, it towered over the music of its time.

BELOW: Wagnerian sopranos, such as Lili Lehmann, shown here in Der Fliegende Holländer, *need a strong vocal range and great stamina.*

HIGH ROMANTIC

1845–1890

after *Rigoletto* he was giving Italian opera a much darker aura, with more incisive characterization and dramatic atmosphere than before. By the time Verdi reached old age, his *Otello* ⇢ **p. 176** and his last work, the comic opera, *Falstaff* (1893) ⇢ **p. 177**, were much closer than his early work to Wagner's idea of a unified work of art.

EPIC IDEAS

For Wagner, however, it was not close enough. Compared to what he had in mind, *Otello* and *Falstaff*, which both depict the vagaries of human behaviour, were too earthbound. Wagner's vision was of epic proportions, involving myths, gods and goddesses, ancient legends, heroic sagas, death and sacrifice – all

GENRES AND STYLES

WAGNER'S INFLUENCE IN FRANCE

The influences that radiated from Wagner's music were immense, even in France where Germans were regarded as politically dangerous and the Teutonic intensity of Wagner's work jarred on aesthetic French tastes. Nevertheless, several French composers took cues from Wagner. For instance, in his *Faust* (1859) ➤ **p. 207**, Charles Gounod (1818–93) emulated him by greatly enhancing the role of the orchestra and scoring recurring motifs for the instruments to play. Gounod adopted Wagnerian harmonies for his love music in *Roméo et Juliette* ('Romeo and Juliet', 1867) and the Wagnerian leitmotif was used by Georges Bizet in his *Carmen*. In all three of these operas, both composers provided opportunities for musical scene-painting and exploration of the public "outer" and secret "inner" life of the characters. Camille Saint-Saëns (1835–1921) wrote Wagnerian love music for Act II of his *Samson et Dalila* (1877) ➤ **p. 211**. In 1884 Ernest Reyer (1823–1909) ventured even further into Wagner territory with his *Sigurd*, a French version of the same Nordic sagas and legends Wagner used for his *Ring* cycle ➤ **p. 184**.

AN ON-STAGE SLICE OF LIFE

Although the monumentally egotistical Wagner regarded his music dramas as the ultimate truth in opera, his concepts were not the only ones at work in the High Romantic era. Italian *verismo* ➤ **p. 190**, which first emerged with *Cavalleria rusticana* ('Rustic Chivalry', 1890) ➤ **p. 252** by

Pietro Mascagni (1863–1945), brought the brutal "slice of life" to the opera stage, with particular emphasis on the crime of passion. *Verismo* also made principle characters out of villains once avoided by composers for fear of offending audience sensibilities – pimps, prostitutes, criminals, murderers and other squalid, violent low-life characters

OPERETTA – JUST FOR FUN

However, this emphasis on brute reality, tragedy, death and larger-than-life legends did nothing to

dent, and probably increased, the popularity of an established genre of a different kind: operetta, the escapist "little opera" which majored in fun, fantasy and romantic high jinks. Operetta evolved in the mid-nineteenth century from the French *opéra comique*. The genre enjoyed a very long – and still continuing – life, changing its name on the way to musical comedy or simply, the musical. Subsequently, operetta spread from France to Vienna and on to England where it appeared in a delightful and quintessentially English version known as the

ABOVE: English operetta found a home at the Savoy Theatre, where the D'Oyly Carte Theatre Company performed works by Gilbert and Sullivan.

THE BANDA

The *banda* was an onstage band, which originated in the eighteenth century and by the nineteenth comprised around 20 brass and woodwind players. Although essentially a military band, the *banda* was used for ballroom scenes or on-stage parades or processions. The on-stage band was not part of the regular orchestra, but was recruited by the theatre impresario. Consequently, its musicianship was not always expert. The *banda* appeared occasionally at first, but after Rossini used it in his *Ricciardo e Zoraide* ('Ricciardo and Zoraide', 1818), it became a regular feature of Italian opera performances.

The *banda* was later taken up by Giuseppe Verdi and in his operas it assumed various guises depending on the on-stage action. It was raucous and somewhat vulgar in *Nabucco* and in *I Lombardi*, very much in keeping with the mood of patriotic fervour that gripped Italy during the *Risorgimento* (1820–70). Verdi's music for the *banda* in the ballroom scenes of *Rigoletto* and *Un ballo in maschera* ('A Masked Ball', 1859) was much more subtle. However, in the *auto-da-fé* – act of faith – scene in *Don Carlos* (1867), depicting the burning of heretics, the *banda*'s music acquired a strident urgency that matched this particularly horrific spectacle.

PARIS OPÉRA

The Académie Royale de Musique (now known as the Paris Académie de Musique or the Paris Opéra), has had many homes. The Académie opened in 1671, and from 1672–87 was largely controlled by Lully. In 1763 the building was destroyed by fire, as was the next building in 1781. The Opéra moved to rue de Richelieu as Theatre des Arts in 1794, to the rue Favart in 1821, and then to rue Lepeletier in 1822 where it experienced a golden age in its history. Operas by Meyerbeer and Daniel Auber

"Savoy operas" by the librettist Sir William Gilbert (1836–1911), a well-known wit, and playwright and the composer, Sir Arthur Sullivan (1842–1900).

SATIRE AND SHOCK TACTICS

The "father" of French operetta was Jacques Offenbach (1819–80), a French composer of German origins, whose declared aim was to take the pretensions and seriousness out of *opéra comique* and inject it with fun and satire. In 1857 Offenbach announced a competition for new operettas, which was won jointly by the then-19-year-old Georges Bizet with his *Le Docteur Miracle* ('Doctor Miracle') and Charles Lecocq (1832–1918). The following year, Offenbach produced his own satirical operetta – *Orphée aux enfers* ('Orpheus in the Underworld') ➼ **p.208**, which was premiered at his theatre, the Bouffes-Parisiens, on 21 October 1858. Offenbach's *Orphée* shocked critics rigid by poking fun at ancient Greek gods and goddesses, the hallowed heroes and heroines of Baroque and later opera, and by debunking Gluck's (1714–87) work on the same subject. Offenbach was unfazed: he took a second swipe at ancient Greece with *La belle Hélène* ('Beautiful Helen', 1864) ➼ **p. 208**.

Meanwhile, in Vienna, Franz von Suppé (1819–95) produced several light-hearted one-act operettas that prepared the ground for *Indigo und die vierzig Räuber* ('Indigo and the Forty Robbers', 1871) by Johann Strauss II (1825–99). This ended Offenbach's virtual monopoly of full-length operetta productions.

RIGHT: The Palais Garnier at the Place de la Bastille, Paris, France: the home of the Paris Opéra.

(1782–1871) were performed, as well as specially commissioned works by Rossini (*Guillame Tell*, 1829) and Verdi (*Don Carlos*, 1867 and *Les vêpres siciliennes*, 1855). The Palais Garnier, or Salle Garnier, designed by architect Charles Garnier, opened in 1875 and could seat 2,600. This fairy-tale venue, with its myriad underground vaults and passages, inspired Gaston Leroux's novel *The Phantom of the Opera* (1910), and also showcases the famous Chagall ceiling. The new house, Opéra Bastille, opened in 1990 and able to seat 2,700, is located at the Place de la Bastille.

Strauss, the eventual composer of 16 operettas, was the son and namesake of the so-called "Waltz King", Johann Strauss I (1804–49) and recast operetta as a vehicle for exotic settings and dances. Strauss' best-known and most enduring operetta, *Die Fledermaus* ('The Bat', 1874) ➼ **p. 213** was full of comic intrigue, mistaken identities, flirtations and, of course, a generous helping of the Strauss family hallmark, the waltz.

BELOW: A satirical cartoon on Offenbach's opera Orphée aux Enfers, *from* L'Illustration, *February 1866.*

KEY COMPOSERS

Giuseppe Verdi

Giuseppe Verdi (1813–1901) was that rarity, a modest, diffident genius. He was so unaware of his powers that he called himself "the least erudite among past and present composers". Born in Le Roncole, near Busseto, Parma, Verdi was eight when his talents were noticed by a local merchant and patron of music, Antonio Barezzi. In 1832 Barezzi paid for Verdi to attend the Milan Conservatory, but he failed to be accepted, partly due to "lack of piano technique and technical knowledge" and "insufficient" gifts.

A MODEST START

Verdi took private lessons to improve his musical skills and the same year he married Margherita, Barezzi's daughter, he completed his first opera, *Rocester* (1836). It was never staged, but much of its music went into a second opera, *Oberto, Conte di*

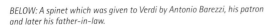

BELOW: A spinet which was given to Verdi by Antonio Barezzi, his patron and later his father-in-law.

San Bonifacio (1839). *Oberto* was so well received at La Scala, Milan, that Verdi was contracted to write more.

HIS TRAGIC FAMILY LIFE

However, Verdi's first work under contract, a comic opera *Un giorno di regno* ('King for a Day', 1840) was overshadowed by tragedy: both his children had died in infancy, and in 1840, he also lost his young wife. *Un giorno* was a fiasco, withdrawn after only one performance and the grieving Verdi was ready to give up. Fortunately, the impresario and librettist Bartolomeo Merelli (1794–1879) perceived his genius and persuaded him to try again. Merelli's faith was more than justified. Verdi's next opera, *Nabucco*, produced at La Scala in 1842, was a splendid success, and also signalled his emergence from the influence of Rossini and Donizetti. From now on, musically speaking, Verdi was his own man.

A POLITICAL TROUBLEMAKER?

Nabucco made Verdi's name known throughout Italy, not only in the opera houses,

but also in the political talking shops where the *Risorgimento*, the movement for the unification and independence of Italy, was being brewed. Even though Verdi had no interest in active politics, there is no doubt that he supported the *Risorgimento* and the censors, for their part, marked him down as a potential revolutionary. Verdi's long and fractious involvement in censorship was at least partly the result of these suspicions.

THE CREAM OF HIS CONTEMPORARIES

Verdi's *Ernani* was another brilliant success. Subsequently, Verdi was deluged with commissions and entered what he called his *anni di galera* – his "galley years", in which he composed 16 operas in 11 years – 1842 to 1853

VERDI AND HIS LIBRETTISTS

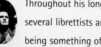

Throughout his long career, Verdi worked with several librettists and gained a reputation for being something of a tartar. Sometimes he would even write the text himself, only allowing his librettist to put it into verse. The composer had strong ideas about what he wanted from the text to his operas; in the early compositions this was a dramatic series of confrontations, perfectly set by Temistocle Solera in *Nabucco*, *I Lombardi*, *Giovanna d'Arco* ('Joan of Arc', 1845) and *Attila* (1846), and set by Salvatore Cammarano in *Luisa Miller* (1849), the celebrated *Il trovatore* ('The Troubador', 1853) and others.

Verdi worked more comfortably with Francesco Maria Piave (1810–76), a personal friend who was responsible for *Ernani* (1844), *I due Foscari* ('The Two Foscari', 1844), *Macbeth* (1847), *Il corsaro* ('The Corsair', 1848), *Stiffelio* (1850), *Rigoletto*, *La traviata*, *Simon Boccanegra* (1857) and *La forza del destino* ('The Force of Destiny', 1862). Another librettist who did not give in to Verdi's bullying was Eugène Scribe; they clashed on several occasions, but Scribe usually won. A more congenial librettist, Camille du Locle, wrote *Don Carlos* and provided the original libretto of *Aida* (1871), which was translated into Italian by Antonio Ghislanzoni, a former baritone who had sung in *Ernani* in Paris.

Operas

1839	*Oberto, conte di San Bonifacio*
1840	*Un giorno di regno*
1842	*Nabucco*
1843	*I Lombardi alla prima Crociata*
1844	*Ernani; I due Foscari*
1845	*Giovanna d'Arco; Alzira; Attila*
1847	*Macbeth; I masnadieri; Jérusalem*
1848	*Il corsaro*
1849	*La battaglia di Legnano; Luisa Miller*
1850	*Stiffelio*
1851	*Rigoletto*
1853	*Il trovatore; La traviata*
1855	*Les vêpres siciliennes*
1857	*Aroldo; Simon Boccanegra*
1859	*Un ballo in maschera*
1862	*La forza del destino*
1867	*Don Carlos*
1871	*Aida*
1887	*Otello*
1893	*Falstaff*

Timeline

1813	Giuseppe Verdi is born, Le Roncole
1825	Begins studying music under Ferdinando Provesi
1828	Composes a new overture for a performance of Rossini's *Il barbiere di Siviglia*
1832	Travels to Milan to study under Vincenzo Lavigna
1836	Marries Margherita Barezzi, the daughter of his patron
1839	*Oberto* premieres at La Scala in Milan
1840	Death of Margherita sends Verdi into a spiral of despair
1842	*Nabucco* triumphs at La Scala, with Giuseppina Strepponi singing Abigaille
1847	Verdi and Strepponi become lovers
1848	Donizetti dies and Verdi becomes the leading Italian composer
1851	*Rigoletto* is a raging success at La Fenice
1854	Verdi and Strepponi move to Paris
1857	*Simon Boccanegra* and *Aroldo* receive cool reviews
1859	Verdi marries Strepponi
1861	Stands for parliament in the newly unified Italy, and is elected
1864	Becomes a member of the French Académie des Beaux-Arts
1871	After a delay caused by the Franco-Prussian War, *Aida* opens in Cairo
1879	Meets Arrigo Boito in Milan
1884	Begins work on *Otello*
1887	*Otello* premieres at La Scala to a standing ovation
1893	*Falstaff* receives a similar reception at its opening
1897	Giuseppina Strepponi dies
1901	Verdi dies, Milan

– half of them produced between 1844 to 1847 alone. Writing under pressure meant mixed results. The "galley years" produced inspired achievements like *La traviata* p. 170 and *Il trovatore*, both of which premiered in 1853, but also included *Stiffelio*, which was unloved by audiences despite Verdi's extensive revisions. By the time the "prison years" ended, Verdi, aged 40, eclipsed all others as the most highly acclaimed living composer of opera. However, he was not sitting on his laurels. In 1871 his *Aida* p. 175, which was set in ancient Egypt, had its premiere in Cairo and although his *Requiem* (1873), which he wrote after the death of the Italian poet and patriot Alessandro Manzoni (1785–1873), was his last for 13 years, there were more achievements to come. In an astoundingly creative old age, Verdi produced

two operas based on Shakespeare's plays – the tragedy *Otello* and the comic opera *Falstaff* – and, in 1897, his *Quattro pezzi sacri* ('Four Sacred Pieces') for voices and orchestra. His second wife, the soprano Giuseppina Strepponi (1815–97), had died the same year, and the frail Verdi, with failing eyesight and hearing, did not survive her long. He died on 27 January 1901 in Milan, after donating 2.5 million lire to found a home for infirm musicians. Some 28,000 people lined the streets as his cortege passed by.

ABOVE RIGHT: The house in Le Roncole, near Busseto, Italy where Verdi was born in 1813.
ABOVE FAR RIGHT: Giuseppe Verdi, who had a long and successful career and wrote his last opera at the age of 80.

Nabucco

Nabucco by Verdi

Composed	1841
Premiered	1842, Milan
Libretto	by Temistocle Solera, after Auguste Anicet-Bourgeois, Francis Cornue and Antonio Cortesi

Nabucco was originally named *Nabucodonosor*. An opera in four acts set in Jerusalem and Babylon in the sixth century BC, *Nabucodonosor* was first produced at La Scala, Milan on 9 March 1842 with Giuseppina Strepponi, who later became Verdi's second wife, as Abigaille. The opera was not billed as *Nabucco* until 1844. The opera occasioned Verdi's first serious brush with the censors, who criticized *Nabucco* because of its biblical sources. The real message, though, was their concern for the way the opera's theme of a people enslaved by a cruel conqueror could be used to further the *Risorgimento* movement.

'VA PENSIERO'

In *'Va pensiero'*, from *Nabucco*, the Hebrews exiled in Babylon send thoughts to their faraway homeland. Italians under foreign rule identified with them and the chorus became the anthem of the *Risorgimento*, the movement for Italian unification and independence. It was sung by the crowds at Verdi's funeral in Milan in 1901.

POPULAR MELODY

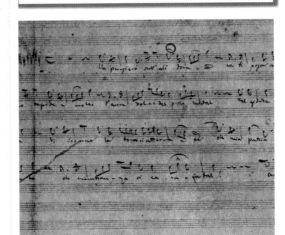

ABOVE: The score for the beautiful chorus 'Va pensiero' from Verdi's Nabucco.

𝒮*ynopsis*
Nabucco by Verdi

ACT I ❧

The Israelites lament their fate at the hands of Nabucco, King of Babylon. The high priest Zaccaria enters with a hostage: Nabucco's daughter Fenena. She is entrusted to Ismaele, who loves her; she freed him in Babylon and he intends to return the favour. Abigaille, Nabucco's elder daughter, enters and offers to free the Hebrews if Ismaele returns her love; he refuses. Nabucco enters. Zaccaria threatens Fenena but Ismaele saves her. Zaccaria declares him a traitor and Nabucco orders the temple to be destroyed.

ACT II ❧

Abigaille finds out that she is actually a slave's daughter and swears vengeance on Nabucco and Fenena, who is regent during the war. Encouraged by the high priest of Belo, Abigaille considers killing Fenena and announcing that Nabucco is dead. Zaccaria converts Fenena to the Hebrew faith and Ismaele is pardoned for saving her. Abdallo, a royal advisor, warns Fenena to flee but it is too late; Abigaille arrives. Nabucco returns, declaring himself king and god. Lightning knocks the crown from his head and sends him mad. Abigaille grabs the crown.

ACT III ❧

In Babylon, Abigaille is hailed as queen. She tricks Nabucco into sealing a death warrant for all Hebrews. He realizes too late that Fenena will die. He threatens Abigaille with revealing her lowly birth, but she destroys the documents. Pleading with her to spare Fenena's life, Nabucco is taken away and imprisoned. The Hebrews lament the loss of their homeland. They pray for help and Zaccaria foresees their revenge.

ACT IV ❧

The imprisoned Nabucco tries to escape and begs forgiveness from the Hebrew god, promising to convert the Babylonians. He is released and sets out to rescue Fenena and reclaim the crown. The executioners prepare to kill the Hebrews. Nabucco arrives, ordering the idol of Belo to be destroyed; it shatters of its own accord. Praying to the Hebrew god for forgiveness, Abigaille poisons herself and dies. Nabucco declares his new faith and commands the Hebrews to return to their homeland.

Ernani

Ernani by Verdi

Composed	1843
Premiered	1844, Venice
Libretto	by Francesco Maria Piave, after Victor Hugo

Verdi's four-act opera *Ernani*, which has been called his "most romantic" work, was first performed at the Teatro La Fenice in Venice on 9 March 1844. An immediate success, it was based on the tragedy *Hernani* by the French writer Victor Hugo (1802–85). Politically, the treatment of the subject was far more overt than *Nabucco*, featuring a revolutionary outlaw as its eponymous hero and the King of Spain as the conniving villain. The fifth of Verdi's ultimate total of 28 operas, *Ernani* was the first of them to be performed in England, at Her Majesty's Theatre, London on 8 March 1845.

𝒮*ynopsis*
Ernani by Verdi

ACT I ❧

Ernani, an outlawed nobleman, is leading a group of rebels in a plot to overthrow the king Don Carlo, to avenge his father's death. Ernani is in love with Elvira, but she is being forced to marry Don Ruy Gomez da Silva and is living in his castle where she awaits Ernani. Don Carlo also loves Elvira and arrives at the castle to claim her. Ernani arrives at the same time and da Silva enters Elvira's room to find her two suitors. Furious, he challenges them to a duel, but calms down when he recognizes the king. Don Carlo saves Ernani from da Silva's wrath by introducing him as a royal messenger.

ACT II ❧

Elvira's wedding to da Silva is approaching. Ernani's conspiracy to dethrone Don Carlo has failed. He takes refuge in da Silva's castle. Although displeased to find Ernani with Elvira, da Silva adheres to the rules of hospitality and protects Ernani when the king comes in search of him. The king leaves with Elvira; da Silva and Ernani, realizing that Don Carlo is their common foe, join forces against him. Da Silva agrees to help Ernani

ABOVE: Sandra Ford and Alan Opie in a 2000 production of Verdi's Ernani.

Macbeth

Macbeth by Verdi

Composed	1847–47; rev. 1864–65
Premiered	1847, Florence
Libretto	by Francesco Maria Piave and Andrea Maffei, after William Shakespeare

Verdi was an enthusiastic admirer of Shakespeare and *Macbeth* was the first opera based on his work. It premiered at the Teatro della Pergola in Florence on 14 March 1847, with Verdi himself conducting. Performances followed throughout Europe, including Madrid (1848), Vienna (1849), and New York (1858). For the premiere in Paris, at the Théâtre Lyrique on 21 April 1865, Verdi revised the opera. This included several additions: an extra aria in Act II for Lady Macbeth, '*La luce langue*' (The Weak Light), two new choruses, a new duet for the Macbeths, a battle fugue and a ballet.

ABOVE: A striking ensemble scene from a 1986 production of Verdi's Macbeth, *based on Shakespeare's play of the same name.*

Synopsis
Macbeth by Verdi

ACT I ❧

Macbeth and Banquo encounter three witches, who declare that Macbeth will become Thane of Cawdor and then king of Scotland, while Banquo will father many future kings. The news arrives that Macbeth is to succeed the comdemned Thane of Cawdor. Lady Macbeth receives a letter from her husband about the predictions. The king, Duncan, is staying at their castle and she plots his murder. Macbeth returns and his wife reveals her plans. He is persuaded to carry out the murder but is racked with guilt. Lady Macbeth goes to incriminate the guards with the king's blood. Banquo and Macduff arrive and discover Duncan's body. All mourn and swear vengeance.

ACT II ❧

Macbeth feels uneasy as king, although Duncan's son Malcolm has fled to England. Remembering the witches' predictions for Banquo, he schemes with his wife to kill him and his children. Assassins carry out the murder but Banquo's son Fleance escapes. That night the ghost of Banquo appears at a banquet. Only Macbeth can see the apparition. Macduff resolves to join Malcolm's forces.

ACT III ❧

Macbeth revisits the three witches. They tell him to beware Macduff, but that he is safe until Birnam Wood rises against him. Macbeth enquires about Banquo and his apparition appears, along with royal sons. Lady Macbeth encourages him to murder Banquo's offspring, as well as the family of Macduff.

ACT IV ❧

Macduff laments the loss of his wife and children. Malcolm arrives from England with a troop of soldiers and encourages Macduff to join him in his plan to kill Macbeth. Macduff joins the troops and, concealing themselves with branches, they approach the castle.

Lady Macbeth is guilt-ridden over her crimes. As she sleepwalks and describes the murders, she is overheard by members of staff. Macbeth, fearing his own death, is unmoved by the news that Lady Macbeth has killed herself. Soldiers inform him that Birnam Wood appears to be approaching the castle.

The English troops storm the castle and Macduff confronts Macbeth. They fight and Macbeth dies, cursing the witches. Malcolm is crowned king.

on one condition: if he wants Ernani to die, he need only blow his hunting horn and the deed is done.

ACT III ❧

The election of the emperor is imminent. By the tomb of Charlemagne, Don Carlo, having heard rumours of a conspiracy, conceals himself. Ernani and da Silva arrive with the rest of the rebels and Ernani is elected to kill the king. Da Silva promises Ernani his life if he will let him carry out the task instead, but Ernani refuses.

Don Carlo is elected emperor and confronts the rebels. Elvira persuades him to spare their lives and, realizing that she will only ever love Ernani, Don Carlo allows the couple to marry and restores Ernani's property and status. Da Silva is furious.

ACT IV ❧

At the palace of Ernani, who is in fact Don Giovanni d'Aragona, wedding guests celebrate his marriage to Elvira. The servants are made uneasy by the presence of a masked man in a black cloak. As Ernani and Elvira declare their love for one another, they hear the sound of a hunting horn. Ernani sends Elvira away; Da Silva reveals his identity and reminds Ernani of their pact. Despite the pleas of Elvira, who has returned, Ernani remains true to his word and kills himself.

Rigoletto

Rigoletto by Verdi

Composed	1850–51
Premiered	1851, Venice
Libretto	by Francesco Maria Piave, after Victor Hugo

Verdi's three-act opera *Rigoletto*, based on Victor Hugo's play *Le roi s'amuse* ('The King Amuses Himself', 1832), was originally entitled *La maledizione* ('The Malediction') a reference to the curse placed on the superstitious court jester Rigoletto, which fulfills itself in the final scene. The first performance of *Rigoletto* took place at the Teatro La Fenice in Venice on 11 March 1851. The London premiere followed on 14 May 1853 and the first performance in New York on 19 February 1855. *Rigoletto* is a superb example of the integrated opera in which

Rigoletto, **Vienna Philharmonic Orchestra**
Carlo Maria Giulini, **conductor**
Deutsche Grammophon 415 288-2GH2
Soloists: Ileana Cotrubas (Gilda), Elena Obraztsova (Maddalena), Placido Domingo (Duke), Piero Cappuccilli (Rigoletto), Nicolai Ghiaurov (Sparafucile), Kurt Moll (Monterone)

RECOMMENDED RECORDING

action, music and characterization combined to create dramatic unison. This, even though the opera's five most famous numbers, including the great quartet from the last act, are often detached and performed separately. *Rigoletto* is also an unconventional opera, based on what Verdi called a "series of duets". He also used a reminiscence motif, repeating the chilling, doom-laden phrase introduced in the prelude to the opera to represent the jester's terror at the curse laid on him. The motif made its own subtle contribution to the famous aria '*La donna è mobile*', which tells Rigoletto that his planned murder of the licentious Duke of Mantua has failed.

ABOVE: Paolo Gavanelli as Rigoletto in a 2001 London production.

◆Synopsis

Rigoletto by Verdi

ACT I 🎵

In the court of Mantua, the duke tells the courtiers of his success with women. Rigoletto, the duke's jester, taunts Count Ceprano about the duke's interest in his wife. The count plots revenge on Rigoletto with some other courtiers; the jester is believed to keep a mistress at his house and they plan to abduct her. A nobleman, Monterone, enters, intending to denounce the duke for seducing his daughter. Rigoletto mocks him and Monterone is arrested; as he is led away, he curses the horrified jester. The curse worries Rigoletto as he returns home. He is approached by the assassin, Sparafucile, who offers his services, but Rigoletto refuses and muses on how words can be as harmful as a dagger. He is welcomed home by his daughter, Gilda, whom he keeps hidden from the world and, more importantly, the philandering duke. Rigoletto laments the death of his wife and, fearing for Gilda's safety, orders her nurse Giovanna to prevent anyone from entering the garden.

As Rigoletto leaves, the duke, having bribed Giovanna, enters the garden. He introduces himself to Gilda as Gualtier Maldè, an impoverished student, and declares his love for her. She has seen him in church and, after he leaves at the sound of approaching footsteps, dreamily muses over his (false) name.

Ceprano and the courtiers stop Rigoletto and enlist his help in abducting Ceprano's wife. They blindfold him and, confusing him, trick him into putting a ladder up against his own wall. The courtiers then abduct Gilda and make off with her. Hearing her cries for help, Rigoletto removes his blindfold and sees that everyone has vanished. Finding Gilda's scarf, he laments Monterone's curse.

ACT II 🎵

The duke is concerned about Gilda's abduction, picturing her crying alone, but cheers up when his courtiers reveal that they have her and that she awaits the duke in his chamber. He rushes off to seduce her. Rigoletto arrives in search of Gilda and the courtiers are surprised to learn that she is in fact his daughter and not his mistress as they had assumed. Despite his pleas, however, they refuse to let him pass. Gilda runs from the duke's room, telling her father of her abduction and explaining that she has been courted by the duke over a long period of time, during their visits to church. As Monterone is led past on his way to the dungeons, Rigoletto swears vengeance on him and the duke, whom Gilda begs him to forgive.

ACT III 🎵

Rigoletto and Gilda stand outside the inn owned by Sparafucile and his seductive sister Maddalena. As the duke drinks and flirts with Maddalena, singing of the fickleness of women, Rigoletto comforts Gilda. He sends Gilda away to disguise herself as a boy, arranging to meet her in Verona where they will be safe. He then pays Sparafucile to murder the duke and departs. Maddalena, who has fallen for the duke, pleads with her brother to kill Rigoletto instead. He refuses, but is eventually persuaded to kill the next person to enter the inn, in the duke's place. Overhearing this, Gilda resolves to sacrifice herself for the duke, whom she still loves despite his infidelity. She enters the inn and Sparafucile stabs her and puts her in a sack. Rigoletto comes to collect the body and takes it to the river to dispose of it. But, suddenly, he is horrified to hear the presumed-dead duke singing in the distance. He opens the sack to reveal his dying daughter, who begs forgiveness. Rigoletto cries that Monterone's curse has been fulfilled.

Il trovatore
('The Troubadour')

Il trovatore by Verdi

Composed	1851–52
Premiered	1853, Rome
Libretto	by Salvatore Cammarano and Leone Emanuele Bardare, after Antonio García Gutiérrez

Of all Verdi's operas, *Il trovatore* ('The Troubadour') provides the fullest panorama of melodies, each of them memorable in its own right. *Il trovatore* did not have the subtle characterization of *Rigoletto*, and suffered from an all but impenetrable plot, but nonetheless became as frequently played. The *Miserere* (meaning 'Have Mercy') sung by a chorus of monks in Act IV was for some time the best-loved number in any opera. *Il trovatore* was one of Verdi's speediest creations: he wrote its four acts in only 30 days, between 1 and 29 November 1852. Less than two months later, on 19 January 1853, the premiere

took place in at the Teatro Apollo in Rome followed by New York and London in 1855. The menacing mezzo-soprano role of the gypsy Azucena was a new departure for singers in Italian opera and may have been influenced by a similar character in Meyerbeer's *Le prophète* ('The Prophet', 1849), which premiered in Paris.

Il trovatore, **New Philharmonia Orchestra**
Zubin Mehta, **conductor**
RCA RD86194
Soloists: Leontyne Price (Leonora), Fiorenza Cossotto (Azucena), Placido Domingo (Manrico), Sherrill Milnes (Conte di Luna), Bonaldo Giaiotti (Ferrando)

RECOMMENDED RECORDING

BELOW: Dolora Zajic as Azucena in a 1986 production of Il trovatore.

Synopsis
Il trovatore by Verdi

ACT I ﻩ

Count di Luna waits beneath the window of his love Leonora. Meanwhile, Ferrando, the captain of the guard, entertains the soldiers by telling them of how the count's brother was bewitched as a child by a gypsy, who was subsequently burned at the stake. Her daughter, to avenge her death, kidnapped the child and is thought to have killed him. Leonora reveals to her confidante Inez that she has fallen in love with an unknown troubadour, who serenaded her at a tournament. The count arrives to court Leonora and the troubadour, Manrico, also arrives. He serenades Leonora and she confuses him with the count in the darkness. When she realizes her mistake, she declares her love for Manrico. Manrico and the count threaten to kill each other.

ACT II ﻩ

In a camp, the gypsies go about their work. Azucena, the daughter in the tale related by Ferrando, recalls her mother's dying call for vengeance. and laments

accidentally throwing her own son into the flames. Manrico, who has been brought up as Azucena's son, overhears. She encourages him to exact revenge on the count, but Manrico relates that, during battle, he was about to kill him in a duel, but something held him back. He agrees to help his "mother" to avenge her mother's death. A messenger brings the news that Leonora, thinking Manrico dead, is entering a convent. Ignoring Azucena's pleas, Manrico leaves.

Under the count's orders, Ferrando and his men wait by the convent to abduct Leonora. When she appears, Manrico arrives and a fight breaks out. Leonora and Manrico escape together.

ACT III ﻩ

In the count's camp, near where Manrico has taken Leonora, the soldiers prepare to besiege the castle; count laments the loss of his love. Ferrando announces that a gypsy woman has been taken prisoner; Azucena is brought in, explaining that she is looking for her son. On realizing the count's identity, she reveals that she was his brother's abductor. The count orders her burned at the stake. Assuming that Manrico is her true son, he

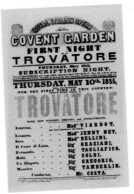

hopes to trick his rival into leaving Leonora, while also avenging his brother. Manrico learns of Azucena's imminent execution; he rushes to her rescue.

ACT IV ﻩ

Outside the tower where Manrico is being held prisoner, Leonora sings of her love for him. A chorus prays for the condemned Manrico and he bids farewell to Leonora. Leonora offers herself to the count in exchange for Manrico's life; he agrees. She takes a slow-working poison. In the prison, Manrico comforts Azucena. Leonora enters and urges Manrico to flee, but adds that she must remain behind. Manrico, guessing the bargain that she has struck with the count, is further horrified when she reveals that she has poisoned herself and dies in his arms. The count, realizing he has been tricked, is furious and orders Manrico's immediate death. Azucena tries in vain to dissuade the count. As the axe falls on Manrico, Azucena informs him that he has killed his own brother. Her mother's death is finally avenged.

La traviata
('The Fallen Woman')

La traviata by Verdi

Composed 1852-53]
Premiered 1853, Venice
Libretto by Francesco Maria Piave, after Alexandre Dumas

La dame aux camélias ('The Lady of the Camellias') by Alexandre Dumas (1824–95) had barely been staged in 1852 before Verdi took it up for *La traviata*, one of the great operas from his middle period. It premiered at Teatro La Fenice, Venice on 6 March 1853, and the first performance was disastrous. Verdi blamed the singers and the audience burst out laughing in the final scene when the hefty soprano playing the heroine, Violetta, was supposed to be "wasting away" from consumption. *La traviata* managed to salvage success from its unfortunate beginnings, but it was still controversial. Violetta was

La traviata, **Royal Opera, Covent Garden**
Georg Solti, **conductor**
Decca 071 431–9 (DVD Region 0, NTSC)
Soloists: Angela Gheorghiu (Violetta), Leah-Marian Jones (Flora), Frank Lopardo (Alfredo), Robin Leggate (Gastone), Leo Nucci (Germont)

RECOMMENDED RECORDING

modelled on the consumptive Parisian courtesan Marie Duplessis (1824–47) who, together with other dubious, immoral characters of the demi-monde, offended the puritan tastes of the nineteenth century. Opera houses reacted by substituting a seventeenth-century setting to place *La traviata* at an acceptable distance. However, in retaining a courtesan as heroine despite the moralists, Verdi was anticipating the *verismo* of later nineteenth-century opera. In addition, Verdi experimented by changing the vocal music as the

RIGHT: Beverly Stills as Violetta in a 1973 San Francisco Opera production of Verdi's La traviata.

tragedy developed: the fun-loving Violetta of Act I, for instance, acquired a passionate intensity in Act II and ended in Act III as a fragile, fading shadow of her former self. In 1854 it was restaged at another Venetian theatre, and this time had been thoroughly rehearsed and better cast. It was a resounding success.

Synopsis
La traviata by Verdi

ACT I

Violetta, a high-class prostitute, is holding a party in her Parisian home. She indulges in a gay lifestyle, partly in order to distract her from the fact that she is suffering from the early stages of consumption. The nobleman Gastone introduces her to his friend Alfredo, who admires her. As the other guests go into another room to dance, Violetta is seized with a coughing fit and stays behind; Alfredo remains with her. He tends to her and expresses his love for her; she is touched. Left alone, she confesses that she has fallen in love for the first time.

ACT II

Violetta has given up her life in Paris and is living with Alfredo in a small house in the country. Annina, a servant, informs Alfredo that they have no money left; in order to pay for the house, Violetta has been selling her jewellery. He leaves immediately for Paris, in order to raise the money to repay her.

Violetta receives an invitation to a party from Flora, a friend from Paris, and reminisces about her

life there. Giorgio Germont, Alfredo's father, arrives on a visit. He at first accuses her of dragging his son into poverty, but she explains that she has been supporting them herself. He urges her to break off her relationship with Alfredo, as her sullied reputation is ruining that of his family. Furthermore, Alfredo's sister wishes to marry and the family's link to Violetta might prevent the match from going ahead.

Violetta realizes that leaving Alfredo will be in everyone's best interests. She writes to Flora, accepting the invitation, and then composes a farewell letter to Alfredo. When he returns, he informs her that his father is coming to persuade him to end their relationship. Violetta, suggesting that the two men be left alone, departs. She sends her farewell letter to Alfredo via a messenger. He is devastated; his father comforts him.

Violetta attends Flora's party with her former lover, Baron Douphol. Alfredo, who discovered Flora's invitation and guessed that Violetta would attend, arrives in search of her. He has won large amounts of money while gambling at the party. On seeing Violetta with Douphol, Alfredo insults her. Douphol challenges him to a game and Alfredo wins. Alone with Alfredo, Violetta pleads with him to leave

the party, as she fears a duel between him and Douphol. Alfredo insults her, accusing her of infidelity. Unable to disclose Germont's orders, Violetta confesses that she has sworn to break off their relationship but lets him believe that it was at Douphol's request. Calling the guests in, Alfredo publicly insults Violetta and proclaims her faithlessness. Throwing his winnings at her feet, he declares his debt to her repaid. Germont enters and scolds Alfredo for being so hard on Violetta; however he does not reveal the truth about his involvement.

ACT III

Violetta is now very ill with consumption and is confined to her bed. Her doctor offers her words of encouragement but she knows the end is near. A letter arrives from Germont; he begs forgiveness for his actions. He has revealed the truth of Violetta's sacrifice to Alfredo, who was horrified and is hurrying over to visit her. As she lies in bed, doubting he will arrive in time to see her alive, he enters. Overjoyed to see him, Violetta finds the strength to sit up and they sing ecstatically of their future together. The doctor then enters, accompanied by a regretful Germont. Unfortunately, Violetta's recovery was only temporary and she dies in Alfredo's arms.

Les vêpres siciliennes
('The Sicilian Vespers')

Les vêpres siciliennes by Verdi

Composed	1854
Premiered	1855, Paris
Libretto	by Eugène Scribe and Charles Duveyrier

Verdi inherited the libretto for *Les vêpres siciliennes* ('The Sicilian Vespers') from *Le duc d'Albe* ('The Duke of Alba'), an opera left unfinished when the composer, Donizetti, died. Verdi made it a five-act work and it had its first performance at the Paris Opéra, for which it was commissioned, on 13 June 1855. It was well received, but the Italian censors made difficulties, objecting to Naples as a setting for a massacre. The locale was changed to Sicily, then Portugal. The Italian title, *I vespri siciliani*, was replaced by *Giovanna di Braganza*, *Giovanna de Guzman* and *Batilde di Turenna*, before its rightful name was reinstated in 1857.

ABOVE: Renato Bruson in a 1980 production of Simon Boccanegra.

Simon Boccanegra

Simon Boccanegra by Verdi

Composed	1856–57; rev. 1880
Premiered	1857, Venice
Libretto	by Francesco Maria Piave and Giuseppe Montanelli, after Antonio García Gutiérrez

Verdi's dark, brooding opera *Simon Boccanegra* had a tortuous history before 24 March 1881, when its final version premiered at La Scala, Milan. Originally, Verdi composed *Boccanegra* in 1857, but the Venetian audience reacted coolly; an anti-Verdi claque sabotaged the performance and a false rumour spread, claiming that Verdi had written the libretto and made a mess of it. A quarter century passed before *Boccanegra* reappeared with extensively revised music and libretto. This time, the opera ran for 10 performances in Milan, but New York had to wait until 1932 and London until 1948.

Synopsis
Les vêpres siciliennes by Verdi

ACT I

The Duchesse Hélène laments the execution of her brother, encouraged by Robert, a French soldier, and stirs emotions amongst the crowd. A fight breaks out between the French and the Sicilians. The unpopular governor of Sicily, Guy de Montfort, tries to calm them and interrogates Henri, a Sicilian who wants to speak to Hélène. Suspecting him to be an anarchist, Montfort warns him against involvement with the duchess. Henri ignores his orders.

ACT II

Jean Procida, a returning exile, reveals that there is little support for the Sicilian cause. Henri declares his love to Hélène; she asks him to avenge her brother's death. Henri is arrested for declining a royal invitation. To annoy the Sicilians, Procida persuades French soldiers to abduct some local girls.

ACT III

Guy de Montfort learns that Henri is his son. Neither of them is pleased. Procida tells Henri that they must put their plot to assassinate the governor into action. Wanting to protect his father, Henri prevents the assassination from going ahead. Hélène and Procida are arrested, while the Sicilian people revile Henri's treachery.

ACT IV

Henri visits Hélène and Procida in prison and explains his reasons for defending Montfort. Hélène forgives Henri; he pledges to rejoin the conspirators now that he has saved his father's life. The weapons for the uprising arrive. De Montfort promises to free Hélène and Procida if Henri publicly acknowledges him as his father; Henri agrees. Montfort blesses Henri's marriage to Hélène, which he hopes will unite France with Sicily; Hélène feels uneasy.

ACT V

The marriage celebrations are underway. Procida informs a horrified Hélène that the wedding bells will be the signal for the uprising to begin. Montfort, sensing that something is wrong, rings the bells to start the ceremony. At this signal, the armed Sicilians burst in on the unsuspecting French.

Synopsis
Simon Boccanegra by Verdi

PROLOGUE

Paolo and Pietro hope to gain power by electing Boccanegra as doge. He hopes it will enable him to marry Maria, the mother of his child, imprisoned by her father Fiesco. As Fiesco laments Maria's death, Boccanegra arrives to make peace. Fiesco demands his grandchild, but the child is missing. As Boccanegra mourns Maria, he is hailed as doge.

ACT I

25 years later, Amelia Grimaldi awaits her lover, Adorno. Boccanegra arrives; Amelia fears he will force her to marry Paolo. Adorno asks Amelia's guardian Andrea (in fact Fiesco) for her hand; he consents. The doge sees a portrait of Maria and realizes that Amelia is his daughter. He refuses Paolo her hand, so Paolo plots her abduction. Adorno suspects Boccanegra of the attempted kidnap, but Amelia intervenes. Adorno is imprisoned and Paolo forced to curse the kidnappers; he obeys, cursing himself.

ACT II

Paolo sends Pietro to free Adorno and poisons Boccanegra's drink. He tries to persuade Andrea to kill Boccanegra and suggests to Adorno that Amelia and the doge are lovers. Amelia arrives; Adorno berates her, hiding as the doge enters. Boccanegra allows Amelia to marry Adorno and drinks the poison. Adorno goes to stab Boccanegra but Amelia prevents him. Learning that Boccanegra is her father, he pledges his life to him. An uprising is heard; if Adorno calms the people, Amelia will be his.

ACT III

The rebellion is suppressed. The condemned Paolo tells Andrea about the poison; Andrea makes his peace with Boccanegra. The doge blesses Amelia and Adorno, naming the latter his successor before dying.

Un ballo in maschera
('A Masked Ball')

Un ballo in maschera by Verdi

Composed	1857
Premiered	1859, Rome
Libretto	by Antonio Somma, after Eugène Scribe

In 1857, Verdi was virtually asking for censorship trouble when he chose *Gustavuse III, ou Le bal masqué* ('Gustavus III, or The Masked Ball') for his next work. In 1792 King Gustavusus III of Sweden had been shot dead at a masked ball in Stockholm. Regicide was a taboo subject and the Neapolitan censors immediately demanded radical changes. They objected to the Swedish location because it was too close to home – and shooting the king dead on stage was too much like the real-life event, although stabbing with a knife would be permitted. Verdi refused the censors' demands and left Naples for Rome, where he accepted a change of locale to Boston in the USA and exchanged "Riccardo Count of Warwick" for "King Gustavus III" for the premiere at the Teatro Apollo on 17 February 1859. Further alterations were made for the Paris premiere in 1861 – for instance "Boston" was relocated to "Naples". Despite this tinkering, *Un ballo's* splendidly varied music and mixing of comic and tragic elements, the beautiful love duet in Act II and imaginative effects like the assassins plotting on stage, while a stately court dance is played, combined to make the opera an enduring success.

ABOVE: Patricia Payne as Mlle Arvidson (Ulrica) in a 1977 production.

Un ballo in maschera, **Teatro alla Scala**
Claudio Abbado, **conductor**
Deutsche Grammophon 453 148-2
Soloists: Katia Ricciarelli (Amelia), Edita Gruberova (Oscar), Elena Obraztsova (Ulrica), Placido Domingo (Riccardo), Renato Bruson (Renato)

RECOMMENDED RECORDING

Synopsis
Un ballo in maschera by Verdi

This synopsis uses the Swedish character names from the original Scribe libretto. Where necessary, the names used in the revised US version are shown in brackets.

ACT I

Courtiers await the arrival of Gustavus III (Riccardo). Among them are the Counts Horn and Ribbing (Tom and Samuel), who are plotting his downfall. Gustavus arrives; Oscar, his page, hands him a list of guests for a masked ball. Gustavus, seeing the name of Amelia, sings of his concealed love for her; she is the wife of Anckarstroem (Renato), Gustavus's secretary. Anckarstroem enters and warns Gustavus of a conspiracy against him; the king does not heed his words.

A judge brings Gustavus a document to sign, banishing Mademoiselle Arvidson (Ulrica), a fortune-teller. Oscar advises Gustavus against signing the order. The king suggests they pay her a visit. He will disguise himself as a fisherman.

Mlle Arvidson invokes the devil to aid her prophesies. A sailor, Christian (Silvano) hears that he will soon find promotion and wealth, which comes true since Gustavus has slipped some money and a recommendation into his pocket.

Amelia arrives. She reveals to the fortune-teller that she is in love with the king and wishes to calm her feelings. Mlle Arvidson instructs her to pick a herb at midnight. Overhearing, Gustavus is overjoyed to learn that his love is reciprocated and resolves to meet Amelia at midnight. He requests his fortune. Mlle Arvidson recognizes his hand as that of a great man, but is unwilling to disclose what she reads there. Once persuaded, she tells him that his death is imminent. His assassin will be a friend, more specifically, the next person to shake his hand. Unconvinced, Gustavus offers his hand to the assembled crowd, but no one will shake it. Seeing Anckarstroem approaching, Gustavus runs to offer him his hand. This must disprove the fortune-teller's

prediction, since Anckarstroem is his best friend. Everyone realizes Gustavus's identity and Mlle Arvidson repeats her warning.

ACT II

As Amelia seeks the magic herb, Gustavus arrives and declares his love for her. She admits that she returns his love but does not want to betray her husband. Anckarstroem enters, fearing for Gustavus's safety; Amelia covers her face with a veil. Gustavus leaves, insisting that Anckarstroem returns the woman to the city without lifting her veil. The conspirators arrive and find Gustavus gone. They mock Anckarstroem, demanding to know the woman's identity; Amelia intervenes and drops her veil. The conspirators are amused but Anckarstroem is furious; he arranges a meeting with the Counts Ribbing and Horn.

ACT III

Anckarstroem has resolved to kill Amelia, who begs to see her child before she dies. She leaves and Anckarstroem addresses Gustavus's portrait, realizing that it is he that should be punished, not Amelia. Horn and Ribbing arrive and Amelia returns; she is asked to draw lots to see which of the men will kill the king. Anckarstroem is pleased when his name is pulled out. Oscar arrives with invitations for a masked ball; the conspirators realize that this is the perfect opportunity for the assassination.

Gustavus reluctantly signs a document to send Anckarstroem and Amelia abroad. Oscar enters with an anonymous letter, which warns Gustavus to avoid the ball. Not wanting to appear cowardly and desiring to see Amelia one last time, Gustavus ignores the note.

At the ball, Anckarstroem tricks Oscar into revealing which of the masked figures is Gustavus. Amelia tries to warn Gustavus but he will not listen and tells her that he is sending her away. Anckarstroem stabs Gustavus. As he dies, the king assures Anckarstroem of his wife's innocence, shows him the document he has signed for the couple's emigration and forgives the conspirators. Full of remorse, Anckarstroem and the courtiers lament the death of the magnanimous king.

LEFT: Nicolai Gedda plays King Gustavus III in a 1970s Royal Opera House production of Un ballo in maschera.

La forza del destino
('The Force of Destiny')

La forza del destino by Verdi

Composed	1861–62; rev. 1869
Premiered	1862, St Petersburg
Libretto	by Francesco Maria Piave, after Angel de Saavedra and Friedrich von Schiller

La forza del destino ('The Force of Destiny') was commissioned by the Imperial Theatre, St Petersburg (➤ p. 194) where it premiered in 1862. Verdi and considered the opera an "excellent success" with "opulent" settings and costumes, although critics thought the tragic, lugubrious love story had a depressing effect on the audience. It was first performed in New York in 1865 and London in 1867. Verdi had composed *La forza* in only two months, and it represented a

RIGHT: Martti Talvela as Padre Guardiano and Leontyne Price as Leonora in a 1979 production.

CENSORSHIP IN OPERA

Opera censorship was a fact of life for nineteenth-century composers and librettists. Libretti were minutely picked over for anything that might give offence, encourage sedition or create public disorder. Censors even attended dress rehearsals to make sure there was no "improper" scenery, costumes or stage business. The Spaniards, Austrians and French who occupied Italy at various times suspected the natives of sedition, rebellion or worse and fancied that they were at their most dangerous en masse. This made the opera house potentially dangerous, since it was virtually the only place in the Italian peninsula where large gatherings were permitted. Censorship came in various forms. Political censorship, which intensified after the revolutions of 1848, forbade operas to depict regicide or any behaviour that put royal personages in a bad or insulting light. Operas could also be censored on moral grounds, for example when the Roman censor baulked at the crystal shoe in Rossini's *La Cenerentola* because fitting it exposed a naked foot in public. Verdi's *La forza del destino* got into trouble for religious reasons; *forza* could mean "power" as well as "force" and, according to the censors, "destiny" was not a power: the only power was God's will.

"halfway house" in his development as an opera composer. The music recalled his earlier, lyrical melodies and instrumentation but also contained the rich orchestration and the darker, more intense atmosphere of his later work. In particular, the tense urgency and rising four-note pattern of the overture offered a foretaste of Verdi's later music. Despite its success, *La forza* had a worrying effect on performers: a superstition arose that it was unlucky to mention the opera's title inside a theatre. In 1869 it was extensively revised for its Milan production.

Synopsis
La forza del destino by Verdi

ACT I

Leonora is preparing to elope with Alvaro. Her father, the Marquis of Calatrava, considers Alvaro unworthy. Leonora regrets having to leave her home and family, but when Alvaro arrives she agrees to leave with him. Her father enters and demands an explanation. Alvaro declares that he is abducting Leonora, who is innocent. He then throws down his pistol in a gesture of surrender. The gun goes off, fatally wounding the marquis. He curses Leonora and Alvaro.

ACT II

Leonora is looking for Alvaro. Disguised as a man, she enters an inn, observed by Preziosilla, a gypsy girl. Leonora's brother Carlo also enters the inn, disguised and in search of the couple; he intends to kill them to avenge the death of his father. He questions Trabuco, a muleteer, about the person he has just seen enter the inn. Preziosilla sings of the wars in Italy and pilgrims pass by, on their way to a nearby monastery. Carlo continues to ask Trabuco about the traveller and identifies himself as a student, Pereda, who is helping a friend to track down his sister and her lover who killed their father; the man is thought to have escaped abroad.

Leonora overhears and feels betrayed by Alvaro's flight abroad. She goes to the monastery and is admitted by brother Melitone. She begs the Padre Guardiano, to whom she reveals her true identity, for forgiveness. He allows her to live in a nearby cave as a hermit. He summons the monks and bids them respect the new hermit's solitude.

ACT III

In war-torn Italy, Alvaro sings of his wretched life and asks Leonora – whom he assumes is dead – to look down on him from heaven. Hearing a cry, he hurries to help. A quarrel has broken out over a card game and Carlo is in danger. Alvaro saves him and the men introduce themselves – Alvaro as Federico Herreros, and Carlo as Felice de Bornos. The two men swear eternal friendship and go into battle. Alvaro is badly wounded; Carlo fetches the surgeon. Alvaro gives Carlo a package and asks him to destroy it. Carlo wants to open the package; his sense of honour prevents him, but he discovers a portrait of Leonora nearby and the truth dawns. He receives the news that Alvaro will live and is overjoyed, as he can now kill him.

When Alvaro returns, Carlo challenges him to a duel and the men fight until a patrol separates them; Alvaro departs to join a monastery. At dawn, the soldiers and vivandières go about their duties. Preziosilla tells fortunes, while Trabuco strikes bargains among the soldiers and brother Melitone sermonizes.

ACT IV

At the monastery, brother Melitone distributes food to the poor. With the Padre Guardiano, he discusses the new monk, brother Rafaello, who is in fact Alvaro in hiding. Carlo has tracked Alvaro down and arrives at the monastery asking to see Rafaello. He announces to Alvaro his intention of killing him. Alvaro tries to avoid conflict, but Carlo remains unmoved by his piety and hurls insults at him. Unable to ignore Carlo's slighting of his family, Alvaro takes the sword Carlo has brought for him and the fight begins.

Leonora, who has been unable to forget Alvaro, emerges from her cave. She hears the sound of fighting and Alvaro arrives, asking her to give Carlo his last rites. The lovers recognize each other and Alvaro reveals that her brother lies dying. Leonora runs to him but Carlo, still intent on revenge, stabs her before he dies. The Padre Guardiano offers Leonora comfort as she dies and Alvaro laments that he, guilty and alone, must live.

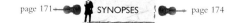

1845–1800   HIGH ROMANTIC

KEY COMPOSERS

173

Otello

Otello by Verdi

Composed	1884–85
Premiered	1887, Milan
Libretto	by Arrigo Boito, after William Shakespeare

Verdi's late masterpiece, *Otello*, completed when he was 74, was the second of his three operas taken from the plays of Shakespeare. The libretto by Arrigo Boito (1842–1918) dispensed with the Shakespeare's opening scene, set in Venice and concentrated the action on Cyprus, giving it an almost claustrophobic intensity. Long considered Verdi's greatest opera and his most outstanding achievement, *Otello* was written at a time when the composer believed he had reached his peak with *Aida* and was being upstaged by the Teutonic grandeur of Richard Wagner, whose operas were dominating the European music scene. Verdi was wrong on both counts. His *Otello* fulfilled Wagner's concept of a "total work of art" in more ways than one. Music fused with drama and each scene with the next, with few set-piece arias or ensembles like those found in Verdi's previous works. The orchestral picture of a storm off the coast of Cyprus has thrilled

PREMIERE OF OTELLO

The opening of *Otello* at La Scala on 5 February 1887 was a major occasion, which musicians and critics attended from all over the world. People's excitement mounted to fever pitch, both inside and outside the opera house. They were not to be disappointed. The seamless continuity of the opera, the lavish costumes, the richness and sophistication of the orchestral settings and the perfect harmony of the poetry and music guaranteed the opera's instant success. The audience was captivated from the opening lines and at the final curtain both Verdi and his librettist Boito received a standing ovation. It is reported that even after Verdi had retired for the night, crowds thronged around his hotel "shouting and yelling" in appreciation.

Verdi himself was reputed to have been unhappy with the premiere of *Otello*, which is not surprising given the perfectionist stance he had taken with this particular work all along. However, despite the composer's dissatisfaction, the opening of the opera was greeted with worldwide acclaim and was recognized as an event of great significance in the shifting trends of operatic style.

audiences ever since the opera was first performed at La Scala, Milan on 5 February 1887 ➡ **p. 158**. Yet there are also intimate moments and sublime expressions of love between Otello and his doomed wife Desdemona that scale great heights of lyricism and melodic beauty.

LEFT: Ermanno Mauro as Otello and Katia Ricciarelli as Desdemona in a 1989 production of Otello.

Synopsis
Otello by Verdi

ACT I

The island of Cyprus is under Venetian rule. The people wait at the port for their governor, Otello. The ship arrives and the people rejoice as Otello announces their victory. Iago, Otello's ensign, swears revenge on his master for promoting Cassio to captain. He conspires with Roderigo, who loves Otello's wife Desdemona, to wreak revenge on Cassio and cause Otello's downfall. Iago insinuates to Roderigo that Cassio admires Desdemona and provokes a duel between them. The retiring governor Montano intervenes, while Iago causes a commotion. Otello arrives, angry that Montano has been wounded and Desdemona's sleep disturbed. He retracts Cassio's promotion and bids everyone leave.

ACT II

Iago reveals to Cassio that Desdemona alone can persuade Otello to restore his promotion. Iago muses on his nihilistic view of the world. He sees Cassio approach Desdemona in the garden and suggests to Otello that Cassio has designs on his wife. Desdemona pleads Cassio's innocence but Otello is inflamed by jealousy. Desdemona offers to wipe his brow with a handkerchief – an early love token from Otello.

He snatches it and throws it to the ground; Emilia, Iago's wife, retrieves it. A bewildered Desdemona begs forgiveness, while Iago procures the handkerchief with a view to planting it in Cassio's house. Otello asks to be left alone but Iago remains behind to inform him that Cassio has spoken of Desdemona in his sleep. He also mentions having seen Cassio in possession of the handkerchief. Furious, Otello swears vengeance.

ACT III

Iago tells Otello that he can prove Desdemona's infidelity. Desdemona again approaches Otello about pardoning Cassio; he demands to see the handkerchief. When she admits she cannot produce it, he accuses her of infidelity and sends her away. Iago persuades Otello to hide while he speaks to Cassio about Desdemona. Iago then engages Cassio in conversation about a courtesan and manipulates the discussion so that Otello, unable to hear every word, belives them to be discussing Desdemona. A confused Cassio produces the lost handkerchief, further infuriating Otello. Trumpets announce Venetian ambassadors; Otello resolves to kill Desdemona. Lodovico, an ambassador, brings the news that Otello is to return to Venice and Cassio is to become governor. Otello begins to lose his mind and strikes Desdemona, while Iago encourages Roderigo to murder Cassio. Otello orders everyone to leave and curses Desdemona, before collapsing in a fit. Iago exults in his triumph.

ACT IV

Emilia helps Desdemona prepare for bed. Desdemona is upset by Otello's unprovoked anger towards her. She says her prayers and bids farewell to Emilia before going to bed. Otello enters and, kissing her, orders her to repent her sins. He berates her infidelity and, ignoring her protestations of innocence, smothers her. Emilia enters to announce that Cassio has killed Roderigo and is horrified to discover the dying Desdemona. She calls Cassio, Iago and Lodovico to the chamber and reveals the truth to Otello; Iago flees. Realizing that Desdemona was innocent, Otello is distraught. He kisses her and Lodovico seizes his sword but Otello, drawing a dagger, kills himself.

1845–1890   HIGH ROMANTIC

KEY COMPOSERS